Urban Development and Housing in India

1947 to 2007

Urban Development and Housing in India

1947 to 2007

Incorporating

An Introduction to Urban Development and Housing in India

Edited Extracts on Urban Development and Housing in India's Five Year Plans (I Plan to X Plan and Approach Paper to XI Plan)

Select Urban Development and Housing Schemes in Operation

Edited by

Rishi Muni Dwivedi
Assistant General Manager
Indian Overseas Bank
Regional Office
New Delhi

New Century Publications
New Delhi, India

NEW CENTURY PUBLICATIONS
4800/24, Bharat Ram Road,
Ansari Road, Daryaganj,
New Delhi-110 002

Tel.: 23247798, 65396605
E-mail: indiatax@vsnl.com
www.newcenturypublications.com

Editorial office:
34, Gujranwala Town, Part-2,
Delhi - 110 009
Tel.: 27247805, 27464774

First Published - May 2007

ISBN: 81-7708-123-3 (*10 digit*)
978-81-7708-123-7 (*13 digit*)

Published by New Century Publications and printed at Singhal Print Media, New Delhi -110 005

PRINTED IN INDIA

About the Book

Urbanisation is a natural consequence of economic changes that take place as a country develops. At the same time, urbanisation helps to contribute to the growth process at large. This is manifest in the increasing contribution of urban sector to national income.

The positive role of urbanisation is often over-shadowed by the evident deterioration in the physical environment and quality of life in the urban areas caused by widening gap between demand and supply of essential services and infrastructure. This results from increasing population, pressure on urban centres, most of which are financially and organisationally ill-equipped to respond to infrastructural needs. Public investment in urban infrastructure has also been less than adequate. The challenge of reorienting the urbanisation process, thus, lies in overcoming the infrastructural deficiencies and taking the best advantage of economic momentum inherent in urbanisation. The broad objective of urbanisation policy should be to secure balanced development between large, medium-sized and small industries, and between rural and urban areas.

Housing is an activity that is typically labour intensive and, therefore, fits in well with the pattern of development envisaged for India. The provision of shelter is a basic need which must be met. Housing construction also creates much-needed employment for the unskilled and, therefore, income for the relatively poor.

Urban and housing policies have been witnessing a continuous change since the launching of the First Five Year Plan in 1951, and particularly so since 1991. Part I of this work provides a detailed introduction to urban development and housing policies in India. Part II of the book presents edited extracts on the subject from India's Five Year Plans. Part III contains select schemes of urban development and housing which are presently in operation.

Editor's Profile

Dr. Rishi Muni Dwivedi holds M.Sc. (Agriculture) and Ph.D. degrees. His professional qualifications include C.A.I.I.B and Certificate in Rural Banking from Indian Institute of Banking and Finance, Mumbai and Certificate in Project Planning and Management from Development and Project Planning Centre, Bradford, U.K. He has 30 years of experience in Indian Overseas Bank as officer in various capacities. He has to his credit about 170 articles, mainly on agriculture and rural development finance. Presently, he is Assistant General Manager, Indian Overseas Bank, Regional Office, New Delhi and is also heading the Retail Loan Processing Centre.

Editor's Note on the Book

Urbanisation is an important aspect of the process of economic and social development and is closely connected with many other problems such as migration from villages to towns, levels of living in rural and urban areas, relative costs of providing economic and social services in towns of varying size, provision of housing for different sections of the population, provision of facilities like water supply, sanitation, transport and power, pattern of economic development, location and dispersal of industries, civic administration, fiscal policies, and the planning of land use. These aspects are of special importance in urban areas which are developing rapidly.

Urbanisation is a natural consequence of economic changes that take place as a country develops. At the same time, urbanisation helps to contribute to the growth process at large. This is manifest in the increasing contribution of urban sector to national income.

The positive role of urbanisation is often over-shadowed by the evident deterioration in the physical environment and quality of life in the urban areas caused by widening gap between demand and supply of essential services and infrastructure. This results from increasing population, pressure on urban centres, most of which are financially and organisationally ill-equipped to respond to infrastructural needs. Public investment in urban infrastructure has also been less than adequate. The challenge of reorienting the urbanisation process, thus, lies in overcoming the infrastructural deficiencies and taking the best advantage of economic momentum inherent in urbanisation.

Urbanisation: Policy Objectives

The broad objective of urbanisation policy should be to secure balanced development between large, medium-sized and small industries, and between rural and urban areas. While this is by no means easy to realise, the main ingredients of developmental policy should be the following:

- As far as possible, new industries should be established away from large and congested cities.
- In the planning of large industries, the concept of region should be adopted. In each case, planning should extend beyond the immediate environs to a larger area for whose development the new industry would serve as a major focal point.
- In community development projects or other areas within a district the rural and urban components of development should be knit into a composite plan based in each case on schemes for strengthening economic inter-dependence between towns and the surrounding rural areas.
- Within each rural area the effort should be to secure a diversified occupational pattern in place of the present extreme dependence on agriculture.

In considering the nature of the urban problem to be phased over the next decade, it is necessary both to deal with the situation which exists now and to ensure action along the right lines for the future.

In a country still largely rural and agricultural in character, it is natural that programmes for agricultural and rural development should receive the greatest emphasis; in particular those for rural employment creation and assistance to the rural poor. Urban development should, however, be seen as complementary to rural development and policies affecting the process of urbanisation should be such as to strengthen the links between towns and cities and their hinterland. Urban areas of all sizes operate as market centres for agricultural output and provide a variety of service functions in addition to operating as centres of manufacturing activity. These functions should be strengthened such that towns and cities serve the rural areas more effectively. The process of urbanisation should then be seen as aiding employment and income generation in rural areas rather than as a competitive process. Larger towns serve as distribution centres for seed, fertilisers and credit for farmers as well as serving as organised markets for their produce. The bigger cities provide services and facilities to both the smaller towns as well as rural areas in their hinterland. Thus, national policy on urban development should view the whole range of urban settlements as having a role to play in the national development process.

Housing

Housing is an activity that is typically labour intensive and, therefore, fits in well with the pattern of development envisaged for India. The provision of shelter is a basic need which must be met. Housing construction also creates much-needed employment for the unskilled and, therefore, income for the relatively poor.

In fulfilling the basic needs of the population, housing ranks next only to food and clothing in importance. A certain minimum standard of housing is essential for healthy and civilised existence. The development of housing, therefore, must enjoy high priority in a poor society such as ours where housing amenities are far below the minimum standards that have been internationally accepted. Housing activity serves to fulfil many of the fundamental objectives enshrined in India's Five Year Plans:

- providing shelter, raising the quality of life particularly of the poorer sections of the population;
- creating conditions which are conducive to the achievements of crucial objectives in terms of health, sanitation and education;
- creating substantial additional employment and dispersed economic activity;
- improving urban-rural and inter-personal equity through the narrowing down of difference in standards of living and
- last but not least, generating additional voluntary savings.

Urban housing shortage at the beginning of Tenth Plan was assessed at 8.89 million units. As much as 90 per cent of the shortfall pertained to the urban poor, and was attributed to the 'congestion' needs of joint families, obsolescence and replacement of old houses, upgrading of kutcha houses, and provision of housing to slum-dwellers. In urban areas, the problem becomes complex due to two factors: the high cost of land, and the lack of access to institutional credit for workers in the informal sector, including the self-employed. Provision of affordable land requires allocation of Government-owned lands, and cross-subsidization from commercial properties and colonies developed for the affluent, to those for the urban poor.

According to Tenth Five Year Plan (2002-07), "During the Tenth and Eleventh Plan housing shortage would go up further due to population growth, in addition to the backlog of housing shortage in the Ninth Plan. It would be possible to make a more precise assessment of the housing shortage and requirement once details for 2001 are available from the Census. However, in view of the housing shortage even on the basis of 1991 Census, a major thrust to the housing programme would have to be accorded in the Tenth and Eleventh Plan to meet the goal of 'Shelter for All' by year 2012. For this a detailed action plan would have to be drawn up incorporating housing programmes of public, private and household sectors. Nevertheless, it would be necessary to provide free houses under IAY to the shelterless rural poor, with some subsidy for upgradation of kutcha houses. There is also a need to promote credit linked housing in the rural areas for easing the housing shortage for non-BPL families. As regards credit for the urban poor, which is required even in the programmes of slum-rehousing (Valmiki Ambedkar Awas Yojana), there is need for measures to create institutional arrangements. The steps to ensure availability of credit will include strengthening of State Housing Boards, arranging tie-ups between self-help/thrift-and-credit groups of urban poor and Housing Finance Institutions, and promotion of co-operative housing schemes for the benefit of urban poor." (Tenth Plan,, vol I, p. 18)

The objective of the National Housing and Habitat Policy, 1998 was to provide shelter to all, especially to the poor and the deprived. The policy envisaged construction of 2 million additional houses annually. Of these, 1.3 million units were to be in rural areas and 0.7 million units in urban areas.

The dimensions and problems of housing need to be viewed in the overall environment of human settlement. The physical dwelling unit is not the sole element of housing; equally important is the provision of basic services like potable water, sanitation, drainage and electricity. Further, the type and location of housing is inextricably linked to the employment and affordability of the occupant.

Housing has been primarily self-help activity for the majority of the households. Increasing population pressure on land and infrastructure and associated high cost have made proper housing inaccessible to the poorer segments of the population, necessitating State intervention initially as a welfare activity and now recognised as a social and economic imperative. In a developing country like India, problems of urban housing have been more evident, both because of exponentially increasing land and construction cost and deteriorating quality of life in congested urban pockets. Sheer number of additional housing required to meet the needs of the growing urban population presents a formidable task. If we add to this the unserviceable housing stock in rural areas the task assumes frightening proportions. However, the facts that housing is one of the major employment generators and that motivation for ownership of housing is an important element in the mobilisation of domestic savings, make the task worth our endeavour. Housing is not to be treated as a marginal or welfare sector which is a drain on productive resources but to be recognised as a major economic sector.

In this context, the housing policies and programmes, while accepting that housing is essentially a private activity, have to recognise that State intervention is necessary to meet housing requirements of a majority of vulnerable sections as well as to create an enabling environment for accomplishing the goal of "Shelter for All" on a self-sustaining basis.

The Housing and Habitat Policy, 1998 has specifically advocated that Government create a facilitating environment for growth of housing activity instead of taking on the task of housing itself. Housing is largely a private sector activity in both the rural and urban sectors. This is not to rule out the need for a high degree of involvement of the Government and its agencies in meeting the housing needs of the urban poor. The nature of this involvement - it may in some instances extend to house construction itself - is to be determined by the needs of a given situation.

Housing Finance

Housing Sector is a very crucial sector as far as the interest rates on the loans are concerned. The growth of housing finance segment in India has accelerated in recent years. Many supporting policy measures (like tax benefits) and the supervisory incentives instituted had played a major role in development of housing finance. Housing development creates business for many sectors like brick kilns, cement industry, iron and steel industry, skilled and unskilled labour, carpenters, wooden furniture, etc. In view of its backward and forward linkages with other sectors of the economy, housing finance in India is seen as a social good.

At one time the interest on housing loans was to the extent of 18 to 19 %. It dropped to 7 percent in the year 2005-06. Now again it has started rising and may settle for some time.

The interest for various periods has gone slow changes to the extent of 3 percent in last 5 years. For example, for a loan repayable in 20 years, the interest rate percentage was 8.25 (April 2002), 7.75 (November 2002), 7.50 (January 2003), 7.00 (January 2004), 7.50 (November 2004), 8.00 (June 2005), 8.50 (February 2006), 9.50 (July 2006), 10.00 (December 2006).

In February 2007, the Public Sector Banks have been advised to hold the home loan rates at the current levels. Provisioning and risk weight has been increased for credit card receivables, loans and advances qualifying for capital market exposure, personal loans (excluding housing loans and real estate sector. These have been treated as considerable risk prone sectors and provisioning for standard assets on these four segments has been increased from one percent to two percent. Housing loans are not included in these segments. This is an encouragement to the banks continue finance to housing sector as usual.

The housing loan exposure of the Public Sector Banks grew to 111 per cent from Rs. 53,737 crore in March 2004 to Rs. 1,13,230 crore in September 2006. Direct housing loans up to Rs. 15 lakh irrespective of the location now qualify as priority sector lending. From a very low base, housing credit has increased substantially over last few years. During the period 1993-2004, outstanding housing loans by scheduled commercial banks and housing finance companies grew at a trend rate of 23 per cent. The portion of housing loans in total non-food credit of scheduled commercial banks was about 3 per cent in 1992-93 which has gone up to about 7 per cent in 2003-04. Non-priority sector housing loans outstanding as on February 18, 2005 were around Rs. 74,000 crore, which is, however, only 8.0 per cent of the gross bank credit.

Housing loans are understood to form a large component of such lending. In addition, housing credit is also being provided by housing finance companies, which in turn are also receiving some bank finance. Thus the exposure of the banking sector to housing loans has gone up substantially.

The housing sector was in boom due to rising employment bin IT, BPO and other sectors with good pay packets. There was a sudden increase in demand for housing in last 3-4 years. Many people invested in housing for speculative reasons. The bullish trend in housing and real estate sector is now heading for price correction. The money of the people, who invested for speculative purposes, is stuck up. For the high value residential units (above Rs. 25 lakh) constructed during 2004-06, in the northern India in the cities of NCT Delhi, Jaipur, Chandigarh, Panipat and Sonipat, the supply exceeds demand as per a study conducted. The demand exceeded supply in the southern and western areas. There is supply of 38,026 units and demand is for 21262 units having a surplus of 16,764 units. More people prefer for the flats as compared to the independent houses for various reasons like safety and security due to old parents living alone, price factor and the various community services available in flats. Many people are investing in bigger houses due to increase in their income. The results of the study reveals that only one percent people invested in housing sector for rental purpose, 23 per cent for investment purpose and rest for residing.

Improving consumer purchasing power, coupled with more liberal attitudes toward personal debt, is contributing to India's retail banking segment including housing. The rise of the Indian middle class is an important contributory factor in this regard. The percentage of middle to high-income Indian households is expected to continue rising. The younger population not only wields increasing purchasing power, but as far as acquiring personal debt is concerned, they are perhaps more comfortable than previous generations.

Urban Governance

Urban governance today is characterised by fragmentation of responsibility, incomplete devolution of functions and funds to the elected bodies and ULBs, unwillingness to progress towards municipal autonomy, adherence to outmoded methods of property tax and reluctance to levy user charges. State governments continue to take decisions on such matters as rates of user charges, property tax, octroi, role of parastatals in water supply and sanitation services, etc., with little reference to the ULBs that are affected by these decisions. Far from strengthening the constitutional role of the elected ULBs, such developments only reinforce the perception that ULBs are subordinate entities under the day-to-day control of the state governments, beholden to them not only for the development of the cities but often for their very survival. There appears to be a lack of confidence that many of the ULBs are capable of meeting their obligations as institutions of local self-governance. In the present set up, initiatives for local developmental activities rarely come from the ULBs. Experience shows that functional autonomy becomes a reality only when it is accompanied by financial independence. State governments, therefore, need to strengthen the autonomous functioning of the ULBs through positive measures, and in particular, ensure their financial self-reliance.

The role of the ULBs in the immediate future will be:

- To be responsive and accountable to the community;
- to develop cities with standards of service comparable to the best in that particular category;
- to constantly improve their capabilities so as to equip themselves to undertake their tasks in resource-raising, service provision, and poverty alleviation,

Good urban governance calls for adequate policy and legal frameworks, the existence of regulatory and planning authorities, human skills, a sound revenue base, accounting and accountability. Substantial work has already been done to upgrade the urban infrastructure and several parastatals and urban development authorities have acquired considerable skills in planning and executing projects. Programmes such as the Mega City project for five selected cities, the Integrated Development of Small and Medium Towns (IDSMT), and the Accelerated Urban Water Supply Programme (AUWSP) have shown varying degrees of success in meeting some of the urban needs. In particular, parastatal agencies and bodies such as development authorities, need to play a supportive role to the elected bodies rather than taking over functions which properly belong to the ULBs. The objective of devolution and decentralisation should be carried forward by making parastatals and authorities partners and agencies of the democratically elected ULBs, thus making a gradual transition to local management while continuing to use the expertise of the organisations set up and supervised by the State Governments. Initiating the necessary processes for partnerships between the State and its agencies on the one hand, and the ULBs on the other, is a part of the exercise of 'capacity building' in the ULBs.

The growing concentration of urban population in larger towns is another urban concern. The tasks are challenging, for it is mainly in the mega and metro cities that land is a major constraint for undertaking development work. A large part of civic amenities, particularly water supply, sanitation and sewerage, are managed with assets that have outlived their operational efficiency. The required massive upgradation and renovation of these assets, is constrained by high population density and concentrated commercial activities at the locations where these service assets are installed. The lack of comprehensive urban planning in the past to promote regular upgradation and renewal has resulted in a large backlog of development activities.

The key urban concern is the growing gap between demand and supply of basic services. While there has been a steady growth in the housing stock, infrastructure and services, the gaps between demand and supply have been rising, even in terms of conservative norms.

Attitudes to urban growth within the country tend to swing between two extremes. Cities are seen either as an unavoidable evil or in a more positive way as 'engines of growth'. The former view is held by those who focus on the growth of slums and squatter colonies, the congestion on the roads and environmental degradation. The others, in contrast, focus on the bustling formal and informal sectors in urban areas and their contribution to the economy, the diversification of occupations away from traditional land-based ones to newer forms of production and services, and the lower levels of poverty as compared to rural areas.

The poor quality of urban infrastructure in our major cities is an aspect of infrastructure deficiency that has come to be increasingly recognised in recent years. Urban infrastructure problems are likely to intensify as our cities expand and our urban population grows. Besides, in an environment in which states are increasingly interested in attracting foreign direct investment, it is inevitable that the quality of infrastructure in urban areas will be one of the critical competitive aspects that investors will consider in making location decisions.

Urban and Housing Policies in Five Year Plans

The policies of urban development and housing in India have come a long way since 1950s. The pressure of urban population and lack of housing and basic services were very much evident in the early 1950s. In some cities this was compounded by migration of people from Pakistan. However, the general perception of the policy makers was that India is pre-dominantly an agricultural and rural economy and that there are potent dangers of over urbanisation which will lead to the drain of resources from the countryside to feed the cities. The positive aspects of cities as engines of economic growth in the context of national economic policies were not much appreciated and, therefore, the problems of urban areas were treated more as welfare problems and sectors of residual investment rather than as issues of national economic importance.

In the First Five Year Plan (1951-56), the emphasis was given on institution building and on construction of houses for Government employees and weaker sections. The Ministry of Works & Housing was constituted and National Building Organisation and Town & Country Planning Organisation were set up. A sizeable part of the plan outlay was spent for rehabilitation of the refugees from Pakistan and on building the new city of Chandigarh. An Industrial Housing Scheme was also initiated. The Centre subsidised Scheme to the extent of 50 per cent towards the cost of land and construction.

The scope of housing programme for the poor was expanded in the Second Plan (1956-61). The Industrial Housing Scheme was widened to cover all workers. Three new schemes were introduced, namely, Rural Housing, Slum Clearance and Sweepers Housing. Town & Country Planning Legislations were enacted in many States and necessary organisations were also set up for preparation of Master Plans for important towns.

The general directions for housing programmes in the Third Plan (1961-66) were co-ordination of efforts of all agencies and orienting the programmes to the needs of the Low Income Groups. A Scheme was introduced in 1959 to give loans to State Governments for a period of 10 years for acquisition and development of land in order to make available building sites in sufficient numbers. Master Plans for major cities were prepared and the State capitals of Gandhi Nagar and Bhubaneswar were developed.

The balanced urban growth was accorded high priority in the Fourth Plan (1969-74). The Plan stressed the need to prevent further growth of population in large cities and need for decongestion or dispersal of population. This was envisaged to be achieved by creation of smaller towns and by planning the spatial location of economic activity. Housing & Urban Development Corporation (HUDCO) was established to fund the remunerative housing and urban development programmes, promising a quick turnover. A Scheme for Environmental Improvement or Urban Slums was undertaken in the Central Sector from 1972-73 with a view to provide a minimum level of services, like, water supply, sewerage, drainage, street pavements in 11 cities with a population of 8 lakh and above. The scheme was later extended to 9 more cities.

The Fifth Plan (1974-79) reiterated the policies of the preceding Plans to promote smaller towns in new urban centres, in order to ease the increasing pressure on urbanisation. This was to be supplemented by efforts to augment civic services in urban areas with particular emphasis on a comprehensive and regional approach to problems in metropolitan cities. A Task Force was set up for development of small and medium towns. The Urban Land (Ceiling & Regulation) Act was enacted to prevent concentration of land holding in urban areas and to make available urban land for construction of houses for the middle and low income groups.

The thrust of the planning in the Sixth Plan (1980-85) was on integrated provision of services along with shelter, particularly for the poor. The Integrated Development of Small and Medium Towns (IDSMT) was launched in towns with population below one lakh for provision of roads, pavements, minor civic works, bus stands, markets, shopping complex etc. Positive inducements were proposed for setting up new industries and commercial and professional establishments in small, medium and intermediate towns.

The Seventh Plan (1985-90) stressed on the need to entrust major responsibility of housing construction on the private sector. A three-fold role was assigned to the public sector, namely, mobilisation for resources for housing, provision for subsidised housing for the poor and acquisition and development of land. The National Housing Bank was set up to expand the base of housing finance. NBO was reconstituted and a new organisation called Building Material Technology Promotion Council (BMTPC) was set up for promoting commercial production of innovative building materials. A network of Building Centres was also set up during this Plan period. The Seventh Plan explicitly recognised the problems of the urban poor and for the first time an Urban Poverty Alleviation Scheme known as Urban Basic Services for the Poor (UBSP) was launched.

As a follow-up of the Global Shelter Strategy (GSS), National Housing Policy (NHP) was announced in 1988. The long term goal of the NHP was to eradicate houselessness, improve the housing conditions of the inadequately housed and provide a minimum level of basic services and amenities to all. The role of Government was conceived, as a provider for the poorest and vulnerable sections and as a facilitator for other income groups and private sector by the removal of constraints and the increased supply of land and services.

The National Commission of Urbanisation submitted its report. The Report eloquently pointed out the reality of continuing and rapid growth of the urban population as well as the scale and intensity of urbanisation, the critical deficiencies in the various items of infrastructure, the concentration of vast number of poor and deprived people, the acute disparities in the access of shelter and basic services, deteriorating environmental quality and the impact of poor governance on the income and the productivity of enterprises.

In the backdrop of this report the Eighth Plan (1992-97) for the first time explicitly recognised the role and importance of urban sector for the national economy. While growth rate of employment in the urban areas averaged around 3.8 per cent per annum, it dropped to about 1.6 per cent in the rural areas. Therefore, the urban areas have to be enabled to absorb larger increments to the labour force. The Plan identified the key issues in the emerging urban scenario:

- the widening gap between demand and supply of infrastructural services badly hitting the poor, whose access to the basic services like drinking water, sanitation, education and basic health services is shrinking
- unabated growth of urban population aggravating the accumulated backlog of housing shortages, resulting in proliferation of slums and squatter settlement and decay of city environment
- high incidence of marginal employment and urban poverty as reflected in NSS 43rd round that 41.8 million urban people lived below the poverty line.

The response of the Plan to this scenario was the launching of Urban Poverty and Alleviation Programme of Nehru Rojgar Yojana (NRY).

The major objectives of urban and housing policies in the Ninth Plan (1997-2002) included the following:

- Development of urban areas as economically efficient, socially equitable and environmentally sustainable entities;
- Accelerated development of housing, particularly for the low income groups and other disadvantaged groups;
- Development and upgradation of urban infrastructure services to meet the needs of a growing population;
- Alleviation of urban poverty and unemployment;
- Promoting accessibility and affordability of the poor to housing and basic services;
- Promoting efficient and affordable mass urban transportation systems in metropolitan cities;
- Improvement of urban environment;
- Promoting private sector participation in the provision of public infrastructure and of the community and NGOs in urban planning and management of specific components of urban services; and
- Democratic decentralisation and strengthening of municipal governance.

The approach to urban management issues in the Tenth Plan (2002-07) revolve around the strengthening of the democratic structure, with the assistance of the very agencies-state governments, parastatals and the urban development authorities - who have continued to take over the functions that rightly belong to the ULBs. The major thrust areas for the Tenth Plan were identified as follows:

- An extra effort has to be made to ensure that the capacities created in such areas as water and sanitation, transport systems, and planned city development are not permitted to degenerate.
- Public-private partnerships should be brought on to the urban agenda for improving efficiency and better service delivery. However, capacity building in the public services has to be given highest priority, through training both elected and appointed officials, and by restructuring of municipal entities for more efficient management. Performance of the ULBs in their allotted tasks, apart from being watched by the citizens, should also be closely monitored by the State Governments.
- Finances of the ULBs need strengthening through smooth working of the SFC awards, rationalisation and improvement of the property taxation system, and a sufficient level of levy of user charges. Transfers from State budget should be linked to defined levels of performance of the ULBs in resource-raising, expenditure control, proper financial management, and transparency in functioning.
- Broad-based urban sector reform measures should commence during the Tenth Plan. The fundamental need is to strengthen the autonomy - functional as well as financial - of the ULBs. There is need for improving the debt-servicing capabilities of ULBs so that investment funds from financial institutions and market borrowings can be made available for urban infrastructure works. Plan support in the form of centrally sponsored schemes should be linked to the willingness in the state and local bodies to implement reform programmes.

- The 2001 Census data provide basic information on the trends in urban growth and this will help establish the needs of the ULBs, which has to be balanced by capabilities. Future programmes of assistance should be based on these two factors. But first, studies to develop the disaggregated picture of urban growth in different size categories, different states and types of cities should be taken up immediately based on the Census data. Planning of urban growth projects should be based on these studies.

Housing is a basic necessity as well as an important economic activity, in that it is a part of the construction industry. Construction activity accounts for more than 50 per cent of the development outlays. A study by the Indian Institute of Management, Ahmedabad, commissioned by HUDCO, to evaluate the impact of investment in the housing sector on GDP and employment, has found that the sector ranks third among the 14 major sectors in terms of the direct, indirect, and induced effect on all sectors of the economy.

The Approach Paper on the Eleventh Five Year Plan (2007-12) released by the Government in November 2006 has also stressed the importance of construction, housing and real estate industry as it provides a large scope for direct and indirect employment of persons with a wide range of skills and also of unskilled persons. It employs over 30 million people and has been growing at over 10 per cent per year over the last five years. It covers rural and urban infrastructure, roads, airports, sea-ports and commercial and residential buildings. The Eleventh Plan has, therefore, put special focus on this sector so that its potential to create employment and growth is fully realised.

Conclusion

When we talk about the housing, it does not mean the house for living alone. There are requirements of buildings for other than living spaces, like schools, factories etc. Like minimum requirement for housing, there are minimum basic requirements for every person, school children and workers in the factory.

These aspects have not yet been dealt in detail. This has resulted in haphazard use of buildings for various purposes not fully suitable for that purpose.

All the basic services, which are the need in the urban area, are also a must for rural areas. In urban areas, the shortage or inadequacy of these survives call for immediate attention, while in then villages; inadequacy of various necessities goes unattended. As the rural people think that they have to live with these inadequacies. All ingredients should be woven in such a manner that need for transport is minimal. Decentralisation of various offices/factories/industries and then housing near the work place can fulfill these objectives. More number of areas to be developed in urban instead of few areas to be in developed in a haphazard manner.

Proper housing assumes more importance in our country where still 26 per cent of the population is living below poverty line. This means that the 26 per cent of the population are not able to afford the basic minimum need of the food. In such condition they can not thing a roof on their head. House is an address, status of the person.

The blue prints of future India are molded in schools. Leave the quality, even the number of schools is not increasing in the same ratio the population is increasing. Result a long queue for admissions. Every child has a right to learn. The planners of various colonies and apartment complexes are not providing the space for schools. Hence the schools are run as commercial ventures. In the spaces that are not sufficient as per the health care requirements of the children. Physical, mental, behavioural and other aspects of life develop in the schools. For this purpose the sufficient space is needed for every child in the schools. We have to keep space for schools also while dealing with the problem of housing.

As urban development is a major area affecting the human life there is a need for more educational institutions to take care of this aspect. A new framework of urban institutions is required, which answers the current and emerging requirements of growing metropolitan cities. There is need for comprehensive planning. A new urban land policy is required which treats the land as a source for creating socially and environmentally harmonious communities. Construction of buildings with natural surroundings of green areas, conservation and development of natural features, development and preservation of open spaces and management of natural resources, automatic rechargeable water reservoirs and related environment infrastructure and services must be the strategies for a good Living environment. Space for marriages and public functions, parking, smokeless and gas less transport are the requirements of a good city.

A new cadre of urban administrators who have the training and motivation to meet new challenges; a new human settlement technology which promotes technological adaptations and focuses on special problems of poor urban migrants and involves a strategy of changing this neglected lot of today into urban pioneers of tomorrow.

There should be department to administer and enforce the City's codes, ordinances and regulations pertaining to planning and development in a professional manner; and to conduct these services with integrity and equality for each resident.

Urban Development is comprised of several sections and units. Urban Development focuses on community development; regulating and enforcing the vast number of codes, laws, acts, regulations and ordinances related to development and construction within the City and maintaining high standards before, during, and after the development process.

The health department is responsible for protecting the health, safety and welfare of the City and its citizens through the enforcement of building, electrical, plumbing, mechanical, and other applicable codes/ordinances adopted by various authorities.

This responsibility requires a team effort and is accomplished with the support of the Building Inspection Unit, Central Permitting Unit, Electrical Inspection Unit, Mechanical Inspection Unit, and Plumbing Inspection Unit.

There should be the Long Range Planning for each city. The Long Range Planning concentrates on long-range planning issues, including periodic updates to the City's Comprehensive Plan, land use surveys, updating community development plans, environmental reviews for projects utilizing community development block grant funds, and professional consultation on special projects. Maintenance of Historic buildings should also consist of the part of urban development. Parks cemeteries and green spaces are an important part of the urban areas and should be maintained properly.

Every city should have the units to work in cases of any type of emergency like storm, hurricane heavy rains, fire, flood, drought etc. One of the tedious jobs for urban area is disposal of litter, trash and debris, junk vehicles, high weeds and grass and substandard and deteriorating structures. This should be also taken care of by the Urban Development Authority. Landscaping, tree planting and tree protection should be taken up simultaneously. All the urban areas should maximize their income resources, improve the services and implement focused and progressive planning.

New Delhi
May 20, 2007

Rishi Muni Dwivedi

Contents

Part III: Select Urban Development and Housing Schemes in Operation

Part I
Urban Development and Housing in India: An Introduction

Urban Development and Housing in India: An Introduction

Planned urbanization can act as a spur to growth, employment and a better quality of life.

1. Urban Development

Over a third of India's population lives in urban areas. There are 35 urban agglomerations with population of more than one million, and about 37 percent of the total urban population live in these million-plus cities. Urbanization in India is proceeding at a modest pace.

The likely increase in urban productivity and population due to the new economic policies of the Government of India will place a heavy demand on all kinds of urban infrastructure and services. The infrastructure bottlenecks in urban centres are likely to pose serious impediments in enhancing the productivity.

The 74th Constitutional Amendment Act, 1992 has given Constitutional status to municipal governments, has defined municipal responsibilities in broad terms and has left the individual State Finance Commissions, both the task of assigning the expenditures and revenues, and the task of defining the nature of financial relations between state and local governments. As a result, there has been considerable variation in the rigor and quality, across states, on the nature of State Finance Commissions recommendations and the extent to which they have been implemented.

In many states, the devolution of administrative powers related to planning, financing and managing municipal services has not yet become effective. The expected improvement in services, as an outcome of decentralization, is based on the notion that as expenditure responsibilities are devolved, local elected representatives would have decision making authority. However, the range of issues on which elected municipal representatives can take a decision is limited. There is a wide variation in availability of infrastructure and services in different cities. The larger cities have the ability to raise resources from the capital market, while smaller towns lag behind because of lack of resources and expertise. Urban Local Bodies (ULBs) and state development agencies have an important role to play in development of urban infrastructure. City Challenge Fund (CCF) was created in the budget 2001-02 to support Urban Local Bodies (ULBs) to undertake reforms. The CCF seeks to directly support the grass-root institutions like ULB, and partially finance the cost of developing a reform program and its implementation.

Programmes such as Mega City Project, Integrated Development for Small and Medium Towns (IDSMT), Accelerated Urban Water Supply Program (AUWSP) have shown some success in meeting the urban needs. IDSMT and Mega City schemes are being implemented in states to meet the requirements of water supply, sanitation, solid waste management, urban transport and development of new extensions like residential colonies and satellite towns to relieve congestion. The IDSMT was launched in 1979-80. 1,310 small and medium towns have so far been assisted under the scheme. Central assistance released under the scheme is Rs. 599.4 crore (up to January 31, 2003). Mega city scheme was introduced in 1993-94, covering five cities namely, Mumbai, Kolkata, Chennai, Hyderabad and Bangalore. The Central assistance released under the Scheme has been Rs. 809.3 crore (up to January 31, 2003). The Central assistance in these schemes has not been adequate in terms of amount and coverage of cities. Moreover, the implementation of the scheme has not been satisfactory in terms of timely completion of projects, augmentation of resources by ULBs, tie-ups of institutional finance etc.

1.1 Need for Urban Development: Over a third of India's population lives in urban areas. There are 35 urban agglomerations with population of more than one million, and about 37 per cent of the total urban population live in these million-plus cities. Urbanization in India is proceeding at a modest pace.

The likely increase in urban productivity and population due to the new economic policies of the Government of India will place a heavy demand on all kinds of urban infrastructure and services. The infrastructure bottlenecks in urban centres are likely to pose serious impediments in enhancing the productivity.

The 74th Constitutional Amendment Act, 1992 has given Constitutional status to municipal governments, has defined municipal responsibilities in broad terms and has left the individual State Finance Commissions, both the task of assigning the expenditures and revenues, and the task of defining the nature of financial relations between state and local governments. As a result, there has been considerable variation in the rigor and quality, across states, on the nature of State Finance Commissions recommendations and the extent to which they have been implemented.

In many states, the devolution of administrative powers related to planning, financing and managing municipal services has not yet become effective. The expected improvement in services, as an outcome of decentralization, is based on the notion that as expenditure responsibilities are devolved, local elected representatives would have decision making authority. However, the range of issues on which elected municipal representatives can take a decision is limited. There is a wide variation in availability of infrastructure and services in different cities. The larger cities have the ability to raise resources from the capital market, while smaller towns lag behind because of lack of resources and expertise. Urban Local Bodies (ULBs) and state development agencies have an important role to play in development of urban infrastructure. City Challenge Fund (CCF) was created in the budget 2001-02 to support Urban Local Bodies (ULBs) to undertake reforms. The CCF seeks to directly support the grass-root institutions like ULB, and partially finance the cost of developing a reform program and its implementation.

Programmes such as Mega City Project, Integrated Development for Small and Medium Towns (IDSMT), Accelerated Urban Water Supply Program (AUWSP) have shown some success in meeting the urban needs. IDSMT and Mega City schemes are being implemented in states to meet the requirements of water supply, sanitation, solid waste management, urban transport and development of new extensions like residential colonies and satellite towns to relieve congestion. The IDSMT was launched in 1979-80. 1,310 small and medium towns have so far been assisted under the scheme. Central assistance released under the scheme is Rs. 599.4 crore (up to January 31, 2003). Mega city scheme was introduced in 1993-94, covering five cities namely, Mumbai, Kolkata, Chennai, Hyderabad and Bangalore. The Central assistance released under the Scheme has been Rs. 809.3 crore (up to January 31, 2003). The Central assistance in these schemes has not been adequate in terms of amount and coverage of cities. Moreover, the implementation of the scheme has not been satisfactory in terms of timely completion of projects, augmentation of resources by ULBs, tie-ups of institutional finance etc.

1.2 Features of Urban Infrastructure Services: Urban infrastructure services have the following characteristics.

- Most urban infrastructure services are natural monopolies and their marginal cost declines over a very large range of output. As such, it has been feared that the private sector might exploit the monopolistic situation. Such services include water, waste water management, telephone, electricity, bridge, and road networks.
- Many services like sanitation and solid waste disposal (SWD) have significant external economies. As a consequence, market-based systems may fail to provide the service in adequate quantity and quality.
- It is difficult to exclude anyone from using say, roads or public lighting. The consumer may refuse to pay for the service since he may be able to use it free of charge legally or otherwise.
- Certain infrastructure services being necessities (like water) have almost inelastic demand. Private provision of these could result in exploitative pricing unless prices are regulated.

- Requirement of heavy investment in capital equipment discourages private sector entry into certain infrastructure segments.

The above mentioned characteristics have for long been used as valid arguments for blocking entry of the private sector into infrastructure. The arguments, however, are slowly losing their validity due to many technological and organizational innovations. Unbundling of services has been a major mechanism through which the misconception about the economies-of-scale argument has been overcome. Technological innovations in the areas of sanitation and sewerage have permitted low-cost supply options. Increasing range and quality of service has reduced the cost of providing the service, making the operation commercially viable and also opening up areas for private sector operations. The recognition of the demand aspect has made remunerative pricing possible in some segments.

Though there are examples of efficient provision of infrastructure services by governments – power in Mexico, most sectors in Korea and Singapore, water in Togo and Botswana – by and large, governments have not been very effective suppliers of many services. The cost of government failures has been much higher than the possible cost of market failure. Commercialisation of infrastructure projects basically means efficient provision of service to the consumers' satisfaction on cost-recovery basis. Since the public sector in most cases is an inefficient provider due to its inherent characteristics, promotion of privatisation itself becomes an instrument for commercialisation.

2. Jawaharlal Nehru National Urban Renewal Mission (JNNURM)

JNNURM was launched by the Prime Minister on December 3, 2005 to encourage cities to initiate steps to bring about improvement in the existing service levels in a financially sustainable manner. The objectives of the mission, *inter alia*, include planned development of identified cities including semi-urban areas, outgrowths and urban corridors and improved provision of, basic services to the urban poor. The duration of the mission would be seven years beginning from 2005-06. The mission has subsumed the following on-going schemes of the Ministry:

- Infrastructure Development in Mega Cities,
- Integrated Development of Small and Medium Towns and
- Accelerated Urban Water Supply Programme.

Cities/Urban Agglomerations/Parastatals will be required to prepare detailed project reports for undertaking projects under identified areas. Funds for the identified cities would be released to the designated State Nodal Agency, which in turn would leverage, to the extent feasible, additional resources from the financial institutions/private sector/capital market. Private sector participation in development, management and financing of urban infrastructure would be clearly delineated.

The admissible components under the mission include urban renewal, water supply (including de-salination plants) and sanitation, sewerage and solid waste management, urban transport, development of heritage areas, preservation of water bodies etc. A provision of Rs. 50,000 crore has been agreed to as Central Assistance for Jawaharlal Nehru National Urban Renewal Mission (JNNURM) for a period of 7 years beginning from 2005-06.

On completion of the mission period of seven years, it is expected that ULBs/Parastatals will achieve the following outcomes:

- Modern and transparent budgeting, accounting, and financial management systems designed and adopted for all urban services and governance functions.
- City-wide framework for planning and governance will be established and become operational.
- All urban residents will be able to obtain access to a basic level of urban services.
- Financially self-sustaining agencies for urban governance and service delivery will be established, through reforms to major revenue instruments.

- Local services and governance will be conducted in a manner that is transparent and accountable to citizens.

e-Governance applications will be introduced in core functions of ULBs/Para-statals resulting in reduced cost and time of service delivery processes.

3. Integrated Development of Small and Medium Towns (IDSMT)

The persons living in big cities are facing a lot of problems due to increasing population and under development of infrastructure. To improve the economic and physical infrastructure and also to provide essential facilities and service and also to slow down the growth of large cities by developing small and medium towns through increased investments in these towns the this scheme was started. This is a Centrally sponsored scheme initiated in the year 1979-80 and is continuing. The development of small urban centres would also help in reducing migration to large cities and support the growth of surrounding rural areas as well.

The scheme has the following objectives:

- Improving infrastructural facilities and helping in the creation of durable public assets in small and medium towns.
- Decentralising economic growth and employment opportunities and promoting dispersed Urbanisation.
- Increasing the availability of serviced sites for housing, commercial and industrial uses.
- Integrating spatial and socio-economic planning as envisaged in the Constitution (74th Amendment) Act, 1992.
- Promoting resource-generating schemes for the urban local bodies to improve their overall financial position.

3.1 Main Features of the Revised Scheme:

- Towns up to population of five lakh are eligible.
- The share of Central and State assistance has been increased and made available as grant.

- The State to prepare the urban strategy for the next 10 years and give justification for selecting priority towns to be included under IDSMT.
- In accordance with Constitution (74th) Amendment Act, 1992, IDSMT Scheme is applicable to those towns where elections to the local bodies are held and elected representatives are in position.
- The State Government to create State Urban Development fund at the State level and Municipal Revolving Fund at the Town level for continuous sustainable infrastructure development.
- A Sanctioning committee at the State level chaired by the Secretary Urban Development/Local Govt. (incharge of IDSMT Scheme) will approve the projects.
- Institutional finance is reduced to 20-40 per cent through HUDCO/Other Institutional Financing Agencies.
- The component of assistance are enlarged and made more flexible.

Central assistance in the from of grant-in-aid would be made available in the ratio of 60:40 (central & State) for the preparation of Project Reports/Urban Development (Investment plan) of IDSMT towns ranging from Rs. 3 to Rs. 6 lakh depending on the size of the town.

3.2 Selection of Towns:

- IDSMT Scheme will be applicable to town/cities with population up to 5 lakh subject to the stipulation that 1/3 of the total amount available each year, for the Scheme as a whole will be allocated to town with less than 50,000 population. While selecting the towns preference will be given to headquarter of districts followed by Mandy towns and Industrial growth centres, tourist places and pilgrim centres etc.
- The IDSMT Scheme will be applicable to only those towns where elections to the local bodies have been held and elected bodies are in position.

3.3 Components for Funding

The components for assistance under IDSMT will include works as per City/Town Development/Master Plans which may have city/townwide significance.

Strengthening of Master Plan road facilities including ring, arterial, bypass/link roads and small bridges, Sites and services, Development of bus/truck terminals, Construction/upgradation of Master Plan drains including Storm water channels, Solid waste management, Development of Market complexes/shopping centres, Provision of tourist facilities, Development of City/Town Parks, Street lighting for Master Plan roads, Slaughter houses, Major public amenities like Gardens, Playgrounds, Marriage halls, Pay-and-use toilets, etc. Cycle/Rickshaw stands, Traffic improvement and management schemes, Construction of retaining walls and slope stability measures in hill station towns, Social amenities, specially for the poorer sections.

4. Prime Minister's Integrated Urban Poverty Eradication Programme (PM-IUPEP)

The scheme commenced on January 16, 1996 with the objectives of effective achievement of social sector goals, community empowerment, convergence through sustainable support systems and employment generation and skill upgradation. It provides for the following.

- **Self-Employment through Setting up Micro Enterprises and Skill Development:** The maximum project cost should not be more than Rs. one lakh. The maximum loan amount is Rs. 95,000. Margin: The applicant has to bring Rs. 5,000 as margin in cash. Subsidy: A subsidy of 15 per cent with the maximum of Rs. 7,500 is available. The subsidy is to be provided by Town Poverty Eradication Cell. An allocation of Rs. 98.60 Crore was made under the programme for the year 1996-97 for 342 class II towns and 72 district towns.
- **Shelter Upgradation:** A maximum of Rs. 7,500 or 75 per cent of the unit cost, whichever is lower can be sanctioned as

loan. 25 per cent of the unit cost/repair/renovation cost is to be provided as subsidy with maximum of Rs. 2,500.

The loan is to be released in 2 installments on verifying the satisfactory progress of the project. Total training expenditure should not exceed Rs. 2,000 per trainee

5. Promotion of Non-Handicapping Environment for Disabled and Elderly Persons

At the meeting held at Beijing in December 1992, to launch the Asian and Pacific Decade of Disabled Persons 1993-2002, Economic and Social Commission for Asia and the Pacific (ESCAP) adopted the Proclamation on the Full Participation and Equality of People with Disabilities in the Asian and Pacific Region. India was a signatory to the said Proclamation. Ministry of Urban Development & Poverty Alleviation was designated as the nodal Ministry for implementation of barrier-free built environment for the disabled and elderly persons as envisaged in "The Persons with Disabilities (Equal Opportunities, Protection of Rights and Full Participation) Act, 1995.

Ministry of Urban Development & Poverty Alleviation also prepared Model Building Bye-Laws which contained a number of provisions for providing accessibilities to disabled persons to various public buildings. These Building Bye-Laws were sent to State Governments, Union Territories, Delhi Development Authority, Municipal Corporation of Delhi, New Delhi Municipal Committee etc. for adoption.

6. Urban Housing

Housing is one of the basic requirements for human survival. For a normal citizen owning a house provides significant economic and social security and status in society. For a shelter less person, a house brings about a profound social change in his existence, endowing him with an identity, thus integrating him with his immediate social milieu. A housing programme for the rehabilitation of refugees was taken up immediately after partition by the Ministry of Rehabilitation and this lasted till around 1960.

Approximately 5 lakh families were housed in various centres mainly located in Northern India. A Village Housing Scheme was also launched as part of the Community Development Movement in 1957, in which loans to individuals and cooperatives were provided up to a maximum of Rs. 5,000 per house. However, only 67000 houses were built under this scheme by the end of the Fifth Plan (1980). In 1972-73, the Estimate Committee of the Lok Sabha in its 37th Report pointed out that "the Committee is distressed to note that although 83 per cent of India's population lives in villages and about 73 per cent of the rural population reside in unsatisfactory kutcha structures, the problem of rural housing has not received the close attention of the Government." Following this, certain initiatives were undertaken by Government including the launching of the House Sites-cum-Construction Assistance Scheme which began as a Central Scheme in the 4th Plan and was transferred to the State Sector with effect from 1.04.1974 on the recommendation of the National Development Council (NDC).

6.1 Indira Awaas Yojana: The scheme was launched during 1985-86 as a sub-scheme of Rural Employment Guarantee Programme. Thereafter it continued as a sub-scheme of Jawahar Rozgar Yojana (JRY) since its launching in April, 1989. 6 per cent of the total JRY funds were allocated for implementation of IAY. From the year 1993-94, the scope of IAY was extended to cover below the poverty line Non Scheduled Castes/Scheduled Tribes families in the rural areas. Simultaneously, the allocation of funds for implementing the scheme was raised from 6 per cent to 10 per cent of the total resources available under JRY at the national level, subject to the condition that the benefits to Non-Scheduled Castes/Scheduled Tribes poor should not exceed 4 per cent of the total JRY allocation. IAY was de-linked from JRY and made an independent scheme with effect from January 1, 1996.

The objective of the Indira Awaas Yojana is primarily to help construction/up gradation of dwelling units of members of Scheduled Castes/Scheduled Tribes, freed bonded labourers and other below the poverty line non-SC/ST rural house holds by providing them a lump sum financial assistance. The house is to be constructed by the beneficiary himself/herself. No contractor shall be involved in the construction of dwelling units under the scheme. The dwelling units should normally be built on individual plots in the main habitation of the village.

The Indira Awaas Yojana is a Centrally Sponsored Scheme funded on cost-sharing basis between the Government of India and the State Governments in the ratio of 75:25. In the case of Union Territories, the entire funds under this Scheme are provided by the Government of India.

The target groups for houses under the IAY are below poverty line households living in the rural areas belonging to Scheduled Castes/Scheduled Tribes, freed bonded labourers and non-SC/ST BPL rural households, widows and next of-kin to defence personnel/paramilitary forces killed in action residing in rural areas (irrespective of their income criteria), ex-servicemen and retired member of paramilitary forces fulfilling the other conditions.

6.1.1 Funds Earmarking:

- At least 60 per cent of the total Indira Awaas Yojana allocation during a financial year should be utilized for construction/upgradation of dwelling units for SC/ST BPL households.
- A maximum 40 per cent for non-SC/ST BPL rural households.
- 3 per cent of the above categories for physically and mentally challenged persons.

If any particular category is exhausted or not available in a district, allocation can be utilized for other categories as per priorities given in the Guidelines after it has been certified to this effect by the Zilla Parishad/DRDA concerned.

Prioritization of beneficiaries will be as follows:

- Freed bonded labourers
- SC/ST household

1. SC/ST households who are victims of atrocity
2. SC/ST households, headed by widows and unmarried women

3. SC/ST households affected by flood, natural calamities like earthquake, cyclone and man-made calamities like riot.
4. Other SC/ST households

- Families, widows of personnel from defence services, paramilitary forces, killed in action.
- Non- SC/ST BPL households.
- Physically and mentally challenged persons.
- Ex-servicemen and retired members of the paramilitary forces.
- Displaced persons on account of developmental projects, nomadic/semi-nomadic, and de-notified tribals, families with physically/mentally challenged members.

The selection of the beneficiaries will be subject to the condition that the households of all the above categories except (iii) are Below Poverty Line (BPL). The District Panchayat/Zilla Panchayat/District Rural Development Agencies (DRDAs) on the basis of allocations made and targets fixed shall decide the number of houses to be constructed/upgraded Panchayat wise under IAY.

6.1.2 Involvement of Beneficiaries: The beneficiaries should be involved in the construction of the house. To this end, the beneficiaries may make their own arrangements for procurement of construction material, engage skilled workmen and also contribute family labour.

6.1.3 Unit Cost for Construction of IAY Houses and Upgradation: The ceiling on grant of assistance per unit cost under the Indira Awaas Yojana for construction of new house and upgradation of unserviceable kutcha house is given as under:

		Plain Areas	Hilly/Difficult Areas
a	Construction of house including Sanitary latrine and smokeless Chulha	Rs. 25,000	Rs. 27,500
b	Upgradation of unserviceable households	Rs. 12,500	Rs. 12,500

6.1.4 Credit-cum-Subsidy for Construction/upgradation of Rural Houses: Up to 20 per cent of the total funds can be utilized for up gradation of existing kutcha houses and toward subsidy for construction of houses with credit from Banks/Financial Institutions. Credit cum-subsidy will be provided subject to the following conditions:

- Rural households having an annual income of up to Rs. 32,000 only.
- Ceiling of subsidy under the Scheme Rs. 12,500 per household.
- The upper limit of construction loan under this scheme will be Rs. 50,000 only.

6.1.5 Criteria for Allocation of Resources: Central assistance under the IAY will be allocated to the States/UTs on the basis of poverty ratio and housing shortage, with each of these variables being given equal weightage. The proportions of rural SC/ST population and housing shortage in a district to the total rural SC/ST population and housing shortage in the State/UT are the criteria of inter-district allocation of the Indira Awaas Yojana funds within a State/UT. Both these variables are given equal weightage in the inter-districts allocation. The targets for the Blocks within a District will be decided on the same principles. Diversion of resources from one district to another is strictly prohibited. Up to 20 per cent of the total funds can be utilized for upgradation of existing kutcha houses and towards subsidy for construction of houses with credit.

A total of 5.86 lakh houses have been constructed during 2002-2003 up to November, 2002, of which 2.71 lakh houses for Scheduled Castes and 8.73 lakh houses for Scheduled tribes.

6.2 Housing Assistance by State Government: Various state governments have responded to the housing programme by placing it at the top end of their development priorities, thereby imparting great vigour to the implementation process. While the implementation lies with the DRDAs, the houses are constructed by the individual beneficiaries themselves, with absolute freedom of choice over the design. The scheme is closely monitored by an extensive network at the district, state and national level to ensure right selection and effectiveness in the implementation mechanism.

Punjab State Housing Corporative Federation has announced in April 2006 that the federation will construct 5000 flats or the poor in the 5 municipalities in the State. The Federations has already constructed the houses for the poor in Amritsar and Ludhiana.

6.3 Bharat Nirman Programme for Rural Houses: Under this Programme 8,70,000 houses have been constructed and a sum of Rs. 2,260 crore has been released till January, 2006. The scheme is to construct 60 lakh pucca houses.

6.4 Valmiki Ambedkar Awas Yojana (VAMBAY): The VAMBAY was launched in December 2001 to ameliorate the conditions of the urban slum dwellers living below the poverty line without adequate shelter. The scheme ahs the primary objective of facilitating the construction and up-gradation of dwelling units for slum dwelling and providing a healthy and enabling urban environment through community toilets under Nirmal Bharat Abhiyan, a component of the scheme. The Central Government provides a subsidy of 50 per cent being arranged by the State Government. There are prescribed ceilings on costs both for dwelling units and community toilets. During 2003-04, Central subsidy to the extent of Rs. 239 crore has been released. Since inception up to May 2004, Rs. 522 crore have been released as Government of India subsidy for the construction/upgradation of 2,46,035 dwelling units and 29,263 toilets seats under the scheme.

7. Components of Urban Development

7.1 Urban Water Supply: As per Census of India, if a household has access to drinking water supplied from a tap, hand-pump/tube well within or outside the premises, it is considered as having access to safe drinking water. Census 1991 reported the coverage of households in India having access to safe drinking water at 62 per cent, comprising over 81 per cent of urban households and around 56 per cent of rural households. The 54th Round of National Sample Survey (July 1999) on drinking water, sanitation and hygiene estimated that 50 per cent of rural households were served by a tube well/hand pump, 26 per cent by a well, and 19 per cent by taps.

Safe drinking water and improved sanitation play a major role in the overall well being of the people, with a significant bearing on infant mortality rate, death rate, longevity and productivity. The poor, both in rural and urban areas, bear a disproportionately higher burden on the non-availability of water, as well as its poor quality. Seasonal disruption of water supply is common, especially during summer months. Fetching of water for domestic use, sometimes from far-flung sources, is a time-consuming physical burden borne by women, particularly in the rural areas.

Apart from repercussions on health, this also affects their overall well-being. Moreover, 70-80 per cent of illnesses are related to water contamination and poor sanitation. Women and children are particularly vulnerable to the effects of water contamination. It is also a matter of concern that despite the progress achieved in provision of water supply, the level of water-related sickness continues to be high.

The Tenth Five Year Plan envisages the provision of potable drinking water to every settlement in the country on a sustainable basis and the pursuit of all possible measures for the rapid expansion and improvement of sanitation facilities in rural and urban areas.

The Accelerated Urban Water Supply Programme was launched in 1993-94. It aims at providing water supply to towns with a population of less than 20,000 as per 1991 Census. 2151 towns qualify for consideration under this scheme as per this criterion. As on December 31, 2002, 736 schemes (223 schemes sanctioned during the Eighth Plan, 437 schemes sanctioned during the Ninth Plan and 76 schemes sanctioned during 2002-03) have been approved at an estimated cost of Rs. 951.16 crore. As against this, the Government of India has released Rs. 435.54 crore and the State Governments have released Rs. 311.41 crore during this period.

As per 2001 Census of India estimates, approximately 20 percent of urban households do not have access to safe drinking water. Only 23.55 per cent had toilet facilities and up to March 1992, 52 per cent of the population was left uncovered by sanitation facilities. The coverage in terms of organised sewerage system ranged from 35 per cent in class IV to 75 per cent in class I cities. The drainage system for rain water disposal covers only 66 percent of the urban population. The city roads are inadequate for traffic requirements, leading to congestion and fast deterioration in quality of roads due to excess loads.

Technological up-gradation and improved design can hike efficiency and rationalise consumption. Regularity in supply could mean lower project cost and greater willingness to pay on the part of the consumers. Micro-level systems need to be designed to recycle water at the household level. The supply should be metered to plug leakages.

Pricing is to be on cost-recovery basis in the long term or over the full life of the project. In the short term, since prices cannot be increased at one go, the government will have to continue to provide subsidies. The water tariff should be increased gradually to reach cost-recovery level. Part of the required increase may be capitalised and charged as connection charges or advance registration charges. Cost recovery may also be made by including water tax, water benefit tax, betterment charges or development charges.

Cross-subsidisation of domestic use of water by commercial and industrial use may prove self-defeating if the latter diversify their sources of water. Metering of water supply must be promoted. To improve monitoring of leakages, bulk metering should be adopted. A block tariff system may be adopted under which consumption of water is picked at a low initial rate up to a specified volume of use and at a higher rate per block thereafter. Differential pricing may also be related to time of use.

Differential treatment of water for different uses. Micro-level systems needs to be designed to recycle water at the household level. The supply should be metered to plug leakages.

7.2 Solid Waste Management (SWM): The cost of collection, treatment and disposal of the solid water is to be reduced through various mechanisms. Technological innovation to improve the reusability of the recycled waste will increase returns and make projects viable. Privatization of as many operations as is feasible in an urban area will improve efficiency and reduce costs.

- Greater attention to segregation of different kinds of waste at the collection point itself will reduce cost of disposal.
- Toxic waste should be collected and disposed of separately. The frequency of collection can be as low as once a month.
- Biodegradable waste should be tackled locally to avoid storage and transportation over longer distances. This waste can also be coupled with the local sewers and horticulture waste from streets in biodigesters. This will produce three important by-products — biogas, compost and recyclable water, which will improve the viability of disposal.
- Building debris (*Malba*) should be kept separately and used for filling building sites and low-lying areas.
- Remaining waste in each Indian city gets recycled by rag pickers. The small components left over can be disposed of through incineration or sanitary landfills.
- Wherever environmentally acceptable, disposal can be decentralised to save on transportation cost.
- Appropriate technologies should be used to improve the quality of processed waste.

An improved quality of compost may fetch a higher price and reduce process time and mechanisation. Similarly RDF (Refuse-derived fuel) seems to have good scope for providing cooking fuel, process steam and power generation. These should be promoted. Converting waste management into biogas with fertiliser as the by-product is a commercially viable VD method. The small scale of operators and pricing structure have been the major constraints in this area. This may be tackled by providing supportive service to start operations on an economical scale. Landfills can be scientifically organised to minimise pollution from leaching. The biogas produced in a properly-designed landfill can be harnessed and utilised.

The 'polluter pays' principle should be applied. Operations which create waste may be charged a levy and the returns from the same may be used for financing waste disposal programmes. The cost of collection, treatment and disposal of the solid waste be reduced. Greater attention to segregation of different kinds of waste at the collection point itself will reduce cost of disposal. Wherever environmentally acceptable, disposal can be decentralised to save on transportation cost.

7.3 Sanitation: Use of low-cost technologies like that of Sulabh Shauchalayas must be promoted. SWD services can be unbundled and most functions entrusted to the private sector. This is one area where privatization has shown consistent productivity gains and cost reductions. Proper packaging – for instance, clubbing water supply and drainage projects together, can reduce project cost and improve viability. Similarly road development and storm-water drain management can be clubbed with commercial development of adjacent areas.

Cost of drainage and sewerage can be piggybacked on to the water tariff since these projects can be taken up as one package. The cost of storm-water drainage projects can be recovered by commercial use of adjacent lands. Taking up of integrated Area Development Schemes rather than isolated water supply or sanitation schemes should be given priority. Even in older areas, augmentation of water supply schemes and other facilities can be financed out of impact fees or valorisation charges or by a temporary surcharge on property tax.

The property tax base needs to be fed from the Rent Control Act. The Rent Control Act should be amended and pending that, the property tax should be made independent of the controlled rent. Resistance to tariff increases may be overcome by providing detailed and well-communicated information about cost of supply to the consumers.

As per Census 1991, less than one-fourth of households in the country had toilet facilities within the premises, the proportion being less than 10 percent for rural and around 64 percent for urban households. The 54th Round of NSS (July 1999) estimated that only 17.5 percent of the rural population were using latrines. In urban areas, 26 percent of households reported using no latrine, 35 percent reported using septic tank and 22 percent used the sewerage system, i.e. 43 percent of households in urban areas either had no latrines or no connection to a septic tank or sewerage.

The Low Cost sanitation Scheme was envisaged to convert the existing dry latrines into low cost pour flush latrines. The objective of the scheme is to eliminate manual scavenging totally. Under the scheme, a loan and subsidy is extended simultaneously by the HUDCO. The Central subsidy is being routed through the HUDCO. Up to December 31, 2002, 860 schemes in 1496 towns have been sanctioned at a project cost of Rs. 1468.72 crore involving GOI subsidy of Rs. 512.24 crore and HUDCO loan of Rs. 514.96 crore for construction/conversion of 36.75 lakh individual units along with 3966 community toilets. Rs. 254.72 crore have been released to the States as GOI subsidy and Rs. 317.48 crore have been released as loan from HUDCO. 387 towns have been declared scavenger free.

While water supply and sanitation facilities are important components of the overall strategy for development social issues such as primary health care, women's welfare, child nutrition, immunization and eradication of illiteracy are equally significant and inter-linked, thus necessitating a convergence of approach in implementation of these programmes.

7.4 Roads: Technological upgradation should be used to reduce maintenance costs. Better co-ordination with other departments like telecom/sewerage boards can reduce frequency and cost of levelling of dug-up roads.

Narrow earmarking of specific taxes and fees that are closely related to use of facilities help overcome resistance to taxes. Apart from taxation/user charges and impact fees, costs may be recovered by giving advertisement rights, limited development or license rights (like running kiosks), long lease for trees and the right to use their product.

In the roads sector, apart from taxation/user charges and impact fees, costs may be recovered by giving advertisement rights, limited development or license rights (like running kiosks), long lease for trees and the right to use their product.

7.5 Mass Rapid Transport System: Little attention has been paid to development of mass rapid transport systems in most major cities. In fact, urban transport is one of the most important components of urban infrastructure which has been neglected due to various reasons. Bus services and urban rail services have been extremely limited. Only seventeen largest cities of the country have organized bus services, and only three cities – Mumbai, Kolkata and Chennai have a suburban rail system. A good network of roads coupled with efficient mass urban transport system makes a substantial contribution to the efficiency of the cities and enables them to become a catalyst of economic and social development. The capital city of Delhi has experienced a phenomenal growth in population, from 57 lakh in 1981 to 138 lakh in 2001. The City however, lacked an efficient mass transport system. The setting up of the Delhi Metro Rail Transit System which was inaugurated on December 24, 2002, is expected to bring about a great improvement in efficiency and quality of life of the citizens of Delhi.

7.6 Delhi Metro Rail Transit System: Delhi Metro Rail Transit System (DMRTS) is a joint venture between Government of India and Delhi Government. DMRTS is one of the largest infrastructure projects being undertaken, and is being developed on lines of mass rapid transit systems in Hong Kong and Singapore. The first phase of the project comprises of three routes totaling 62.16 km due to be completed in March 2005. The entire project is expected to be completed by 2008 and this will be the first mass rapid transport system in the country that will match international standards and incorporate new technologies. The project is expected to bring about substantial reduction in pollution, reduction in accident rates and improvement in quality of life. As of March 2004, 3 stretches of Metro Rail in Delhi are operational.

7.7 Scheme for Urban Micro Enterprises (SUME)

Scheme for Urban Micro Enterprise (SUME) was implemented as a third component of Nehru Rozgar Yojana. The scheme was launched in the year 1989. This scheme was under Nehru Rozgar Yojana for the people living below poverty line.

The objective of the scheme is to encourage unemployed and under employed urban poor living below poverty line in metropolitan areas, cities and towns with population exceeding 10000 according to 1981 census, to take up self employment ventures with the help of subsidy and bank loan. The scheme commenced on October 11, 1989. The Urban Local Body will provide subsidy.

7.8 Disaster Management: Social security schemes are designed to provide relief against economic and social distress caused by a variety of contingencies. One such contingency is the occurrence of natural disasters which affect a large number of people at the same time. It is said that in 1943, when the Great Bengal Famine occurred, over 5 million people died. It is common knowledge that in India, natural calamities in the form of drought, famine, cyclone, floods, earthquakes etc. have been occurring every year, in one part of the country or the other. Every such disaster attracts every form of social security, namely, medical care, invalidity benefit, survivors benefit, maternity protection, child care etc. It is therefore, necessary to design an appropriate National Scheme for providing relief and rehabilitation assistance to the affected people.

An appropriate organization is required to handle the crisis situations, and adequate funds should be allocated for this purpose.

It would be worthwhile to think in terms of creating an auxiliary task force specially trained to handle such situations. The Army could provide the necessary training for the task force. Retired army personnel could be of immense help in such agencies. Units of this task force must be in a state of continuous preparedness, ready to swing into action as soon as a disaster strikes.

It is also necessary to have a computerised data base which would be available to the bureaucracy as well as to the task force. The database would contain information about where the members of the local task force are located, the means of getting in touch with them and the instructions that are to be issued to them. An inventory of the various types of transport available in each district as well as the kind of assistance that could be provided by the railways, the air force, and the navy would be a vital part of the database.

Special equipment would be necessary to rescue people. Lists of the equipment required and its location must be prepared. Building and highway contractors could post a list of their equipment and its locations electronically. Exercises could also be done to find quick ways of transferring this equipment. Large industrial houses and computer professionals can get together to evolve this system in collaboration with government institutions.

Estimates of the kinds of drugs and equipment needed for different types of disaster per 100 persons need to be kept ready with disaster research centres. Such information is now available. All decision makers should be aware that it exists, and where it can be accessed. Large hospitals need to have lists of private doctors and individuals in their neighbourhood who would be willing to volunteer professional and nursing help and equipment. Regional consortia can be set up for outdoor wards and operational facilities with the help of tent houses etc. There is a great deal of medical expertise internationally available on dealing with these exigencies and issues, and we must set up systems that can meet our needs.

The all-important question of where the money for all this work will come from will also have to be addressed at the outset.

The role of the NGOs would be very crucial in this context. The data base should also list all the NGOs in each region and the kind of help they would be able to render in a crisis situation, be it in terms of human resources, materials or money, or all three.

Blueprints for dealing with disasters have been evolved. Institutes for disaster management have also been set up. But most of this work remains at a sub-critical level, and is not given importance. Not enough has been done to involve all sectors of society, and the arrangements have not been rehearsed from time to time.

Detailed scientific post-analyses need to be undertaken after every disaster to understand what worked and what did not work, and why. The results of such exercises will have to be shared with the departments and groups concerned so that responsibilities can be assigned by each agency. If this were done periodically, people would know how to act constructively when a natural or man-made disaster strikes.

A permanent Commission for disaster management should be set up on the lines of the Election Commission. It should be responsible for the management of relief and rehabilitation after every drought, loss of crops, floods, cyclones, earthquakes and other disasters. This body could study how disasters are managed in other countries and suggest the equipment to be purchased. It should also be empowered to seek help from the Army, Police and other personnel in times of acute distress due to calamities.

The enormity and complexity of the problem would suggest the need for initiating action on many fronts. The starting point for such action would be to develop a comprehensive disaster response and mitigation policy, and a legal and administrative framework to implement it.

In the UK, a set of guidelines have been issued by the Home Office for dealing with disaster. These guidelines identify the agencies responsible for handling situations arising out of disasters, and how they should function. The guidelines also set out the command and control mechanism to be set up for handling disasters. Similar arrangements need to be made in India.

8. Financing of Urban Infrastructure

Urban infrastructure services are provided by local level agencies. Funds have generally been in the form of loans/grants from the Central and state governments. The ULBs own resources have been insufficient even to meet the O&M requirements of these services. Since most urban infrastructure services have been treated as public services and the concept of cost recovery has never been considered relevant, a commercial approach to these services has not developed. Even if the facilities were funded by loans, the repayment of loans generally took adjustments or paid out of grants made by state governments. Even when user charges are levied, the price per unit is too low to cover even the variable cost of providing the service.

The fact that infrastructure services do not pay for themselves and the government does not have the financial capacity to continue to subsidise the beneficiaries has resulted in low availability of funds. With increasing requirements, this has meant deficiency in volumes as well as quality of service. Consequently, a parallel unorganised sector for provision of many of these services has developed, resulting in high prices and qualitatively deficient services. From a societal point of view, these are expensive solutions. It is high time that a commercial approach is adopted.

In order to augment resources in the urban infrastructure, 100 percent foreign direct investment (FDI) has been permitted in the development of integrated township since 2001. However, investments have not materialized because of very rigid existing conditions relating to land procurement specially in urban areas, where land revenue and land reform legislation have precedence over organization. Moreover, there are problems relating to lack of clear titles, old protective tenancy and rent control. The system of maintenance of land records need to be improved through computerization. This, together with rationalization of stamp duty, will make things easier for those interested in entering into partnership for development of townships.

8.1 Costing and Cost Effectiveness: The major demands of the strategy to minimise cost should be technological appropriateness, proper attention to maintenance, curbing misuse of services and efficient institutional arrangements for providing services. To promote cost effectiveness, different infrastructure projects may be packaged together like water supply and drainage projects. Coordination between different departments providing different services will also reduce overall cost of production and should be encouraging.

The supply orientation in infrastructure policy has not succeeded having been unable to respond adequately to the evolution of demand. A commercial approach requires that demand-orientation service should be supplied in response to demand rather than in anticipation of demand. This will also improve cost recovery and financial viability of such projects.

Proper packaging – for instance, clubbing water supply and drainage projects together – be used to reduce project cost and improve viability.

8.2 Institutional Structure: Urban Local Bodies (ULBs) should be made responsible for providing all urban infrastructure in the city area and entrusted with the functions of planning, co-ordination and policy for supply of services. The multiple agencies in charge of providing various services should be merged under the ULB. The ULB will be responsible for deciding on the operations to be contracted out carrying out preliminary preparation of contract documents and monitoring of private operation. The ULB may coordinate with the metropolitan or regional/state level agencies and with other ULBs whenever required.

The government should set up a state level Nodal Infrastructure Financing Corporation which will channelise funds available from various sources and under various programmes to smaller municipalities. The bigger municipal corporations may access funds directly from the financing institutions.

An Infrastructure Fund may be set up for the transition period till the debt market is developed. A facility to provide guarantees to private sector investment may also be set up. The seed money for the same may be provided by the government. The existing financing institutions should set up separate departments or cells to promote commercialisation of projects. This would entail providing information about technologies, cost and remunerative pricing of different projects, preparation of feasibility reports, carrying out demand surveys and providing consultancy to infrastructure agencies in project design formulation and implementation.

Lastly, a state level regulation body be set up to monitor quality of service provided and price charged. This regulatory agency can have separate departments for each infrastructure segment.

The ULB should be responsible for providing all urban infrastructure in the city area. The multiple agencies in charge of providing various services should be merged under the ULB.

A state-level Nodal Infrastructure Financing Corporation be set up to channelise funds available from various sources and under various programmes to smaller municipalities.

In water supply projects, it is possible to privatise sourcing, treatment and bulk supply. The retail distribution and pricing may remain with the public sector. Low-cost sanitation may be privatised fully on the model of Sulabh Shauchalaya. Maintenance of roads can be entrusted to the private sector subject to quality control.

Part II
Five Year Plans on Urban Development and Housing

First Five Year Plan: 1951-56

Introductory

The housing problem has become acute in most industrial regions of the world since the last war. There is increasing recognition everywhere of the close relation between housing and the health and well-being of the people. Actually, over a number of years, shortages on a large-scale have developed and conditions worsened a great deal. Efforts made to solve the problem were handicapped by the difficult economic situation prevailing during these years. Private enterprise has proved incapable of meeting the needs and the State has had to assume direct initiative and responsibility in this field to an increasing extent. In some highly industrialised countries, housing accommodation has been provided to a large extent by heavy subsidies from the State in respect of houses of standard design for low-income groups which are not an economic proposition in most countries at present on account of the high cost of construction, building materials and development.

Conditions in India

In India the situation has become particularly serious on account of the large increase of population since 1921. The percentage increase of population in the last three censuses has been 11 per cent, 14'3 per cent and 13'4 per cent respectively. During the same period the growth of population in urban areas is estimated at 21 per cent, 32 per cent and 54 per cent respectively. The heavy shifts of population from the rural areas reflected in these figures have occurred on account of the lack of adequate opportunities for employment in the villages and the growth of industry and business in towns with the attraction of relatively high wages and various kinds of amenities. The second world war helped the growth of urban population by setting up a number of war production plants. The labour population engaged in them did not, as a rule, go back to the villages when these plants ceased to operate at the end of the war. The increasing unemployment and underemployment in agriculture have helped this tendency. Since 1947 when the country was partitioned there has been a very heavy influx of refugees who have, on the whole, tried to settle in the urban areas. The supply of houses on the other hand did not keep pace with the increasing demand. Private enterprise, which has been the primary source of building activity so far, tended to shrink on account of scarcity and high price of building materials during and immediately after the war. The enactment of legislations controlling rents and requisitioning premises had also a deterrent effect on private enterprise in building. Pressure on the existing accommodation, therefore, progressively increased leading to evils of over-crowding, deterioration of housing .estates and a variety of malpractices in relations between landlords and tenants.

Most of the towns in India have grown up haphazardly. They have a large proportion of sub-standard houses and slums containing insanitary mud-huts of flimsy construction poorly ventilated, over-congested and often lacking in essential amenities such as water and light.' This is specially so in the large industrial cities. The disgraceful sights presented by the ahatas of Kanpur and the bustees of Calcutta are conspicuous examples of this state of affairs. These conditions have developed because of insufficient control over building activity by the State or municipal authorities. Local authorities have been generally indifferent to enforcing such bye-laws regarding building and sanitation as have existed. Their own resources have been too meagre to permit any development work worth the name.

Rents have been generally high, but in pre-war years sharing of tenements by several people or even families in conditions of extreme over-crowding reduced the burden on the individual to some extent. But during and after the war, landlords, fully conscious of the scarcity value of accommodation, began to realise rents at much higher rates, sometimes wholly out of proportion to the capital outlay. Very often consideration money or premium, known as pugree or salami, was charged for letting out house property. The State Governments attempted to control rents and to prevent eviction of tenants by means of special legislations. While the tenants could be given some protection against eviction, the attempt to control rent, specially in the case of new comers, did not prove very successful, generally for the same reasons which led to the failure of price control of essential commodities. Requisitioning of house properties by Governments, both Central and State, during and after the war to accommodate their offices as well as officers and, in some cases, for allotment to private citizens led to a further contraction of building activity of private landlords and thus aggravated the shortage.

Housing by Governments and Public Bodies

In India, the necessity of providing accommodation for their own employees specially in smaller towns or out of the way places has been long recognised by Governments, both Central and Provincial, and some housing activity of this description has been a regular feature throughout. Of late, it has also been realised that housing for low-income groups, who are not necessarily Government servants, will have to be undertaken, at least in the bigger cities, to cope with the acute shortage of accommodation. Among the State Governments, Bombay took a lead in 1921 by establishing a Development Department to reclaim land, to construct 50,000 one-roomed tenements and to organise the supply and distribution of building materials to cope with the growing shortage of houses in Bombay city. This Department had to be closed down soon after it had built only 15,000 tenements. The cost of construction proved very high and workers could not afford to pay the rent which was fixed by the Department to cover the interest and maintenance charges of these buildings.

The Bombay Government resumed their activity in this field in 1949 by setting up a special Housing Board with the object of building houses for industrial workers and other low-income groups, developing land, and assisting in the production and distribution of building materials. The Board, which was set up by legislation, was given a loan of Rs. 4-37 crore up to March, 1952 to provide its initial capital. It has constructed 7,000 tenements for industrial workers and low-income groups and over 9,000 tenements for displaced persons out of an allotment of Rs. 2 crore by the Central Government. At present it is engaged in developing an area of about 400 acres of khassan land for co-operative housing societies at a cost of about rupees one crore.

Of late, the activities of the Board have been considerably curtailed because loans and subsidies expected from the Central Government have not materialised. Other State Governments have not so far taken very active steps in the sphere of housing. Some of them such as Uttar Pradesh, Madhya Pradesh and Hyderabad have set up Housing Boards quite recently. Others such as Bihar and Mysore are considering similar measures. None of these Boards appears to have started functioning yet except in Uttar Pradesh where construction of houses for workers of sugar factories has been taken up out of a special cess levied by the State Government.

Improvement trusts in Bombay, Calcutta, Madras and Kanpur have undertaken housing schemes to some extent. Very often these are rehousing schemes for persons displaced by the activities of these trusts in opening up and clearing residential localities. Municipalities have also constructed a certain number of houses, generally for their own essential staff but occasionally for other low-income groups as well. The total number of houses constructed by local authorities is reported to be 18,771. The main difficulty in the way of a more ambitious programme of construction has been the lack of funds. Most of the improvement trusts have no independent sources of revenue and have to depend on grants from State Governments or subventions from municipalities. As for municipal finance, it is generally in such a deplorable condition that few municipalities can provide even the minimum service to which the rate-payers are entitled, and can scarcely venture into such costly projects as housing schemes for low-income groups.

The activities of the Central Government till quite lately were confined to providing houses for their employees, particularly in essential services connected with communications and transport. The Indian railways have done pioneering work in this line and the total number of houses constructed by them up to the end of March, 1951, was 2,75,917 of which as many as 1,97,535 were meant for low-paid railway employees. The Railway Board have a further programme of construction of accommodation for their staff at a cost of about Rs. 3 -7 crore in 1952-53 and about Rs. 4 crore a year for the rest of the period of the Five Year Plan. The Ministry of Defence also provide accommodation for their employees in various parts of the country. Up to 1949 the number of houses constructed for ordnance workers, for instance, was 22,340 the total labour employed in ordnance factories being only 52,864. The Posts and Telegraphs Department have also undertaken construction of houses for their staff. State industrial undertakings, such as the fertilizer factory at Sindri, the locomotive works at Chittaranjan and the aircraft factory at Bangalore have also constructed houses to accommodate their staff.

It is in connection with the construction of houses for refugees from Pakistan that the Central Government first undertook a large-scale housing programme for persons other than their employees. A major situation was created when as a result of the partition of the country about 75 lakh of displaced persons came to India from Pakistan and had to be provided with accommodation of some sort. The problem has been tackled to a great extent and well-planned colonies and town-ships in various parts of the country have been developed where not only reasonably comfortable accommodation but also local employment in industry and trades has been provided. The total number of houses completed up to June, 1952, was 94,200 for displaced persons from Western Pakistan. Another 17,300 houses were under construction. In addition, individual displaced persons constructed 37,000 houses with financial assistance from Government. Among major colonies which have been set up are Ulhas Nagar near Bombay and Sardar Nagar near Ahmedabad;

Gobindpur and Hastnapur in Uttar Pradesh; Chandigarh, Faridabad and Nilokheri in the Punjab.

For the displaced persons from Eastern Pakistan, townships are under construction at Fulia and Habra in West Bengal and others in Assam and Bihar. Up to the end of June 1952, 7667 houses had been constructed by Government for the displaced persons from Eastern Pakistan. The total expenditure on housing for displaced persons incurred up to the end of March 1952, by the Central Government, was Rs. 48 crore. The efforts of Government to rehabilitate displaced persons are not yet over and additional funds are being allocated for the purpose. One outcome of this activity is the impetus for bold experiments in new materials and modes of construction with a view to effect utmost economy. Thus, the Punjab Government built nearly 4,000 houses in stabilised soil with cement plaster on both inner and outer wall. The Ministry of Rehabilitation experimented with the construction of traditional types of houses at Nilokheri, Faridabad and a number of other towns in the Punjab and West Bengal, by organizing the production of all building materials and components and labour under Government auspices, thereby eliminating the services of contractors. The cost of construction was considerably reduced as a result; at Nilokheri it came to Rs. 4/8/- to 4/12/- per sq. ft. of the plinth area as against Rs. 7 per sq. ft. with standard materials and Rs. 6 per sq. ft. with inferior specifications by the Central Public Works Department. In West Bengal also housing at Fulia showed the cost to be Rs. 4/13/- per sq. ft. of the plinth area.

Private Enterprise

In respect of provision of houses for their workers, the employers have not a uniform record. A number of them have appreciated the necessity of providing accommodation for their workers in and around the work-site in the interest of efficiency as well as for securing a steady supply of labour. During and immediately after the war, several large concerns which had made considerable profits during the period invested part of their earnings in providing better living conditions for their workers. Some of them were prevented from doing so because they could not obtain land at reasonable cost and municipal services could not be assured. On the whole, construction of houses by employers in post-war years has fallen short of expectation. Where accommodation has been provided it has not always been of sufficient size or of satisfactory quality. The employers have generally taken the stand that not they but the State has the responsibility for providing houses for the working class and that apart from their other handicaps, they have not sufficient means for investing in house building.

A few instances of the efforts made by the employers to solve the housing problem of labour may be referred to here. In November, 1950, the Industrial Committee on Plantations decided to adopt two-room standard for all housing in plantations in Northern India and called upon planters to put up houses for 8 per cent of their labour every year. About 25,023 houses were built in 1950-51 in accordance with this scheme which's still in progress, the From Coal Mines Welfare Fund construction of standard types of houses for miners in a big colony at Bhuli near Dhanbad was undertaken and in 1948-49, 1566 two-room tenements were constructed at a cost of about Rs. 54 lakh. These tenements were let out at a concessional rate of Rs. 8 per month, of which the worker paid only Rs. 2, the balance being met by the mine-owners. The jute industry appears to have put up the largest number of houses for its workers. Statistics of houses constructed by different industries are not available but, some time ago, a total of 4,28,970 workers were reported to have been provided with accommodation by employers.

Co-operative housing societies have attempted, to a limited extent, to provide accommodation for middle and low-income groups. The Madras and Bombay States have been the centres of co-operative activity in this direction. In Madras about 4,000 houses were constructed up to August, 1950, by 273 co-operative building societies. About 12,000 houses were also under construction. In Bombay 3,500 houses were constructed in 1948 and 229 houses were under construction by 315 societies. In Uttar Pradesh 136 societies were registered by 1949 and were provided with facilities by way of sites and loans at low rates. The Textile Labour Association at Ahmedabad constructed 200 tenements and organised workers into co-operative housing societies for providing suitable accommodation for them on hire purchase system. Originally 8 such societies were formed to which 8 more were added after the last war. The major difficulty which faced the Association was paucity of funds and the inability of the Bombay Government to provide substantial assistance. Similar difficulty about obtaining loans at low rates has been experienced by co-operative building societies in other States as well.

The bulk of the building activity throughout has been in the hands of private enterprise. But for a long time it has not been able to keep up with demand. The trade depression of 1931 dealt a severe blow to the building industry; the level of construction fell between 1931 and 1939. During the war years and immediately thereafter both manpower and materials became scarce and the situation was further aggravated by a phenomenal growth of the urban population. A great defect in private construction, particularly for the low-income groups, is that too often only the barest amenities and services are provided and sometimes, as in the slum areas, even such minimum amenities are altogether absent. The lack of vigorous enforcement of building regulations by municipal authorities has been a potent source of evil and private builders have generally put up houses with little regard for sanitation and comforts of tenants.

Estimate of Housing Shortage

Reliable statistics of the number of houses in urban areas are not available. While construction of houses remained almost at a standstill for several years on account of the war and post-war difficulties, urban population grew steadily. The advance census figures of 1951 show that in the decade 1941-51, while the rural population increased by 7-4 per cent the urban population increased by 53.77 per cent. The corresponding figures of the previous decade were 12 per cent and 32-1 per cent respectively. The Planning Commission made an attempt to obtain a rough estimate of housing shortage in the principal industrial towns. Information received in respect of 37 such towns with a total population of 17,14,560 engaged in large-scale industries shows that the approximate number of industrial workers, who are in immediate need of accommodation, is 4,54,900. The Environmental Hygiene Committee estimated the shortage as 18-4 lakh houses in urban areas in addition to 10 lakh houses for displaced persons from Pakistan. According to the advance census figures of 1951, the population of 74 cities with one lakh or more inhabitants increased in the decade ending in 1951 by about 74 lakh. Population of towns with 5,000 to one lakh inhabitants increased by 140 lakh. It will thus be seen that to house this increased population considerable building activity will have to be undertaken.

Housing Policy

The subject of housing is not specifically mentioned in the seventh schedule of the Constitution of India which deals with matters coming within the purview of the Union and State Legislatures. In so far as housing for industrial labour is concerned, item 24 of list III may be said to cover it because it deals comprehensively with welfare of labour. That would bring the matter in the Concurrent List with which both the Union and the State Governments are concerned. The residuary power in relation to subjects not mentioned in the Concurrent List or the State List, however, vests in the Union Legislature. As such the Centre may be said to be directly concerned with the subject of housing in general. In these times, the State cannot afford to confine its role in this field to planning and regulation. Private enterprise is not in a position to do the job so far as low-income groups are concerned. They cannot afford to pay the economic rent for housing accommodation of even the minimum standards. The State has, therefore, to fill the gap and assist the construction of suitable houses for low and middle Income groups both in urban and rural areas as a part of its own functions. This would involve a large measure of assistance which may take the form of subsidies on a generous scale and the supply of loans on a somewhat low rate of interest. In view of the gravity and vastness of the problem and the financial condition of the States, the Central Government have to accept a large measure of responsibility for financing housing programmes in the industrial centres where congestion and shortage have become very acute in recent years. Provision should also be made to find funds for middle-class housing schemes, preferably through co-operative building societies.

We would, however, suggest that the State Governments, who are being relieved to a large extent of the responsibility for industrial housing, should concentrate on ameliorating conditions of housing in rural areas. Although a great deal cannot be expected in view of the financial limitations, a beginning can be made in taking up pilot schemes of model housing and better living conditions in selected rural areas.

The principle of interest-free loan and subsidy for housing schemes are not novel ideas as far as the Central Government are concerned. The Industrial Housing Scheme, which was formulated in 1949, envisaged the issue of interest free loans by the Central Government to the State Governments or private employers sponsored by the latter to the extent of two-thirds of the cost of an approved housing scheme, on condition that the rent charged would not exceed 21 per cent of the capital cost subject to a maximum of 10 per cent of the workers' wages, the employer contributing 3 per cent of the cost of the houses. Early in 1952 a new policy was announced whereby the Central Government were prepared to pay a subsidy up to 20 per cent of the cost of construction, including the cost of land, provided the balance was met by the employers who would also let out the houses to genuine workers at rates suggested under the earlier scheme. The houses thus constructed would remain the property of the employers.

That these concessions have not produced the desired effect seems to indicate that the policy of paying subsidies, which has already been accepted, will have to be further liberalised as well as supplemented by loans. We recommend that subsidy should be paid to the State Governments up to 50 per cent of the total cost of construction including the cost of land. The State Governments in their turn will allocate the grant to the statutory housing boards. The subsidy admissible to private employers of labour and co-operative societies of industrial workers under this scheme should be limited to 25 per cent of the total cost of construction including the cost of land. In addition to the subsidies, loans should be made available to the State Governments for the balance of the cost at a rate of interest which should only take into account the cost of servicing the loans above the current rate of the Central Government borrowing. Such loans should be repayable in 25 years. The State Governments in their rum are expected to make funds available to statutory housing boards out of the Central loan.

Loans should also be admissible to co-operative housing societies of industrial workers and to private employers up to 37! per cent of the actual cost of construction including the cost of land. Interest should be charged at a reasonable rate having regard to the rate at which similar loans are advanced to the State Governments. The period of repayment in these cases should, however, be 15 years. In regard to the co-operative societies, we would further suggest that as far as possible, the subsidy should take the form of grant of developed lands of equivalent value. It will also be necessary in these cases to provide sufficient safeguards in regard to transfer of shares of the members so that by a change in the composition of the society the houses do not come into the possession of a class for whom they are not intended. We further suggest that where co-operative building societies of industrial workers are not in existence, developed building sites may be made available to individual workers who are willing to construct houses of their own under this scheme on the same terms as are admissible to industrial co-operatives.

At the same time we think that provision should be made for loans to co-operative building societies of middle class and other low-income groups who are also in need of financial accommodation no less than industrial workers, though they may not be considered eligible for the payment of subsidy. In their case we think it would be sufficient if loans are made available at reasonable rates of interest. For this purpose we recommend that the Central Government should provide funds for issue of loans to co-operative building societies through the State Governments, who will make the money available to such societies through the State co-operative organisations. The important point is that the difference between the rate of interest at which such loans are made available by the Central Government and the rate at which the co-operative societies are asked to pay should not be more than half per cent in order that the scheme is of substantial assistance to such societies. We lay special emphasis on co-operative housing societies not only because they can mobilise private capital, which otherwise would remain dormant, but because they open the way for aided self-help in the construction of houses which should be encouraged for reducing the cost as much as possible.

We recognise, however, that for years to come the bulk of the building activity will still have to be undertaken by private enterprise. In building works on a small scale the private builder can often construct at a rate cheaper than public bodies on account of economy in supervision and personal attention to details. We think that the encouragement to private builders should take the following forms:

- provision of suitable building sites, where possible, at reasonable cost;
- empowering the statutory housing boards to guarantee loans which a private builder may obtain from a bank or an insurance company to finance construction of buildings, the buildings in such cases being hypothecated to the housing boards;

- reorganising the present system of distribution of essential building materials, such as steel, cement, coal, etc., and taking steps to reduce the high prices of these materials which are all subject to price control, and for this purpose conducting necessary investigation ; and
- provision on the lines of section 39 of the Delhi and Ajmer Rent Control Act XXVIII of 1952, which exempts premises constructed between certain periods, from the operation of the rent fixation law.

At the same time we would suggest that while private builders should be encouraged to the maximum, steps should be taken to eliminate the speculative element inland and to discourage land hoarding in urban areas, for which purpose the taxation structure on vacant lands should be so designed as to make all land hoarding unprofitable. We under stand that steps in this direction have been taken in certain States.

Building cost can be substantially reduced by adopting improved techniques which have already been tried in other countries. For instance, production of bricks can be mechanised, at least in the bigger cities, by use of power and improved types of continuous process kilns. Similarly building components such as door and window frames and other building equipment can be standardised, thus making mass production possible. Use of modern implements and machinery in building construction has not been introduced in India to any appreciable extent. The attention of the building trade is drawn to the possibility of using various types of machinery and tools which are at present employed in advanced countries abroad for construction purposes.

Housing Standards and Estimates of Cost

The immediate need is the construction of a maximum number of houses for removing congestion and providing reasonably decent accommodation in the urban areas within the limited funds available for the purpose. The standards and specifications proposed by various commissions and committees in the past will, therefore, have to be re-examined. The situation being what it is, it seems to us impracticable to insist on standards which it is difficult, if not impossible, to achieve in the present conditions of building cost. All that we can .aim at is that the minimum, from the point of view of health and privacy, is provided, at least for the next few years. On this basis our suggestions are that houses should be built of the two following types:

- In smaller towns, where land value is low and permits a less intensive development: a single-storeyed tenement with a carpet area of 220 sq. ft. and an enclosed space of about 250 sq. ft. The tenement will comprise a living-room, a kitchen, a verandah and a water-flushed latrine.
- In larger cities where land value is relatively high: multi-storeyed buildings in which each tenement should have a carpet area of about 240 sq. ft. comprising a living-room and a kitchen. The bath-rooms and latrines will have to be shared by a group of flats. In these constructions density of development should not exceed 20 tenements or 100 persons per acre. As far as possible ramps should replace staircases. It is not desirable to build more than 3 storeys unless lifts can be provided.

The minimum standards of services should be as follows:

1. every unit should have at least one water-tap for drinking-water;
2. the latrine should be preferably of the water-borne sanitary type which in a single-storeyed unit may have to be shared between two tenements,
3. effective provision should be made for disposal of kitchen and bath-water through the water-borne system; and
4. electricity should be provided for lighting, wherever possible.

We do not favour temporary constructions for relieving housing shortage, because in the long run the recurring liability proves heavier. It is not necessary that construction should aim at long life of houses but that it should provide adequate safeguard against instability and risk of fire.

Careful calculations have been made of the cost of construction of tenements of the types proposed. According to an estimate prepared by the Central Public Works Department, the cost of construction of a single-storeyed tenement in the smaller towns would be about Rs. 2,200. The cost of land would vary according to locality, but it may be expected that for a plot of about 55 sq. yds., which is the size contemplated, the cost would not exceed Rs. 500. In the case of multi-storeyed buildings in larger cities, the calculations of the Report of the Environmental Hygiene Committee have been followed with an additional provision of 20 per cent as the cost of staircase, balcony, etc, necessary in vertical development. In general the construction of a multi-storeyed unit would cost about 51 per cent more than a single-storeyed tenement. The cost of land may be assumed as Rs. 700 to Rs. 1,000 per unit. The total cost of a tenement in a multi-storeyed building in the larger cities should, therefore, be about Rs. 4,500.

In calculating rent the subsidy is not taken into account. On the balance a return of 61 per cent is considered adequate to meet the interest charge on the loans which may be obtained from the Central Government or other sources, cost of maintenance at 1 per cent of the cost of construction and municipal rates and taxes at 12 per cent of rent in the case of single-storeyed tenements and 25 per cent of rent in the case of multi-storeyed tenements. The calculation takes into account the sinking fund charge on the net cost calculated on 40 years' basis. From the point of view of the workers care has been taken to see that, in general, rent does not exceed 10 per cent of the average family earnings. On the basis proposed, the rent of a single storeyed tenement would amount to about Rs. 10 per mensem and of a tenement in a multi-storeyed building about Rs. 18 per mensem in both cases inclusive of municipal taxes. It may be pointed out that even now the worker pays as rent Rs. 10 per mensem for such inferior accommodation than is envisaged under the scheme. There should not, therefore, be any reasonable grievance in the matter of fixation of rent.

In this connection we would like to refer to the objections raised in certain quarters to the proposal for, subsidising constructions by employers for housing their workers. It has been urged that as the houses will belong to private employers, there can be no justification for subsidising them from public revenues. A closer examination will show that the subsidy, in fact, does not amount to any substantial concession. We do not propose that the employers should have absolute right of ownership in these houses. We suggest that the management of these houses should vest in a committee consisting of the representatives of the employer and employees concerned together with a chairman nominated by the State Government. Tills committee will be responsible for allotment of tenements and generally for the management of the housing estate. We also propose that a tenant, who ceases to be in the employment of the employer who owns the property, must be given a reasonable time for vacating the tenement. The ordinary trade union rights of access to the workers must similarly be guaranteed.

These provisions should be laid down in the agreement to be entered into by the employers when obtaining subsidy and loan from the Central Government. Later, it may be desirable to have the provisions incorporated in the proposed legislation on housing or in statutory rules framed there under. It will thus be seen that the ownership which we envisage is of a limited, indeed nominal, character. The employer owns the building only in the sense that his own employees, and not others, are housed therein. The employer also should have no objection to these provisions because by obtaining subsidy and loan at a cheap rate, he can provide accommodation for his employees, which is ultimately to the benefit of his concern. Even the fact that about 37 per cent of the total cost will have to be initially borne by him does not mean any loss. The provision whereby the sinking fund charges are spread over 40 years, ensures recovery of the outlay, because the houses of the specifications proposed would last longer than 40 years.

From the point of view of the State too, there should not be any objection to what seems, on the face of it, to be an outright grant to private employers because the immediate object is to house as large a number of industrial labour as possible and it can only be done by inducing capital to be invested in such schemes by an offer to meet a part of the initial cost. There is no other way in which large scale house-building can be undertaken for low-income groups in the present situation. It may be pointed out that the argument has no application in the case of the houses constructed by the State Government and the housing boards which will remain public property or the houses constructed by co-operative societies of industrial workers which will be owned by the society on what amounts to a hire-purchase basis.

Housing Finance

Originally the provision of the Central assistance towards industrial housing in the five year period was Rs. 13.5 crore and it was expected that a contribution of Rs. 15 crore each would be forthcoming from the employers and workers and that the State Governments would provide an amount of Rs. 37 crore. It was, however, suggested that an alternative scheme for raising finance would be to utilize money in the provident fund accounts created under the Employees, Provident Fund Act. We have reviewed our recommendation in this regard and we are now of the opinion that advantage should be taken of the alternative scheme which was put forward by us, namely, to utilize the provident fund deposits without imposing any additional burden on the industry.

It is expected that contribution of the workers and employers to the provident fund scheme will amount to Rs. 15 or 16 crore annually, out of which, after meeting the cost of administration and withdrawals, a substantial amount can be expected to be available for investment every year. It is also expected that subsidies to the extent of about Rs. 2 crore per annum will be available from the Central revenues. A provision of Rs. 38.5 crore is accordingly suggested in grants and loans by the Central Government for housing schemes during the period of the Plan.

Loans will be advanced to private employers and to workers' co-operatives repayable in 15 years and to the State Governments repayable in 25 years but the standard rent for housing estates will be calculated so as to spread over the period of the redemption of loans to 40 years in all cases.

Loans at reasonable rates should also be made available (a) to co-operative housing societies of middle and low income .groups referred to in paragraph 16, and (b) to local authorities, for clearance of slums and development of land, which, as will be explained subsequently, is considered an essential part of the housing policy.

Town and Country Planning

The solution of the housing problem on a permanent basis has to be linked up with town and country planning. We have already seen how haphazard growth and ribbon development have been caused by inadequate legal powers to control use of land and construction of buildings, though it must be admitted that neither the State Governments nor local authorities have shown a full appreciation of the situation or utilised such powers as they already have to arrest the unhealthy growth. In some States, legislation on town planning has been enacted or is contemplated. It is, however, desirable that there should be a uniform policy in the matter and we recommend that there should be a National Town and Country Planning Act, which would provide for zoning and use of land, control of ribbon development, location of industries in areas considered suitable, clearance of slums, carrying out of civic and diagnostic surveys and preparation of Master Plans.

Regional planning has become even more important in view of the implementation of the several river valley schemes and community development projects. Such regional planning should take into account the population, agricultural condition, industries, and communications of a region with a view to secure a balance of population in the particular area between villages, market towns and industrial centres. Such plans will aim at integrating agriculture and industry in rural areas, and will provide for dispersal of industries from existing centres, development of cottage and small-scale industries, services like medical aid, education and recreation facilities.

Slum Clearance

Slums have grown up in practically all the major industrial cities of India as a result of laxity in enforcing building regulations, the indifferent attitude, till recently, to conditions of living amongst industrial workers and the high land values prevalent in certain cities which led the landlords to exploit their advantage to the fullest. These slums are a disgrace to the country and it is a matter of regret that Governments, both Central and State, have so far paid little attention to this acute problem. No city can be considered healthy which tolerates within itself the existence of a highly congested area with only the minimum amenities of life where some of the poorest elements of population are huddled together in almost sub-human conditions. It has been observed that slums are a national problem. A person who becomes a juvenile delinquent or a tuberculosis case because of slum conditions is no less a national than a local liability. From the national point of view it is better to pay for the cost of clearing slums than to continue to pay the mounting cost of slums and suffer their destructive effects upon human lives and property indefinitely.

In certain cities, improvement trusts have made some efforts at slum-clearance. There efforts have been rather sporadic in character, mainly because the improvement trusts, to a greater degree than other local authorities, suffer from limitation of funds. Few of them have independent sources of income and have generally to depend on uncertain grants and subventions from the State Governments and local authorities. The initial cost of acquiring slum areas which under the present state of the law have to be compensated not only at their market value but with an additional surcharge in consideration of the compulsory nature of acquisition, is almost prohibitive, in most areas, for improvement trusts to undertake any large scale clearance of slums. We consider the clearance of slums to be an essential part of a housing policy because the housing we propose is meant for the class of people who are now generally dwellers of slums. In our view the schemes of housing should proceed pari passu with the scheme of slum clearance, at least in the major industrial cities, so that when a housing estate is ready, steps should be taken to remove the slum dwellers to the newly built houses and to proceed with the clearance of the slum area in question.

The procedure to be adopted in such cases should be simple and of a summary nature. The competent authority should, after proper survey and enquiry, issue a clearance order. Compensation should be assessed on the basis of the use to which the land was put on the date of the issue of the clearance order. We suggest that no additional compensation on account of the compulsory nature of acquisition should be allowed in case of acquisition of slum areas, because we believe that such compensation ought not to be admissible to properties which are not put to social use. We do not think that the owners of slum areas perform any social service by accommodating large number of the poorest sections of the community in conditions of squalor and filth and we do not see why such social abuse of property should be compensated for over and above the actual value. We agree, however, with the suggestion that where the owners of slum areas themselves come forward to rebuild and develop their properties within a specified period, on standard plans to be approved by the competent authority, there may be no need for acquiring such lands for the purpose of clearance of slums. We understand that in certain municipal acts provisions to this effect already exist.

We have already pointed out that the main difficulty which hampers a large-scale clearance of slums is insufficient financial resources of improvement trusts and local authorities. We, therefore, suggest that out of the provision of Rs. 38.5 crore for housing schemes in the period of the Plan a certain amount should be set apart every year for issue as loans by the Central Government to improvement trusts and other local authorities through the State Government concerned for providing the initial capital for acquisition and demolition of slums. We recommend that this loan should bear a low rate of interest not exceeding half per cent above the rate at which the loan is made available to the State by the Central Government.

Rural Housing

The problem of housing in rural areas is a vast one as even now 83 per cent of the entire population of India live in villages. Having regard to the limitations of financial resources, a satisfactory programme of rural housing during the period of the Plan cannot be envisaged. It should, however, be appreciated that the pressure of population shifts towards cities and the slum problems resulting there from cannot be solved without ameliorating rural living conditions. Some opportunities for planning in the villages have arisen of late due to reforms in the land tenure system and establishment of community development projects. The problems which confront the rural areas are, however, somewhat different in character and do not call for expenditure of large slums for individual housing units. Unlike in towns, land value, and consequently congestion, is not a principal factor.

The immediate needs of the villagers are primarily adequate water-supply, improved communications and arrangements for disposal of sewage and waste-products. Improvement in standards of rural housing should be aimed at primarily by utilising labour and materials locally available with only a modicum of technical assistance. By the use of aided self-help technique, preferably promoted through the Community Projects Administration wherever possible, a significant increase in the standard of living in the villages may be accomplished and the pressure on the cities relieved to a large extent. It seems to us that there are two principal ways in which Government can attempt to improve the standards of housing in the villages, e.g. by demonstrating improved standards through model houses built in selected areas and by assisting the villager to build better types of houses within his means and with the resources readily available to him through methods of aided self-help. Aided self-help housing should, however be planned in such a way that improvement over existing conditions is achieved without prematurely advancing beyond the living habits and means of the villagers.

With regard to model houses in selected villages, the fifty-five community development projects taken up under the Indo-American Technical Aid Programme offer the most suitable venue for demonstration of improved techniques and designs for rural housing. Emphasis should be laid on the use of local materials with the object of teaching the villagers how cheap houses can be built which would provide adequate ventilation, remove the proximity of cattle and other animals and provide manure-pits, sanitary latrines and such other simple and essential amenities of decent living. The other method we advocate is, in many respects, a corollary of the first; that is to say, when the villager has learnt the technique of constructing a cheap and decent house within his means, there should simultaneously be a scheme to give practical effect to his desire to build along the lines he has been shown.

Self-help in putting up houses has been a feature in Indian villages for generations. It is only necessary to encourage and foster the habit of the villager to build his own house by utilizing local building materials but providing greater amenities than are now available to him. Certain improvements can be readily effected without much additional cost, such as, improved floors by stabilization, simple devices for ventilation, provision of chimneys in the kitchen to draw away smoke, use of erosion-resistant mud plaster for walls and roofs of improved materials and designs. Aided self-help in housing aims at helping people to build their shelters out of materials available in their community. Generations of trials and error have produced very practical ways of using many kinds of local resources including timber, bamboo, lime, clay, stone, gypsum, sand, kaolin, murram, junglewood, grass and waste products of various types.

It is, however, necessary to see that use of local materials does not degenerate into use of unsuitable materials like galvanized iron sheets, packing boxes, salvaged lumber etc. A practical approach, in our opinion, would be for Government to provide technical assistance in the form of skilled supervision and equipment. Pilot projects in selected villages can be taken up to teach the use of local materials. Since our proposals on urban housing practically relieve the State Governments from their share of the expenditure, we think they may be expected usefully to concentrate on improving standard of housing and living conditions in the rural areas. The provision for housing in the State Plans is of the order of Rs. 10.19 crore. The State Governments may, therefore, provide funds for house-building in rural areas by issuing interest-free or long term loans. The money cost of a house built with the villager's own labour is not likely to exceed Rs. 200 to 300 per unit. The State Governments may also perform a useful function by disseminating information regarding experiments in cheap housing which are taking place in other parts of India, such as, the pot-tiled vaulted roofing in Hyderabad State and stabilized soil construction in the Punjab.

In this connection we should like to cite the example of aided self-help in Puerto Rico as being worthy of emulation in India. Conditions in Puerto Rico are similar in many ways to those obtaining in this country. There, a rural development programme included secure tenure of building-cum-garden plots with aided self-help in house construction, in gardening, in water-supply and sanitation development and in multi-purpose co-operative activities. The aid given by the State consisted of equipment, materials and skilled assistance costing $ 300 per housing unit. The equipment consisted of a truck for hauling gravel and .sand from nearby sources, concrete mixers, hand-operated cement block machines and wheel barrows.

Building materials in the form of lumber, Portland cement and reinforcing steel were also supplied. The estimated cost of each housing unit, viz., $ 300 was advanced to the villager as a loan with provision of repayment in easy instalments of about $ 2.50 a month. The subsidy involved in the housing aspect of the scheme was the absence of interest on the loan. The cost of the house, if purchased, would have been $ 1,500. Thus by investing his own labour and with a certain amount of help from the State, the villager in Puerto Rico saved $ 1,200 or 80 per cent of the cost of a house of much better quality than he could otherwise afford. Owing to the shortage of cement and steel in India, we shall have to emphasize the need for using local materials. But the principle of aided self-help, as practised in Puerto Rico can, if adopted, result in great improvement in quality at a very low cost.

Research

Research in building techniques and materials is necessary for achieving reduction in cost and improving the quality of work. It is also necessary to standardize building components and invent new materials or synthetic substitutes. In the West, building research has made considerable progress and has resulted in the discovery of new building techniques and finish without any substantial increase in cost. Problem of design, functional requirements of buildings, basic studies of structures, nature and properties of clay, minerals and soil are matters of very great importance which requires research and further study.

In India, facilities for such research are provided in universities, such specialized institutions as the Central Building Research Institute at Roorkee, the Forest Research Institute and colleges at Dehradun, The Indian Standards Institution in Delhi, the Government Test House at Alipore, the Engineering Central Laboratory at Hyderabad, the Soil Mechanics Laboratory at Karnal in the Punjab, and the Road Research Institutes in Delhi and Bangalore. There are also the recognized institutes of engineers, architects and town-planners and the association of builders. Industrial undertakings which manufacture building materials such as the Associated Cement Company, the Tata Iron and Steel Company and the Indian Steel and Wire Products also provide facilities for research. There is, however, considerable scope for expansion and consolidation of the work which is being done by these institutions. In particular, stress should be laid on research in the following subjects:

- basic building materials such as bricks, tiles, high tension steel, laminated timber, calcination of ordinary soil for use as bricks and the possibility of utilizing indigenous materials as building components;
- possibility of use of substitutes such as timber, bamboo etc. for steel and other traditional building materials;
- revision of building codes, specifications and factors of safety; and
- standardisation and mass-production methods of building components and materials.

In India, experiments in cheap housing have been undertaken in stabilised soil construction in Mysore and the Punjab, hollow sand-cement block construction at Chittaranjan, Bangalore and Ahmedabad, pot-tiled vaulted roof construction in Hyderabad State and cement united wall construction by the Western Railways in Bombay. The Government Housing Factory in Delhi has produced prefabricated panels. These experiments offer scope for further research. Constructions in stabilised soil and sand-cement blocks for walls and pot-tiled roofs are specially suited for aided self-help housing. In India, although prefabricated housing has made very little progress so far, there is little doubt that manufacture of prefabricated building components offers considerable scope.

It is also desirable to organize the building trade in all its aspects including training of labour and technical personnel of all grades. It is unfortunate that importance of technical training in house-building labour is yet insufficiently realized. In Europe and America, it has been found that training of personnel not only improves the quality of work but expedites the process of building. In India, the building activity in the public sector as a whole is estimated to involve an annual expenditure of Rs. 150 crore. The need of a requisite organisation for training facilities both to economise cost and to intensify the building programme can, therefore, easily be appreciated.

National Building Organisation

Though research is being carried on in different institutions for cheapening cost and improving building techniques, there is no authority to co-ordinate the results of such research and to make it available in a form which would have ready acceptance with Governments as well as private firms and individuals engaged in building activity. It is for this reason that the setting up of a National Building Organisation as an important activity connected with housing has become necessary. We suggest that such a body should be set up with the following principal objectives:

1. to co-ordinate and evaluate results of research on building materials and technical development now being carried on in different institutions;
2. to suggest from time to time subjects of further research and development with due regard to their relative importance and urgency ;
3. to incorporate the results of such research in actual building practice;
4. to ensure effective utilisation of all available building materials including non-traditional materials;
5. to guide industry and public in general on the use of new materials and techniques in building construction;
6. to initiate proposals for increased production of building materials and their proper distribution;
7. to examine building costs with a view to reduction in overheads and other expenses particularly in the public sector;
8. to provide museums or standing exhibitions where methods of cheap houses and techniques for economic building can be displayed, explained and demonstrated;
9. to take necessary steps for the standardisation of building components and to organise production and distribution of such standardised components on a large scale;
10. to advise Government on technical matters including experiments, research, bull ding education and new techniques; and

11. to provide for training in building work and improved techniques and to organise refresher courses for engineers and architects.

Such a body should consist of persons who are eminent in their professions and whose decisions would carry weight. It must also have facilities for experiments in various types of building materials and it must be associated with a Ministry of the Central Government which should act as its executive wing to translate its recommendations into actual practice. We are, therefore, of the opinion that the Council of the Organisation should consist of such persons as the Chief Engineer, Central Public Works Department, the Director-in-charge of Civil Engineering in the Railway Board, the Road Development Adviser to the Central Government, the Engineer-in-Chief at the Army Headquarters, the Director of the Forest Research Institute, Dehradun, and the Director of the Central Building Research Institute, Roorkee. The Council should be assisted by an advisory body consisting of three experts, respectively on steel and concrete, clay products, and timber and forest products. There should be a whole-time Chairman who will coordinate the work of the Council and the advisory body.

The National Building Organisation should hold annual conferences on building techniques and designs to which may be invited not only all those who are interested in the subject but, in particular, the Chief Engineers of Roads and Buildings of the State Governments. We consider that dissemination of new ideas through such conferences is of considerable value specially when persons in charge of large constructions are themselves convinced of the suitability of the new techniques and processes.

We also recommend the establishment of a permanent museum, or preferably several regional permanent museums, where exhibits of cheap housing can be displayed and the comparative costs, building techniques and methods, use of substitutes for traditional building materials can be studied with profit by engineers, industry and the general public.

Housing Boards

We recommend the setting up of housing boards which would be statutory autonomous bodies appointed by Government and responsible for implementing the housing programme. Such boards should be both Central and Regional and should have an executive body with a president, a whole-time secretary and not more than five other members, some of whom at least should be specialists in town-planning, architecture, and the social, economic and financial aspects of housing problems. The boards may have associated with them advisory bodies consisting of representatives of employers, tenants, building trade and the general public.

The principal functions of the Central Housing Board may be indicated as follows:

1. to administer the Central Housing Fund,
2. to activate housing programmes;
3. to administer such housing projects as are directly entrusted to it by the Central Government;
4. to lay down principles for the guidance of the Regional Boards, regarding selection and development of sites for housing schemes and fixation of priorities in the allotment of tenements;
5. to advise on rationalisation on building legislation and to prepare model building bye-laws for adoption by regional and local authorities;
6. to suggest action in regard to slum clearance and improvement in environmental conditions of housing; and
7. to recommend from time to time any legislation or amendment of existing legislations which have a bearing on the problems of housing, town and village planning, fixation of rents and such allied subjects.

There should be a Regional Housing Board for each State where there is an active housing programme; but in suitable cases, there may be more than one board in a State. The principal functions of these boards may be indicated as follows:

1. to administer the Regional Housing Fund;

2. to activate the State building programme;
3. to collect information regarding housing needs of different classes of people and to undertake surveys for the purpose;
4. to undertake the construction of houses in selected areas according to approved plans;
5. to allot tenements to workers and other low-income groups in accordance with the policy laid down by Central Housing Board;
6. to establish new townships and industrial suburbs and to prepare Master Plans for the same;
7. to undertake and encourage slum clearance and improvement of existing-conditions of housing within their jurisdiction;
8. to undertake maintenance of houses and other properties belonging to the Board and to realise rents for the same;
9. to encourage self-builders both in the shape of co-operatives and individuals;
10. to organise building trades and to provide facilities for vocational training for building labour;
11. to guarantee loans taken by private builders for house-building, provided adequate securities are furnished; and
12. to organise training for building-labour generally and in specialised types of work, such as laying patent-stone floors, reinforced cement concrete roofs and beams, etc.

The housing boards which we envisage should be statutory autonomous bodies. It will, therefore, be necessary to provide them with independent sources of income in addition to grants and subsidies which may be made available from the Central or the State Exchequer. While it is true that for many years, the Central Government will have to subsidise the construction of houses for the lowest-income groups and also to provide funds in the shape of loans, it is our intention that the housing boards should be financially self-supporting to a large extent so as to undertake housing programmes on their own, if not for the lowest-income groups, at least for the middle classes. In States where improvement trusts have been set up, it may be considered whether their functions cannot conveniently be amalgamated with those of housing boards, the aims and objectives of both the organisations being more or less similar.

The principal sources of revenue of housing boards may, therefore, be stated as follows:

1. grants from the Central or State Governments and municipal authorities;
2. rents and recoveries from housing estates constructed by the boards;
3. sale proceeds of lands acquired for development by the boards;
4. betterment levies which the boards may be authorised to charge from persons benefiting from an improvement scheme;
5. terminal tax on passengers and goods, arriving by road or rail, in cities where housing programmes have been undertaken within the jurisdiction of the boards;
6. issue of housing bonds with the consent of the Central or the State Government, as the case may be, at rates half per cent above the current rate of Government borrowing; and
7. loans from banks, insurance companies and such financing institutions on terms to be approved by Central or State Governments;

An additional surcharge on stamp duty on the value of immovable property transferred or mortgaged within the State is also recommended for those States where there is still scope for an increase in the rate of stamp duty.

Legislation

We have already indicated the lines on which the proposed Housing Act and the Town and Country Planning Act should proceed. Here we shall confine our remarks to certain amendments in the existing legislation, which are considered desirable. We are of the opinion that the basis of assessment of compensation in the Land Acquisition Act of 1894 requires modification in respect of acquisition of slum areas as well as of lands which will be needed for the housing schemes. At present the cost of acquiring slum areas is prohibitive because not only their market value but an additional compensation at 15 per cent has to be paid in consideration of the compulsory nature of acquisition. It may be that when a slum has been demolished and the area cleared and developed, the land can sometimes be disposed of at a reasonable price, especially if it is situated in the heart of a city. It is not, however, possible for housing boards and improvement trusts with their meagre resources, to make a considerable outlay for the purpose of acquiring slum areas and demolishing slums in the expectation of a reasonable return at a distant date. We, therefore, suggest that the Act should be modified in respect of payment of compensation which should be on the basis of the use to which the land was put on the date of the issue of the preliminary-notification. We do not think that any additional compensation should be admissible for acquiring either slum areas or lands required for housing scheme for the industrial workers and low-income groups. The Act should also be amended so as to provide for a speedier procedure for taking possession of lands on which housing projects are contemplated or where slum areas are lo be cleared. Without such a provision neither the housing schemes nor schemes for clearance of slums will be expedited as the normal procedure of land acquisition is often very protracted.

We would also suggest that the various State legislations on the control of rent should be made uniform. In order to encourage private construction, without which the problem of housing cannot possibly be solved in the near future, provision may be made to exempt newly-constructed houses from the operation of the rent control legislation for an initial period of, say, 4 years. The civil courts, however, should have jurisdiction, on the application of parties, to fix fair rents (excluding municipal rates) even in such cases on the basis of a reasonable return on the cost of construction, including services. With regard to the acquisition of premises for public purposes, we would recommend that the practice should be resorted to only exceptionally. It cannot be denied that requisitioning of premises on an extensive scale in recent years has had a deterrent effect on the building activity in the private sector. We would, therefore, urge upon Governments, both Central and State, to be cautious in having recourse to requisitioning house properties in times of peace.

Second Five Year Plan: 1956-61

The period of the first five year plan witnessed the first steps in a national housing programme which will assume growing importance in future plans. This included a subsidised industrial housing scheme and a low income group housing scheme. Housing schemes for plantation labour and for labour in coal and mica mines were also implemented as part of the programme. These programmes are being substantially expanded during the second five year plan, in the course of which it is proposed to take up three new programmes, namely, rural housing, slum clearance and sweepers' housing and middle income group housing. The tasks undertaken through these programmes, and the proposals formulated for the second five year plan are explained briefly below.

Housing schemes for workers in the coal industry are financed from the Coal Mines Labour Welfare Fund which is expected to provide over the five-year period about Rs. 8 crore. Housing schemes for mica and coal mines are the responsibility of the Ministry of Labour, the other schemes being administered by the Ministry of Works, Housing and Supply.

In addition to these schemes, substantial housing programmes are undertaken by the Ministries of Rehabilitation, Defence, Railways, Iron and Steel, Production, Communications, Works, Housing and Supply etc. State Governments and a certain number of local authorities also have their own housing programmes. It is estimated that during the first five plan the Ministry of Rehabilitation provided 3,23,000 houses or tenements in urban areas and State Governments and Central Ministries other than the Ministry of Works, Housing and Supply about 3,00,000 unit Including the other housing schemes mentioned above, public authorities provided during the first plan about 7,42,000 houses or tenements. It is difficult to estimate the extent of private construction. An enquiry carried out for the Taxation enquiry Commission indicated that the total investment on urban housing during 1953-54 was about Rs. 125 crore. If this is taken as a kind of average for the five year period, and the average cost of a house is assumed to be about Rs. 10,000, it would appear that during the first plan about 6,00,000 units have been provided in the private sector. Thus, during the first plan about 1.3 million urban houses were added. In the nature of things, the estimate of private construction is liable to vary according to the assumptions which are made.

Programmes undertaken by other Central Ministries, by State Governments and local authorities and those pertaining to coal mines labour are expected to provide 7,53,000 units, in addition to private construction, which was been reckoned for the second plan period at 8,00,000 units. Thus, the total programme for the second plan envisages the construction of about 1.9 million units as compared to about 1.3 million during the first plan.

Subsidised Industrial Housing Scheme

The subsidised industrial housing scheme was at first "approved for industrial workers governed by the Factories Act, but now includes also mine-workers other than those engaged in the coal and mica industries for whom there are separate schemes. Under the industrial housing scheme loans and grants are given by the Central Government to State Governments and public authorities, to employers and to co-operatives of industrial workers. For one-room tenements, the maximum cost prescribed is Rs. 4,500 for multi-storeyed tenements in Bombay and Calcutta and Rs. 2,700 elsewhere. For two-roomed tenements the corresponding figures are Rs. 5,430 (now raised to Rs. 5,930) in Bombay and Calcutta and at other places Rs. 3,340 for single-storeyed tenements and Rs. 3,490 for double-storeyed tenements. For State Governments 50 per cent of the cost is given by way of loan and 50 per cent as subsidy; for co-operatives 50 per cent as loan and 25 per cent as subsidy; and for employers 37 per cent per, cent as loan and 25 per cent as subsidy. The period of repayment is 15 years in the case of employers and 25 years in other cases.

In the course of the first five year plan a total construction programme for 79,679 tenements was approved. Of these, 19,195 were planned for construction Bombay, 21,709 in Uttar Pradesh, 5,629 in Hyderabad, 5,181 in Madhya Pradesh, 3,444 in Madhya Bharat and smaller numbers in other States. The number of tenements completed before the end of the first five plan is estimated to be about 40,000. Out of the total number of tenements approved, 68,200 or about 85 per cent are being constructed by State Governments, 10,161 or about 13 per cent by private employers, and 1,318 or 1.6 per cent by co-operative societies of industrial workers. When the scheme was formulated a larger response was expected from employers and from co-operatives. This aspect of the scheme is under investigation and steps necessary for securing a greater response from employers and from co-operatives of industrial workers are being studied.

Low Income Group Housing

The low income group housing scheme, which was introduced towards the end of 1954, provides for the grant of long-term house building loans at a reasonable rate of interest to persons whose income does not exceed Rs. 6,000 per annum. Loans are given to individuals as well as to co-operatives whose members fulfil this condition. The assistance is restricted to 80 per cent of the estimated cost of construction, including land, and is subject to a maximum of Rs. 8,000. The scheme also provides for loans to State Governments at 3 per cent interest repayable in three years for acquisition and development of land by local authorities and its allotment to prospective builders. Local bodies, charitable institutions, hospitals, etc., can obtain assistance under this scheme for building houses to be let to their low paid employees or on hire purchase terms. By the end of the second plan loans amounting to about Rs. 21.5 crore had been sanctioned for about 40,000 houses and for various land development schemes. The low income-group housing scheme has tried to meet a widely felt need and large numbers of persons have sought to take advantage of it. However, on account of high land prices and the lack of suitably developed sites, progress in the construction of houses under the scheme has not been as rapid as was hoped for.

The provision of developed land on an adequate scale and at reasonable cost is crucial to the success of all housing programmes; for, besides low income group housing, sites have to be provided for private individuals, for co-operatives and for private businesses. Private construction, especially amongst people of small or moderate means is likely to make greater progress if developed sites can be made available by local authorities at low rates, which may be subject to appropriate conditions regarding resale. High land values and a general scarcity of plots are an important reason for the slow progress of housing in recent years, especially in towns which have grown rapidly.

It would therefore, appear desirable to provide assistance to State Governments and local authorities for developing sites for sale to persons who have low incomes and wish to build houses for their own use, whether or not they are applicants for loans under the specific low income group housing scheme which is being implemented. It is further suggested that a proportion of funds available under the scheme for low income housing might be used for land development on a planned basis, special attention being given to those towns where considerable congestion exists and to towns which are likely to develop more rapidly on account of development programmes to be undertaken during the second five year plan. State Governments may examine in consultation with individual local authorities how far action can be pursued along these lines. Sites might also be developed for lease as distinguished for sale.

Rural Housing

A large proportion of the 54 million houses in rural areas need to be rebuilt or substantially improved. Sooner or later, every village should have a plan which provides for wide streets with drains, proper spacing of houses, the location of community buildings and a playground for children. While the improvement of rural housing is an aspect of general rural development and there will be greater progress in housing as rural prosperity increases, there are certain directions in which specific action is called for. Such action may be on a small scale at first but can be readily extended in due course. In rural housing, the bulk of the materials employed are locally available, and fuller use can be made of them. There is considerable scope for voluntary co-operative labour and local community action and, if the right approach is adopted from the beginning, fairly rapid progress can be achieved. Increase in population has intensified the problem of congestion and additional sites are required almost everywhere.

The worst congestion exists in the case of scheduled castes and tribes and other backward classes and artisans and, generally, among landless sections of the village population, although the problem is by no means confined to them. The housing conditions of under-privileged sections in village communities are often extremely bad and need urgent attention. Artisans live and work under, conditions which are already a serious impediment to the adoption of improved techniques, besides being injurious to health. The traditional designs of houses in villages, even for sections of the population which are somewhat better off, do not provide for the minimum requirements of light, ventilation and drainage. In all villages the need for introducing improved methods of excreta disposal is being increasingly felt and the time has come for a large-scale effort in this direction. Finally, improved lay-outs for village abadis have to be introduced, both for new villages and for expansions of existing villages.

These are some of the principal tasks to be undertaken for bringing about better living conditions in villages, and in all of them a great deal can be done in the course of the second plan if various rural programmes are implemented at the district arid village level in a coordinated manner with maximum cooperation from the people. Improvement of rural housing has to be viewed, not as an isolated objective, but as a part of the larger scheme of rural reconstruction, which includes improvement of agricultural production, cooperative working in as many fields as possible, rural water supply, drainage, sanitation, village roads, welfare programmes for scheduled castes and other backward classes and programmes for providing more work and better living conditions for village artisans. During the second plan, resources have been allocated for these and other activities.

As the rural community programme succeeds and village communities assume larger responsibilities, improvements in village housing conditions are to be expected. At this stage, what is required is that in each national extension and community project area and elsewhere, village communities should be made fully conscious of the housing problem and those steps which are urgent should be initiated, such as expansion of the village abadi provision of sites and other assistance for Harijans and the various backward sections, adoption of better standards for houses constructed in the future and introduction of better lighting ventilation and drainage in existing houses.

During the first plan, some steps have been taken towards the improvement of living conditions in villages. In community project areas, 58,000 rural latrines, 1,600 miles of drains and 20,000 wells have been constructed and 34,000 wells renovated, the corresponding figures in national extension areas being 80,000 rural latrines, 2,700 miles of drains, 30,000 new wells and 51,000 renovated wells. In national extension and community project areas, about 29,000 houses were constructed and about the same number reconditioned. In a number of States, brick kilns are being established in rural areas, in some cases through cooperatives. In Uttar Pradesh, for instance, 16 cooperative brick kilns were established in 1950-51; by 1954-55 the number had risen to 752, and in villages within easy reach of brick kilns, improved types of houses are being built to an increasing extent. In several States attempts are being made to improve housing conditions of Harijans through allotment of sites and formation of co-operative housing societies. At the Centre, the Ministry of Works, Housing and Supply has set up a Rural Housing Cell with the object of studying various problems in this field and evolving better designs, lay-outs and methods of construction and better utilisation of local materials.

A rural housing programme is necessarily in the nature of an aided self-help programme in which education and guidance play a large part. Assistance from Government will mainly be in the form of technical advice, demonstrations of model houses and model villages, provision of improved designs and lay-outs, pilot experiments relating to the uses of local materials, organisation of co-operative village programmes based on voluntary labour and, in some measure, provision of financial assistance, especially for Harijans and other backward classes. It would be desirable for every State to have a small technical unit in its Housing Department for evolving designs of houses and lay-outs suited to local conditions, and for studying possible uses for local materials. Further, the various agencies of Government which are concerned with one aspect or the other of rural development should co-ordinate (heir efforts with one another and with the national extension service. In respect of Harijans and other backward classes, extension workers should take steps to see that village communities try to provide free plots of land for house construction by landless agricultural workers. Wherever provisions for financial assistance exist, for instance, for improving housing conditions of Harijans and other backward classes and for setting up rural community .workshops, co-operative societies should be constituted and mutual aid teams organised. Rural housing programmes on these lines can help not only to raise rural living standards but also to increase rural employment and bring about fuller utilisation of the available man-power resources.

Slum Clearance and Sweepers' Housing

The existence of slums in every large town is a matter of serious concern. During the past two or three years a fraction of slum dwellers have been moved out of their habitations as a result of the subsidised industrial housing scheme. But, on the whole the slum problem continues much as it was. Unless steps are taken to make it impossible for new slums to come into existence, the problem of slums will become even larger. For preventing the growth of slums there are two sets of measures to be taken. In the first place, municipal by-laws must be enforced with the utmost strictness. In the enforcement of municipal by-laws the support of enlightened public opinion should be mobilised and potential slums should receive immediate attention. Secondly, master plans should be approved for every town, beginning with towns which are already large or have expanded much in recent years or are likely to grow rapidly in the next few years. For enforcing master plans, local authorities should have the requisite powers to implement zoning schemes, control the use of land and prevent ribbon development. Where necessary, new authorities may be set up. In Delhi a special development authority has been recently constituted.

While action is taken to prevent the development of slums in the future, it is also essential to tackle the problems of existing slums. To a large extent there is no alternative to their demolition and clearance, but there may be cases where measures for improvement are feasible. Hitherto proposals for slum clearance have been held back because of three difficulties, namely, the high cost of acquisition of slums, the unwillingness of slum dwellers to move to distant places on account of the fear that their social and economic life will be dislocated, and the need for subsidising the construction of houses so that they can be let to slum dwellers at rates which they can afford to pay. These aspects have been kept in view by the Central Government in evolving a new scheme for slum clearance and sweepers' housing for which a total provision of Rs. 20 crore has been made in the second five year plan.

With the object of reducing the cost of acquisition of slums, which are disproportionately high at present, especially in the larger towns, it has been recommended that State Governments should take advantage of the provisions of Article 31 of the Constitution. Delays which occur in land acquisition proceedings should also be eliminated through appropriate modifications in the legislation. Under the slum clearance and sweepers' housing scheme which is now to be implemented. State Governments are being asked to undertake social and economic surveys of their worst slum areas in the larger towns and to draw up phased programmes of slum clearance. The scheme is based on two main principles. The first principle is that there should be the minimum dislocation of slum dwellers and the effort should be to rehouse them as far as possible at or near the existing sites of slums, so that they may not be uprooted from their fields of employment

The second principle is that in order to keep rents within the paying capacity of the slum dwellers, greater emphasis should be on the provision of minimum standards of environmental hygiene and essential civic amenities rather than on the construction of elaborate structures. Within the allocation made in the plan, it is proposed that the Central Government should provide 25 per cent of the cost as subsidy and 50 per cent by way of loan repayable in 30 years. State Governments being required to find the remaining 25 per cent of the cost as subsidy from their own resources. It is proposed that wherever practicable, and especially where the rent paying capacity of the slum dwellers is extremely small. State Governments and local bodies should provide slum dwellers with developed and demarcated plots of land varying from 1,000 to 1,200 sq. ft. in area as well as limited quantities of building materials, leaving it to slum dwellers to build houses for themselves as far as possible on the prescribed pattern and under appropriate guidance on a self-help and mutual aid basis. Standard costs of slum clearance and slum improvement projects have been worked out for the guidance of State Governments.

The rehousing benefits to be provided under the scheme are intended for those slum families whose income does not exceed Rs. 250 per mensem in Bombay and Calcutta and Rs. 175 per mensem elsewhere. Families with higher incomes are to be encouraged to take advantage of loans under the low income group housing and other schemes and it is also proposed that they should be given assistance in procuring land and some part of the land developed by States may be set apart for them. Since a large proportion of slum dwellers in most towns are sweepers, it is expected that under the new programme large numbers of sweepers will be able to move to new houses from their present habitations.

Other Housing Schemes

In accordance with the provisions of the Plantation Labour Act, 1951, it is obligatory for every plantation to provide houses of prescribed standards for workers and their families residing in the plantations. While the larger plantations are able to fulfil this condition, for the smaller plantations Government assistance by way of loans is needed. During the second five year plan Rs. 2 crore are to be provided for this purpose. About 11,000 houses are expected to be built under this scheme.

For several years attempts have been made to provide improved houses for labour in the coal mines. In view especially of the large expansion programmes of the coal industry, the provision of houses for miners has considerable importance during the second five year plan. On the basis of the experience gained in working earlier proposals a new scheme has been recently formulated. The scheme is financed through a cess of six annas per ton of coal and coke despatched from the collieries, the annual income being almost Rs. 1 crore. Under the scheme the Coal Mines Labour Welfare Board will obtain land from colliery owners on lease for a period of 40 years free of cost or at nominal rent. Houses will be constructed by the Board and the colliery owners will pay the Board rent at Rs. 2 per tenement per month and workers will be charged rent not exceeding the contribution made to the Board. About Rs. 8 crore are expected to be made available for this purpose, and it is hoped to construct about 30,000 houses during the plan period.

The Mica Mines Labour Welfare Fund Act, 1946 has prescribed an ad valorem excise duty of 2 per cent per cent on mica exported from India. The annual income of the fund is about 15 lakh. A subsidised housing scheme for mica miners was approved in 1953.

With effect from 1956-57, the Central Government have revived the scheme for the grant of house building advances to Central Government servants which was discontinued some years ago. Under the present scheme, advances up to 24 months' pay, subject to a maximum of Rs. 25,000 for new houses and Rs. 10,000 for extensions can be made. These will be repayable at 4Vt per cent interest per annum over a period of 20 years.

A provision of Rs. 3 crore has been made in the second plan for a middle income group housing scheme. The scheme envisaged collaboration with insurance companies and, according to the terms originally proposed, each loan was to be jointly approved by Government and an insurance company, the loan being limited to 80 per cent of the cost of a house, including the cost of land, of which Government was to provide 25 per cent and the insurance company the balance of 75 per cent Following the nationalisation of life insurance, further details of the scheme are at present under consideration.

Housing Statistics and Surveys

The housing problem has grown steadily over the past few decades, both in rural and in urban areas. There have been few systematic surveys of housing conditions in India. Housing statistics are also extremely deficient and incomplete and data are not available showing either the progress of new construction or the extent of shortage. For organising housing programmes on any scale it is essential that accurate statistics should become available at regular intervals. The Central Statistical Organisation are taking steps, in collaboration with State statistical bureaux, to collect data on housing and building materials, both in the public and in the private sectors. Increasing building activity and construction will come to be an important factor in the regulation of the economy. The importance of statistical information in this field cannot therefore be too much stressed.

In its seventh round (October 1953 to March 1954) the National Sample Survey investigated housing conditions in 943 sample villages as well as in 53 sample towns and in the four cities of Bombay, Calcutta, Delhi and Madras. Of the 53 sample towns 14 had a population of 100,000 and above, 9 of 50,000 to 1,00,000,14 of 15,000 to 50,000 and 16 had a population of less than 15,000. The data obtained in the survey have been recently tabulated and, although they are still provisional, they throw light on certain aspects of the housing situation in the country. The investigation showed that in rural areas about 85 per cent of houses have mud plinths, 83 per cent walls of mud, bamboo and reed and about 70 per cent roofs of straw, grass, reed, mud etc. About 7 per cent of the houses have plinths and walls of brick, cement or stone and roofs of corrugated sheets, tiles etc. More than 95 per cent of the houses have no latrines attached to them. As regards sources of drinking water, about 70 per cent depended on wells, 13 per cent on tanks and ponds, 12 per cent on natural sources like lakes, springs and rivers, 3 per cent. on tubewells, less than 1.5 per cent on tap water supply and about 1.5 per cent on other sources. About 81 per cent of the houses had three rooms or less, one-roomed houses accounted for 34 per cent and two roomed houses for 32 per cent of the houses studied in the survey. About 38.5 per cent of the households had less than 100 square feet per head of floor space and about 32.5 per cent between 109 and 200 square feet.

In the urban areas studied during the investigation, nearly one-fourth of the houses had plinths, walls and roofs of mud. The study confirmed the impression that over the past two decades new construction has not kept pace with the growth of urban population. From the data available it appears that as against increase in urban population at a rate varying from 3 to 4 per cent. per annum new houses have been built at a rate varying, say, from 2 to 2.5 per cent About 44 per cent of the houses in urban areas have only one room, 28 per cent two rooms, 12 per cent 3 rooms and 16 per cent 4 or more rooms. About 46 per cent of houses had less than 100 square feet per head. These facts illustrate the congestion which exists in urban areas and, as matters stand, is likely to increase further.

The extent of the housing shortage which exists in urban areas can only be broadly estimated. For an urban population of 62 million there were in 1951 about 10 million houses. The shortage of houses in that year was roughly reckoned at about 2.5 million. The population of towns increased by 10.6 million between 1931 and 1941 and by 18.1 million between 1941 and 1951. During these decades the number of occupied houses in urban areas increased respectively by 1.8 and 1.7 million. Even apart from the question of the quality of housing, the quantitative shortage increased considerably during the period 1941-51. Alongside post war developments and targets there has been accelerated urban growth. Between 1951 and 1961 the total urban population is expected to increase by about 33 per cent so that in the absence of effective measures and carefully formulated programmes of urban development, the shortage in 5961 may be twice as much as in 1951. Comprehensive housing policies and programmes are likely to emerge only after a few years of practical experience in working various housing schemes in the private sector and through public authorities. In this chapter an attempt is made to formulate a broad approach to housing policy and urban development in the context of economic planning and programmes for the development of both large-scale and small-scale industries.

Housing Problems

Programmes for the expansion of housing to be implemented during the second five year plan by various public authorities and the anticipations in regard to construction in the private sector have been described earlier. In expanding housing facilities, during the past two or three years the main problems which have arisen and to which attention has to be given are the following:

1. in rapidly growing towns developed sites are not available to a sufficient extent,
2. construction in the private sector tends to concentrate on expensive houses intended to fetch high rents and the needs of

the lower middle and middle classes are not adequately catered for;

3. apart from assistance which the Government now provides, adequate institutional arrangements for housing finance do not exist;
4. cooperative housing has made comparatively little progress;
5. there is considerable need for research in building materials, and techniques and for prescribing standards of construction with due regard to the availability of local materials and the economic use of scarce materials; and
6. with a few exceptions. State Governments are not yet adequately organised for undertaking and assisting extensive housing programmes.

The question of providing sites or plots for the construction of houses especially by persons of small or moderate means has been mentioned earlier. It has been suggested that a proportion of funds provided under the low income group housing scheme may be used on land development on a planned basis, so that plots can be made available at reasonable prices to persons who apply for loans under the scheme as well as to other persons with low incomes. Speculation in land, which occurs frequently, should be dealt with through control of land use and regulation of transfers of land.

The greater part of construction which occurs in the private sector is for rent and generally rents are high in relation to the rent-paying capacity of the vast majority. In developing private construction, the emphasis should be on providing facilities to enable persons of moderate means to build houses for themselves, and public authorities should take the necessary initiative. In the nature of things, the low income-group housing scheme introduced by the Central Government can meet only a fraction of the total demand. There is need for adequate arrangements of an institutional character for housing finance. In 1955 the Housing Ministers' Conference suggested examination by States of the possibility of constituting State Housing Finance Corporations. In the past a limited amount of housing finance has been made available by insurance companies. In view of the nationalisation of life insurance and the urgent need for the provision of additional housing in most urban areas, we recommend that a special study should be undertaken by the Central Government of the institutions and methods which could be best developed in the special conditions of India for providing real estate credit on an adequate scale.

House building has an important role in expanding employment opportunities and stimulating capital formation and private saving. From this aspect also it is desirable to take early steps to evolve appropriate institutions for providing financial and other assistance. In this connection, the experience of cooperative housing societies in various urban areas and amongst industrial workers should be examined with a view to determining the directions in which cooperative housing schemes may be pursued with special advantage and the character of the institutional and other facilities required for the development of cooperative housing.

In accordance with a recommendation in the First Five Year Plan, for developing building research and techniques, the National Buildings Organisation was established in 1954 in the Ministry of Works, Housing and Supply. The functions of the Organisation are to recommend measures for promoting quicker, cheaper and better construction and economy in the use of scarce materials and manpower. The Organisation is also attempting to compile and collect statistics relating to building activity and building materials and to serve as a clearing house for information regarding the technology of building designs, materials and construction. The National Buildings Organisation has drawn up a comprehensive programme of research through the various research laboratories and institutions.

On the development side, the problems under investigation include measures to improve the quality of bricks, the manufacture, of boards, partition walls, tiles, hollow bricks, etc. The use of seasoned and treated timbers and bamboos in construction, cheap methods of fixing doors and windows to masonry, current uses of scarce materials in construction and possibilities of reducing the use of cement and replacing it by lime where possible, are also being studied. The National Buildings Organisation is also investigating the production of kankar lime and other limes. Work on mud plaster is being undertaken from the point of view of moisture resistance. In view of the need to economise in the use of scarce materials and reduce housing costs, steps are being taken to evolve standards of housing which will be satisfactory without being expensive or ostentatious and will involve the use of the maximum extent of local materials after appropriate processing.

The question of organisation for carrying out housing programmes was considered at the Housing Ministers' Conference which was held in 1955. The Conference recommended that in each State there should be a department or agency to coordinate the various aspects of housing, especially, in regard to the assessment of housing needs, preparation of master plans, acquisition of land and implementation of house building programmes. As housing and other construction programmes are undertaken on a large scale, the need has been felt for organising systematic training of masons, brick-layers, carpenters, plumbers and other personnel. Some steps in this direction have been recently taken both by the Ministry of Works, Housing and Supply and by a few States, but considerable expansion of training programmes is required.

Urban Development

The shortage of housing in urban areas calls for a series of measures for the expansion of housing facilities. If attention is concentrated only on these measures, in face of the present trends in urban development, the shortage of housing will continue to be accentuated. It is necessary, therefore to consider urban housing, not merely as a problem by itself or as an attempt continually to catch up with events but as part of the wider problem of the planning of urban areas and of their economic and other relationships with the regions in which they are situated.

Between 1921 and 1951, the urban population rose from about 27 million to about 62 million, the proportion of the urban to the total population increasing from about 11 to more than 17 per cent As the national economy has become more closely integrated, the economic, social and political importance of towns has increased. In the nature of things, much of the development in the past has been of an unplanned character. Large towns have attracted to themselves new industries and services and the problems of providing housing and other amenities have become increasingly acute. Rise in land values, speculative buying of lands in the proximity of growing towns, high rentals and the development of slum areas are features common to most large towns.

Few municipal administrations have been able to cope with the problems which have thus grown cumulatively. With a view to the closer understanding of those aspects of urban growth which bear specially on rural-urban migration and the development of employment opportunities, the Research Programmes Committee of the Planning Commission has initiated surveys of 21 leading cities and towns. In recent years, much thought has been given to problems of rural planning; similar attention has now to be given to the complex problems of urban development and re-development. India is on the threshold of rapid industrial development. Unless there is adequate forethought and planning, industrial progress will be accompanied by serious social and other problems in urban areas which may become increasingly difficult to manage. It is, therefore, necessary that from now on the future course of urban development should be viewed by public authorities at the Centre, in the States and in each region in its correct perspective. Even though quick results may not be forthcoming, appropriate policies should be laid down from the start and determined efforts should be made to follow them with the support of enlightened public opinion.

If urban development and re-development and housing policies are viewed in the context of planned economic development and rapid industrialisation, three problems claim special study, namely, (a) methods of securing planned development in urban areas, (b) expansion of housing facilities, and (c) development of civic administrations along sound and progressive lines. The second problem has been examined at some length in this chapter. On the third aspect, it is sufficient to remark here that- for urban development to proceed on desirable lines, competent municipal administrations with adequate powers, resources and administrative and technical staffs are essential. Urban development and redevelopment throws increasing responsibility on municipal administrations which few of them are at present able to discharge. In many western countries, local authorities are the principal agencies for implementing housing and other civic programmes. In India also, it is essential to use local authorities more and more as agencies of the State for providing housing and other civic amenities in keeping with the requirement of economic development

If planned urban development is to be undertaken and the lines along which various urban or potentially urban centres are to develop over the course of the next ten or fifteen years, there is need for a clear conception of the pattern of economic development and especially of industrialisation which is to be followed in determining the distribution, location and size of various industrial and other undertakings. These questions have been considered in the appropriate chapters. Within the framework of plan's drawn up on the basis of territories such as districts and States and for different sectors of development such as agriculture, industry, transport, etc. and-for their more efficient implementation, it is also necessary to work out physical and economic plans based upon the study of urban-rural regions, viewing each region as an area for integrated, local planning. The regional planning approach is required especially for large and growing towns and for river valley areas which are being developed through new irrigation and power projects. The aim ultimately must be to evolve balanced urban-rural regions which would provide stable and diverse employment and, through the provision of the necessary economic and social over-heads, achieve development at reasonable social and economic cost

To achieve this objective, action has to be taken in each State along five principal directions:

1. Each State should have a phased programme for the survey and preparation of master plans for all important towns. These should provide for integration of land use and zoning principles in each town or area with a view to obtaining the maximum amount of efficiency and economy in working and living conditions. In this connection towns and cities such as Delhi, Bombay, Calcutta, Madras, Ahmedabad, Hyderabad, Kanpur, Lucknow, Poona etc. would require early attention.
2. A number of new towns have recently come into existence; others are likely to develop rapidly during the second and subsequent plans as industrialisation proceeds. Sindri, Durgapur, Bhilai, Rourkela, Chittaranjan and Neiveli are illustrations of towns in this group. As early as possible, the preparation of regional plans for such towns should be taken in hand.
3. Development of river valley areas should be based on careful surveys of their topography, resources and development needs and potential. A pilot project for a regional planning survey of the Damodar Valley are will shortly be undertaken. Surveys on similar lines are required, for instance, in areas served by the Bhakra Nangal, Hirakund, Chambal, Tungabhadra, Koyna and other important projects.
4. Town and country planning legislation has been so far enacted in four States, namely, Madras, Bombay, Hyderabad and Saurashtra. Uttar Pradesh has such legislation under consideration. It is recommended that town and country planning legislation should be enacted in all States and the necessary machinery for its implementation should be set up. The preparation of town plans is at present often held up for lack of qualified personnel. The expansion of existing facilities for the training of town planners and architects has been provided for in the plan.

5. There are a number of programmes in the second five year plan which have considerable bearing, on urban development and re-development, such as, large industrial and other undertakings whose location is determined or influenced by the Government, development of village and small industries and of industrial estates and townships, major irrigation and power projects, small town an rural electrification schemes, establishment of warehouses and marketing centres for agricultural produce, urban water supply and sanitation schemes, industrial and low-income group housing schemes, expansion of transport facilities etc. These and other programmes should be implemented in an integrated manner with careful attention to their impact on urban and regional development and with reference to the present and future requirements of planning in different parts of each State or region. Such coordinated planning will ensure that the resources devoted to these programmes will yield satisfactory results, and the costs of economic development as well as of providing civic amenities will be reduced.

Third Five Year Plan: 1961-66

Housing and Urban and Rural Planning

The housing programme which had its beginning in the First Five Year Plan was directed mainly towards housing for industrial workers and low income groups. The programme was considerably expanded during the Second Five Year Plan with the introduction of schemes of slum clearance and slum improvement, plantation labour housing, village housing and land acquisition and development.

A few other specific schemes designed to benefit sections of the community like scheduled castes, scheduled tribes and backward classes in rural areas, handloom weavers, displaced persons etc., were undertaken. The housing programme for workers in the coal and mica industries was implemented with resources provided by the labour welfare funds for these industries. During the Second Plan the Life Insurance Corporation began to provide funds for house building to middle income groups and to State Governments for undertaking rental housing for their low paid employees. Housing on a considerable scale was also undertaken by the Central Government Departments and public enterprises for their employees. The total outlay on public housing during the Second Plan was of the order of Rs. 250 crore and about 5,00,000 houses were constructed.

Although efforts on an increasing scale have been made in housing during the First and Second Plans, the problem of catching up with the arrears of housing and with the growth of population will continue to present serious difficulty for many years to come. Between 1951 and 1961 there was an increase in population of nearly 40 per cent in towns with a population of 20,000 or more. It was reckoned in the Second Plan that the shortage of houses in urban areas might increase by 1961 to about 5 million as compared to 2.5 million houses in 1951.

The growth of population and, in particular, of the urban population suggest, at least three genera], considerations in relation to the directions in which housing programmes should be developed during the Third and subsequent Five Year Plans. Firstly, housing policies need to be set in the larger context of economic development and industrialisation, both large-scale and the problems likely to emerge over the next decade or two. Proposals relating to location and dispersal of industries will; therefore, be of increasing importance in the solution of the housing problem. In the second place, it is necessary to coordinate more closely the efforts of all the agencies concerned, whether public, cooperative or private. The need to undertake the preparation of master plans for urban areas becomes all the greater, for without these plans there is no means of bringing together and maximising the contribution of different agencies towards well-defined common objectives pursued systematically over a long period. In the third place, conditions have to be created in which the entire programme of housing construction, both public and private, must be so oriented that it serves specially the requirements of the low income groups within the community. In working out the housing programmes for the Third Plan an attempt has been made to bear these considerations in mind.

The housing schemes, which have been operating in recent years, namely, those relating to subsidised industrial housing, low income group housing, slum clearance, plantation labour housing, land acquisition and development and village housing will be continued and expanded in the Third Plan. There will be special emphasis on land acquisition and development as this is basic to the success of all housing programmes. New programmes for housing economically weaker sections of the community, dock labour and pavement dwellers will also be taken up. Concerted efforts will be made to prepare master plans and regional development plans of metropolitan and industrial cities and resource regions. Provision has also been made in the Third Plan for undertaking experimental housing and research in building techniques and for collecting housing statistics, the absence of which has been a great handicap in the past.

Outlay and Targets

For housing and urban development programmes, the Third Five Year Plan provides Rs. 142 crore as against the revised outlay of Rs. 84 crore in the Second Plan. In addition, funds for housing are also expected to be provided by the Life Insurance Corporation, whose contribution is estimated at about Rs. 60 crore.

Besides the provision for housing mentioned above, there are certain additional housing programmes financed from other sources. The coal and mica mine welfare funds are expected to provide in the Third Plan about Rs. 14 crore for the construction of 60,000 houses. The programme for the welfare of backward classes includes allotments for housing. Tentative estimates of the Ministries of Railways, Commerce and Industry, Communications and others suggest that over the plan period they may build about 3,00,000 houses for their employees at an approximate cost of Rs. 200 crore. Broadly, in the course of the Third Plan, under various housing schemes and the construction programmes of Ministries, 9,00,000 houses might be constructed as compared to about 5,00,000 in the Second Plan.

In the private sector there has been an increasing amount of construction, but it is difficult to estimate its precise magnitude. The net investment on housing and other private construction, which was reckoned at Rs. 900 crore in the First Plan, is estimated at about Rs. 1,000 crore in the Second Plan. In the Third Plan private investment on housing and other construction is placed at about Rs. 1,125 crore.

Housing Boards

In the present stage of development, finance provided directly by Government can meet only a fraction of the demand for housing. Institutional arrangements are, therefore, required which will enable large numbers of persons, many of them with small incomes, to build for themselves. In this connection, the possibility of setting up a Central Housing Board is at present under study. Such an organisation could help to channel additional funds into housing, encourage the flow of credit on easy terms amongst other things by means of insured mortgages, improve lending practices and provide the machinery needed for the creation of a sound mortgage market in housing. It could, for instance, raise finance, directly to some extent and provide loan assistance to State Governments or State Housing Boards for purchase and development of land, construction of houses and acquisition and redevelopment of slum areas. Funds obtained from the Life Insurance Corporation and from the Central Government could be channelled through it. In States where Housing Boards already exist, they generally serve as construction agencies for implementing the State housing programmes. The existence of a Central Housing Board and of Housing Boards in the States could in due course, secure for the development of housing resources which might not be otherwise readily available. Together these institutions could assist in evolving housing policies which would facilitate construction of houses by persons of limited means for their own use and also enable banks and other financial institutions to undertake various services. It is proposed to consider these aspects further with a view to implementing the housing programmes of the Third Plan and laying the foundations for larger development in the future.

Land Acquisition and Development

Availability of building sites in sufficient numbers and at reasonable rates is essential for the successful implementation of the housing programme. During the Third Plan, therefore, a fair share of the resources available for housing is being devoted to land acquisition and development. A scheme was introduced in 1959 for giving financial assistance to Start Governments in the shape of loans repayable over a period of 10 years for acquiring and developing lands in selected places. The land acquired is to be utilised for house building under different schemes and for the provision of related community facilities like parks, playgrounds, schools, hospitals, shops, post offices etc. In the Third Plan a programme entailing an outlay of Rs. 26 crore (inclusive of the contributions to be made by the Life Insurance Corporation) is envisaged for land acquisition and development. The resources made available under this programme could serve as nuclei for 'revolving funds' in the States and be utilised for bulk acquisition and development of land.

Housing of Industrial Workers

Under the subsidised industrial housing scheme which was formulated in 1952 for providing housing to industrial workers employed in factories and mines, mainly in the private lector, the Central Government provides to State Governments, State Housing Boards and municipal bodies 50 per cent of the cost as loan and 50 per cent as subsidy. Industrial employers and cooperative societies of industrial workers are given financial assistance to the extent of 75 per cent and 90 per cent respectively, the extent of subsidy in both cases being 25 per cent. To enable industrial workers to provide the remaining 10 per cent of the cost, they have been allowed to draw non-refundable loans from their provident fund accounts. By the end of the Second Plan, the construction of about 1,40,000 tenements costing Rs. 45 crore had been approved. About 1,00,000 tenements had been completed and the rest were under different stages of construction.

The scheme should have made greater progress if even the subsidised rate of rent had not proved a comparatively high charge for workers, with the result that in some areas the tenements which have been constructed have not been occupied by industrial workers. The question of bringing down the rent so that it should be within the paying capacity of workers needs further study. Along with it, arrangements should be made to provide cheap transport for taking workers to their places of work. Certain aspects of the scheme have been revised already. Workers have a larger measure of choice as between different types of accommodation. Open developed and demarcated plots of land along with some building and roofing materials can be taken up by workers, so that they may build huts of the prescribed pattern themselves. For those who do not wish to go in for 'self-built' huts on open developed plots, 'skeletal' housing with the necessary foundation, plinth and roof to form a stable structure is provided.

The rent for open developed plots is about Rs. 2 to Rs. 3 per month, whereas for skeletal housing it is about Rs. 8 per month. For non-family workers hostel or dormitory accommodation is built. A few other modifications such as extension in the period of repayment of loan, increase in the ceilings of standard costs to fit in with the rise in prices of building materials and labour, liberalisation of allotment rules and provision of developed sites to employers and cooperatives have been introduced. Recently employers have been granted a concession in income-tax in the shape of an initial depreciation allowance of 20 per cent on the cost of construction of new houses for their low-paid employees, in addition to exemption for three years from payment of income tax on the rental value of small houses.

Despite the steps which have been taken to make the industrial housing scheme more attractive to employers, much progress cannot be achieved without the employers generally accepting the housing of a substantial portion of workers as an essential obligation. It is necessary to remember that housing conditions for industrial workers have continued to deteriorate and that without improvements in this direction efforts to increase industrial efficiency and productivity will also be affected. The problem is, therefore, one of working out arrangements for new industries as well as for the established industries which might be feasible from the financial and other aspects and would also result in an effective contribution towards the solution of the housing problem. For instance, new establishments with a prescribed limit of paid-up capital (say, Rs. 20 lakh or more) could be placed under the obligation of constructing one-half of the housing required by their labour over a period of perhaps 10 years.

In the case of the older establishments, in any specific scheme that is worked out the contribution already made by an employer to provide housing for their workers should be taken into account. In these industries also, over a period, the aim might be to ensure that about 50 per cent of the housing required is made available directly by the industries and the rest as part of the general scheme of housing development. To the extent the employers are unable to construct directly the Government or the Housing Boards may take up construction. In such cases, the employers could contribute towards the cost of construction. These and other suggestions should be considered jointly in consultation with representatives of employers and workers with a view to evolving a satisfactory scheme.

Housing of Dock Workers

A provision of Rs. 2 crore has been made in the Third Plan for giving loan assistance to Dock Labour Boards at Bombay, Calcutta and Madras to enable them to build houses for workers registered with them. A suitable approach might be for Government to grant loans to the extent of 80 per cent of the cost of construction. With the provision made in the Plan, it should be possible to build about 5,000 houses. In recent years port development has been undertaken on a large scale, and in cooperation with the port authorities a coordinated view of the housing problems in the ports should now be taken.

Holding For Low Income Groups

The low income group housing scheme provides for grant of loan assistance up to 80 per cent of the cost of the dwelling, subject to a maximum of Rs. 8,000, to persons whose income does not exceed Rs. 6,000 per annum. Assistance on this scale is also given to local bodies, public institutions run on no-profit-no-loss basis, recognised health, charitable and educational institutions and cooperative societies.

Since the scheme began in 1954, loans for about 85,000 houses have been sanctioned, and by the end of the Second Plan about 53,000 houses were completed. There is considerable demand for loans under this scheme. Progress has been greater in towns where developed sites are available. It is felt that in the Third Plan special steps should be taken to enable those sections of the community which are economically weak to obtain clue benefits from the scheme, such as those with an annual income of Rs. 1,800 or less. Persons in this category are in a position to pay rent in the range of Rs. 10 to 12 or, at the most, Rs. 15 per mensem. The principal methods for providing housing for diem would appear to be either through construction of rental housing mainly by Housing Boards and local bodies or through housing cooperatives.

As a basis for further consideration, it might be possible to provide local bodies with loans at a concessional rate of interest repayable over a long period. Apart from pucca houses, the question of providing open developed plots or skeletal housing on the lines of the industrial housing and slum clearance schemes could be considered. Housing cooperatives comprising economically weaker persons could also be given similar assistance. Roughly about a third of the provision under the low income group housing scheme could be earmarked for economically weak persons. Exemptions from State and local taxes would also need to be considered. As more institutional finance for the housing of low income groups generally becomes available, larger proportion of the funds provided by Government could be utilised for housing schemes for the economically weaker sections.

Plantation Labour Housing

The Plantation Labour Act, 1951, requires every employer of plantation labour to provide and maintain for all workers and their families residing in plantations, necessary housing accommodation, at the rate of at least 8 per cent of the workers every year, until all such workers have been provided for. A number of planters, particularly the smaller ones, found it difficult to discharge this obligation due to inadequacy of financial resources. Accordingly the plantation labour housing scheme was introduced in 1956 for assisting such planters as needed financial help Under this scheme, loans are given to the extent of 80 per cent of the cost of construction of the dwelling, excluding the cost of land and its development, subject to a maximum of Rs. 2,400 per house in North India and Rs. 1,920 per house in South India. The planters are required to contribute the balance of 20 per cent from their own resources.

By the end of the Second Plan only 700 houses costing Rs. 14 lakh had been sanctioned and 300 houses completed. The main difficulty in the way of the scheme has been the inability of the planters to furnish adequate security for the loan. The scheme requires the planters to mortgage to the State Governments land and houses built on it as security for the loan. The planters are not in a position to comply because their land and other properties are usually mortgaged with banks as security for the loans advanced to them for the normal working expenses of the plantations.

To make it easier for planters to avail of the loans, some State Governments have relaxed the security conditions. A "Pool Guarantee Fund" is also proposed to be set up with an additional-per cent interest charged on loans to the planters and the interest earned thereon' from year to year. This Fund will serve as collateral security for the grant of loans and the losses, if any, in excess of the assets in the Fund will be shared equally by the Central Government, the State Government and the Commodity Board concerned.

Middle Income Group Housing

A scheme for providing loans to middle income groups was introduced in February, 1959, with funds provided by the Life Insurance Corporation and is meant for persons whose income is between Rs. 6,000 to Rs. 12,000 per annum. Loans to the extent or 80 per cent of the cost of the house subject to a maximum of Rs. 16,000 (Rs. 20,000 in the case of those who do not already possess a plot of land) are provided under the scheme. The loans are advanced to individual borrowers through the State Governments at the rate of 5 per cent per annum. By the end of the Second Plan a sum of Rs. 10.5 crore was disbursed to State Governments and Union Territories. Loans were sanctioned to 3,600 applicants and about 500 houses were constructed. Progress was comparatively small in the initial stages as this was a new scheme for which rules for the grant of loans had to be drawn up and other arrangements made.

Rental Housing for State Government Employees

The object of the rental housing scheme for State Government employees is to assist State Governments in providing housing accommodation to their low paid employees. Under the scheme, which was introduced in February 1959 the Life Insurance Corporation grants loans carrying an interest of 5 per cent per annum to State Governments, and the loans are repayable over a period of 20 years. A sum of about Rs. 7 crore was given to State Governments under the scheme during the Second Five Year Plan, and 2,500 houses were sanctioned and 735 were completed.

Slum Clearance and Improvement

The Third Plan provides for a programme of about Rs. 29 crore for slum clearance and improvement. A scheme for giving financial assistance to State Governments and local bodies to enable them to clear some of the worst slums in big cities was initiated during the Second Plan. By the end of the Second Plan 208 projects costing about Rs. 19 crore and involving re-housing of 58,200 families living in slum conditions were taken up in different towns and cities. About 18,000 units have been already completed. For such of the families as cannot afford to pay even the subsidised rent of a pucca tenement, the scheme provides for skeletal housing and open developed plots with a separate washing platform and latrine for each family, leaving it to the slum dwellers to build huts of a prescribed pattern themselves on a self-help basis in accordance with the technical directions of the State Government.

Some of the difficulties which came in the way of implementation of the slum clearance and improvement programme were the lengthy and time-consuming procedures of acquisition of slum areas, non-availability and high costs of alternative sites near existing places of work, inability of the slum dwellers to pay even the subsidised rent and their reluctance to move from the areas selected for clearance. Some States like Mysore, Madras, Madhya Pradesh, Assam, Punjab, West Bengal and Delhi Administration have enacted legislation for speedier acquisition of slum areas and for scaling down the rate of compensation. Similar legislation is also needed elsewhere. The scheme was reviewed by the Advisory Committee on Slum Clearance and by a Study Team set up by the Committee on Plan Projects. These Committees recommended that while long-term plans were required, it was even more essential to think of short-term measures to relieve acute distress in the slum areas and, as an immediate measure, minimum amenities like sanitary latrines, proper drainage, uncontaminated water supply, moderately good approach roads, paved streets, and proper lighting should be provided.

Following consideration of the reports of these two committees the scope of the slum clearance programme was extended to include slum improvement. Larger resources were also provided as a matter of immediate priority for dealing with slum problems in six major cities, namely, Calcutta, Bombay, Madras, Delhi. Kanpur and Ahmedabad. In these cities, the total subsidy for slum clearance was raised from 50 per cent to 62 per cent and the Central Government' share in it from 25 per cent to 37 per cent.

The maximum effort under this scheme should continue to be concentrated on the six cities mentioned above. However, it is proposed that in the Third Plan, in principle, slum clearance and improvement work could be taken up wherever State Governments consider that the slum problem exists in acute form. In view of limitations of resources, it is considered that ordinarily towns and cities with a population of 1,00,000 or more should receive priority. It is suggested that State Governments may arrange for surveys of slum areas, classifying them in two categories—areas which may have to be cleared and re-developed completely, and those which can be made habitable through the improvement of environmental conditions. If the owners of slum properties falling within the second category fail to carry out the improvements, these should be carried out through local bodies and the cost recovered from the owners; where necessary, the properties could be acquired or requisitioned. Wherever improvements are carried out by local-bodies in slum areas on public lands or requisitioned lands, it may be necessary to give them grants for providing essential services. The cooperation of voluntary organisations and social workers should be fully enlisted in carrying out the programme of slum clearance.

While steps are being taken to clear or improve the existing slums, it is equally important that new-slums should not be allowed to grow up. This is by no means an easy object to achieve. Besides preparing and strictly implementing master plans for all growing towns and cities, it will be essential to enforce municipal bye-laws and building regulations, and at the same time, to expand housing facilities for low income groups and for economically weaker sections. As transitional measures, night shelters and dormitory accommodation for pavement dwellers and non-family workers have considerable urgency. Similarly, the housing of sweepers and scavengers must receive special attention. In selecting slum areas for clearance and improvement high priority should be given to areas predominantly inhabited by sweepers and scavengers.

Urban Planning and Land Policy

Urbanisation is an important aspect of the process of economic and social development and is closely connected with many other problems such as migration from villages to towns, levels of living in rural and urban areas, relative costs of providing economic and social services in towns of varying size, provision of housing for different sections of the population, provision of facilities like water supply, sanitation, transport and power, pattern of economic development, location and dispersal of industries, civic administration, fiscal policies, and the planning of land use. These aspects are of special importance in urban areas which are developing rapidly. The number of cities with a population of 1,00,000 or more has increased from 75 in 1951 to

115 in 1961, and their population now forms about 43 per cent of the total urban population. Of the aspects mentioned above, in the long run, the most decisive are the pattern of economic development and the general approach to industrial location. The broad objective must be to secure balanced development between large, medium-sized and small industries, and between rural and urban areas. While this is by no means easy to realise, the main ingredients of developmental policy are the following:

- As far as possible, new industries should be established away from large and congested cities.
- In the planning of large industries, the concept of region should be adopted. In each case, planning should extend beyond the immediate environs to a larger area for whose development the new industry would serve as a major focal point.
- In community development projects or other areas within a district the rural and urban components of development should be knit into a composite plan based in each case on schemes for strengthening economic inter-dependence between towns and the surrounding rural areas.
- Within each rural area the effort should be to secure a diversified occupational pattern in place of the present extreme dependence on agriculture.

In considering the nature of the urban problem to be phased over the next decade, it is necessary both to deal with the situation which exists now and to ensure action along the right lines for the future.

Costs of Urban Development: Much of the deterioration which occurs in living conditions in rapidly growing urban areas is due to the high costs of urban development, in particular, the costs of providing housing, water supply, drainage, transport and other services. The situation is further accentuated by the existence of unemployment, overcrowding and the growth of slums and the fact that a significant proportion of the population in many cities is without shelter. The problems to be faced are formidable in size and complexity, and solutions for them can be found only if their nature is fully appreciated not only by the State Governments, but also by municipal administrations and by the public generally and if an increasing amount of community effort and citizenship participation can be called forth within each urban area. There are certain minimum directions in which action should be taken during the Third Plan so that, for the future, at any rate, a correct course is set. These are:

- control of urban land values through public acquisition of land and appropriate fiscal policies;
- physical planning of the use of land and the preparation of master plans;
- defining tolerable minimum standard for housing and other services to be provided for towns according to their requirements and also prescribing maximum standards to the extent necessary; and
- strengthening of municipal administrations for undertaking new development responsibilities.

Control of Urban Land Values: The most important element in raising housing and other costs and in restricting the scale on which improvements can be undertaken in the interests of low income groups is high land prices. Apart from normal increases, a major factor in raising land prices is speculation. In some towns, there are powerful factors like the setting up of new industries and the establishment of new public and other offices which stimulate speculative activity. However, since the rapid economic development of the country as a whole is under way and exerts its influence in all directions, elements of rising land values are present in larger or smaller degree in almost every urban area. In several urban areas, there is need for drastic measures, legislative and others, for freezing land values and also for undertaking large scale public acquisition of land. According to the nature of the situation the need for adequate measures for taxation of urban land and property exists, without exception, in all towns.

Specific measures for checking rise in land values can become effective if there is strict regulation of the uses of land, especially in and around metropolitan cities, large and growing cities and new industrial towns. It is for such towns that the preparation of master plans referred to later is of special importance. The following are the principal steps to be taken for controlling land values:

1. Issue of notifications for freezing land values with a view to early acquisition of land by public authorities.
2. Acquisition and development of land by public authorities in accordance with the interim general plans is essential for preventing speculation. The land should be acquired in bulk, although, depending upon local circumstances, the programme of acquisition would have to be suitably phased. Acquisition proceedings should be speedy and legal procedures should be simplified as far as possible. It is important that development of the acquired lands should be expedited. The essential services have to be provided by public authorities. Besides development undertaken directly by them, under appropriate regulations, cooperative and private agencies should also be utilised
3. Allotment of land on a lease-hold basis. As a rule, lands acquired by public authorities should be given out only on a lease-hold basis so that, besides the recurring income secured on account of the ground rent, a fair share in the increase in the value of land continues to accrue to the community.
4. Betterment levies and taxation of agricultural lands put to non-agricultural users. These are growing sources of revenue for States and local bodies, but in several States the existing provisions are inadequate.
5. Capital tax on transfer of free-hold lands.
6. Taxation of vacant plots in developed areas with power to acquire if they are not built upon within specified periods.
7. Setting a ceiling on the size of individual plots and limiting the number of plots which a single party may be permitted to acquire.
8. Determination of appropriate norms of rent and regulation and control over rents

These measures lie at the base of proposals for planned urbanisation and have therefore to be given concrete shape as a matter of high priority.

Preparation of Master Plans: To secure orderly development of towns and cities, town planning is indispensable. The first step in this direction will be the preparation of interim general plans establishing the broad pattern of land use to which developments should conform. This should be followed by the preparation of detailed master plans for urban and regional development. Master plans should be drawn up in the first instance for metropolitan cities. State capitals, port towns, new industrial centres and other large and growing cities where, in the ordinary course, conditions are likely to deteriorate further. A tentative list of such towns and cities has been drawn up for the Third Plan period. In redeveloping existing cities and building up new towns, it is of the utmost importance that the regional approach should be followed. This is necessary both for securing a proper balance between social and economic development and for achieving greater cultural unity and social integration in the life of developing urban communities. Greater attention to the environment and appreciation of the day to day needs of the people can go a long way to give to all citizen a sense of community in urban life.

The primary responsibility for the preparation of master plans lies with State Governments and the local administrations concerned. For the Third Plan, limited provision has been made at the Centre for assisting the State Governments in the preparation of master plans for these cities and towns. An essential preliminary is the enactment of suitable legislation on town and country planning. It is also necessary that State Governments establish Town Planning Organisations with adequate trained personnel. The Central Regional and Urban Planning Organisation can assist State Governments and organisations concerned with the establishment of new towns, in the preparation of master plans and in formulating suitable urban and regional development policies.

Standards: For the solution of the housing problem for the bulk of the population and for the elimination of slums and other evils, it is essential that certain minimum standards of residential and office accommodation and other services are set, keeping in view the requirements of the community as a whole and the limited resources available. It is also desirable that maximum standards should be prescribed. This will go some distance in making the investment on housing yield more socially desirable results. Luxury housing and waste of urban land should be prevented so that larger numbers of modest dwelling units can be constructed for the same investment. For achieving this objective, the principal methods are (a) adoption of fiscal measures including local taxation, aiming at discouraging diversion of funds for luxury housing, (b) advice on building designs, (c) modifications in existing building bye-laws of local bodies so as to facilitate construction of low cost housing in accordance with austere standards and specifications, (d) prefabrication of building components, and (e) greater use of locally available cheaper materials. The systematic study of standards and advice relating to them constitute important aspects of the work of the National Buildings Organisation.

Strengthening Municipal Administration: At the local level, municipal administrations alone can undertake satisfactorily the task of providing the services needed for development in urban areas, expansion of housing and improvement of living conditions. Most municipal administrations are not strong enough to carry out these functions. They should be sufficiently strengthened by increasing their resources and personnel and by enlarging their jurisdiction and functions. Where the present limits of the selected urban areas are insufficient to cope with the problem, they should be extended. In the case of growing towns, it would be desirable from (he beginning to provide for larger rather than smaller municipal areas, so that these towns and the rural areas surrounding them can be developed together in a coordinated manner without having to face difficulties later on account of separate jurisdictions. Inevitably, municipal administrations have larger functions than in the past for providing civic services. It is envisaged that a large proportion of towns will in future have separate development plans of their own and these will be integrated with the plans of States. In this context, a careful review of the administrative and financial measures which should be taken in cities with a population of one lakh or more other than the metropolitan areas should be undertaken in each State.

Rural Housing and Planning

Improvement in housing conditions in the villages has a manifold significance. It raises the level of living, provides greater opportunities for work and is a vital element in the transformation of rural life. Yet, because of the magnitude of the problem and its inherent difficulties the task of improving housing conditions in the villages has to be viewed, not as an isolated objective, but as a part of the larger scheme of rural development. Consequently, rural housing is intrinsically a part of community development and village planning. The specific programme for rural housing as such is intended to supplement the resources of the community development movement at the level of the block and the village by way of assistance in the form of technical advice, demonstration, provision of improved designs and lay-outs, better use of local materials and, to a limited extent, provision of finance. Its essential object is to help create healthy environmental conditions for all sections of the village population and for balanced development of rural life as a whole. It is against this background that the village housing scheme which was introduced in 1957 has to be considered and its working reviewed.

The village housing scheme provides for the selection of villages in groups of four to six and the preparation of lay-out plans for these villages after carrying out physical and socio-economic surveys. The implementation of lay-out plans and rebuilding of houses is taken up in stages so that the entire village is remodelled over a period of 8-10 years. Cooperatives for the manufacture of different building components are organised.

Assistance in the shape of loans up to 66.6 per cent of the cost of construction subject to a maximum of Rs. 2,000 per house is given for building of houses. Loans are also given for carrying out improvements in existing houses in accordance with the standards prescribed by the State Governments. Provision has also been made in the scheme for acquisition of land required for streets, community buildings, new house sites and for thinning out densities etc. Research-cum-training centres have been established at six centres for promoting research in improving local building materials and construction techniques and for training personnel required for executing the scheme. The rural housing cell set up in the States for preparing lay-out plans and model designs etc. have been further strengthened.

During the Second Five Year Plan about 3,700 villages were selected and socio-economic and physical surveys of about 2,000 villages were completed. Lay-out plans of 1,600 villages were drawn up and loans amounting to Rs. 3-6 crore were sanctioned for construction of about 15,400 houses. About 3,000 houses were completed and the remaining houses were under different stages of construction.

In the working of the village housing scheme during the Second Plan it has been observed that as a rule the scheme has been taken up in isolated villages and not in groups of villages as was envisaged in the scheme. The latter aspect is important because it is only when a small group of villages is taken up together that it is possible to arrange to set up a brick kiln or arrange for the supply of components on a cooperative basis to meet a continuing demand. The full impact of a housing programme in the rural area by way of increase in employment and improvement in environmental conditions cannot be obtained unless the programme is undertaken systematically in groups of adjoining villages. Lay-out plans are at present prepared generally for selected villages. They provide for the extension of the village site, improved village streets and drainage and land for such common amenities as the village school, the playground for school children and the panchayat bhavan.

However, not enough is being done in these directions, and the available funds tend to be devoted mainly to the construction and improvement of a small number of houses. It is suggested that the first claim on the resources provided for the village housing scheme should be on account of the extension of the village site, improvement of roads and drainage and allotment of land for essential purposes of interest to the community as a whole. The key to improved housing is the availability of land for the extension of village site.

To the greatest extent possible, the community itself, through mutual arrangement, should be expected to provide the additional land required. However, for assisting the community to acquire land for providing house sites for agricultural workers and Harijans it may be useful, as suggested later, to provide for a limited measure of assistance. The first place in the programme for improving village housing should be given to housing for Harijans, agricultural workers and those sections of the community whose housing conditions are specially deplorable. For scheduled tribes and scheduled castes in particular, besides funds available under the village housing scheme, assistance by way of subsidy is also given under the programme for the welfare of backward classes. Provisions under the two programmes should be utilised in a coordinated manner.

Rural housing cells, which have been set up in the States, and research-cum-training centres are already engaged in designing, houses suited to different parts of the country, and involving the use of local materials. Work in these directions has to be intensified. There is frequently a temptation to resort to houses on urban patterns constructed in brick and cement without sufficient emphasis being placed on the use of local materials, economy of construction cost, cultural traditions and background of the locality and functional requirements of rural life. There is also inadequate stress on community effort in improving roads and drainage, contribution by way of land for the extension of the village site and mutual aid in constructing improved housing. The scale of the rural housing problem is so vast that provision of additional funds by itself, necessary as this may be, can produce only a small impact. In the main problem is one of creating a widespread desire for better living, evolving practical methods for improving the village environment and building better houses at relatively small cost based mainly on cooperative self-help, community effort and contribution and the use of local building materials.

In the Third Plan it will be essential to link up the programme more closely with different schemes of community development such as provision of water supply, roads, drainage, public health, education etc. It is also necessary that rural housing activities should be effectively coordinated with other connected programmes of rural development so as to ensure that the villages selected under the village housing scheme derive the maximum benefit from the limited resources which are available. For example, the subsidy admissible under the programme for ameliorating the living conditions of scheduled castes and scheduled tribes should be made available to members of these communities residing in the villages selected under the scheme. Village and small industries should also be set up to the extent possible in the selected villages. Special attention has to be given to the setting up of brick-kilns and local production of building components, such as doors, windows, etc. For this purpose, cooperatives should be organised, and they should be given technical assistance and materials such as wood and coal-dust.

A number of new villages are coming up on account of reclamation of large tracts of land and development of new areas for agriculture. It should be ensured that the lay-out plans of such villages are prepared in advance and they develop in a planned way. In the case of existing villages where the problem is, in part, one of redevelopment, the success of the programme will depend upon their proper selection. The scheme already lays down that amongst other considerations preference will be given to

- villages which are situated in flood-affected areas,
- villages which have substantial populations of backward classes and agricultural labourers,

- villages in which consolidation of holdings has been completed or in which programmes for increasing agricultural production are being successfully implemented, and
- villages whose inhabitants happen to be displaced because of major development projects or natural calamities.

Villages which have concentrations of artisans should also be given preference. Evidence of cooperative self-help and willingness on the part of the village community to contribute land for the extension of the village site and to give priority to the housing of Harijans and other backward classes should be important considerations in the selection of villages suitable for a programme of village housing. In selected villages in which these conditions are fulfilled, with a view to facilitating the total effort that is called for, it may be necessary to give a limited amount of assistance by way of grant to the village panchayat for undertaking the improvement of village streets and drainage as an essential step in the programme for replanning village as a whole.

House Sites for Agricultural Workers: In the land reform legislation enacted in some States provision has been made for conferring rights of occupancy or ownership on tenants of village house sites. In a few States there are provisions for transferring ownership on payment of compensation. It is essential that priority should be given to the provision of land for families of landless agricultural workers. Wastelands and bhoodan lands should be used for this purpose to the extent possible. In some congested villages, while emphasising the obligations of the village community, it may be necessary to supplement its contribution in providing the land needed for extension of the village site, through acquisition of additional land for house sites for agricultural labourers. It is proposed to earmark Rs. 5 crore by way of grant under the village housing scheme for assisting States in securing house sites for landless agricultural workers in villages in which they form a fairly large part of the population.

Housing Statistics

The present position of housing statistics is unsatisfactory in relation to the needs of planning. Except for data regarding the total number of houses and house-holds in the country thrown up by the decennial census there are no proper statistics on such aspects as current building activity, additions to houses made each year, quantity and cost of materials used, production and consumption of building materials and prices of building materials. Certain basic items of information on housing conditions have been collected in the population census 1961. These will facilitate compilation of an inventory of housing in the country and throw useful light on structural, functional, size and tenure characteristics.

The National Buildings Organisation is arranging for the collection of housing statistics in the public sector through various construction agencies such as the Central and State Public Works Departments and others. In other fields, the actual collection of statistics has to be undertaken by the appropriate agencies, while questions of method and approach have to be considered by the National Buildings Organisation and the Central Statistical Organisation. In view of the unsatisfactory state of statistics regarding building and construction, in November, 1960, the Central Council of Local Self-Government proposed that local bodies should modify their bye-laws so as to make it incumbent on applicants, both at the time of applying for building permits and for issue of completion certificates, to provide detailed information about investment and other aspects. In February 1961, the Central Statistical Organisation requested State Statistical Bureaus to initiate the collection of information from corporations and municipalities on a uniform pattern. The forms suggested by the Central Statistical Organisation provide for a common classification of buildings and seek information regarding the nature and type of construction, area, estimated cost, number of dwelling units in the case of residential construction, and materials used for walls, roof and floor. As the subject is one of considerable complexity and large numbers of cities and towns are involved, it would be desirable first to establish an adequate system of building statistics in a small number of cities and towns and to phase the programme for extending it to other centres. To be useful, it is important that the returns should flow at regular intervals and in the ordinary course of administration of building rules and bye-laws.

Statistics of production and consumption of building materials are also needed from time to time to survey the supply and demand position of materials of building construction. While figures of production are already available in the case of organised industries such as steel, cement, etc., no reliable estimates of materials such as bricks, lime etc. produced in the unorganised sector are available. These may be collected through periodic sample surveys. Statistics of consumption and requirements of building materials could, however, be developed through the use of technological ratios related to value of construction on the basis of certain type studies. Some type studies have already been carried out in the country and there is need to increase their scope and coverage. Prices of selected building materials and wage rates at selected centres in the country should also be collected regularly and published by the National Buildings Organisation and State Statistical Bureaus.

Research and Training

A considerable volume of research in the field of housing and construction has been undertaken in recent years at the Central Building Research Institute and at other centres. Since its establishment in 1954, the National Buildings Organisation has also sponsored a series of research projects and endeavoured to make the results of research more widely available. Thus, investigations have been carried out regarding techniques and materials for water proof renderings for mud walls, effect of wall thickness and ceding heights on thermal insulation, utilisation of low-grade gypsum for light weight partitions, masonry mortars, hollow bricks and tiles, utilisation of waste products like blast furnace slag for the production of light weight aggregates and the influence of climatic and regional factors in relation to designs of houses and other aspects. Research in housing and construction is essential for reducing building costs and improving the quality of construction, and programmes now in hand should be further intensified. The training of different types of construction workers is an important factor in securing these objectives and has to be organised much more extensively and systematically than in the past. The work of research-cum-training centres for rural housing has far-reaching interest, and the results achieved in evolving new designs of rural houses and fuller use of local building materials should be carried into the field through education and practical demonstration.

With the growth of population in towns and cities and the progress of the economy, problems of housing and urban and regional development will come to occupy an increasingly critical place in the successive Five Year Plans. The right solutions to these problems are of great consequence both for social stability and for general welfare. In varying degree, these problems are faced both by advanced and by less-developed countries, and over the years a considerable body of knowledge and experience has been built up by the United Nations and other international agencies as well as by research centres and institutions abroad. The National Buildings Organisation, which already serves as a Regional Housing Centre for research and study of the problems of hot and arid zones in the ECAFE region can make the results of studies and experiments undertaken by other countries and international organisations available to construction agencies and organisations in different parts of India.

Fourth Five Year Plan: 1969-74

Housing

In the field of housing Government has been giving assistance for the benefit of selected sections of the community and providing accommodation to its employees. Life Insurance Corporation loans, which heretofore supplemented the Plan provisions will now be included therein. Expenditure on housing schemes is indicated in Annexure I. Schemes in the housing sector cover only a small portion of the total effort. Substantial expenditure on housing is made by public sector undertakings, railways, the post and telegraphs and defence. During the Third Plan, it was estimated at Rs. 300 crore. The major share of the investment on housing comes from the private sector. It is estimated at Rs. 1,400 crore in the Third Plan and expected to rise to Rs. 2,140 crore in the Fourth Plan.

The migration of people from villages to towns in search of employment has accelerated the growth of urban population. Adequate facilities and services for the increased urban population are not available. There has been some decline in standards, particularly of housing. The provision of housing through private or co-operative effort is usually directed to the affluent or middle classes and the incoming poor in metropolitan areas give rise to slums.

The experience of public housing so far is that its unit costs are high and that with the constraint of resources it is not possible for public operations to touch even the fringe of the problem. Slum clearance schemes often lead to creation of new slums or deterioration of conditions in some of the older slums. In growing cities of a reasonable size, it should be part of Government policy to encourage, through proper planning and land policy, adequate supply of housing. In cities where the slum population is large, this approach would not be effective and it would be necessary to try to ameliorate the living conditions of dwellers of slums as an immediate measure. Emphasis should be on limiting the rise in the prices of land, providing financial assistance to co-operative and private effort and assuming legal powers for reconditioning of slums

At the end of 1966-67, there were 16 State level co-operative societies and 12,723 primary societies, with a total working capital of Rs. 154 crore. During 1966-67, these societies built 16,000 independent houses and 15,571 tenements. The co-operative form of organisation could be enlarged, especially for low and middle income groups. Where appropriate, an apex cooperative could be set up with the necessary minimum of assistance from Government. State Housing Boards should be encouraged to float bonds and debentures.

Cheaper houses should be provided by organising the supply of material and by pursuing research into practicable schemes of cheaper ways of building. States, local authorities and statutory bodies have to play a more active role in organising this effort. The proposed Central Housing Finance Corporation would also promote the organisation of mass production of cheaper building materials. The private sector should standardise building components and manufacture them on a large scale. At the Centre, the National Buildings Organisation is engaged in the introduction of new techniques and materials in construction to effect reduction in costs and in inducing construction agencies to take up experimental construction for demonstration purposes. Provision has been made for the establishment of a Cellular Concrete Plant at Ennore in Tamil Nadu.

Village Housing

Laws on consolidation of holdings provide for earmarking of land for expansion of abadi sites and for other purposes. Lands which vest in the State as a result of the abolition of intermediary tenures or enforcement of ceiling laws or consequent on the consolidation of holdings, could also be utilised to provide house sites.

The essential tasks in the sphere of village housing will be to get appropriate lay-outs made for the growing villages, to provide basic amenities such as water and sanitation facilities, and to stimulate private building and renewal activity. Encouragement will have to be given to co-operative effort. Special housing schemes in favour of scheduled castes or other disadvantageously placed classes should be integrated into the village lay-out alone with the general housing programmes.

Introduced in 1957, the village housing projects scheme provides for assistance to villagers for construction or improvement of houses, for house sites to landless agricultural workers and for streets and drains in selected villages. The scheme has not made much progress. A study of its working supported by some quick field surveys has brought to light the low priority that is being accorded to it in the States. The machinery for proper administration of the scheme does not exist and there is little co-ordination with the complementary programmes for improvement of rural areas. Many houses remained incomplete. In the next two years, effort should be concentrated on completing the houses under construction. New villages may be taken up thereafter as part of a general programme of development for the villages selected.

It is necessary to protect the homesteads of families of landless agricultural labour, large numbers of whom belong to scheduled castes and backward classes and who live on land belonging to others. Laws conferring proprietary rights in such cases will have to be passed and enforced where this has not already been done. Measures to help these weaker sections in putting up a decent super-structure on these sites have to be adopted by supplying materials and guidance.

Water Supply and Sanitation

In the Third Plan, 529 new urban water supply and sanitation schemes were taken up at a cost of Rs. 13; crore in addition to 53 schemes continuing from the Second Plan period. Most of them were completed. During the three Annual Plans, 150 new schemes were taken up at a cost of about Rs. 39 crore. They are in various stages of execution.

Rural water supply schemes were taken up under the programmes for community development, local development works and welfare of backward classes. These were supplemented by the National Water Supply and Sanitation Programmes of the Ministry of Health. The latter v/as confined to those groups of village', where the tapping of water resources required a measure of technical skill. In executing this programme, emphasis was laid on providing water to areas which suffered from water scarcity and salinity and where water-borne diseases were endemic. At an estimated cost of Rs. 27 crore, 1,764 schemes were completed during the Third Plan. During the three Annual Plan that followed, 478 schemes at an estimated cost of Rs. 21 crore were undertaken and are in various stages of execution. The work done in 1961-69 added 6,000 villages to those having piped water supply.

Programmes under community development local development works and welfare of backward classes included the construction and renovation of wells and installation of hand-pumps. The number of such wells the end of 1968-69 is estimated at Rs. 1.2 million.

The Fourth Plan outlay is Rs. 407.29 crore. In metropolitan areas water supply schemes would, as far as possible, be accompanied by sewerage and drainage schemes. Local bodies will contribute to the programme. In the remaining urban areas, priority will be given to the completion of spill-over schemes. A number of new schemes will be taken up in areas endemic to water-borne diseases. The bulk of the provision for rural water supply, which is of the order of Rs. 125 crore and has been earmarked, will be utilised in areas of acute scarcity. Other areas will meet their need from programmes for community development, welfare of backward classes or through local effort.

It will be Song before urban areas can afford full-fledged sewerage and sanitation systems. The problem of sanitation in towns other than those with sewerage schemes has so far been dealt with from the point of view of improving the conditions of those in unclean occupations; no reference was made to the problem of sanitation in the villages. The overall problems of sanitation require to be dealt with on a long term basis. The efforts made so far to improve the conditions of scavengers under existing arrangements have not had much success. It is necessary to think in terms of doing away with present arrangements by either adopting a proper system of underground sewerage of converting all dry latrines into some type of improved latrines. A number of improved types which are not costly are available. A phased programme has, therefore, to be undertaken by which the transformation can be effectively brought about. As an immediate step, this can, in urban areas, take the form of providing improved sanitary conveniences in all public institutions as also in public places. In villages a similar start can be made with public institutions, particularly schools. Once these reforms are introduced, it may be hoped that they will be gradually adopted by private institutions and the people generally. The initial programme will have to be undertaken by local authorities. It is necessary for public health departments and research organisations to take special interest in the problem.

Under a Centrally sponsored programme, assistance is being given to State Governments for special investigation divisions attached to their Public Health Engineering Departments. They will prepare technical designs and estimates of rural water supply schemes, particularly in difficult areas, making use of the data available from the Exploratory Tubewells Organisation and the Geological Survey of India. In designing these schemes, water available from major or medium irrigation projects would also be integrated hi supplying drinking water. A provision of Rs. 2 crore has been made for this purpose.

A provision of Rs. 3.5 crore has been made in the Central sector to accommodate assistance from UNICEF in the shape of high speed drilling rigs for exploration and exploitation of ground water resources in hard and rocky areas. This equipment will be available to States as and when they need it.

Central assistance is being given to institutions for training in public health engineering. Courses for water works supervisors and other categories of workers are being conducted by the Union Government. The training programme is proposed to be continued with a provision of Rs. 25 lakh.

With increase in industrialisation and urbanisation, indiscriminate discharge of wastes from industrial plants and sewerage effluents from towns and cities is posing problems in some areas. Central legislation for prevention of pollution of water sources is under consideration. It is hoped that all the State Governments will adopt this legislation for enforcement. An allocation of Rs. 7.60 lakh has been made for the establishment of a central board envisaged under the new legislation.

The total provision of Rs. 407.29 crore will meet only part of the needs of water supply and sanitation. In the urban areas, the water supply schemes should be looked upon as a service which has to be paid for the direct beneficiaries through capital contributions and water charges. There is scope for improvement in the realisation of water charges. Sewerage schemes are costly by and by themselves cannot always be self-financing. It should be possible to treat them as a combined utility with water supply.

The rural water supply schemes, in particular the piped water supply schemes, should be maintained properly. Otherwise, they become derelict in course of time, resulting in large waste of public funds. In rural areas also, water supply schemes should be looked upon as a service which has to be paid for. Wherever possible, capital contributions and levies should be collected from the beneficiaries.

Fifth Five Year Plan: 1974-79

Urban Development, Housing and Water Supply

Urban Development: Provision made in the State Plans for integrated Urban Development are being supplemented by funds provided for the scheme of integrated Urban Development in the Central Sector. This scheme provides loan assistance to State Governments for developing the necessary infrastructure. It is expected that over a period of time the State Governments will be able to build up a corpus of seed money for expansion programmes

Urban Development programmes were taken up in the three metropolitan cities of Calcutta, Bombay and Madras and nine other cities in 1974-75. Additional six cities were taken up in 1975-76 and it is expected that six more will be taken up during 1976-77. Work for the preparation of Plans for some other cities is in hand.

In view of the progress made so far, total provision of Rs. 256.13 crore has been made for Urban Development for next two years against a likely expenditure of Rs. 249.33 crore during 1974-77.

Housing: The main thrust of the programmes in the Fifth Plan is directed towards ameliorating the conditions of the backward sections of the society. This is sought to be achieved by augmenting the programmes for the construction of housing colonies by State Housing Boards and by taking up on a large scale a programme for the provision of house-sites for landless labourers in rural areas. While the bulk of this programme is being undertaken in the State Plans, the activities of the Housing and Urban Development Corporation in the Central sector are being geared up to meet the expanding demand. A provision is being made to increase the Equity participation in HUDCO to enable it to generate resources of the order of Rs. 150 crore in the Fifth Plan period. Separate provisions have been made for the scheme of subsidised housing for plantation labourers and Dock labourers. Adequate emphasis has also been placed on research and development activities for generating better and cheaper designs.

Rural Water Supply and Sanitation: The main objective is to provide safe water supply in difficult and problem villages. At the end of the Fourth Plan period, it had been estimated that there were 1.13 lakh of such villages. It is expected that in the first three years of the Fifth Plan with a provision of Rs. 201.10 crore, about 57,800 villages would have been covered. The allocation made for the remaining two years is on the basis of providing safe water supply for additional 53,900 villages. The provision which has been made is of the order of Rs. 180.14 crore (inclusive of Rs. 157.87 crore under the MNP). The revised Fifth Plan outlay would now be Rs. 381.24 crore.

Urban Water Supply and Sanitation: Particular emphasis is being laid on completion of spill over schemes. In the first three years with an investment of Rs. 257.54 crore, about 266 towns are likely to be covered with water supply and 46 towns with sewerage and drainage systems. With an outlay of Rs. 281.63 crore for the remaining two years of the Fifth Plan, about 254 towns are likely to be covered with water supply and 38 with sewerage and drainage systems. The outlay mentioned above will be supplemented from the Central sector scheme of Integrated Urban Development in cities of national importance such as Bombay, Calcutta, Madras, Hyderabad, Ahmedabad, Bangalore, Kanpur, Lucknow, Agra, Allahabad, Varanasi, etc. The outlay in the Fifth Plan amounts to Rs. 539.17 crore against the outlay Rs. 431.00 crore in the Draft Fifth Plan.

The revised Fifth Plan also provides for an outlay of Rs. 10.27 crore for supporting programmes such as public Health Engineering training to train about 3,000 Public Health Engineering personnel and mechanical composting to set up 27 mechanical compost plants along with 60 mechanical sieve plants in different cities. A provision also exist for converting about 30,000-35,000 dry latrines into sanitary latrines.

Sixth Five Year Plan: 1980-85

Housing, Urban Development and Water Supply

The urban population of India is small as a proportion of the total population of the country, estimated to be only about 21.8 per cent of the total in 1980. However, the absolute size of more than 109 million people (in 1971) living in urban areas is large by any standards. Urban development, therefore, requires serious attention in its own right, though in the context of overall development planning. In a country still largely rural and agricultural in character, it is natural that programmes for agricultural and rural development should receive the greatest emphasis; in particular those for rural employment creation and assistance to the rural poor. Urban development should, however, be seen as complementary to rural development and policies affecting the process of urbanisation should be such as to strengthen the links between towns and cities and their hinterland. Urban areas of all sizes operate as market centres for agricultural output and provide a variety of service functions in addition to operating as centres of manufacturing activity. These functions should be strengthened such that towns and cities serve the rural areas more effectively. The process of urbanisation should then be seen as aiding employment and income generation in rural areas rather than as a competitive process. Larger towns serve as distribution centres for seed, fertilisers and credit for farmers as well as serving as organised markets for their produce. The bigger cities provide services and facilities to both the smaller towns as well as rural areas in their hinterland. Thus, national policy on Urban Development should view the whole range of urban settlements as having a role to play in the national development process.

That having been said, it is also important to view the provision of services in rural areas in an integrated manner. Availability of shelter, a safe water supply and facilities for hygienic sanitation are as necessary in the rural areas as in the urban. Owing to different residential densities, however, different technologies can be used in different sizes of settlements in providing these services. The Sixth Plan, therefore, addresses the problems of the spatial distribution of population, housing, water supply and sanitation in an integrated manner. Given the resource constraints, public intervention in these fields has to be highly selective and centred on the areas of greatest need. The thrust of planning measures must inevitably be toward the assistance of the poor— in rural as well as in urban areas. Priority is being given to providing sites to the rural landless along with construction assistance wherever possible. Similarly, priority is attached to providing at least one source of safe water supply in every problem village.

The provision of safe drinking water and of sanitation is essential for all settlements whether large or small. Higher residential densities necessitate greater care in providing for efficient and timely disposal of human wastes. The current methods of excreta disposal are a serious health hazard and until these are improved, the benefits derived from other programmes will be vitiated on account of the propagation of stomach-related infections caused by the existing environmental conditions in the poor areas of our towns and cities. In particular, the health benefits derived from the provision of safe drinking water are nullified unless accompanied by appropriate sanitation measures. The Sixth Plan, therefore views the problems of shelter and urban development as being inexorably connected with the provision of safe water supply and adequate sanitation. It is only through purposive public programmes providing essential services like water and sewerage along with low cost shelter programmes like sites and services that the urban landscape of the country can be improved to enable the urban population to function more efficiently. Particular attention must be paid to the functioning of the small, medium and intermediate cities in order to aid them in their role as market centres and as suppliers of goods and services for agriculture. The environmental and infrastructural conditions in some of these towns and cities have been neglected so long that their efficient functioning is beginning to be hampered.

As in the past, the bulk of housing for the higher income groups will continue to be provided by the private sector. In addition, in view of the constraints on public resources, there should be greater encouragement of the private sector _to step up its activities in the construction of housing for low and middle income groups. Imaginative schemes of improved facilities for financial intermediation in this sector will have to be, investigated in order to achieve this objective

Housing

Review: Housing is an activity that is typically labour intensive and, therefore, fits in well with the pattern of development envisaged in this Plan. The provision of shelter is a basic need which must be met. Housing construction also creates much-needed employment for the unskilled and, therefore, income for the relatively poor.

Over the last three decades, public investments in housing through the Plans have been of the order of Rs. 1,253 crore. In addition, investments by public sector enterprises, departmental undertakings and grants-in-aid institutions were about Rs. 1800 crore. Investment by the private sector during the corresponding period has been estimated to amount to about Rs. 12,740 crore. It is difficult to compile adequate statistics on the number of housing units constructed through planned investments in the public sector. Housing is constructed by all levels of the Government including local Governments, State Housing Boards, State Governments, public undertakings and the Central Government.

Apart from housing constructed for government employees, the role of the public sector in the provision of housing has been small. Subsidised dwellings have been provided to certain selected economically weaker sections of the community. Between 1950-51 and December 1979, 2.05 lakh houses were constructed for plantation labour and industrial workers. Housing for other low income groups totalled 3.36 lakh. Construction of housing under various other schemes for somewhat higher income groups totalled about 1.42 lakh. In the rural areas, about 77 lakh sites have been distributed and about 5.6 lakh houses constructed under the Rural House-Site-cum-House Construction Scheme.

As is evident from the above, the role of Government in the field of housing has necessarily been rather limited. It was only during the Fifth Plan that provision was; made to provide house sites to some of the rural landless as well in addition to the schemes operating in urban areas.

A review of the various social housing schemes implemented by State Governments and their agencies his revealed some problems in these programmes. These schemes were intended to create housing for Economically Weaker Sections EWS) with household income below Rs. 350 per month and households with Low Income Group LIG within incomes between Rs. 350 to Rs. 600 per month. It now appears that houses constructed for a particular Income category are largely occupied by families in the next higher income group since the instalment payments required for the house are clearly beyond the paying capacity of the income groups for which the houses were meant. Those alottees/tenants who do continue to occupy their houses tend to run up payment of arrears of their instalments/rents. This has, therefore, be come a major problem for the State Governments and Housing Boards. As*a result, future provision of social housing schemes will need to make a more realistic appraisal of the paying capacity of the recipients: this will mean a modification of standards with a view to economy. In addition to the groups mentioned above, the only class of people who have benefited substantially from public sector support in housing have been employees of Government, of public sector corporations and other autonomous bodies.

A review of past performance in public sector as well as private sector housing investments makes it clear that the country's housing problems-both rural as well as urban-cannot be solved in the Sixth Plan period. It should, however, be feasible to catch up with the housing requirements of the country if a sustained programme of investment and construction is undertaken over the next 20 years. This programme would attempt to cover 'the existing housing shortfalls as well as providing for the expanding population. For the Sixth Plan period, the combined public and private sector outlay is expected to be about Rs. 12,900 crore; Rs. 3,500 crore for rural housing and Rs. 9,400 crore for urban housing. Such an outlay would yield about 13 million dwelling units in rural areas and 5.7 million units in urban areas. Reliable data on investment in private housing are not easily available.

However, the Central Statistical Organisation (CSO) has estimated that gross capital formation in residential buildings in the private sector (including public sector undertakings) was about Rs. 2,243 crore in 1976-77. If we assume the share of public sector undertakings to be not more than Rs. 50 crore, gross capital formation in housing in the private sector would have been around Rs. 2,200 crore in 1976-77. It is then safe to assume that private sector investment will not be less than Rs. 11,500 crore during 1980-85 Sixth Plan periods. An investment of Rs. 1,302 crore is proposed in the public sector. Additional investments by public sector enterprises, departmental undertakings and grants-in-aid institutions may be of the order of Rs. 250-300 crore. Since the public sector outlay will necessarily be small in relation to the total investment, maximum benefit from such an outlay will be achieved if public resources are largely devoted to low cost schemes such as "sites and services".

Objectives

It is clear that housing conditions in the country are rather poor. A large number of people either live without any shelter whatsoever or in units below the lowest possible standards. The objectives of the Plan are, therefore, to reduce substantially the number of absolutely shelterless people and to provide conditions for others to improve their housing environment. Specifically, the objectives of the Sixth Five Year Plan are as follows:

- Provision of house-sites and assistance for the construction of dwellings for rural landless labourers. This will normally include an element of housing extension services to assist in proper planning of layouts, sanitation. etc.
- In view of the severe constraints of public resources, public sector social housing schemes will be designed to benefit the maximum number of people. They will, therefore, be directed towards the economically weaker sections of the community and designed so that they are within their paying capacity. For the rest, investment policies would be framed so as to promote and encourage self-help housing. In addition, resources of institutional agencies like HUDCO and State Housing Boards will need to be augmented to enable them to provide infrastructural facilities as a means of encouraging housing in the private sector. Care, however, must be taken to avoid subsidies in these activities.
- Specific efforts must be made to secure a reduction in costs in public housing schemes by reviewing standards and by using cheap and alternative building materials. This will necessitate the promotion of research in building technology and the development of cheap and local building materials. Attention should also be paid to the possibilities of energy conservation in construction technology by utilising existing materials in local use in the construction of shelter. The programme for the provision of shelter should be linked with sanitation programmes such that the potential of deriving energy from human wastes can also be realised.

In order to achieve these objectives, specific attention will have to be given to:

- housing activity in small, medium and intermediate towns which have been neglected hitherto;
- low cost housing techniques including existing local methods so as to bring down unit costs;
- the modification of existing building bye-laws, land use controls, minimum plot requirements and land requirements

for roads which often make it difficult to reduce the costs of shelter;

- the avoidance of direct subsidies in urban housing. In the case of higher and middle income housing, subsidies should be totally avoided. For low income housing, where some direct subsidies are inevitable, they should preferably be in the form of infrastructural and sanitation facilities which improve the environment for people to invest in their own shelter;
- greater stimulus and support to private housing in the middle and lower income groups so that there are incentives to channelise savings into housing construction.

Rural Housing

The Minimum Needs Programme places a high priority on the provision of house sites and assistance for construction of houses for the rural landless workers. It is estimated that the number of eligible families needing housing assistance would be around 14.5 million families by March 1985. Of these, 7.7 million landless families have already been allotted house sites, leaving about 6.8 million families who are still without a site. The Plan proposes to provide sites to all the remaining landless families. Of the families who have been provided sites only, about 0.56 million families have so far been given construction assistance. This leaves about 13.9 million families who will still need such housing construction assistance. About 25 per cent of these eligible families, i.e. about 3.6 million families, will be provided assistance with construction during 1980-85, with the balance being provided for in the following years. Provision is being made for Rs. 250 per family for developed plots, approach roads and a masonry tube-well for each cluster of 30 to 40 families. Construction assistance is expected to amount to Rs. 500 per family. This assumes that all labour inputs will be supplied by the beneficiaries. These provisions involve a total outlay of about Rs. 354 crore for the programme, Rs. 170 crore for the provision of sites and about Rs. 184 crore for construction assistance.

It should be the endeavour of all States to provide outlays of at least this magnitude in the Sixth Plan and Annual Plans. While it is expected that all families currently without sites will be provided sites under this programme by 1985, the next Plan will have to ensure that construction assistance is available for those remaining in need.

It is recognised that with this kind of assistance house's will have to be built with only mud walls and tiled roofs but it is essential that an attempt is made in the next five years that this highly deprived group of landless rural labour, who currently have no land, are able to obtain this barest minimum of shelter. Therefore, in order to implement this programme, it is proposed that in every district, organisations are set up at the tehsil, taluka and block level for the disbursement of the housing subsidy to the eligible families. These organisations should assist in developing layouts and housing plans for these clusters of houses such that appropriate access as well as drainage is available for these sites. Where possible and desired, community latrines and bathing places will also be established. Attempts should also be made to obtain all materials locally, e.g., roof tiles and drain tiles from local potteries. It would also help if the beneficiaries of these local organisations can help with guidance in the design of their houses within the given constraints. The National Buildings Organisation, State Housing Boards and the HUDCO have plans on hand to prefer improved design types for use in the rural areas.

In general, the State Governments are implementing the programme on the basis of norms and standards visualised in the Plan. However, some State Governments are currently implementing the programme on a more ambitious scale involving larger amounts of subsidies and loans. Given the limitations of resources, State Governments will make every effort to adhere to the norms and standards suggested in the Plan in order to ensure that the target of constructing 3.6 million houses is achieved during the Plan.

In addition to the requirements of the rural landless under the Minimum Needs Programme, there is obviously need for other housing as well in rural areas. Because of the scarcity of resources there is only very limited additional public provision for rural housing in the State Plans. The Housing and Urban Development Corporation (HUDCO) and General Insurance Corporation (GIC) have also entered the field of rural housing and have begun to provide loans for construction in rural areas.

Urban Housing

The public sector has only a marginal, though promotional, role to play in the provision of urban housing. It is clear, that the need is great for better and more housing in urban areas. As stated earlier, given the overall resources constraints and more pressing competing claims on public resources, the vast majority of additional housing in urban areas will have to be met from private resources. The role of the public sector will have to be restricted to the improvement of slums, the direct provision of housing to some of the urban poor and encouragement of agencies such as HUDCO which can promote the marshalling of private resource into housing in a constructive manner.

It is proposed that the strategy of attempting massive relocation of slums in urban areas should be given up in the future. Such relocation not only involves substantial hardship to those affected in terms of loss of easy access to employment centres and other amenities, but results in unnecessary destruction of existing housing capital, however sub-standard it may be. It is, therefore, important that substantially increased investments be made in the environmental improvement of slum areas. Low cost sanitation and drainage are key areas of much needed investment in the slums of our cities.

Direct public sector assistance is proposed for housing the Economically Weaker Sections (EWS) of the population. The strategy here is to provide 'Sites and Services' Schemes with enough funds for a minimum structure, the beneficiaries to be given loans up-to Rs. 3,000 per unit repayable over a period of 20-25 years at concessional rates of interest. The Scheme relies on the expectation that the beneficiaries will themselves gradually improve the quality of accommodation in course of time. A provision of about Rs. 485 crore has been made in the Plan, with a target of about 16.2 lakh units to be constructed.

Housing and Urban Development Corporation

The bulk of the remaining public sector investment in housing is to be channelled through the Housing and Urban Development Corporation (HUDCO). As on July 31, 1980, HUDCO had sanctioned 1274 schemes in 319 towns and cities in 17 States and 4 Union Territories involving loan assistance of Rs. 600 crore, and has disbursed about Rs. 337 crore. On completion, these projects will provide about 6.8 lakh dwelling units and about 62,000 developed plots and a number of shops and commercial complexes. Of these, about 86 per cent of the plots are for the benefit of the EWS and LIG. During the current year 1980-81, HUDCO is expected to sanction loans of the order of Rs. 160 crore and disbursements are visualised at about Rs. 89 crore. In addition, HUDCO has launched new schemes like financing rural housing, apex cooperative housing societies and urban development schemes.

The Plan proposes an increase in the equity of HUDCO from the present Rs. 25 crore to Rs. 75 crore. Including the recovery of loans, it will then be able to invest about Rs. 600 crore over the next five years in its various housing programmes. Currently, HUDCO is allocating its loan disbursements in the following proportions:

Economically Weaker Section	30 per cent
Low Income Group	25 per cent
Middle Income Group	25 per cent
High Income Group	20 per cent

HUDCO should be encouraged to step up its activities in the provision of EWS and LIG housing in the future, perhaps by utilising elements of cross subsidisation from its high income group housing and commercial activities.

LIC and other Institutional Support

The Life Insurance Corporation (LIC) is the other public financial organisation, which has provided financing for housing. Up to March 1977, the LIC has provided Rs. 728.56 crore in loans for various housing programmes. Its experience with promoting housing by linking it with insurance policies does not appear to have been too successful. Loans advanced so far under this scheme have amounted to only Rs. 53 crore. The scheme should, therefore, be reviewed and amended in order to make it more effective. LIC is statutorily required to invest 25 per cent of the net accretion to its controlled fund in socially-oriented schemes, such as, housing, electricity, water supply, sewerage and industrial estates. If the housing programme is to help the weaker sections of the community, who cannot otherwise benefit from the scheme of loans to policy holders, the LIC would need substantially to increase the allocation of funds for housing for EWS and LIG. A similar principle should apply for investments in housing being made by the General Insurance Corporation.

Cooperative housing programmes represent an ideal form of self-help housing and, therefore, need encouragement. Developed or partially developed land will be allocated to the housing cooperative societies where successful functioning has been hampered due to lack of this facility.

Urban Land Policy

A ceiling on urban land prescribed under the Urban I-and (Ceiling and Regulation) Act 1976 was meant to prevent speculation in land and to ensure the optimal allocation of land to different users. The implementation of the Act has experienced great difficulties and the State Governments have not been able to implement it effectively. A Working Group was set up in the Ministry of Works and Housing with representatives from State Governments to suggest ways and means of improving the Act.

The Report has since been submitted to Government and is being examined. In the meantime, there is a general feeling that costs of land have increased substantially, both of private land as well as of land owned by public agencies. As a result, fears are expressed that urban housing might become too expensive for a large number of people. It would be useful, therefore, to initiate systematic investigations into the functioning of urban land markets and to identify the causes of the increase in the value of land. Measures can then be recommended to promote a more efficient and equitable functioning of the urban land market so that these enormous and unwarranted increases in land values are checked.

Urban Development

Objectives and Strategy: Urbanisation in India has grown at a relatively slow rate throughout this century as well as in the last 30 (years. This is quite consistent with the overall pattern of development that the country has experienced where the proportions of people engaged in agricultural and non-agricultural pursuits have barely changed over this whole period. Despite this slow rate of growth, the country exhibits all the urban problems. that can be found in any part of the world. Moreover, many of these problems are aggravated by the very low per capita income observed even in large cities. Unlike many other countries where their capital cities or other metropolitan cities are excessively dominant, India exhibits a very balanced size distribution of settlements. According to the 1971 Census, out of a total population of 547.95 million, about 109 million were in urban areas. The growth rate of urban population during the 1961-71 decade was about 3.2 per cent per year as compared with about 2.2 per cent per year for the total population.

It would appear that larger towns have grown faster than smaller towns, and it might therefore be concluded that the country is suffering from an unhealthy process of urbanization which must be remedied. The reality is, however, more complex with a great deal of inter-regional variation as well as infra-regional differences.

The process of urbanisation has thus been relatively balanced in India. Within this overall pattern, it is important to distinguish problems as they occur between different regions and different cities. For example, excluding West Bengal, the whole Eastern region (Orissa, Bihar, Assam) was less than 10 per cent urbanised in 1971 as compared with 28 and 31 percent for Gujarat and Maharashtra at the high end. Hence, while in the backward States the problems of urbanisation are caused by stagnation, those in the more advanced States are caused by relatively rapid growth. The articulation of national urbanisation policy should then involve specific consideration of regional problems and urban development should be viewed in the context of its relationship with rural development in each region. The problems of each urban area should be seen in the light of its specific functions within the overall settlement framework.

As in housing, public resources for urban development are necessarily limited and high priority areas for public investment have to be selected for particular attention. The thrust of the urbanisation policy during the next 'decade would be to give greater emphasis to the provision of adequate infrastructural and other facilities in the small, medium and intermediate towns which have been neglected hitherto in this respect. The aim would be to strengthen these market centres to equip them to serve as growth and service centres for the rural hinterland. For this purpose, increased investments are proposed in these towns in housing, water supply and communication facilities. Likewise, facilities for education, medical care and recreation will need to be augmented. Given the economic importance of large, cities, care must be taken to improve the conditions of She urban poor and raise civic services, such that the large capital investments of all kinds that exist in these cities are utilised better Given the constraints on available resources, the only way that the appalling conditions in which the urban poor live today can be improved is to adopt more realistic norms and standards for urban services.

We need to adopt low cost standards for infrastructure so as to benefit the maximum number of urban people.

In order to ensure the continuance of the present balanced distribution of urban population, positive inducements need to be given for setting up new industries and other commercial and professional establishments in small, medium and intermediate cities, taking advantage of the particular special conditions available in each place. These could include appropriate concessions in respect of capital expenditures on housing, schools, entertainment facilities, power, water supply, sanitation and drainage. Power, telephone and telex connections must be improved in these towns. It is essential to strengthen local bodies organisationally as well as financially so that they can themselves improve the infrastructure and services in their towns. While these improvements are being made, tax incentives can also be considered for the location of employment generating, productive activities in these towns.

This kind of balanced approach is essential to ensure an orderly process of urbanisation along-with the overall development of the country. There has been a tendency to neglect infrastructure provision in small, medium and intermediate cities in the past which may have restricted their role as dynamic growth centres. This must be redressed.

Programmes

In the Sixth Plan, the major emphasis is placed on the following measures:

- Instead of attempting a massive relocation of slums, the greater emphasis would be on environmental improvement of slums for which substantially increased investment will be made. A particular area becomes a slum more because of poor environmental conditions, poor drainage, sewerage and sanitation, rather than the poor state of structures. Of the total urban population, nearly a fifth is estimated to constitute the slum population. In 1985, the magnitude of such population needing attention is estimated to be about 33.1 million. Of this, only 6.8 million have been covered so far by the scheme in the earlier Plans. The proposed investment of about Rs. 150 crore will benefit about 10.0 million people, assuming a per capita expenditure of Rs. 150. This scheme will be applicable to all urban areas irrespective of the size of the city/town. This forms part of the Minimum Needs Programme. The facilities that will be provided are water supply, storm water drainage, paving of streets, street lighting and provision of community latrines. Areas inhabited by scheduled castes or scavengers etc. are to be given due priority.

- A provision of Rs. 96 crore has been made in the Central Sector for the Centrally Sponsored Scheme of Integrated Development of Small and Medium Towns. This will be in the form of assistance to the State Governments on a sharing basis. It is visualised that about Rs. 200 crore would become available from the Central, State Governments and implementing agencies for the development of about 200 towns during the Plan period. Small and medium towns with a population of less than one lakh are eligible to receive assistance from the Centre under the Scheme, provided matching contributions are forthcoming from the State Governments/ implementing agencies.
- In the next five years, Rs. 423 crore will be spent by the State Governments in urban development programmes. Besides including the States' share against the centrally sponsored programme of Integrated Development of Small and Medium Towns, the above provision is meant for providing facilities such as roads, pavements, minor civic works as well as such amenities as bus sheds, markets, shopping complex, theatres etc. It is expected that the State Governments would make adequate provisions for the continuing commitments and further activities in respect of the scheme of Integrated Urban Development Programme in Metropolitan Cities and Areas of National Importance, which ceased to be centrally sponsored from 1-4-1979. A sum of Rs. 247 crore is being provided for the continuing development projects in Calcutta being

coordinated by the Calcutta Metropolitan Development Authority and aided by the World Bank. An additional sum of about Rs. 66 crore will be spent on on-going schemes in State Capital Projects in Bhopal. Gandhinagar and Chandigarh. These outlays cover schemes to improve water supply, sewerage, roads, traffic and transportation. Provision is also being made for area development, etc. in these cities.

- For the National Capital Region around Delhi, a provision of Rs. 10 crore has been made. This scheme, the details of which are under review, is expected to de-concentrate economic activity from the core of Delhi into regional towns-located in UP, Haryana and Rajasthan.
- A sum of Rs. 1.60 crore is being provided for research and development in order to improve the formulation of policy on urbanisation and urban development. The roles of different sizes of towns and cities is not well understood; the relationship between urban and rural activities needs to be investigated further in order to improve the links between urban and rural areas; the comparative costs of providing infrastructure and services to large, medium and small cities need to be worked out.

Water Supply and Sanitation

Although a national water supply programme was launched in 1954 during the very First Five Year Plan, and progressively larger allocations were made for water supply and sanitation in the succeeding Five Year Plans, the progress made so far in the provision of safe water supply and basic sanitation can hardly be called satisfactory. The available statistics relating to the status of rural and urban water supply in India present a discouraging picture especially in the rural areas. By March 1980 about two lakh villages in the country with a population of some 160 million were yet to be provided with potable water supply facilities. The situation in the urban areas is relatively better but here too, particularly in the hundreds of smaller towns, water supply and sanitation arrangements are far from adequate. The statistics in fact do not fully portray the hardship and inconvenience that is experienced by the poor, particularly the women and the children, in areas where water is scarce, inadequate or polluted. In terms of mandays lost due to water-borne or water related diseases which constitute nearly 80 per cent of the public health problem of our country, the wastage is indeed colossal.

Until the end of the Fourth Five Year Plan, i.e. during the period 1951-74, the total investment made by the Central and State Governments for providing water supply and sanitation facilities was of the order of Rs. 855 crore, over 65 per cent of it in the urban areas. During this period, the water supply programme was not given a high enough priority in the national planning; process. The constraint of resources in the States and the competing demands for programmes in other sectors compelled the State and local governments to give relatively lower priority to water supply in the allocation of funds. There was also at the same time insufficient appreciation of the magnitude and complexity of the problem.

The importance of providing .safe water supply and sanitation as a basic minimum need without meeting which no improvement m the living standards of the people could take place, was reiterated in the Draft Fifth Five Year Plan 1974-79 which included drinking water for villages .in its Minimum Needs Programme. The Draft Fifth Five Year Plan declared that adequate resources would be allocated for the programme irrespective of the resources constraints of individual States. The objective of the Minimum Needs Programme for drinking water was to provide the facility to all villages suffering from chronic scarcity or having unsafe sources of water. The Plan provided for an expenditure of Rs. 381 crore on rural water supply and sanitation as compared to a total of Rs. 289 crore provided in all the previous Plans.

The Sixth Five Year Plan is being launched at a time of increasing awareness, both nationally and internationally, of the importance of safe drinking water supply in sustaining the processes of economic and human resource development and improving the quality of our environment. The drought of 1979-80, which was accompanied by an acute scarcity of drinking water in many parts of the country where wells, tanks and other sources dried up in large numbers, has added urgency to the search for a lasting solution to the problem. The global concern with the need to provide drinking water and elementary sanitation to the people in developing countries led the United Nations Water Conference at Mar del Plata (Argentina) in 1977 to call for a ten Year campaign by member-countries and international agencies to provide access to safe water and sanitation for all people. The ten years 1981-90 have been designated as the International Drinking Water Supply and Sanitation Decade. India as a signatory to the Resolution has pledged its full support to the action plan under the International Decade.

Considering the magnitude of the problem in a vast country like India and the constraints on resources it is obvious that we cannot afford expensive or sophisticated water supply services. Nor is it possible to have a uniform mode of water supply everywhere. The wide variety of climatic conditions and of the sources of water, surface and underground, should permit the adoption of a variety of solutions which are economical, in keeping with local needs and conditions and capable of speedy implementation. Simple, even austere, standards will be necessary so that maximum population coverage, specially of the poor and the under-privileged sections of the community, can be achieved within the limited funds available.

Rural Water Supply and Sanitation

Until the Third Five Year Plan drinking water supply in the rural areas was a component of the amenities scheme of the Community Development Programme. Besides, the local development works programme, taken up through voluntary labour participation, and the programme of welfare of backward classes also included schemes relating to water supply. These efforts were supplemented by the National Water Supply and Sanitation Programme of the Ministry of Health. It is estimated that by the end of 1968-69 about 1.2 million sanitary wells and hand-pumps had been constructed and piped water supply provided to some 17,000 villages. During the Third Five Year Plan, under a Central scheme, Special Investigation Divisions were established in most States to make an assessment of the water supply situation especially in areas of acute scarcity and those endemic to water borne diseases. In the Fourth Five Year Plan 1969-74, the bulk of the provision for rural water supply was allocated for these areas. For this purpose, a new centrally sponsored scheme was also launched in 1972-73 to accelerate the efforts of the State Governments in meeting the needs of such areas. The programme gained further momentum during the Fifth Five Year Plan which made an allocation of Rs. 381 crore in the State Plans including Rs. 329 crore under the Minimum Needs Programme mentioned earlier. In addition, provision of Rs. 100 crore was made in the Central Sector under the Accelerated Rural Water Supply Scheme. Available information based on reports from State Governments indicates that by the end of 1979-80 about 1.84 lakh villages had benefited from water supply schemes 'of one type or another.

The Special Investigation Divisions established during the Third Five Year Plan period were the first step in identifying villages which could be regarded as problem villages from the point of view of the quality and accessibility of drinking water sources. Preliminary data collected by these Divisions in 1964-65 indicated that about two-thirds of the rural population lived in areas where it was relatively easy to provide safe drinking water from local sources like wells. The remaining one-third lived in villages which suffered from water scarcity and where engineering skills, extra financial outlays, and time consuming works would be called for. These villages were categorised as follows:

- Those which do not have an assured source of drinking water within a reasonable distance of say 1.6 kms;
- those which are endemic to diseases like cholera, guinea-worm etc.; and

- those where the available water has an excess of salinity, iron, fluorides or other toxic elements.

The first category was defined as scarcity and difficult villages and the other two as health problem villages.

In 1971-72 a total of 1.52 lakh villages in the country were identified as being without a safe and assured source of drinking water. Of these, 90,000 villages were classified as scarcity and difficult villages and 62,000 as health problem villages. In addition, it was estimated that there were 1.85 lakh villages with a population of 160 millions which were served by simple wells.

Since 1972-73, as a result of the larger investments made in the rural water supply sector, about 95,000 problem villages have been provided with safe drinking water supply facilities by March 1980. Thus, some 57.000 villages (including those in Sikkim) which had been identified as scarcity or health problem villages in the earlier survey remain to be provided with safe water supply. However, various State Governments have recently reported that the earlier survey did not adequately represent the magnitude of the problem partly because it was not complete and partly because the drought conditions in subsequent years had brought to light fresh areas which were vulnerable to water scarcity. The latest data received from the State Governments show that there are at present about 1.90 lakh villages in the country which need to be provided water supply facilities on a priority basis.

It is worth emphasising that these figures represent only the first step in the evaluation of the problem. The type of water supply system required varies from State to State and often from one area to another within a State. It is necessary for the State Governments to work out suitable engineering solutions for covering all the needy villages so as to ensure that at least one source of potable water is available throughout the year in every such village. Details for requirement of funds, materials and equipment, staff and maintenance arrangements will have to be worked out and annual action plans prepared. The programme envisaged in the Sixth Plan has to be viewed in the perspective of a 10 year plan but during this plan period itself it will have to be limited to assuring water supplies in the rural areas through simple and inexpensive devices. In many areas a simple sanitary well with parapet and with regular cleaning and disinfection will be considered a safe and adequate source of water supply. In hard rock areas or where the water table is low, emphasis will have to be given on deep tube wells with hand-pumps. Power pumps or piped water supply schemes should only be the last alternative.

During the Sixth Five Year Plan the effort will be to cover all the problem villages of the three categories mentioned earlier. With the financial provisions made in the Plan, it will be possible to achieve this objective except in certain difficult areas in the hill and desert regions where, because of physical constraints, the programme may take a longer time. The approach in all the areas will be to provide at least one source of drinking water in every village identified as a scarcity or health problem village. Additional sources may, however, be necessary in villages with large populations or dispersed hamlets. In particular, the needs of the scheduled caste habitations in the rural areas will have to be given priority.

Apart from the problem villages which will be covered under the Minimum Needs Programme, there are other villages where the existing sources of water supply may need improvement or augmentation. The Sixth Plan provides Rs. 128 crore for these areas. Altogether the provision for rural water supply in the Sixth Plan is Rs. 2,135 crore, Rs. 600 crore in the Central Sector and Rs. 1,535 crore in the State/Union Territory Plans.

Poor maintenance of existing water supply systems in the rural) areas continues to be a source of concern in most States. Lack of involvement of the local community in the maintenance arrangements, shortage of staff and inadequate funds for maintenance are the main reasons why the existing water supply schemes have failed to yield the expected benefits. It is clear that the operation of small rural water supply systems can be ensured only with the participation of the village community and institutions. Excepting very large systems covering many villages and requiring skilled supervisory staff, in most cases n should be possible for the block and village level functionaries to take care of the relatively ample operation and maintenance requirements of rural water supply schemes. A three-tier maintenance set up, with a care-taker at the village level, a mechanic at the block level and a mobile repair team at the district level, has been successfully tried in Tamil Nadu and can be adopted in other States with suitable variations. It has been noticed that wherever the maintenance arrangements are adequate, the beneficiaries are not unwilling to pay a nominal charge for the water supplied to them. The effort should in all cases be -to recover at least the operating expenses.

So far little attention has been given to the problem of rural sanitation except for some pilot projects in a few States. It is estimated that almost 98 per cent of the rural house-holds do not have any latrines. Keeping in view the present position of rural sanitation and the limitation of budgetary resources sanitation facilities can be provided to only 25 per cent of the rural population by the end of the Decade. Much more can, however, be done in this area through self-help schemes organised by the village community. Simple low cost designs of water-seal latrines have already been developed in many areas. Extension efforts will need to be made on a large scale to assist the village organisations in the adoption and use of these designs, with such local modifications as may be necessary. The UN Resolution on the International Drinking Water Supply and Sanitation Decade calls for basic sanitation facilities being made available to all citizens by 1990. This objective can be attained only through large scale mobilisation of voluntary effort at the village level. The effort in the Sixth Five Year Plan is to make a modest beginning in this direction by undertaking pilot, projects in all States which would help in making an assessment of the community attitudes in the rural areas to the type of latrines to be provided and the nature of sanitation facilities needed.

Urban Water Supply and Sanitation

Some features of the present coverage of water supply services in the urban areas may be mentioned. Where towns with nearly 84 per cent of the urban population have been provided with drinking water facilities, the population coverage is partial and uneven. Even in the larger cities many of the newer settlements and areas inhabited by the economically weaker sections continue to be without adequate water supply. Further, out of the 1,027 towns still lacking drinking water supply facilities, as many as 902 belong to the group of towns which have a population of less than 20,000. It is in these smaller towns that the population served by drinking water facilities is 50 per cent or even less. In the past, the bulk of plan investments in urban water supply has gone to the larger cities and the smaller towns have in consequence continued to suffer.

The position in regard to urban sewerage and sanitation is even less satisfactory. Out of the 3,119 towns, only 198 have been provided with sewerage facilities. Even in respect of class I cities having a population of one lakh and above, only 46 per cent have arrangements for sewerage and sewage treatment. The overall population coverage in the urban areas is about 20 per cent.

Water supply and sewerage programmes in the urban areas should be considered an integral part of urban development. While the pressing need of providing adequate water supply and sewerage facilities in the larger cities, especially in the high density areas populated by the' low income groups and economically weaker sections, must continue to receive priority, greater attention needs to be given in the Sixth Five Year Plan to the needs of smaller and medium size towns which have been neglected in the past. The Sixth Plan lays considerable emphasis on the integrated development of small and medium size towns and the environmental improvement of slums. Water supply and sewerage schemes have to be dovetailed in this programme. The Town and Country Planning Organisations in the States which have the responsibility of preparing master plans for these areas have to ensure that adequate provision is made for water supply and sewerage facilities in the formulation and implementation of these plans.

Some effort has recently been made to evolve low cost techniques for urban sanitation. The UNDP Global Project in India is intended to assist and promote the installation of water-seal latrines in 110 towns in 7 States, viz., Assam, Bihar, Gujarat, Maharashtra, Rajasthan, Tamil Nadu and U.P. The Project aims at adopting appropriate technologies which would be particularly helpful in the smaller towns. Pilot projects are to be taken up in these States to provide low cost water-seal latrines with on-site disposal of human waste.

During the Sixth Plan, priority would be given to the completion of on-going urban water supply and sewerage schemes, including augmentation of the existing systems in the larger cities. It is expected that about 930 urban water supply schemes and 120 urban sewerage and drainage schemes will be completed during this period. In addition, it is proposed that new schemes of water supply will be taken up in about 550 towns and sewerage schemes in 110 towns.

As in the rural areas, the maintenance of urban water supply schemes, particularly in the small municipalities, is unsatisfactory. The poor quality of maintenance results mainly from the unwillingness of the local bodies to levy water rates and the inability of the State Governments to provide adequate non-plan grants for maintenance purposes. Urban water supply and sewerage schemes are highly capital intensive and there is a strong case for recovery from the beneficiaries at least the interest and operation and maintenance charges to start with.

Seventh Five Year Plan: 1985-90 (Volume I)

Housing and urban development

The Seventh Plan aims at providing housing assistance to 2.71 million poor rural families. The promotion of self-help housing and rural housing for economically weaker sections will stimulate and support private housing, especially for middle and lower income groups. Around 9 million slum-dwellers will benefit from a programme for the environmental improvement of slums.

Seventh Five Year Plan: 1985-90
(Volume II)

Housing

In fulfilling the basic needs of the population, housing ranks next only to food and clothing in importance. A certain minimum standard of housing is essential for healthy and civilised existence. The development of housing, therefore, must enjoy high priority in a poor society such as ours where housing amenities are far below the minimum standards that have been internationally accepted. Housing activity serves to fulfil many of the fundamental objectives of the Plan: providing shelter, raising the quality of life particularly of the poorer sections of the population; creating conditions which are conducive to the achievements of crucial objectives in terms of health, sanitation and education; creating substantial additional employment and dispersed economic activity; improving urban-rural and inter-personal equity through the narrowing down of difference in standards of living and last but not least, generating additional voluntary savings.

The National Buildings Organisation (NBO) have estimated that the housing shortage in 1981 was around 21 million dwelling units (16 million in rural areas and 5 million in urban areas); the shortage at the beginning of the Seventh Five Year Plan has been placed at 24.7 million units (18.8 million in rural areas and 5.9 million in urban areas).

The above estimates of backlog of housing shortage are only rough. But apart from the existing backlog in housing, the increase in population between 1985 and 1990 would generate roughly an additional requirement of housing units to the extent of 16.2 million, of which 12.4 million will be in rural areas and 3.8 million in urban areas. This means that even if the aim is only to prevent an increase in the magnitude of backlog in housing shortage, it would be necessary to build during the Seventh Plan period around 16.2 million dwelling units. This fact makes evident the gigantic magnitude of the housing problem. This problem cannot be tackled in a meaningful way, if housing activities are left to follow the past pattern of slow and unsystematic growth. There is need for radical orientation of all policies relating to housing. The most important among these are: the provision of finance for house construction on a large scale, development of suitable land sites in urban areas, provision of house sites in rural areas, developing and applying low-cost technology in house construction an policies relating to rent control.

While all sectors of the economy—the Government sector, public enterprise sector, the private corporate sector, the co-operative sector and the household sector—would have to participate in housing activities in , coordinated manner, the major responsibility for house construction would have to be left to the private sector, ii particular the household sector. Building houses according to the differing preferences and requirements o different households and economy in house construction can become possible only if the home owner himself participates or becomes responsible for house construction. What has inhibited large scale house construction b} households is the inadequate provision of institutional finance for the housing sector so far. Two major desiderata for a quantum jump in house construction in urban and semi-urban areas are the mobilisation of resources for the housing sector through the establishment of a proper set of institutions and the development of suitable housing sites on a large scale. The poorer sections of the society, however, would need subsidisation and also assistance in house construction from the public sector. In this context, the public sector's role should be three-fold.

First, largely promotional, to initiate steps to mobilise resources for the housing sector on an adequate scale; second to continue the efforts to provide subsidised housing to segments of the rural poor and to other economically weaker sections (EWS) of the community like slum dwellers and dock and plantation workers; and third to undertake land acquisition and development in urban areas and providing house sites in rural areas. Housing authorities and Housing Boards should concentrate on the last activity instead of going in for direct construction of houses. The second activity would be performed mainly by the Housing and Urban Development Corporation (HUDCO) for the poorer sections of the society. For other sections this would be performed through a network of house financing institutions with an apex bank for re-finance.

Public sector Plan expenditure on housing during the Sixth Plan is estimated at Rs. 1,839 crore; in addition, public enterprises are estimated to have spent around Rs. 275 crore on housing. The extent of shortage has been worked out in terms of certain minimum standards; therefore it should not be assumed that an equivalent number of families are entirely shelter less. Nevertheless, the figures fairly reflect the great inadequacy of housing in the country, housing through agencies of the public sector amounted to Rs. 2,114 crore during the Sixth Plan period.

The major part of investment in housing is undertaken by the private sector. Reliable data on investment in private housing are not available. According to the estimates made by the Central Statistical Organisation (CSO), gross fixed capital formation in residential buildings in the private sector, including public sector undertakings, amounted to Rs. 3,054 crore in 1980-81. Assuming that the share of the public sector undertakings in this was of the order of Rs. 70-80 crore, gross capital formation in housing in the private sector would have been around Rs. 2,980 crore in that year. According to CSO figures, private sector investment in housing between 1974-75 and 1979-80 increased by about 62 per cent, or at about 12 per cent per annum. A 10 per cent growth rate could be assumed for the Sixth Plan period.

On this basis, the private sector investment in housing during the Sixth Plan would have amounted to Rs. 18,000 crore. A growth rate in private sector housing in the Seventh Plan period equal to that assumed for the Sixth Plan period would imply an investment of around Rs. 29,000 crore. In fact, if the backlog in housing is to be reduced to any significant extent by the end of the

Seventh Plan, a much larger investment than Rs. 29,000 crore would be called for. This underlines the need for a major effort to mobilise resources for housing and for the Government to take other steps needed, such as to make available developed land on the required scale on the one hand and to make the necessary policy changes to remove obstacles in the way of housing activity, e.g., modification in the rent control laws, on the other.

The time has now come for the Government to set before itself a clear goal in the field of housing and launch a major housing effort: not so much to build but to promote housing activity through the supply of fiscal and financial infrastructure such that every family will be provided with adequate shelter within a definite time horizon. As far as possible, the public sector should not assume direct house construction except in the case of the weaker sections of the society. This is not to minimise the role of the Government. As stated earlier, the Government has to play an active role through developing the necessary delivery system in the form of a housing finance market and taking steps to make developed land available at right places and at reasonable prices.

The most crucial need for housing development at the present time is the establishment of a proper and diversified institutional structure for housing finance and construction. The strengthening of the existing institutions like Housing and Urban Development Corporation (HUDCO) and the creation of new institutions like housing co-operatives and building societies would be necessary. The expansion of the Housing Development Finance Corporation (HDFC) type of activities could also be considered. While HUDCO would concentrate on the provision of subsidised finance to the poorer sections of the society, the HDFC would continue to cater to the clientele coming largely from fairly well-to-do sections of the society. The vast majority of house-seeking individuals and families would have to be looked after through the creation of local level housing finance societies. These societies would raise deposits from the public, mainly from the would-be house owners, and thus stimulate private saving. In addition, they should have access to funds from the capital market through the intermediation of different financial institutions. For this purpose it would be desirable to set up a specialised housing finance institution. In course of time steps should also be taken to develop a secondary mortgage market in housing.

The apex housing finance institution should be able to draw funds from the capital market as well as from financial institutions. Commercial banks should be permitted to participate on a larger scale than hitherto in housing finance activities.

As stated above, the public sector has to concentrate on the provision of houses to the poorer sections of the society. HUDCO, in conjunction with the State Governments, would continue to play an important role in the provision of finance to these sections for house-building activity. In addition, the public sector has to play an important role in the provision of housing sites in the rural areas. There is urgent need to adopt low-cost housing techniques, particularly for mass housing schemes for low income groups. Use of alternative building materials like lime, mortar, surkhi, secondary species of timber, etc. in place of traditional building materials like cement, steel, bricks and primary species of timber should be widely adopted.

Prefabricated technology which has been adopted in some western countries requires to be considered for large scale adoption in our country provided the cost factor is favourable for its adoption. The relative advantages of factory production of prefabricated components of Indian Standards Institution (ISI) standards (like beams and blocks, roofing materials and doors and windows) vis-à-vis traditional building methods, may be assessed. If any fiscal measures stand in the way of adopting large-scale prefab, technology because of its being based on factory production, ways and means may have to be explored to overcome this handicap.

Direct subsidy to urban housing should be avoided as far as possible. Where direct subsidies are absolutely unavoidable, they should be small and be in the form of infrastructure facilities so as not to create large differences between the market values and the subsidised prices.

Against this background, the Seventh Five Year Plan (1985-90) has the following objectives:

- Promotion and encouragement of self-help housing;
- Provision of house sites to the balance of rural families identified so far and assistance for construction of dwellings for those rural families already provided house-sites;
- Cost of housing units under the social housing schemes should be such that they are within the paying capacity of the targeted groups, like Economically Weaker Sections (EWS), Low Income Group (LIG) and Middle Income Group (MIG);
- Providing stimulus and support for private housing especially for the middle and lower income groups so as to channel increased savings into housing. This will have to be accompanied by steps needed for reducing the cost of urban land;
- Securing reduction in construction costs not only by adopting low-cost housing techniques and standards but also modifications in building bye-laws, land use control, minimum plot requirements, etc.; and
- Harnessing science and technology efforts for improving building technology and development of cheap and local building materials.

The programmes for achieving these objectives are as follows:

Rural Housing: The Minimum Needs Programme (MNP) and the 20-Point Programme give a high priority to the rural house-site-cum-house construction scheme. It is estimated that there were 12.2 million landless families as of March 1985. As against this, the number of families provided house-sites is estimated at 13.07 million. The "excess" achievement is due to the fact that in some states the scheme was extended to smaller municipalities, and in some states the beneficiaries included some belonging to the upper income strata of the rural community. However, state-wise analysis reveals that still 0.72 million landless families among the total estimated landless families of 12.2 million require to be provided with house-sites. It is felt that before extending the coverage of the scheme to smaller municipalities and to those belonging to the upper income brackets of the rural community, efforts should be made to provide construction assistance to those families already provided house-sites according to the original criteria of the scheme. The Sixth Plan envisaged provision of construction assistance to 3.6 million families; in fact only 1.9 million families could be assisted.

Even though the Sixth Plan envisaged a modest level of Governmental assistance under the scheme, many State Governments were providing substantially higher levels of assistance. In order to make the operation of the scheme more realistic, it is proposed to provide assistance to the extent of Rs. 500 per family for provision of developed house-sites of 90 sq.m. each and assistance of Rs. 2,000 per family towards construction cost. All labour inputs will have to be provided by the beneficiary. The Seventh Plan includes a provision of Rs. 577 crore for this programme. Of this, Rs. 36 crore would be utilised to provide house-sites in respect of those states where there are landless families still to be provided house-sites and Rs. 541 crore would be utilised for the provision of construction assistance to 2.71 million families. Needless to say that if the above targets are to be achieved during the Plan, the State Governments will have to adhere to the norms and standards envisaged in the Plan. These have been considerably liberalised compared to the Sixth Plan.

On account of the resource constraint, only a limited provision is made in this regard in the State Plans. Besides this, HUDCO has been providing funds for rural housing. This would continue. A specified proportion of General Insurance Corporation (GIC) funds are also earmarked for rural housing. Taken together, the funds for rural housing from public institutions (HUDCO and GIC) would roughly amount to Rs. 240 crore during the Seventh Plan.

Urban Housing: As already stated, Government's role in the field of urban housing has per force to be promotional. The major effort will have to come from the private sector, Government's role will have to be restricted to the improvement of slums, direct provision of housing to the weaker sections of the society and encouragement and support of housing finance institutions that promote channelling of private resource into housing in a constructive way.

Urban Development

The Sixth Plan recognised that although the share of urban population of India was small, estimated to be only a little over 20 per cent of the population of the country, the absolute size of about 107 million people living in urban areas in 1971 was large by any standards. The urban growth registered in 1971 -81 has followed the pattern of growth in the previous decade. As a percentage of total population, the increase has been from 20.22 per cent to 23.73 per cent. In absolute terms it has meant an increase in urban population from 107 million in 1971 to 156 million in 1981 (provisional). Certain important aspects of this increase require to be noted. While the growth of urban population as a whole was 3.86 per cent, Class I cities grew by 4.6 per cent and Class II cities by 4.2 per cent. The number of towns increased from 2581 in an increasing proportion and area of urban conglomerations are being turned into slums.

In view of the extremely serious situation in which the urban bodies find themselves, a vigorous multi-pronged attack is needed to reverse the trend and to restore conditions of healthy growth. The following may be identified as the major constituents of a comprehensive plan for urban development:

- the planned and integrated development of small and medium towns and cities along with slowing down of the growth of big metropolises;
- revitalisation of civic bodies;
- thorough-going reforms of municipal tax systems and municipal administration in general;
- concentration on the improvement of slums and the provision of basic municipal services; and

- for this purpose to work out schemes of regular devolution of funds from State Governments and to establish the necessary institutional framework for channelling capital funds for the improvement of urban infrastructure.

A thorough re-examination of the procedures currently used in the planning of metropolitan areas and the evolution of approaches and methods more suited to the new imperatives arising from the intensification of urban growth all over the country are called for.

Urbanisation is a phenomenon which is part and parcel of economic development in general. Certain activities are best performed in, indeed require, agglomeration of people. Planning of urban development should essentially be supportive of the economic development in the country, state or sub-region, be it in agriculture, extractive industry, manufacturing industry or in the tertiary sector. The provision of urban services such as transport, communication, water, sanitation and shelter alone is usually unlikely to stimulate large-scale urban development. It is important to time investments in urban services and shelter to coincide with investments in agriculture and industry, mining and commerce which provide sources of permanent employment. Therefore, a proper urban development approach must consist of two constituents. The first is the interaction between physical and investment planning and the second is the preparation of regional and sub-regional urban development plans to make the first possible. Industrial location policy must be made to subserve regional and urban planning. During the Seventh Plan a concerted effort should be made to channelise private industrial investment in the vicinity of small and medium towns so that migration of population is diverted to these from going to the metropolises. The same principal should be applied to public sector investment.

Regional urban systems can be identified according to their economic, climatic, geographical and transportation characteristics. Planning for urban development can be done on the basis of such regions and according to the relative need and function of each town in its regional context. Thus, within each planning zone allocation to towns should be made more on the basis of their functions with particular emphasis on their respective industrial and employment potential than on their sizes.

Within towns and cities there is a much greater need for community participation and for more private initiative and investment in urban development than existing at present. The delivery of basic public services to everyone is simply not feasible without such an approach. Slum improvement, sanitation, garbage removal, etc. can be organised and even paid for at the community level. Resources for urban development are very limited and will continue to be so in the foreseeable future given the existence of wide-spread rural poverty and lack of basic services in rural areas. This would call for better allocation of existing funds and mobilisation of additional funds by the municipal bodies themselves. A realistic assessment of needs for basic infrastructure and services is, therefore, a pre-requisite for efficient and effective planning.

The planning for metropolitan development should provide for:

- coordination of city level investment plans with higher (State and Central) level planning and resources allocation exercises;
- coordination of city level investment plans with resource availability and with physical planning; and
- the fostering of a close relationship between the norms and standards used in physical planning with the socio-economic realities prevailing within our cities. More explicitly the needs of the poor must be taken account of more specifically in all physical planning exercises.

In the small towns and the new centres, the strategy should be to purchase lands in concentric circles, at short notice, before land values begin to rise, quickly providing the infrastructure facilities within a period of 2 to 3 years and then selling the land to the public and private sectors. In this way, the public authority could make two major gains: (i) the profit from site development and (ii) the gains through passage of time. The gains could be used for various purposes. If the public authority makes non-speculative purchases continuously, withdraws land for short periods and continuously puts these back into the land market, there need not be an inflation of real estate prices. In that case, the rise in the costs and rents of houses would be limited.

While making provision for urban development schemes due attention should be paid to the needs of the minority concentration areas and their development in the context of their socio-cultural milieu.

As pointed out earlier, municipal bodies are not able to play their due part in providing the needed services to urban dwellers and in developing urban infrastructure commensurate with the growth of urban population. They are politically, administratively, and financially in a week condition. The restoration of health to local bodies is the pre-requisite for the efficient management of our towns and cities. At the first stage the aim should be to provide to all citizens the minimum of essential services. All obligatory functions should be reverted to municipal authorities. The strategy for urban development would include a package of measures to strengthen the capability of local bodies comprising the restoration of popular Government (except in states where abnormal conditions exist), structural reforms, improvement in general and financial administration and reform of the tax system. While the State Governments have to shoulder the major responsibility for putting through these measures, the Central Government as well as autonomous institutions at the Central level should actively participate in developing programmes of revitalisation and reform. In particular, the Central Government should extend aid to a selected number of institutions for promoting research in the area of urban administration, urban finances, and the planning of the development of urban infrastructure, and to strengthen their capability to provide technical assistance in these areas to State level institutions as well as to the local bodies.

As the problems created by rapid urbanisation are stupendous and have wide-ranging social and political ramifications, there is national concern for checking the deterioration of conditions in our cities and towns. In this context, central participation and assistance in this vital area is justified. For this purpose it is proposed to set up a National Urban Infrastructure Development Finance Corporation with an initial Plan provision of Rs. 55 crore in the Urban Development Sector and Rs. 20 crore in the Water Supply and Sanitation Sector.

In the Seventh Plan 1985-90 emphasis is placed on the following major programmes:

- The Environmental Improvement of Slums (EIS) programme has to be continued with greater vigour and steps should be taken to provide security of tenure to the slum dwellers so that they may develop a stake in maintaining and improving their habitat. Of the total urban population, nearly a fifth is estimated to constitute the slum population. The Sixth Plan had estimated that in 1985 the magnitude of such population needing attention would be about 33.1 million. Of this, up to March 1985, about 15.6 million slum dwellers would have been benefited, leaving a balance of 17.5 million people yet to be provided relief. Per capita assistance which was only Rs. 120 in 1972 has been stepped up from time to time and the present rate of Rs. 250 was fixed in 1984. Since many State Government considered this quantum inadequate it has been decided to step up the per capita expenditure to Rs. 300. The total outlay for EIS in State Plans works out to Rs. 269.55 crore for the Seventh Plan. On the basis of a per capita expenditure of Rs. 300, this order of total outlay would benefit about 9 million slum dwellers during the Seventh Plan.
- In order to ensure a balanced distribution of urban population and to slow down the growth of metropolises, a centrally sponsored scheme of Integrated Development of Small and Medium Towns (IDSMT) was introduced during the Sixth Plan to provide infrastructure and other facilities in these towns. The Sixth Plan made a provision of Rs. 96 crore in the Central sector with a matching provision in the States' sector

for the development of about 200 towns. During the Plan period, Central releases amounted to about Rs. 61 crore in respect of 235 towns. It is proposed to continue this scheme during the Seventh Plan with a Central provision of Rs. 88 crore. During the Sixth Plan the scheme was applicable to small and medium towns having a population of less than one lakh. It is now proposed to extend the coverage to towns having a population of less than three lakh. In selecting the towns for assistance under the scheme an additional criterion based on the towns' antiquity, aesthetic character, historic association, etc. requires to be adopted.

- The Plan includes a provision of Rs. 930 crore in the States' sector for provision of infrastructure facilities like roads, pavements, minor civic works as well as such amenities as bus sheds, market and shopping complexes and theatres. This provision also includes the States' contribution against the centrally sponsored scheme of IDSMT. A provision of Rs. 317.58 crore is included for the development projects being undertaken in the Calcutta Metropolitan Development Area (CMDA) as part of the externally aided programmes and for the development of State Capital Projects of Gandhi Nagar, Bhopal and Chandigarh.
- An outlay of Rs. 35 crore has been included in the Plan of the Ministry of Works and Housing for the development of the National Capital Region (NCR) around Delhi. This will be in addition to the provisions included in the plans of other Central Ministries like Railways, Shipping and Transport, etc. The NCR Plan envisages deconcentration of economic activity from the core of Delhi into regional towns located in Haryana, Rajasthan and Uttar Pradesh. A statutory Planning Board for NCR has been constituted under the Chairmanship of the Minister for Works and Housing and a detailed Plan for Development for NCR is under preparation.
- In India, the use of development banks to finance development oriented sectors in the national economy has proved to be quite successful. It is proposed to set up an

Urban Infrastructure Development Finance Corporation to deal with the emerging urban problems that the country is and will be facing. The Plan provides Rs. 35 crore in the Urban Development Sector and Rs. 20 crore in the Water Supply and sanitation Sector, as initial capital for the Corporation which would augment its resources by raising funds from institutional sources. The proposed Institution would finance the development of urban infrastructure including water supply and sewerage schemes. The National Housing Bank also proposed to be set up in the Seventh Plan and the Urban Infrastructure Finance Corporation would together play an important role in promoting housing and urban development on an adequate scale and on a sound basis.

Water Supply and Sanitation

With the increasing awareness of the vital importance of the provision of potable water to all citizens in the general move towards social justice, allocation to this sector, particularly to the programme for the provision of potable water supply in rural areas, was increased substantially and also rural water supply was included in the Minimum Needs Programme in the Fifth Year Plan and in the Revised 20-point Programme in the Sixth Plan.

A massive programme for providing safe drinking water facilities in the rural areas was launched during the Sixth Five Year Plan. The results achieved were truly impressive, as 1.92 lakh villages, out of a total number of 2.31 lakh identified problem villages, as well as 47,000 other villages were provided water supply during the Sixth Plan. The significant step-up in the central assistance for this purpose during the Seventh Plan indicates the high priority attached to the provision of the basic amenity of potable water supply to every citizen, especially in the rural areas.

Review of Sixth Plan

Despite the resource constraint, the Sixth Plan provided for a substantial outlay on water supply and sanitation amounting to Rs.

3,922.02 crore—Rs. 3,307.80 crore in the State sector and Rs. 614.22 crore in the Central sector. Within the sector, high priority was accorded to the provision of drinking water to what were identified as problem villages; for this purpose an outlay of Rs. 2,007.11 crore was provided - Rs. 1,407.11 crore in the State sector (MNP) and Rs. 600 crore in the Central sector. The following criteria were used to identify the problem villages:

- those which do not have an assured source of drinking water within a reasonable distance of say, 1.6 km;
- those in which diseases like cholera, guineaworm etc. are endemic; and
- those where the available water has an excess of salinity, iron, flourides and other toxic elements.

This programme got further impetus when it was brought under the Revised 20-Point Programme in 1982-83. In 1983 a new Incentive Bonus Scheme was started by the Ministry of Finance in order to further accelerate the programme of water supply to problem villages. Under this Scheme a provision of Rs. 75 crore was made during 1983-84 and Rs. 50 crore during 1984-85.

At the time of the formulation of the Sixth Plan the identification of problem villages had not been completed. With the data then available the Sixth Plan ha< aimed to cover 1.9 lakh villages; when the task o identification was completed, this figure went up to 2.3 lakh. A massive programme was launched to provide potable water in most of the identified problem villages. The results have been impressive. Out of the total of 2.31 lakh villages identified as problem villages 1.92 lakh of such villages and 47,000 other than problem villages are estimated to have been provided with water supply facilities by the end of the Sixth Plan. With this, 54 per cent of the population in rural areas has been covered by Rural Water Supply Schemes by the end of the Sixth Plan. The achievement was made possible by investment on a scale larger than originally envisaged amounting to Rs. 2,485,3; crore - Rs. 1,566.68 crore in the State sector (MNP; and Rs. 918.65 crore in the Central sector (ARP), including Rs. 116.11 crore under the Incentive Bonus Scheme.

There was an investment of Rs. 3,977.59 crore; (Rs. 3,053.68 crore in the State sector and Rs. 923.9 crore in the Central sector), during the Sixth Plan under the Water Supply and Sanitation Sector.

Seventh Plan

As pointed out above, although the major areas of the rural population have been now provided with potable water supply as a result of the massive effort during the Sixth Plan period, there are still a sizeable number of problem villages. During the Seventh Plan, in line with the objective of International Drinking Water Supply and Sanitation Decade (1981-91), the aim would be to provide adequate drinking water facilities for the entire population and to provide sanitation facilities to 80 per cent of the urban population and at least 25 per cent of the rural population. Although the task ahead is of a stupendous magnitude, an earnest endeavour would be made to fulfil the objectives set out in the 31st UN General Assembly Resolution in regard to the provision of water supply for the total population.

In view of the constraint of resources, it will not be desirable to go in for expensive or sophisticated water supply and sanitation services. Simple and low-cost methods should be preferred. Also, it must be noted that it will not be possible to introduce a uniform mode of water supply everywhere in a vast country like India. The wide variety of climatic conditions and of the sources of surface and underground water require and should permit the adoption of different types of solutions which are economical and in keeping with local needs and conditions.

Experience has shown that in a programme of this kind and magnitude reaching out to all the regions and remote corners of the country, community involvement is essential in all stages-formulation, execution and maintenance of water supply schemes. A considerable amount of pilferage and wastage of water could be avoided if local involvement and cooperation in enlisted.

The burden on the exchequer could be reduced to the extent that the beneficiaries are asked to pay. Water supply is a service to be paid for by the direct beneficiaries. In urban areas in particular there is scope for enhancing water rates; there is also scope for improving the realisation of water charges. The State Governments and local bodies should explore the possibility of raising funds for water supply schemes through suitable levies (capital charges) on the potential beneficiaries. Even in rural areas, while the poorer sections cannot be expected to pay for the water, in many villages through local initiative it is possible to collect a small charge which would cover at least a part of the maintenance expenses.

It is also important that the State Governments, who are the implementing agencies for water supply and sanitation programmes, should pay attention to the organisational and administrative structures at various levels, in order to utilise the Plan funds more efficiently and productively. The organisational pattern for execution of water supply and sanitation schemes varies not only between different States but also within the State itself in the case of many States. Though many States have now set up Water Supply and Sewerage Boards, in some States different agencies like PHED, panchayati raj, community development department, rural engineering department/RIDP/ PWD and CPWD are responsible for the execution of water supply and sanitation schemes. It is necessary to have uniform approach in this regard and as far as possible, the same administrative department should supervise the various aspects of design, execution and maintenance. The monitoring and evaluation systems need to be made more efficient and effective at the Central, State and District levels.

Keeping in view the overall constraint on resources as well as the other competing demands, the Seventh Plan provides for an outlay of Rs. 6,522.47 crore - Rs. 5,285.64 crore under State/UT sector and Rs. 1,236.83 crore under the Central sector—for the water supply and sanitation programme. This works out to 3.62 per cent of the total Plan outlay of the Seventh Plan. This includes loan assistance from the LIC, as well as the external agencies like World Bank, IDA/Bilateral Agencies. The emphasis is considerably greater in respect of rural water supply and an increased outlay of Rs. 3,454.47 crore has been envisaged for this programme in the Seventh Plan.

Rural Water Supply and Sanitation

As in the Sixth Plan, the rural water supply continues to be a part of the Minimum Needs Programme as well as the revised 20-Point Programme during the Seventh Plan. However, in order to achieve the maximum coverage of rural population during the Seventh Plan, the scope of rural water supply under MNP needs to be extended to all villages, whereas it was restricted to identification of problem villages until the end of the Sixth Plan. It may be noticed that, during the Sixth Plan period, there has been a quantum jump in investment in this Sector, especially with regard to the provision of rural water supply. The priority given to this programme is clearly seen from the fact that the Central Government has given a big helping hand to the State Governments in providing the problem villages with water supply by progressively increasing the central assistance under the Accelerated Rural Water Supply Programme (ARP). The amount under ARP and incentive schemes given to the states for the implementation of rural water supply programme in the Sixth Plan amounted to Rs. 918.65 crore and during the Seventh Plan, it is likely to be about 1.5 times that amount.

Some of the policy issues with regard to the rural water supply programme in the Seventh Plan are as follows:

- Whether a re-definition of the problem villages or problem areas is required for the Seventh Plan and if so, what should be the new definition?
- What should be the per capita norm for water supply for rural areas?
- Difficulties which are peculiar to certain areas such as Rajasthan, Haryana and hilly areas and methods of tackling such difficulties.
- Delegation of powers for giving technical approval to State Chief Engineers - extent of delegation.

- Making available adequate funds for the maintenance of completed schemes and assets created.

In view of the resources constraint, the coverage of villages with water supply schemes during the Seventh Plan will have to follow a certain order of Priority. The spill over of identified problem villages (39,000) based on the existing criteria will in any case have to be covered before other villages can be taken up. The next priority will have to be given to those villages which have been identified as problem villages subsequent to April 1, 1980 on the basis of the existing criteria. Once this task is completed and every village is provided with at least one source of water supply, water supply facilities will have to be further expanded in order to provide for adequate water supply to the villagers. This will naturally result in the liberalisation of the present norms and level of satisfaction in the rural areas so far as water supply is concerned.

Attempts would be made to cover all those villages which do not have an assured source of water supply within a distance of 0.5 km (as against the present norm of 1.6 km) and also to enhance per capita norm for water supply from 40 litres per capita per day (Ipcd) to 70 Ipcd during the Seventh Plan, as recommended by the Estimates Committee.

It is also essential to ensure that the poorer sections of the society like Scheduled Castes, Scheduled Tribes and landless agricultural labourers have equal access to this facility. In this context, the location of the source/water collection points is important. This calls for greater attention to the matter of selection of location- o the sources/water collection points. Where necessary additional sources/water collection points for enabling the poor to obtain access to safe drinking water should be separately provided if access to the community source; provided under the general scheme for drinking water supply to village is difficult for them.

A new policy is also being evolved in the Seventh Plan to tackle special problems of water soppy which are peculiar to certain States Rajasthan Haryana and Madhya Pradesh) and to hilly areas. The problems o such States and areas will receive special attention in the Seventh Plan. Administrative bottlenecks in the execution of schemes will be removed by delegation of power to the State chief engineers.

While impressive results have been achieved in providing water supply facilities in the rural areas in the Sixth Plan, the maintenance of these facilities, mostly the hand pumps, has been badly neglected, partly because of lack of adequate funds for maintenance and partly because of the lack of suitable machinery for their maintenance. It has been realised that the assets created for provision of water supply in the rural areas at huge cost cannot be allowed to go waste or even become partially defunct. For the first time, therefore, a maximum of 10 per cent of the Plan funds under MNP is being earmarked for the maintenance of the water supply systems in rural areas. The State Governments are also being advised to create a suitable machinery for the regular maintenance of the water supply schemes in rural areas by actively encouraging community participation in this vital programme.

Sanitation

Lack of a good sanitation system is one of the factor affecting the quality of life of the rural population. Because of resource constraint, considerable backlog in the provision of sanitation facilities in rural areas has arisen. Less than 1 per cent of the rural population is reported to have been covered by sanitation system at the end of the Sixth Plan. This programme is yet to gather momentum. It is possible to start and implement the programme only with people's participation. Much more can be done in this area through self-help schemes organised by the village community and large-scale mobilisation of voluntary effort at the village level through attempts of the State Governments and local bodies. Simple low-cost design of pour flush latrines has already been developed in many areas through UNDP assistance. It is estimated that each individual sanitary toilet would cost about Rs. 100 per head. Extensive efforts would, however, need to be made on a large-scale to assist the village organisations in the adoption and use of these designs with such local modifications as may be necessary.

Urban Water Supply and Sanitation

The Sixth Plan document had noted that "while the pressing need of providing adequate water supply and sewerage facilities in the larger cities, especially in the high density areas populated by the low income groups and economically weaker sections, must continue to receive priority, greater attention needs to be given in the Sixth Five Year Plan to the needs of smaller and medium size towns which have been neglected in the past (p.400). Unfortunately, during the Sixth Plan also, the water supply needs of the smaller and medium towns continued to suffer because of the constraint of resources and the emphasis on provision of water in the rural areas. Although the constraint of resources still continues, it is felt that the needs of the smaller and medium size towns with regard to water supply and sanitation facilities can no longer be ignored. Therefore, augmentation and improvement of water supply facilities in the urban areas, especially in medium and smaller towns, will also have to be attempted during the Seventh Plan to the extent possible.

According to the available information, about 115.48 million people in urban areas (77.8 per cent of urban population) had been provided with water supply facilities at the end of March, 1981. It is expected that the coverage would have been 133.91 million (81.1 per cent of urban population) by the end of the Sixth Plan. Although the average coverage in the country is above 81 per cent, it is below 50 per cent in certain States. The above figures also do not reflect properly either the inadequacy of the water supplied or the deprivation of the urban poor. The urban poor,-due to their low paying capacity and also due to the peculiar conditions governing their settlement patterns, are generally deprived of adequate water and sanitation facilities. Water and sanitation, therefore, has been accorded a high priority in the programme of Environmental Improvement of Slums. The high rate of incidence of death and disease in urban poor settlements can be attributed largely to the poor quality of water and sanitation facilities.

As regards sanitation, reports indicate that by the end of Sixth Plan only 57.27 million (33 per cent of the urban population) people could be provided with sanitation facilities. In view of the huge backlog and the severe overall resource constraint as well as the poor financial condition of the local bodies, it is necessary for the smaller towns other than Class-I cities to adopt cheaper methods of sanitation. Several feasibility studies have been carried out in the area of low-cost sanitation technology in urban areas with the UNDP assistance. These techniques should prove useful in achieving the maximum coverage possible. Central assistance is provided to the low-cost sanitation schemes under the Centrally sponsored scheme of Integrated Development of Small and Medium Towns. Following the recommendation of the conference of State Ministers held in New Delhi in January 1983, that additional resources for the programme be mobilised, HUDCO has agreed to finance 50 per cent of the cost of the low-cost latrines projects.

Central Sector

Water supply and sewerage are the principal infrastructure facilities having a direct bearing on the quality of life of the urban people. The provision of these facilities in urban areas is highly capital-intensive and has a fairly long gestation period. At present, the capital expenditure of local bodies is met mainly from Plan funds. However, Plan funds are limited in magnitude. Hence even dynamic local bodies which have the capacity to undertake new projects are seriously constrained in their efforts to improve services. To overcome this situation, as already indicated, it is proposed to set up a National Urban Infrastructure Development Finance Corporation.

In order to give a boost to the low-cost sanitation schemes in the rural areas, a specific provision of Rs. 4 crore has been made.

For monitoring and development of management information system, a provision of Rs. 1 crore has been included for strengthening and expanding the existing monitoring cells. In view of the large magnitude of work to be done in the areas of water supply and sanitation to fulfil the Plan objectives, a considerable amount of research is called for. The fields which need to be explored in particular are testing of improved simple and effective treatment methods including desalination, re-use of backwash water and more effective methods of low-cost sanitation in rocky and other difficult hydro geological formations. The Plan, therefore, makes a provision of Rs. 6 crore for this purpose.

A new scheme to involve the voluntary agencies to implement Plan programme thereby enlisting community participation in the execution and maintenance of water supply schemes in the rural areas is being introduced in the Seventh Plan, for which a provision of Rs. 2.5 crore has been made.

Eighth Five Year Plan: 1992-97 (Volume I)

Housing

The overall magnitude of the housing problem confronting the country, viewed over a span of 20 years from 1981 to 2001, is estimated to be 23.3 million dwelling units in terms of backlog and 63.8 million new dwelling units 1.omprising of 32.6 million in rural areas and the balance 31.2 million in urban areas to meet incremental housing needs.

The role of the Government in this area would be to create an enabling environment, to remove constraints to housing activity of various sections of the population, to promote a substantial increase in the supply of housing and basic services, to support standardisation and upgradation of the housing stock and to stimulate rental housing. The State would address specifically to the needs of the houseless, poorer households, SC/ST, women and other vulnerable groups. The long term objective is provision of "Shelter for All". Given the competing demands on available resources, however, the achievement on this score will inevitably need to he spread over a reasonable span of time.

Urban Development

The present urban pattern, its form, composition and distribution is such that, unless positive public interventions are made, the present differential and disparities cannot be mitigated. A well-coordinated strategy for promoting development of the small and medium towns, together with a strategy for a sustainable and self- supporting nature of development of metropolitan cities, should form the focus of urban development strategy for the Eighth Plan. An Action Plan to operationalise the development strategy for small and medium towns should consist of strengthening the regulatory/ organisational base of urban local bodies and providing an appropriate investment package on related infrastructure and employment promoting activities. This may require pooling of programmes of different sectors.

Financing of metropolitan development should, in principle, he through internal resources and self-sustaining in nature.' However, significant efforts are required in terms of institutional strengthening, resource mobilisation and also legislative support.

Eighth Five Year Plan: 1992-97 (Volume II)

Introduction

Urbanisation is a natural consequence of economic changes that take place as a country develops. At the same time, urbanisation helps to contribute to the growth process at large. This is manifest in the increasing contribution of urban sector to national income. For instance, in 1950-51 the contribution of urban sector to India's GDP was estimated at only 29 per cent, which increased to 47 per cent in 1980-81 and is likely to rise to 60 per cent by the turn of the century.

The positive role of urbanisation is often over-shadowed by the evident deterioration in the physical environment and quality of life in the urban areas caused by widening gap between demand and supply of essential services and infrastructure. This results from increasing population, pressure on urban centres, most of which are financially and organisationally ill-equipped to respond to infrastructural needs. Public investment in urban infrastructure has also been less than adequate. The challenge of reorienting the urbanisation process, thus, lies in overcoming the infrastructural deficiencies and taking the best advantage of economic momentum inherent in urbanisation.

Urban Scene

The urban population of India according to the Population Census 1991 was 217.18 million spread over 3768 urban agglomerations/towns. The urban population has been growing at a much higher rate than the total and the rural population and as a result, its proportion in the total population has increased from around 11 percent in 1901 to about 26 percent in 1991. Also, the rate of growth of population has steadily risen from decade to decade except during 1981-91 when it was lower than the earlier decade.

There are wide variations amongst regions/States in the level of urbanisation. The Union Territories of Delhi (92.73 per cent) and Chandigarh (93.63 per cent) are the most urbanised in the country and the urban proportion is the lowest (8.47 per cent) in Dadra and Nagar Haveli. Among the major States, Maharashtra is the most urbanised with 38.73 per cent of its population living in urban areas, followed by Gujarat (34.40 per cent) and Tamil Nadu (34.20 per cent).

Inter-state variation in the annual rate of growth of urban population and urban-rural growth differential (URGD) is more revealing. Except in Kerala, Gujarat and Maharashtra, the URGD is lower in all other States during 1981-91 than in 1971-81. Conspicuous deceleration of urban growth during 1981-91 was noticed in Bihar, Orissa, Karnataka and Uttar Pradesh.

The urban areas in the country, excluding Assam, Jammu and Kashmir, consist of 300 Class 1 urban agglomerations/cities, 345 Class II urban agglomerations/towns, 947 Class III urban agglomerations/towns, 1,167 Class IV urban agglomerations/ towns, 740 Class V urban agglomerations/towns and 197 Class VI urban agglomerations/towns, making in all 3,696 urban agglomerations/towns. The distribution of urban units among States and Union Territories is quite uneven. A comparison of decadal growth rate of urban population by size classes suggests significantly higher growth rate (46.9 per cent) in class I towns compared to negative growth rate in class V and VI towns. However, if adjustment is made for re-classification of towns in different size classes in 1981 and 1991 censuses the difference in the decadal growth rate among the different size classes of towns is less marked.

The Class I urban agglomerations/cities accounted for 65.20 percent of the urban population of the country in 1991. A further break-up of the population of cities indicates that a majority (50.5 per cent) of the population of Class 1 urban agglomerations/cities lives in 23 metropolitan urban agglomerations/cities with a population of more than a million each. These cities account for roughly one-third of country's urban population. Furthermore, in India there are four mega cities namely Bombay, Calcutta, Delhi and Madras, with a population of more than five million each in

1991. Almost one-fourth of the population living in Class I urban agglomeration/cities in the country lives in mega cities.

The population in Class I urban agglomerations/cities has continued to increase at a faster rate (46.87 per cent) during 1981-91 than other towns. Considering the common set of towns, the decadal growth rate is 34.5 per cent.

Growth of employment (main workers in urban India during 1981-91 is recorded at 38.0 per cent as against 26.1 per cent in the country as whole. The population growth in urban areas (36.2 per cent) is close to that of employment growth, as the growth rate of labour force during the same period is expected to be higher than that o1 total population growth in urban areas, unemployment/underemployment rate might have gone up. With regard to the composition of main workers for which only four broad categories (cultivator, agricultural labour, household industry and other workers) are available, there is no perceptible change between 1981 and 1991. However, percentage employed in Household industry has increased to 5.6 per cent from 4.9 per cent in 1981.

Thrust of Urban Development Policy

The Seventh Plan asserted that planning of urban development should essentially be supportive of the economic development in the country. It urged making use of industrial location policy to subserve regional and urban planning and suggested that a concerted effort should be made to channelise private industrial investment in the vicinity of small and medium towns to check migration of population to the metropolises. The identification of regional urban systems was suggested on the basis of regional characteristics and needs and functions of each town in its regional context. More explicitly, the needs of the poor were to be taken into account in all physical planning exercises. The following were identified as the major constituents of a comprehensive plan for urban development:

- Planned and integrated development of small and medium towns and cities along with slowing down of growth of the big metropolises;

- Revitalisation of civic bodies;
- Thorough reforms of municipal tax systems and municipal administration in general;
- Concentration on the improvement of slums and the provision of basic municipal services;
- Working out measures for regular devolution of funds from State Governments and
- Establishment of the necessary institutional framework for channelling capital funds for the improvement of urban infrastructure.

Programmes in the Seventh Plan

The Plan emphasised the following major programmes:

- Environmental Improvement of Urban Slums (EIUS) Scheme has been in operation in the State sector since 1974. The scheme bone-fitted about 10 million slum dwellers during the Seventh Plan and another 3.3 million during two Annual Plans (1990-91 and 1991-92).
- A Centrally Sponsored Scheme known as Urban Basic Services was introduced in 1986, with the primary objective of enhancing the survival and development of women and children of urban low income families. During 1990-91, the scheme was revised to bring about functional integration with EIUS and came to be known as Urban Basic Services for the Poor (UBSP) with 100 per cent Central funding.
- Scheme for Integrated Development of Small and Medium Towns (IDSMT) to provide complementary infrastructural support of critical significance was continued. During the Seventh Plan period 145 additional towns were covered.
- Development of National Capital Region around Delhi was aimed at providing infra-structural support to priority towns and the region as a whole.
- In the State sector, provisions were made for infrastructure facilities, civic amenities, and development of State capital projects.

- The Nehru Rojgar Yojana was launched in October, 1989. It is targeted. Towards persons living below the poverty line in urban areas. It has three components viz. Micro-enterprises, Wage employment and Shelter Upgradation.

A significant source of funding in the urban development sector during Seventh Plan and the Annual Plans 1990- 91, 1991-92 was external assistance. Total utilisation of external aid in 1990-91 alone was approximately Rs. 280 crore.

Emerging Issues

The review of urban policy framework in historical perspective indicates that until the Sixth Plan (1980-85), the urban policies mainly addressed problems like housing, slum clearance, slum improvement and upgradation, preparation of Master Plans, development of small and medium towns, strengthening of municipal civic administration etc. The Seventh Plan made a new beginning by explicitly recognising the problems of urban poor which were seen to be linked with creation of employment opportunities. It is now being recognised that urban policies can directly contribute to achieve the goals of poverty reduction and removal of unemployment and under employment. During the last decade, the growth rate of employment in the urban areas averaged around 3.3 per cent per annum, while the employment growth rate in the rural areas dropped to about 1.6 per cent for males.

Thus, urban areas have to be enabled to absorb larger increments to the labour force. Further, promotion of non-agricultural activities, Upgradation of skills and infrastructure development of smaller towns will need added impetus.

The most glaring problem has been the high incidence of marginal employment and urban poverty. It is estimated on the basis of NSS 43rd round (1987-88 data) that 41.8 million people are below the poverty line. It is recognised that the incidence of marginal and low income employment is mostly in the informal sector, which accounts for large share of total employment in large cities. What is needed is Upgradation of informal sector occupations and their integration with the urban economy at large.

The gap between demand and supply of infrastructural services has been continuously widening. Increasing pressure of population, particularly concentration of urban population in large cities and metres and escalating per capita cost of providing urban services account for deterioration of infrastructure services and amenities. The worst sufferers are the poor, whose access to the basic services like drinking water, sanitation, education and basic health services is shrinking.

Unabated growth of urban population has made the problems of urban housing more severe. The accumulated backlog in the urban housing along with the housing needs for the additions to the urban population has aggravated the problem further, resulting in proliferation of slums and squatter settlements and decay of city environment.

Fast growth of urban population, spread of urban areas and spurt in secondary and tertiary activities have led to urban transport problems like severe traffic congestions, slowing down of vehicular movement, high air and noise pollution, longer journey hours, increasing costs of travel etc. Urban transport is an important service sector and plays a crucial role in the development of the urban economy and the time has come to take stock of the urban transport scenario.

In the context of the growing demand for urban services, the rationalisation and the augmentation of revenue system have not made commensurate progress resulting in increasing dependence of urban local bodies (ULB) on the financial assistance from the States and Central Government. Own revenues of the local bodies are not adequate even to meet operation and maintenance expenditure. In the case of smaller LJLB's, the weak financial position is also combined with lack of organisational and technical capabilities.

The weak financial and organisational base of ULB's has, in turn, led to highly subsidised and inequitable supply of various urban services with critical dependence on State grants.

Much of the ills of urban housing and resource mobilisation in larger urban areas can be perhaps attributed to the problems inherent in the urban land market. While urban development programmes have to depend largely on a well coordinated land development programme, the existing legal and administrative machinery has impeded supply and development of serviced land. Also, very little efforts have been made to mop up the large appreciation in values of real estate particularly in metropolitan cities.

The role of ULBs has weakened progressively over the last two or three decades. In recent years, some of the functions performed earlier by the ULBs have been transferred to State level bodies, including Urban Development Authority and Functional Bodies. This process needs to be reversed so as to foster stronger and more responsive local governments, reflecting local initiatives, perceptions and priorities.

A corollary to the above process is exploration of avenues through which private initiatives can find a greater role in urban development programme. The role of private sector needs to be expanded. The extent and the manner in which private developers can contribute to urban renewal and squatter settlements and peripheral areas in metropolitan regions (including residential and trunk infrastructure development) needs assessment.

Attention needs to be focussed not only on the growing challenges of urbanisation but on the relationship between urban and rural development. The rapid transformation in the country's urban scenario must be taken into account and provided for, in order that urban growth becomes compatible with healthy socio-economic development of the nation. It will be necessary to take note of the prevailing dichotomy in rural and urban development and evolve a mechanism for bringing about rural-urban cohesion in the management of growth. This can be achieved through the process of spatial planning, which is an integrating concept that makes it possible to achieve the composite development of human settlements while stimulating economic growth. Spatial development plans would need to be prepared keeping in view the "growth centre" concept. This will provide a framework for identification of "nuclei of development" and lower order centres" where investments could be attracted, depending upon their infrastructure level and growth potential.

The Perspective

Population projections made by the Expert Committee, indicate doubling of India's urban population in two decades i.e. 1981-2001. Growth rate of labour force in urban areas is expected to be even higher. However, the 1991 census recorded significantly lower urban population than that projected. Yet, it may not be prudent to be guided by this transitory trend. Population projections, have been made on the basis of a longer term trend of annual growth of urban population with base year population corrected on the basis of 1991 census. The overall level of urbanisation by the turn of the century is likely to be less than that projected earlier, but absolute addition will still be quite large (148 million during two decades). Moreover, a higher share of population in "million plus" cities imply proportionately higher burden of demand for urban services and also higher per capita cost in real terms.

Thrust Areas in the Eighth Five Year Plan

In the light of experiences gained during the Seventh Plan and the two Annual Plans and also taking into consideration the emerging issues and perspective as indicated above and as elaborated in the Report of National Commission on Urbanisation (1988), the thrust areas for the Eighth Plan will consist mainly of more effective implementation of the strategies adopted during the Seventh Plan and partly in formulation of new strategies. The overall Seventh Plan strategy of urbanisation being supportive of economic development with appropriate location of industry and other employment generating activities will be continued. The programmes for the urban poor and for the small and medium towns will have the same focus, but the content and manner of implementation of these programmes will be made more comprehensive and compatible with the overall strategy at the State level. Resource mobilisation and programmes aimed at strengthening of institutions will be given a concrete shape. The distinctive features of the Plan are as follows:

- Spatial and economic dimension of planning for the urban sector needs to be consolidated and operationalised.
- Convergence of all related programmes to create the desired impact in small and medium towns beyond the threshold level is necessary.
- The key to success of urban development strategy lies in taking measures-legal, financial and organisational — for enhanced and equitable supply of urban land.
- Private and public sectors have to act in tandem for urban infrastructure and housing. Innovations in funding pattern and role of private developers in specific areas need to be explored.
- In view of the deteriorating environmental conditions caused by both natural and man-made factors, the conventional city plans should be modified to incorporate the measures needed for restoration of healthy environment.
- Programmes to deal with the problem of urban poverty should be developed in integrated manner emphasising both employment generation and access to basic services involving community level organisations.

Specific Thrust Areas of Eighth Five Year Plan:

1. Macro strategy for urban development with explicit recognition of rural-urban linkages has to be evolved. In particular, the benefits of accelerated pace of agricultural development should be taken advantage of through appropriate utilisation of backward and forward linkages. This, together with appropriate location policy for development of industry and other major employment generating non-agricultural activities, can provide an effective avenue for absorption of surplus rural labour force.
2. As a corollary to the above macro level strategy, an integrated plan of hierarchy of rural and urban settlements needs to be

evolved. This will imply introducing explicitly spatial dimension.

3. Particular emphasis will be placed on the development of small and medium (S and M) towns which serve as an important link between the village and the large cities. In order to realise the objective of more balanced distribution of urban growth both in terms of its distribution over space and also by size class of urban areas, the small and medium towns have to act as important centres of attraction, in terms of economic opportunities, to the potential migrants not only from villages but also from urban areas to large cities. To operationalise this planning approach, the integration of this strategy for development of small and medium towns in a spatial context with the existing district planning process may be attempted. The concept of GEMS as identified by the National Commission on Urbanisation will be kept in view for this purpose.
4. The programme implementation approach has accordingly to undergo a change from the present practice of implementing urban development programme in an ad-hoc and isolated manner. Not only the physical infrastructure but also the economic infrastructure should form part of urban development programme. The policy of locating industries in rural areas only at a short distance away from the metropolitan or large cities is only symbolic of dispersal policy. Instead, it will be worthwhile to promote industries in small and medium urban centres having the desired impact on decentralisation of urban growth. It would also be necessary to plan for more efficient land use and economic regeneration of old city areas in the metro region keeping in view the new Industrial Location Policy which aims at more flexible approach to location of industries in the metro region. Similarly, the programmes of the Ministries of Agriculture, Rural Development and Telecommunication need to be oriented to small towns which primarily serve as Rural Service Centres.

5. In order to achieve better co-ordination of various related programmes within the Ministry of Urban Development, the programme of IDSMT, housing and infra-structural development programmes of HUDCO, and also employment generation scheme under NRY can be suitably integrated. Identification of towns and cities should be made on a selective and priority basis and the investment plan properly coordinated and placed above the threshold level to have the desired impact. Prioritization should be done in the first instance, with regard to primary economic functions (eg. rural growth centres, service towns, tourist towns, industrial towns, etc.) and later integrated with service level deficiency in the urban areas.
6. Increasing reliance on institutional finance which needs to be dovetailed to an overall plan of infrastructure support in the urban areas is necessary.
7. With regard to the problem of urban poverty and unemployment, the NRY can be made more effective by identification of potential and more appropriate activities, and by suitable organisation at the district/local level and people's participation.
8. With regard to the access of the urban poor to basic services like water supply, sanitation, health and education, a combined package of UBSP and EIUS may provide effective means of overcoming the problems.
9. Resource mobilisation measures of the metropolitan Governments, including rationalisation of existing tax and non-tax resources, and the need for devolution of funds from the State to the Local Government need an urgent plan of action.
10. Legal bottlenecks (for example, Urban Land Ceiling and Regulation, Transfer of Property, Land Acquisition and Rent Control Acts) need to be removed. This aspect has been examined in detail by the National Commission on Urbanisation and also incorporated in the draft National Housing Policy. A time bound action to effect necessary

amendments to these Acts is now called for. Rationalisation of regulatory framework is also necessary as a complementary measure.

11. A decentralised framework of urban Government with necessary participation of local communities and opinion leaders in planning, implementation and monitoring of urban development programmes is another prerequisite for the success of urban development strategy. In addition to the enactment of the Nagar Palika Bill, which is a necessary but not a sufficient condition for efficient urban development, other normal management improvement schemes, including national and local level training programmes and delegation of administrative functions and responsibilities, will help the process. In case of large city government, shift from one centralised authority to a system of smaller area-based committees may be more effective in delivery of urban services.
12. In view of the large size and the complexity of urban development programmes, institutional support and delivery systems at town and area level (for large cities) need to be developed in the immediate future.
13. It is necessary to examine the feasibility of developing appropriate specialised organisations at the Centre and State level to deal with financing and development of urban infrastructure.

Eighth Plan Programmes

Given the above thrust areas of the Eighth Plan, the Plan programmes, covering both the State and the Central sectors have been worked out in detail. While most of the programmes are extension of those of the Seventh Plan and 1990-91/91-92 Annual plans, the content, physical coverage and funding pattern have been revised in most cases in accordance with the thrust areas of Eighth Plan.

Integrated Development of Small and Medium Towns: The Integrated Development of Small and Medium Towns

(IDSMT) scheme was initiated by the government in 1979-80 with a view to reducing the migration of population from rural areas to large cities, generating employment by creating resource generating ventures in the small and medium towns and providing sufficient infrastructure facilities in these towns. The scheme provided for Central assistance on matching (50:50) basis with a ceiling of Rs.40.00 lakh, which assumed the form of a loan repayable in 25 years. Until March 31, 1991, a total of 457 towns had been covered under the scheme for which the loan assistance released was Rs. 162.73 crore.

The scheme has broadly served its objective but it has not had the desired impact on the hinterland. Delays in land acquisition and4ffvel-opment and inadequate counterpart funding by the States/UTs have been identified as major bottlenecks in the scheme.

Therefore, the Eighth Five Year Plan envisages a fresh approach to the development of the towns, dovetailing the activities under the employment generation programmes into the supportive infrastructure development programme with a view to:

i generating employment opportunities to reduce the rural-urban and urban-urban migration;

ii developing growth centres for the betterment of rural hinterland adopting a regional approach;

iii providing infrastructural facilities to support such employment generation activities; and

iv evolving resource generating schemes for local bodies for meeting the expenditure on operation and maintenance of the infra-structural facilities so created. The IDSMT scheme is intended to cover objectives (ii), (iii) and (iv) and objective (i) forms part of larger framework of employment generation.

To overcome the financial constraints inherent in the original IDSMT, the reformulated approach envisages that the scheme should not depend solely on budgetary finance but should seek support from institutional finance. The budgetary provisions should be used mainly for the provision of seed capital to the

State Corporation/local bodies for generation of funds and for critical infrastructure which does not have any direct return.

The coverage of the scheme will be in towns with population between 20,000 to 3 lakh.

The guidelines for the scheme indicate the criteria and the order of priorities for selection of towns. The actual selection of the towns is, however, being left to the State Governments.

The scheme will make the towns with a population of 20,000 to 50,000 the prime target, while the inclusion of towns in 50,000 to 3,00,000 category and less than 20,000 category will be on a selective basis.

The schemes eligible for central assistance will depend on the category as well as special characteristics of the town. Central assistance will be available in general for the following activities:

1. Strengthening of link road facilities;
2. Provision of bus terminals;
3. Development of market yards;
4. Industrial sheds;
5. Water supply;
6. Construction/upgradation of road and side drains;
7. Development of Shopping Centres;
8. Provision of tourist facilities; and
9. Localised drainage works.

Land acquisition and development have been a bottleneck. The modified scheme seeks to tackle this problem by excluding payment of land acquisition cost from the Central share and by stipulating that land for the scheme is to be made available within a year of approval. Access to institutional funds need not be limited to local bodies and urban development authorities. Moreover, the borrowers are expected to adopt a basket type approach so that the expenses incurred on the non-remunerative side and for the weaker sections are made up through adequate returns from the remunerative components. The projects under the scheme will have to be comprehensive covering all facets of development including social services and amenities, and be based on the long term Master Plan/Development Plan of the town within its district or regional context.

Environmental Improvement of Urban Slums: The scheme was made an integral part of the Minimum Needs Programme in 1974 and transferred to the State Sector. The scheme is applicable to notified slums in all urban areas and aims at provision of basic amenities like water supply, services, storm water drains, community baths and latrines, widening and paving of existing lanes and pathways and street lighting. During the Seventh Plan, the scheme provided for a per capita expenditure of Rs.300 against the target of 76.91 lakh slum dwellers, 99.78 lakh slum dwellers were covered during the Seventh Plan. During 1990-91, the targeted number of beneficiaries was 15.40 lakh, against which the achievement was 19.35 lakh. The per capita expenditure was enhanced to Rs.525 from 1991-92. During the Eighth Plan, the scope of the EIUS is being widened to ensure that the EIUS, the Urban Basic Services Programme, the NRY and the Scheme of Liberation of Scavengers form a coordinated whole. Assurance of providing tenurial rights and evolving feasible cost recovery mechanism are important pre-conditions for the success of the programme in a longer term context.

Urban Basic Services for the Poor: The Urban Basic Services Scheme (UBSS) was initiated on a pilot basis in 1986, with the involvement of UNICEF and the State Governments. The Programme aimed at child survival and development; provision of learning opportunities for women and children and community organisation for slum population. The services, meant to be delivered, included environmental sanitation, primary health care, pre-school learning, vocational training and convergence of other social services at the slum level.

The Urban Basic Services for the Poor (UBSP) is a revised scheme based on the experience of UBSS. The revised scheme includes assistance to mentally retarded and handicapped children, rehabilitation of alcoholics and drug addicts, and special programmes for street children. It also enables formation of registered societies/cooperatives of slum dwellers at the community level. The scheme is to operate on the principle of convergence of programmes aimed at the urban poor and limited to those slums covered by EIUS. The Central Government will give Rs. 175 per capita for provision of social services in the first year of a new project. In addition, the State Government will provide Rs. 525 per capita for physical amenities. From the second year onwards the per capita provision will be limited to the recurring component of Rs. 88 per capita. This will be shared on matching basis between the Centre and the State. The scheme will also include provisions for strengthening of Urban Local Bodies, NGOS, some physical works, and creation of an organisation for monitoring and evaluation and organisation of marketing assistance.

Nehru Rozgar Yojana

The Nehru Rozgar Yojana was launched in October, 1989. It is targeted towards persons living below the poverty line hi urban areas (i.e. households with an annual household income of Rs.11,850 at 1991-92 prices). Within the target group of the urban poor the Scheduled Castes and the Scheduled Tribes will have special coverage through earmarking of funds for these sections. The NRY consists of the following three schemes:

Scheme of Urban-Micro Enterprises (SUME)

The SUME is designed to encourage unemployed and under-employed youth to take-up self-employment ventures in all urban settlements. The scheme envisages that 30 per cent of beneficiaries should be women. The scheme has loan-cum-subsidy component and the training and infrastructure component. Under the loan and subsidy component, 25 per cent of the project cost is given as a subsidy, subject to a ceiling of Rs.5,000 for SCs/STs and women and Rs.4,000 for others. It is now proposed that loans up to Rs.30,000 per unit may be given by banks. The training component is aimed at up-gradation of technical and commercial skills of the beneficiaries. Infrastructural support in relation to common facility centres, job centres, design centres technology upgradation, marketing etc., is provided. Up to 30 per cent of the funds earmarked for training and infrastructure support can be used for this purpose.

Scheme of Urban Wage Employment (SUVVE)

This scheme is designed to provide employment to the urban poor through the creation of socially and economically useful assets in the low income neighbourhoods in towns with a population below one lakh. Works like community centres, common work sheds, common selling places for the poor, paving of lanes, low cost water supply, construction of drains and sewers, pay and use community baths cum latrines and children's ponds could he included in the scheme. The material labour ratio is 60:40. While the unskilled labourers are to be paid statutory minimum wages, the skilled labourers would receive market wages. The beneficiaries of the scheme would be the urban poor. The works under the scheme have to be departmentally executed.

Scheme of Housing and Shelter Upgradation (SHASHU)

The scheme aims at providing employment for persons involved in housing; and building activities. The scheme has two components viz. training and subsidy cum-loan assistance. The training component is meant for skill upgradation of masons, carpenters, plumbers, sanitary workers, electricians and others engaged in construction trades as well as infrastructure support for common facilities to beneficiaries and machinery equipment to training institutions. The scheme is operative in urban settlements having a population between 1 lakh and 20 lakh with relaxation in the population criteria for hilly states, UTs and new industrial townships. HUDCO is monitoring this component of NRY and also provides the requisite institutional finance.

Sharing of Expenditure and Operation: The training component of SUME and SHASU has been entirely provided for by the Central Government. The remaining expenditure under SUME and SHASU has been shared on 50:50 basis respectively between the Central Government and the State Governments. The

SUWE expenditure has been shared on 80:20 basis between the Central Government and the State Governments. During Eighth Plan period, the expenditure under all the three schemes is proposed to be shared between the Central Government and the State Government uniformly on 60:40 basis. At the State level, a State Urban Development Agency will monitor the NRY. At the district level, the District Urban Development Agencies will be entrusted with the implementation of the scheme, while at the town level it will be entrusted to the Urban Local Bodies. The community structures created under Urban Basic Services for the poor will be mobilised for the NRY, as it will be implemented in convergence with other schemes.

Scheme for Educated Unemployed of Employment Generation in Urban Localities (SEEGUL)

This scheme (which is under review) in towns with a population above one lakh seeks to provide self employment opportunities for the educated unemployed. The scheme aims at providing training to beneficiaries for the enhancement of their technical skills. The scheme is targeted at all the unemployed persons who are matriculates, ITI diploma holders or have attended a Government sponsored technical training course of at least six months duration and whose family income does not exceed a specified level.

National Capital Region Planning Board (NCRPB)

The Regional Plan - 2001 for the National Capital Region approved by the National Capital Region Planning Board (NCRPB) has the following objectives:

- reducing pressure of population in Delhi and
- achieving a balanced and harmonious development of the National Capital Region.

The specific aims of the NCR Plan are:(i) containing the growth of Delhi UT within a manageable population size of 112 lakh by 2001 AD, (ii) moderate growth of Delhi Metropolitan Area (DMA), excluding Delhi UT, to accommodate a total population of 38 lakh by 2001 AD, and (iii) induced growth of the rest of the region to hold 49 lakh of urban population in towns/complexes identified for priority development i.e. 19 lakh additional population in priority towns between 1990 and 2001 AD.

The main thrust areas during the Eighth Plan are as follows:

- Large scale employment generation in priority towns by making available developed land;
- Development of Regional infrastructure: Transport, and Telecommunications;
- Development of local infrastructure in priority and DMA towns; and
- Development of State highways and transmission and distribution system for power in the State grid.

The NCR Plan envisages that the State Governments will play a role in operationalising the programmes, conceiving appropriate schemes/projects, financing and implementing the programmes. The Central Government is expected to play a lead role in the implementation of the development programmes. A conducive financial and legal climate will be created to enlist the participation of the private sector. The HUDCO and other financial institutions are also expected to finance the infrastructure development programmes in the NCR sub-regions.

The activities proposed to be taken up during the Eighth Plan are as follows:

- Land Acquisition and Development for residential use and economic activities;
- Development of Sub-Regional Centres;
- Development of Counter Magnet Areas;
- Institutional strengthening for Plan Implementation;
- Upgradation of regional roads;
- Development of Power Transmission and Distribution; and
- Augmentation and Rehabilitation of Urban Infrastructure in DMA and Priority Towns.

The NCRPB is to be provided outlays, through the budget of Ministry of Urban Development, for extending loan assistance to

States/Implementing Agencies. The States/Implementing Agencies will have to provide funds on a matching basis for land acquisition and development, development of regional centres and development of counter magnet areas while financial institutions such as HUDCO will be involved in local infrastructure schemes. In addition, schemes relating to National Highways, Expressways, Railways, Telecommunications and Power are proposed for which funds may be provided by the Central Ministries.

Urban Mapping and Research and Training

There is presently no agency to compile and maintain the requisite data and maps for preparation of developmental plans of towns. In order to fill this gap, a three tier Urban and Regional Information System is proposed to be created at the national, the state and the local levels. Preparation of large scale base maps with the help of aerial photographs for about 50 fast growing towns is proposed. These maps may also be used for assessment and monitoring of property values in large cities.

Spatial Planning Approach, to achieve maximum coordination between the sectoral and spatial plans as well as total investment plan for the region is to be adopted during the Eighth Plan. This will require preparation of regional plans by States, in which endeavour the Central Government will extend necessary technical assistance for carrying out pilot studies in representative regions/districts and for drawing up an Implementation Plan linked with various programmes.

The planning units will also be strengthened to carry out this task of preparation of an Urban Development Strategy Paper for the State which will outline the developmental priorities of each town based on the economic function and role of the town within its district/regional context.

It is expected that during first three years of the Eighth Plan, exercises under the above two paras will provide the base for orienting future programmes of urban development sector to a long-term development plan of each priority town/city in a regional centre.

Urban Transport

The transport problems of urban areas, and specially those of the metropolises, have not received due attention in the past. Meanwhile, the traffic has continued to multiply with the result that the urban transport infrastructure in almost all large cities is on the verge of a breakdown. In the absence of reliable public transport, people are compelled to resort to private vehicles, which has aggravated congestion, pollution and energy intensity. There is no single agency to plan, coordinate or execute transport policies and programmes in urban areas.

It is in this context that the subject of planning and coordination of Urban Transport was entrusted to the Ministry of Urban Development in 1986 and in 1988-89 an Urban Transport Consortium Fund was created, which has since been employed to assist State Governments in taking up feasibility studies for Urban Transportation Systems. This appears to be a modest achievement because the objective of this was to involve the concerned Ministries of the Government of India, State Governments, financial institutions and local bodies in planning, coordination and execution of urban transport projects.

The Eighth Plan will continue the Consortium Approach initiated earlier. It may be worthwhile to consider the creation of a financial institution for funding urban transport projects on soft terms as also to explore involvement of private/joint sector agencies in the development of transport systems. The research and development priorities during the Eighth Plan include - development of Urban Bus and introduction of energy efficient transit systems. The participation of the Ministry of Railways in developing mass rapid transport system in mega cities appears to be crucial. A comprehensive study of urban transport is also long overdue and is proposed to be undertaken during the Eighth Plan.

Eighth Plan Outlay

The outlays on urban development sector during the Eighth Plan reflect the reorientation of urban development strategy and thrust areas. Thus, the IDSMT for which actual expenditure during the Seventh Plan (1985-90) was Rs. 80.03 crore is being enhanced to Rs. 145 crore as central assistance in its modified form. This will be supplemented by larger loan assistance from HUDCO. A complimentary programme in the water supply sector for towns below 20,000 is also envisaged with Central assistance of Rs. 50 crore. For the scheme of UBSP, an amount of Rs. 100 crore has been earmarked. The outlay on NCRPB will be Rs. 200 crore as compared to Rs. 35 crore during the Seventh Plan. This Central assistance has to be matched by contribution from the State Governments in accordance with the investment plan prepared by the NCRPB. The outlay on urban development in the State sector is also being raised from Rs. 1,633 crore in the Seventh Plan to Rs. 3,984.88 crore during the Eighth Plan. Similarly, for the Central sector, the budgetary support is being raised from Rs. 168 crore in the Seventh Plan to Rs. 692.10 crore during the Eighth Plan.

Housing

Introduction: The dimensions and problems of housing need to be viewed in the overall environment of human settlement. The physical dwelling unit is not the sole element of housing; equally important is the provision of basic services like potable water, sanitation, drainage and electricity. Further, the type and location of housing is inextricably linked to the employment and affordability of the occupant.

Housing has been primarily self-help activity for the majority of the households. Increasing population pressure on land and infrastructure and associated high cost have made proper housing inaccessible to the poorer segments of the population, necessitating State intervention initially as a welfare activity and now recognised as a social and economic imperative. In a developing country like India, problems of urban housing have been more evident, both because of exponentially increasing land and construction cost and deteriorating quality of life in congested urban pockets. Sheer number of additional housing required to meet the needs of the growing urban population presents a formidable task. If we add to this the unserviceable housing stock in rural areas the task assumes frightening proportions. However, the facts that housing is one of the major employment generators and that motivation for ownership of housing is an important element in the mobilisation of domestic savings, make the task worth our endeavour. Housing is not to be treated as a marginal or welfare sector which is a drain on productive resources but to be recognised as a major economic sector.

In this context, the housing policies and programmes, while accepting that housing is essentially a private activity, have to recognise that State intervention is necessary to meet housing requirements of a majority of vulnerable sections as well as to create an enabling environment for accomplishing the goal of "Shelter for All" on a self-sustaining basis.

Housing Scene

Housing stock in urban areas was estimated at 54.1 million in 1961. This increased to 18.5 million in 1971 and further to 28.0 million by 1981. In the rural areas, housing stock grew from 65.2 million in 1961 to 74.5 million in 1971 and 88.7 million in 1981. The earlier projections of National Buildings Organisation (NBO) put the 1991 housing stock of rural and urban areas in 1991 at 106.2 million and 42.6 million respectively.

A comparison of housing condition in rural and urban areas over the last 10 years, as revealed from the different NSS rounds data, suggests that while proportion of pucca houses has increased over time, the service level has not improved. For example, between 38th and 44th round (1988-89) percentage of pucca house in rural areas has increased from 16.7 per cent to 27.1 per cent and in urban areas from 57.6 per cent to 71.0 percent. In rural areas 'no latrine' households have marginally decreased from 91.4 per cent to 89.2 per cent.

According to the National Buildings Organisation the total backlog of housing is estimated at 31 million in 1991, of which 10.4 million is in urban areas. Taking into account the revised figures available from 1991 census, the backlog of housing shortage in urban areas is going to be little lower. Absolutely houseless families were, however, only 6 lakh in 1981 and are likely to be only a little higher in 1991.

Service deficiency is equally alarming. In 1985, only 28 per cent of urban population had access to proper sanitation and 27 per cent of the urban population did not have a source of safe water within reasonable distance. Urban housing crisis has manifested itself in many ways of which the most significant is the growth of slums and squatter settlements. It is estimated^ that about 48.8 million persons are living in" slums in 1990. About 40 per cent of this population will be in million plus cities.

As against the above magnitude of shortage, it would be useful to understand the capital formation process in this sector and particularly the relative role of public and private .sector in the creation of housing stock.

An attempt was made by the Sub-Group on Housing Finance (1990-95) to estimate the share of formal sector in total housing investment. The 'formal sector' includes direct budgetary allocations and also net financial assistance through financial agencies like GIC, LIC, UTI, Commercial Banks, Provident Fund and also HFIs like HDFC. This share was estimated at 16 per cent in 1987-88, which leaves a balance of 84 per cent to the 'informal sector' that includes households themselves and public and private sector employers extending housing loans to their employees.

Review of Seventh Plan and Annual Plans (1990-92)

Social housing programme in urban areas and rural housing programme for landless labourers and artisans under the Minimum Needs Programme (MNP) formed the thrust of the Seventh Plan. Role of institutional finance and promotion of building material technology was also given due priority in the Seventh Plan. However, the Plan outlay of the order of Rs. 2424.34 crore, comprising Rs. 2168.34 crore in the State Sector and Rs. 256.00 crore in the Central sector, was only 1.1 per cent of total public sector Plan outlay. Including Indira Awas Yojana under rural development, the outlay works out to about

1.3 percent. Even within the social service sector, housing accounted for only 7.63 per cent of Plan outlay. During the two Annual Plans of 1990-91 and 1991-92, while the Central sector outlay was raised to Rs.128 crore, the State sector outlay remained at the same level.

Rural Housing

The scheme of allotment of house sites and construction assistance to rural landless workers and artisans including SCs and STs was initiated in 1971 as a Central sector scheme which was later transferred to State sector in 1974. This scheme is a part of the Minimum Needs Programme. Under the MNP, higher priority was accorded to this scheme during the Seventh Plan, setting apart a sum of Rs.576.9 crore. As many as 43.2 lakh house sites, as against the target of 29 lakh, were allotted and construction assistance provided to 22.5 lakh families. During 1990-91 and 1991-92 the outlay provided was Rs.129.65 crore and Rs. 128.91 crore respectively. An estimated 7.74 lakh additional beneficiaries got House-sites in 1990-91 and 4.24 lakh received construction assistance.

Indira Awas Yojana

The Ministry of Rural Development is operating this fully subsidised rural housing scheme as part of rural employment programme for providing houses to the SCs/STs and freed bonded labour. It now forms a part of Jawahar Rozgar Yojana (JRY). The objective of this scheme is to develop a viable micro- habitat, provide housing and ensure a base for higher level of earning for the beneficiaries. A sum of Rs. 12,700 per unit for plain areas and Rs. 14,500 per unit for difficult hill areas is given as grant under this scheme to the State Governments for housing, sanitation and infrastructure. During the Seventh Plan, 6.87 lakh dwelling units were constructed at an estimated expenditure of Rs. 699.58 crore and for the year 1990-91 the target achieved was 1.71 lakh, at an anticipated expenditure of Rs. 187.96 crore.

Housing and Urban Development Corporation (HUDCO) has been financing several rural housing schemes by earmarking 15 per cent of its resource allocation to such schemes. Till June 30, 1991, 2.15 million houses entailing project cost of Rs. 1247.80 crore were sanctioned under these schemes. The loan releases worked out to Rs. 503.17 crore. About 1.6 million units were completed which accounted for 46 per cent of the total units funded by HUDCO. In addition, HUDCO is financing other shelter options like village abadi improvement and building materials.

Urban Housing

Housing schemes in the urban areas were as under:

- Social housing schemes for different income groups, operated by the States and city level agencies with budgetary -support and loans from HUDCO, LIC and other financing agencies;
- Housing and shelter upgradation scheme for the urban poor, as part of Nehru Rozgar Yojana (NRY) introduced in November, 1989 in cities with population between 1 and 20 lakh;
- Footpath Dwellers Night Shelter Scheme introduced in 1988-89 to provide shelter, and later on also sanitation facility, to the pavement dwellers in cities;
- Scheme taken up by the cooperatives for different income groups with the help of Apex Federations and loans from LIC, HUDCO and scheduled banks;
- Various other schemes including ownership housing scheme for Central Government employees, working women scheme, environmental improvement of urban slums and home improvement schemes, rental housing schemes for employees of public sector undertakings, sites and services schemes operated by various State Governments.

The EWS housing was the most significant component of social housing scheme, as part of the 20-Point Programme during the Seventh Plan. It was contemplated that the public sector would provide sites and services to the beneficiaries. In addition, the beneficiaries would be provided a loan of Rs. 5,000 per unit repayable in a period of 20-25 years at a concessional rate of interest. In practice, however, the scheme operated in a different manner - State agencies either promoted housing units on HLJDCO norms or plots plus cost loan up to HUDCO prescribed ceiling. During the Seventh Plan, 7.14 lakh EWS and 1.67 lakh LIG units have been constructed under the 20-point programme.

Achievement under NRY has also been quite significant. Total subsidy and loan through HUDCO under this component are estimated at Rs. 196 crore for the period 1989-90 to October 1990 covering 5.73 lakh units. The impact of Night Shelter Scheme has so far been limited with an estimated outlay of only Rs.2.27 crore during the last two years benefiting 26,200 pavement dwellers.

During the Seventh Plan, 2.3 lakh dwelling units have been completed under cooperative housing schemes with a total investment of Rs. 1087 crore.

It has been estimated that under the various programmes in Public Sector about 10 lakh houses have been constructed/upgraded each year during Seventh Plan.

New Initiatives in Housing Finance

There has been a marked growth in the flow of credit from the financial institutions and banks to the housing sector during Seventh Plan period. The contribution of LIC increased from Rs. 185 crore in 1984-85 to Rs. 825 crore in 1990-91, Provident fund advances from Rs. 153 crore to Rs. 478 crore during the same period and banking sector's contribution from Rs.186 crore in 1986-87 to Rs.387 crore in 1990-91. The most important development in strengthening the housing finance in recent years has been the setting up of an apex institution - the National Housing Bank (NHB) - as a subsidiary of the RBI under the NHB Act, 1987. The important activities of the NHB are:

- establishing Home Loan Account System - a contractual deposit scheme linked to guaranteed loan from scheduled banks. Till December 1991, 5.5 lakh accounts have been opened in various commercial banks and housing finance institutions;

- liberalised lending guidelines and increased funding from banks; .
- refinance at less than commercial rates of interest of HUDCO and bank's scheme as well as land development and shelter programme of public and private agencies; and
- guidelines for regulation of housing finance.

During 1990-91 total refinance of HFIs was put at Rs.478.39 crore including Rs.161.10 crore for rural housing.

Larger flow of institutional finance has been most evident in relation to the phenomenal growth in HUDCO's operations during the Seventh Plan as well as two Annual Plans. During the Seventh Plan, HUDCO's sanctions for various shelter related schemes totalled Rs.2834.18 crore and loan release Rs. 1796.85 crore, facilitating construction of about 20 lakh dwelling units. Loan operations of HUDCO registered a growth of-133.5 per cent compared to previous Plan.

The Life Insurance Corporation of India (L1C) has also emerged as an important contributor to the housing finance. The contributions by LIC comprising of direct lending, hulk loans and assistance to State Government apex bodies and loans to its own housing finance subsidiary totalled around Rs. 1,570 crore during the Seventh Plan. The contribution was as high as Rs. 825 crore during 1990-91.

A number of specialised housing finance subsidiaries have been floated by the scheduled commercial banks. There has also been spurt in the number of housing finance companies operating in the private sector.

Building Materials, Technology Promotion and Extension

Efforts to effect savings in construction cost through promotion of low-cost and innovative building materials and technology are important as building materials account for a major part of the total cost of construction. Some of the efforts made during the Seventh Plan and two Annual Plans in this direction were:

- setting up of Building Materials and Technology Promotion Council (BMTPC) to provide an appropriate platform for technology transfer and application in the shelter sector and promoting commercial production of innovative materials, with use of industrial wastes like flyash, red-mud, phospho-gypsum as well as agricultural wastes;
- conducting experimental housing projects in different geo-climatic regions by NBO and developing appropriate design and safety measures in zones prone to land slides;
- setting up a network of building centres as a Centrally Sponsored Scheme, under which over 200 Building Centres have been identified out of which 77 are operational; and
- increasing involvement of non-Governmental organisations in supplementing Governmental efforts in the field of technology transfer.

National Housing Policy

The Global Shelter Strategy adopted by the United Nations in November. 1988 calls upon different Governments to take steps for the formulation of a National Housing Policy (NHP) to achieve its goals. The Ministry of Urban Development prepared a draft NHP which was tabled in both Houses of Parliament in 1988. Subsequently, another draft was prepared and widely circulated and discussed and broadly endorsed by Urban Development and Housing Ministers' Conference held in Delhi in October, 1990. The objectives of draft NHP and the major components are described below:

The basic objectives of the policy are:

- to assist all people and in particular the houseless, the inadequately housed and the vulnerable sections, to secure for themselves affordable shelter through access to developed land, building materials, finance and technology;

- to create an enabling environment for housing activity by eliminating constraints and by developing an efficient system for the delivery of housing inputs;
- to expand infrastructure facilities in rural and urban areas in order to improve the environment of human settlements, increase the access of poorer households to basic services and to increase the supply of developed land for housing;
- to undertake, within the overall context of policies for poverty alleviation and employment, steps for improving the housing situation of the poorest sections and vulnerable groups by direct initiatives and financial support of the State;
- to help mobilise resources and facilitate expansion of investment in housing in order to meet the needs of housing construction and upgradation and augmentation of infrastructure; and
- to promote a more equal distribution of land and houses in urban and rural areas and to curb speculation in land and housing in consonance with macro-economic policies for efficient and equitable growth.

Supply and Management of Land

Inadequate and inequitable supply of serviced land particularly in urban areas has been the most significant bottleneck for the promotion of housing activities and urban development at large. The aspect of supply and management of land needs to be viewed both from a larger dimension of regional development and city/town level growth. It would imply that all development in city/region should take place within the framework of a comprehensive development plan with spatial linkages and with planned provision of basic services. At the local level, an appropriate policy package incorporating the following is envisaged:

- control of unregulated peripheral development on agricultural lands;
- optimising overall land use; and
- appropriate urban redevelopment policy.

Rural Housing

The two central measures with regard to rural housing are:

1. Promoting use of local building materials and technologies suited to different geoclimatic regions and preventing indiscriminate and commercial exploitation of such materials;
2. Creating an enabling environment for primarily self-help housing including new construction, additions and upgradation by the rural people through enactment and effective implementation of laws for conferment of homestead rights and provision of house sites with minimum infrastructure.

A few other specific measures suggested as a part of NHP are:

- Prevention of alienation of homestead on tribal lands;
- Avoidance of unnecessary displacement of rural settlements due to developmental projects;
- Rehabilitation of households affected by natural calamities;
- Rural housing/development agencies for supply of credit and materials on flexible terms suitable to local requirements;
- Giving special attention to the needs of Scheduled Castes, Tribes and other disadvantaged groups;
- Linking Rural housing with the programmes of IRDP and JRY for accentuating the pace of rural housing and also other related programmes of asset creation and employment generation; and
- Setting up of a suitable institutional structure for strengthening existing rural development agencies at State, district and local level to meet the needs of the housing sector.

Legal and Regulatory Framework

Creation of appropriate legal and regulatory framework is perhaps the must important contributing factor for enhancing supply of land and housing. The NHP has taken cognizance of it while specifying measures under each component (eg. Rural Housing, Supply and Management of Land). Specified measures suggested in draft NHP are:

- Provision in the land reforms and other relevant acts for conferment of homestead rights to the occupants, and ensuring proper rehabilitation of those dehoused;
- Review of slum improvement laws to provide for conferment of occupancy rights;
- Revision of Master Plan standards, building byelaws, laws and infrastructural standards to reduce cost of land and construction and promote low cost materials and technology;
- Amendments to the Land Acquisition Act for quick acquisition of land in public interest and negotiated compensation to the landowners, delinking provision of land from determination of compensation;
- Amendments to Urban Land (Ceiling and Regulation) Act, to remove inhibiting effects of legislation on enhancing supply of land without diluting its social purpose and also as a specific measure, imposing vacant land tax;
- Amendments to Rent Control Laws to promote investment in rental housing; and
- Procedural simplification measures including building approval procedure, flexible collateral requirements, amendments to NHB Act to provide for speedy foreclosure of mortgages of HFIs refinanced by NHB and introduction of a secondary mortgage system.

Housing Finance

The measures to he taken with regard to housing finance are as under:

- Evolving, over a period of time, a non-subsidised housing finance system the integral linkages of the housing sector with the rest of the economy.
- Targeting of the available capital and interest subsidies to rural and urban poor.
- Introduction of innovative savings and lending instruments to help integrate the housing finance system into the capital markets, by enabling HFIs' access to the funds on a competitive basis with other financial institutions.

- Creating innovative banking/institutional arrangements to cater to the housing credit needs of low income groups in the informal sector through community based system.
- Creation of a suitable environment for developing a secondary mortgage market in order to attract funds from a wide range of investors, including insurance and provident/pension funds and to integrate housing finance with the overall financial system.

The Perspective

According to the estimates made by the Sub-Group on the "Magnitude of Housing Problems" 64.4 million new houses will be needed by 2001. Besides in 1981, there were 14 million units needing upgradation, 1.23 million requiring renovation and 7.5 million needing extension/expansion. To achieve the goal of elimination of houselessness by the turn of the century, it would be imperative to step up investment, public and private in housing.

Taking into account the availability of physical inputs, the Sub-Group had concluded that it would be feasible to construct 21.77 million units with an investment of Rs. 77,590 crore at 1989-90 prices during 1990-95. For the same number of units assumed for 1992-97, the investment requirement would be of the order of Rs. 97,530 crore at 1991-92 prices. If adjustment for 1991 actual population and projected urban population for the year 2001 is made, the target for urban areas will require to be marginally reduced with corresponding increase in rural areas. The requirement of investment in housing (public and private) works out at 12.2 per cent of the total outlay during Eighth Plan.

As against the projected requirement of Rs. 77,590 crore for housing during 1990-95, the overall flow from the formal sector as per existing norms is estimated at around 16 per cent and the Sub-Group on Housing Finance had recommended that the credit support may be increased to at least 20 per cent. It is expected that a large part of the credit flow from the formal sector would come from LIC followed by the commercial banks and provident funds.

The total flow of credit from the formal sector during the Eighth Plan is projected in the range of Rs. 20,000 to Rs. 25,000 crore (at 1991-92 prices).

Core Strategy of Eighth Plan

In line with the National Housing Policy which is a statement of the long term objective, the core strategy of the Eighth Plan consists of creating an enabling environment for housing activity, viewed as an important component of the national economy, by eliminating various constraints and providing direct assistance to the specially disadvantaged groups including rural and urban poor households, SC/ST, physically handicapped, widows and single women. The first objective is intended to be achieved through a set of sub-tasks or instruments as specified below:

1. Expand the provision of basic infrastructure facilities in rural and urban areas in order to improve the overall environment of habitat and enable appropriate conditions for the majority of the households to have access to housing;
2. Remove major legal constraints to increase supply of serviced land as well as rental housing by way of substantially amending the existing statutes like Urban Land (Ceiling and Regulation) Act, Land Acquisition Act, Transfer of Property Act and Rent Control Act;
3. Provide stimulus and support for housing on expanded scale through enhancing the flow of credit both by way of mobilisation of additional resources for housing by tapping capital markets and additional savings and by directed credit from public financial institutions. The Planning Commission had set up a Working Group on Finance for Housing sector for the Eighth Five Year Plan (1992-97) to consider ways and means to step-up flow of institutional finance to the housing sector. The group has made a number of recommendations in its report including projection of flow of credit from various financial institutions and HFIs and greater access of EWS rural households to the institutional credit. Fiscal incentives, procedural simplification and setting up of a wider network of

HFIs particularly in remote areas will act as enabling factors to achieve the objective.

4. Role of private developers in fringe area development of metropolitan region/large cities, while keeping safeguards including environmental standards for the majority of present residents, not only in housing hut also in trunk infrastructure needs to be explored;
5. Promote use of low cost building materials and cost effective technologies intended for both saving in use of scarce resources like brick, cement and steel and provision of affordable housing to poor segments of population;
6. Promote self-help housing as well as shelter upgradation, which is as important as creation of new housing stock, by providing better access to finance, land, materials and technology through appropriate delivery systems to the poorer segment of the rural population;
7. Establish links between formal and informal credit network including community level association and voluntary agencies operating in the housing sector;
8. Provide financial and institutional support, through both formal and informal systems, to environmental improvement and in-situ upgradation programme in the slum areas and other low income congested pockets in urban areas; and
9. Establish an effective Management Information System for housing and urban infrastructure accessible to both private and public development agencies With regard to the second objective of direct assistance, disadvantaged groups;
10. Evolve special assistance programme in the form of subsidy preferably in kind, differential rate of interest and delivery support system for specially disadvantaged groups including vulnerable sections of SCs/STs, widowed women of poorer sections of the society and also those affected by natural calamities.

Eighth Plan Priorities and Programmes

The most significant aspect of the Eighth Plan, compared to the Seventh Plan, in respect of housing sector is that it is set against a definite National Housing Policy, Thus, the priorities and programmes of the Eighth Plan are to be viewed as a sub-set of the long-term policy document. Two other related dimensions that need to be taken into account are: the focus on liberalisation of the economy in the recently announced macro economic policy and directed attention to rural housing.

With the above mentioned thrust areas, the important programmes in the housing sector are described in the following sections. Some of the programmes overlapping with urban development and water supply and sanitation sectors, e.g. NRY, Environmental Improvement of Urban Slums (EIUS), Low Cost Sanitation Programme need to be cross referenced.

Rural Housing

House Sites and Construction Assistance: The scheme was included in the State Sector as a part of MNP and formed the core of the rural housing programme during Seventh Plan. This scheme has two components-provision of free House Sites and construction assistance with varying proportion of subsidy and loan in different States. Construction assistance is planned to benefit 3.5 million families directly as part of MNP. This is exclusive of other special rural housing programmes intended for specific beneficiary groups.

While the scheme will be continued in the Eighth Plan, it would be appropriate to take up fresh surveys and enumeration of the landless families to assess the need for continuing the scheme in the light of the fact that at the beginning of the Seventh Plan, as against the balance of 13.67 lakh identified (in 1971) landless labourers and rural artisans, the coverage during Seventh Plan was much higher at 43.21 lakh. However, construction assistance programme of the component seems to be lagging behind and thus needs stepping up. There is also a need to revise the cost norms of dwellings, the subsidy and beneficiary component of the most of the rural housing schemes of the State Government so as to bring an element of uniformity and achieving the intended coverage of rural households. The following specific measures are suggested during the Eighth Plan:

- Construction assistance (subsidy component) to the poorest section of the rural poor should preferably be given in kind supported by an appropriate delivery system covering all regions of the country;
- All schemes should have loan and beneficiary contribution to promote self-help;
- This programme should he tied with that of building centres so as to promote low-cost housing and locally available material/appropriate material and technology. Training of masons and other construction workers should be an integral part of this scheme;
- Innovative housing finance system should be set up in rural areas and more difficult regions like North Eastern States not only for facilitating supply of credit but also to mobilise the rural savings.

Indira Awas Yojana (IAY)

The Indira Awas Yojana was introduced in the Central Sector in 1985-86 as part of the Rural Landless Employment Guarantee Programme and has continued as part of JRY. The objective was to enable the construction of houses for SCs/STs and freed bonded labourers based on the wage-employment programme.

The endeavour during the Eighth Five Year Plan period will be towards evolving an approach to rural housing which leads to setting up of truly integrated micro-habitats and address this scheme to specially disadvantaged group including the poorest segment of SC/STs and freed bonded labour.

Housing and Urban Development Corporation (HUDCO)

HUDCO was incorporated in 1970, with the mandate to ameliorate the housing conditions of low income and weaker sections. HUDCO finance is available to institutions like State Housing Boards, Development Authorities, Improvement Trusts, Cooperative Societies etc. HUDCO is earmarking 55 per cent of its sanctions for EWS and LIG housing projects and balance 45 per cent for MIG, HIG, rental and commercial housing projects. HUDCO is the only national agency with predominant consideration for EWS both in terms of loan operations and design/technology adoption.

HUDCO is supporting the State Plan programme in housing and urban infrastructure sector through the following broad components:

- Rural housing;
- Urban housing;
- Slum upgradation; and
- Urban infrastructure schemes.

HUDCO has been getting equity support from the Government of India. Up to the end of Seventh Plan period, the equity support to HUDCO by the Government totalled Rs. 457.77 crore and another Rs.46 crore during 1990-91 and 1991-92. The subscribed capital up to November 91 was Rs. 165 crore. HUDCO has also built up reserves and surpluses. In addition to this, HUDCO has been getting funds from LIC, GIC, UTI, and NHB. HUDCO has been permitted to raise funds through tax free bonds from time to time.

From 1989-90, HUDCO is undertaking lending for the following Plan schemes:

- Shelter Upgradation Component of Nehru Rozgar Yojana.
- Low Cost Sanitation Scheme for Liberation of Scavengers.
- Night Shelter Scheme for Pavement Dwellers

The subsidy component in case of the above mentioned schemes is also being routed through HUDCO so that loan releases can be linked with the release of subsidy.

Eighth Plan Perspectives

HUDCO: With the public sector going in for less and less of direct house construction activity and with emphasis on its role as facilitator and enabler, the lending activities of HUDCO during the Eighth Plan are expected to concentrate more on land and infrastructure development and direct support to EWS schemes in rural and urban areas. After taking into account the repayments of loan receivable during Eighth Plan and also internal reserves, equity support to HUDCO and its access to Internal and Extra Budgetary resources (IEBR) would need a step-up during the Eighth Plan.

With manifold step-up in bar operations for urban infrastructure including low-cost sanitation, there is a need for adopting a finalised approach to this activity, has been proposed to strengthen the infrastructure wing of HUDCO, create a specialised technical and management group and eventually set up a separate organisation in near future.

Income Norms and Ceiling Costs: The income limits for eligibility and the existing cost of construction have been revised for various housing schemes for the Eighth Plan as compared to those in the Seventh Plan.

Cost Reduction Measures: Scarcity of conventional building materials like cement, brick and steel and the high energy intensity of the modern construction activity have pushed up construction cost. Thus, the average cost of construction at 1990-91 prices of the lowest design housing in urban areas using the traditional building materials is estimated at Rs. 15,000 and Rs. 30,000 for EWS and LIG category respectively, which may be well beyond the means of the poorer segment of this group of population. Therefore, it is imperative to change over to appropriate and cost-effective technologies which bring down the costs.

Large scale application of low-cost technologies has been hindered by lack of interface between developers of technology and users, lack of standardisation, and lack of an incentive structure.

Building Centres: The question of S and T activities in the housing sector has assumed crucial importance in view of scarcity of building materials, high energy intensity of construction activity and rising cost of development of land. While research endeavour in previous plans has helped in the evolution of appropriate design and development of innovative building materials, the technology has not been accepted due to lack of interface between users and innovators and an incentive mechanism. To foster the technology transfer to the grass root level, a centrally sponsored scheme for establishment of Building Centres was initiated in 1988. The Building Centres are intended to promote the use of new alternate materials and construction techniques through demonstration, production and training in different rural/urban regions. About 213 Building Centres have been established so tar out of which 77 are fully operational. An outlay of Rs. 1 crore each during 1990-91 and 1991-92 was provided for the scheme. The Ministry of Urban Development has constituted an Expert Committee to review this scheme.

Building Materials and Technology Promotion Council: To bridge the gap between laboratory development and large scale field application of innovative materials and technologies, facilitate mass production on commercial scale and develop an integrated system for technology transfer and delivery, the Government of India set up in 1990 the Building Materials and Technology Promotion Council (BMTPC). This Council is an inter-ministerial and apex institution. The Council is coordinating with Central and State agencies to evaluate, validate and adopt new technologies to scale up proven ones and to facilitate the setting up of production units. During the Eighth Plan, the Council will focus on technology transfer and promotion of building materials, venture capital and other support to entrepreneurs in innovative materials, sponsoring of R and D studies, taking up prefabrication technology and dissemination of technology.

Eighth Plan Thrust Areas

The following are major thrust areas during the Eighth Plan:

- Strengthening of Building Centres to provide effective means of propagating low cost building materials and construction technologies at grass root level with at least one building centre in each district and in addition there could be specialised rural/regional building centres;

- Promotion of large scale production of building materials based on industrial and agricultural wastes through an appropriate incentive structure and by achieving target utilisation of wastes like flyash, phopsho-gypsum, agricultural residues and natural fibres;
- Increasing use of locally available building materials in rural housing programmes;
- Development of planning and design norms and codes of practices to promote low-cost energy-efficient technologies and to reduce the cost of housing; and
- Promotion of cost-effective industrialised construction systems to the extent of 10 to 15 per cent dwellings to be set up by public housing agencies.

Strengthening Management Information System

The Draft National Housing Policy has stressed the need for the setting up of an appropriate management information system at various levels for housing and urban services in order to support policy formulation, monitor implementation of various schemes and periodically evaluate their impact. A Sub-Group on Housing Statistics set up by the Planning Commission had identified various gaps in the data collected at present and had suggested strengthening of the present system of data collection. The Sub-group proposed a Housing Census by the Registrar General of India (RGI) and periodic surveys on important indicators of housing conditions, access to service, expenditure and savings pattern and residential pattern and land prices etc. It is proposed that the RGI will take up the census in 1995 in urban areas.

For effective flow of data from all the areas in a State, it has been proposed to strengthen the present three tier system operated by NBO starting at city level which involves additional technical support at central and state level, data processing facilities and incentives at local levels for data reporting. It is proposed to identify the responsibilities of different data collecting agencies in the sector in the Central Government, Reserve Bank etc. and coordinate their efforts through the strengthened set-up for MIS in the Ministry.

Eighth Plan Outlay and Physical Target

An attempt has been made to indicate the contribution of formal sector as defined in an earlier para. The contribution of formal sector is estimated to be about 10 lakh new units annually during the Seventh Plan. This is expected to increase to 13 lakh annually during Eighth Plan. This includes loan assistance through State and Central Plan, HUDCO and other HFIs (Public Sector) as well as fully subsidised Indira Awas Yojana (IAY). Share of the rural sector in terms of units, mostly contributed through state sector programme, is estimated at 51 per cent which is higher than that of the Seventh Five Year Plan. The proportion of EWS Housing is derived from the existing norms of HUDCO. In case of Upgradation, the projected units include kucha and semi-structures only with rural sector receiving greater thrust during Eighth Plan. The projected number of building centres implies that there will be at least one centre in each district.

The Plan outlay is estimated at Rs. 6377.02 crore of which as much as Rs. 3581.67 crore will be in State Sectors. Emphasis during the Eighth Plan will be to promote and provide housing through institutional finance and other instruments. Accordingly, in the central sector, equity support to HUDCO will be about Rs. 155 crore and Internal Extra Budgetary Resources (IEBR) will be around Rs. 860 crore. A new scheme of Rural Housing aimed at supplementing the efforts of State Governments in provision/upgradation of housing units, has been proposed by the Ministry of Rural Development for implementation during Eight Plan. The support provided will be in the nature of equity/financial assistance to HUDCO as also State organisations and for improvement of supply of delivery system.

Water Supply and Sanitation

Introduction: Safe drinking water supply and basic sanitation are vital human needs for health and efficiency. Disease and death, particularly of children, every year and drudgery of women are directly attributable to lack of these essentials.

The requirement of drinking water is at present only 7 to 10 per cent of water available on the surface and 4 to 5 per cent of the ground water potential. The National Water Policy announced in 1987 gives the highest priority to drinking water supply. Since substantial quantities of water are consumed by several other users, it is necessary that the competing demands for water such as for irrigation, industry and domestic use etc. are balanced and fully taken into account while drawing up a comprehensive plan for water management.

Sanitation, both in urban and rural areas, continues to remain neglected. Funds availability has been a constraint in the urban areas, while schemes for rural sanitation were not able to evoke response. These, therefore, require restructuring based on the lessons learnt from the good work done in certain places in Gujarat, Tamil Nadu, West Bengal, Bihar, Uttar Pradesh, Andhra Pradesh, Rajasthan, Madhya Pradesh and Maharashtra.

Review of Performance: Drinking water supply and sanitation are State subjects. The Ministry of Urban Development (MUD) was the nodal agency for this sector at the beginning of the Seventh Plan. Subsequently, rural water supply and sanitation have been transferred to the Department of Rural Development (DRD), while the administration of urban water supply and sanitation has been retained with the MUD. Rural water supply was an important constituent of the State sector MNP during the Seventh Plan. In 1986, the National Drinking Water Mission (NDWM), popularly known as the "Technology Mission" was launched in order to provide scientific and cost-effective content to the Centrally Sponsored Accelerated Rural Water Supply Programme (ARWSP). In 1986, it was decided that a portion of the funds, made available under the rural. employment programme and the Indira Awas Yojana, should also be utilised for rural sanitation. Rural sanitation programme was also added to the State sector MNP from 1987-88. In November 1986, a new Centrally Sponsored Rural Sanitation Programme (CRSP) was launched. In the later half of the Seventh Plan, the UNICEF also came forward to support Government efforts for provision of rural sanitation in Andhra Pradesh, Uttar Pradesh, Rajasthan, West Bengal, Gujarat, Madhya Pradesh, Tamil Nadu and Maharashtra.

An analysis of the performance revealed that:

- Based on the available indicators, performance of the Centrally Sponsored Accelerated Rural Water Supply Programme and National Drinking Water Mission appears to be satisfactory;
- Concept of "total environmental sanitation" was absent. Linkage of rural sanitation programme with primary health care, water availability, removal of illiteracy and women welfare needed attention. Sanitation Programme should have been taken as a package of service rather than mere construction of latrines;
- In actual implementation of water supply schemes, the needs of backward and poorer classes of population were often neglected;
- There was a wide gap between provision for safe disposal of waste water and drinking water supply in urban areas;
- Pricing of water, implementation of billing and collection mechanism for water tariff, etc. needed considerable improvement;
- Wastage and leakage of water was substantial and needed corrective action;
- There was need for greater cost-effectiveness in the existing programmes and its possible integration with similar programmes.

Arising from the analysis, the following issues emerge as areas of concern:

- Operations and maintenance of water supply and sanitation installations in the country is badly neglected. A huge backlog of maintenance is building up at a time when resources are scarce;
- Due to inadequate sewerage and lack of waste treatment facilities, pollutants which enter ground water, rivers and

other water sources contribute to increased incidence of water-borne diseases. It is necessary to take timely steps to prevent further pollution and at the same time provide for progressively cleaning of existing rivers and water resources;

- Water supply and sanitation needs of small towns, particularly in the range of population up to 20,000, received inadequate attention. These towns have a poor financial base and can, therefore, not execute and maintain appropriate water supply and sanitation schemes. The endeavour would, therefore, be to ensure that water supply is provided in all towns, including small towns which are essentially over- grown villages and potential urban nodal centres for the rural hinterland surrounding them;
- It has been recognised that the earlier efforts to discourage manual scavenging and liberate families engaged in this inhuman task have not borne satisfactory results. Therefore, it is suggested that ongoing programme for liberation/rehabilitation of scavengers should be streamlined to cover legislation, involvement of NGOs and adequate funding;
- There are a number of externally aided projects, mainly based on IDA credit and bilateral assistance for undertaking water supply and sanitation projects. Very often the projects are delayed due to inadequacy of counterpart rupee funding and also due to the projects being poorly implemented. It would, therefore, be quite desirable, that before any such new project is taken up, its funding requirement vis-à-vis resources position and committed liabilities of the State Government and local bodies are examined in depth.

Eighth Plan Approach

The approach to the Water Supply and Sanitation Sector will take into account the following guidelines given in the New Delhi Declaration, which was adopted by the U.N. General Assembly in December 1990:

- Protection of the environment and safeguarding of health through the integrated management of water resources and liquid and solid wastes;
- Organisational reforms, promoting an integrated approach and including changes in procedures, attitudes and behaviour and the full participation of women at all levels;
- community management of services, backed by measures to strengthen local institutions in implementing and sustaining water and sanitation programmes;
- Sound financial practices, achieved through better management of existing assets and extensive use of appropriate technologies.

Objectives: Based on the perceptions gained from an analysis of the performance of the water supply and sanitation sector in the past and the overall approach and strategies adopted in New-Delhi Declaration, the following objectives have been visualised for the next five years:

Rural

- Highest priority to be given to ensure that the remaining about 3000 'No-Source' hard-core problem villages in some states are provided with sustainable and stipulated supply of drinking water by March 1993;
- Equally important would be to ensure that all the partially covered villages having a supply level of less than 40 litres per capita per day numbering about 1.5 lakh including hamlets, are fully covered with safe drinking water facilities by the end of the , Eighth Plan on sustainable basis;
- Ensure that SC/ST population and other poor/weaker sections are covered fully on a priority basis;
- The stipulated norms of supply would be 40 Ipcd of safe drinking water within a walking distance of 1.6 kms or elevation difference of 100 metres in hilly areas, to be relaxed as per field conditions applicable to arid, semi-arid and hilly areas. At least one hand-pump/spot-source for every 250 persons to be provided. Additional 30 Ipcd in DDP/DPAP areas, for cattle to he provided;

- Achieve zero incidence of Guinea worm disease by 1993 and total eradication by 1995, besides progressively finding solutions for other bacteriological and chemical problems like excess fluorides, salinity and iron in water sources;
- Achieve coverage of about 5 per cent of rural population (cumulative) with their full involvement with sanitation facilities by the end of Eighth Plan. Information, Education and Communication(IEC)should be an integral part of rural sanitation programme. In this context, it is desirable to adopt a concept of 'total environmental sanitation' and provide guidelines to the rural population in regard to proper environmental sanitation practices, including disposal of refuse, garbage and waste-water through the mechanism of local village leaders and community organisations and construct bio-gas plants adjacent to the sanitary complexes.
- Convert all existing dry latrines into low-cost sanitary latrines.

Urban

1. Extend safe drinking water facilities to the remaining urban population, so as to achieve the goal of 100 per cent coverage of population by turn of the Century with the following norms and standards:

- 125 Ipcd for urban areas where piped water supply and underground sewerage system are available.
- 70 Ipcd for urban areas provided with piped water supply but without underground sewerage system.
- 40 Ipcd for towns with spot-sources/stand posts. One source for 20 families within a maximum walking distance of 100 metres.

2. Provide a special thrust to drinking water supply in small towns with population up to 20,000 and evolve scheme with appropriate financial support to initiate efforts towards the goal of 100 per cent coverage of population by turn of the century.
3. a. Convert all dry latrines into low-cost sanitary latrines, so that the present scavenging system is completely eliminated in

urban areas. b. Cover the outskirts and fringe areas of big cities with low-cost sanitation facilities either on individual household basis or community basis with "pay and use" system, as appropriate.

4. Execute financially viable sewerage schemes in big cities, State capitals, important pilgrim/tourist centres with cost-recovery from beneficiaries to create waste treatment facilities, with adequate thrust on recycling of treated effluents for horticulture, irrigation and other non-domestic purposes.
5. In major metropolitan cities, take steps to evolve and create a scientific and effective mechanism for the collection, transportation and disposal of solid waste and in the process, convert as much of the bio-degradable material as possible into organic manure. During the Eighth Plan, a few cities having population more than 5 lakh each (as per 1991 census) would be covered with the restructured schemes.

Thrust and Strategies: Based on the experience gained in the recent years and taking note of the issues which have emerged, strategies and Plan thrusts have been evolved to cope with the challenges.

With regard-to operation and maintenance, the following aspects need to be emphasised:

- Water has to be managed as a commodity in exactly the same way as any other resource;
- Supply of water to consumers should normally be based on the principle of effective demand which should broadly correspond to the standard of service, that the users are willing to maintain, operate and finance;
- To ensure that in urban areas, Municipalities/local bodies are free to levy and raise appropriate user- charges for drinking water and sanitation facilities in order to strengthen the financial position of the urban local bodies/Municipalities whereby at least the operation and maintenance costs, if not further development, become self-sustaining;

- In rural areas, water-tariff may not be feasible in all places. However, wherever house- service connections are given, it is suggested that appropriate water-tariff is levied and realised whereby operation and maintenance becomes self-sustaining to the extent possible;
- Private Sector efforts for construction and maintenance of drinking water projects should be encouraged and mobilised to the maximum extent feasible;
- Local bodies, whether in rural or urban areas, should be made responsible for the operation and maintenance of the system installed, with technical guidance from government agencies;
- Appropriate links should be forged between water supply and environmental sanitation (solid and liquid waste management) in the planning of new programmes.

Development has, in its wake, led to increasing pollution of water resources. It is, therefore, suggested that in the Eighth Plan, it should he ensured that the pollution, which is presently taking place, is progressively eliminated through provision of industrial waste and sewage treatment facilities. At the same time, preventive measures will have to be taken to see that new physical assets created as a part of the planning process or otherwise do not add to the problem of water pollution.

The concept of "total sanitation" - covering primary health care, water availability, women's welfare, immunization and provision of sanitation facilities, all linked to cleanliness as a basic human need - will be emphasised. Every effort will be made to adopt a low-cost approach, employing technical and scientific know-how and the experience already gained by several non-Governmental organisations in this regard.

In order to reduce costs, it is desirable that the programmes of drinking water supply and sanitation, both in rural and urban areas, are implemented in a more decentralised manner with the involvement of the people and local institutions at all stages — planning, project formulation, execution, operation and maintenance and monitoring and evaluation. It is also desirable that the district planning machinery is used to provide the necessary technical support to the local bodies for creation and maintenance of installations. While emphasising on efficient exploitation of available water for various uses, it is necessary to take timely steps to see that the sources are recharged and rejuvenated. It will, at the same time, be necessary to ensure appropriate linkage between soil-conservation and land/water management and drinking water supply schemes in order to provide for sustained supply.

While the ARWSP has been operative for almost 15 years now, no detailed evaluation of the programme has yet been carried out. It is desirable that the Programme Evaluation Organisation or some similar body undertakes an evaluation in order to identify changes, if any, required in the concept, the content or the manner of implementation of the programme including the schemes undertaken under Mini-Mission and Sub-Mission Projects of National Drinking Water Mission.

In order to ensure effective operation and maintenance of assets created as in the Seventh Plan, a maximum of 10 per cent of funds under MNP and ARWSP each could be utilised for operation and maintenance. Most States face resource problems and, therefore, tend to neglect maintenance. It is necessary to evolve an effective mechanism for ensuring proper operation and maintenance of existing assets. "Village-water-committees" should be actively involved in the maintenance of drinking water supply schemes and a system of beneficiary participation introduced. Participation of village women and NGOs/voluntary organisations should also be encouraged. The mechanism and the funds available under TRYSEM should be used to impart training, so that trained manpower can be locally mobilised for the maintenance of the assets.

After a careful consideration of the situation as regards rural sanitation, it is suggested that the Rural Sanitation Programme be restructured providing for the following elements:

- all activities under this programme will be undertaken through local body/village panchayat and with beneficiary participation.

- wherever feasible, NGOs will be involved in the implementation of the programme.
- women will he actively associated with the implementation of the programme.
- some contribution should be solicited from the beneficiaries, at least in the form of physical labour, in order to engender among them the realisation that the assets created belong to the local community.

Rural water supply and rural sanitation facilities are essential ingredients in the total programme for rural development. There are many other allied elements which go into the total process of rural development. These include infrastructural aspects like land management, soil conservation, afforestation etc. and social aspects like primary health care, removal of illiteracy, women's welfare, child nutrition, immunisation etc. It is desirable that the thrust and implementation of as many of these programmes as possible get converged, in order to provide for integrated rural development with 'village' as one unit on the one hand, and ' area' comprising of several adjacent villages together, on the other.

Urban water supply and sanitation schemes form part of the State Sector Plan. There has been no direct Central funding during the Seventh Plan. The MUD started dealing with installation of low-cost sanitary latrine and conversion of dry latrines into sanitary latrines under a Centrally sponsored scheme since 1990-91. This programme will be a major thrust in the Eighth Plan. The strategy to be adopted will include:

- change in the municipal bye-laws, wherever necessary, to prevent construction of dry latrines in future.
- conversion of all existing dry latrines into low- cost sanitary latrines by the end of the Eighth Plan.
- introduction of legislative measures, whereby employment of manual scavengers becomes an offence beyond a specified date, well before the end of the Eighth Plan.
- A suitable coordination mechanism will be evolved to ensure that the programme is executed in an integrated and effective manner. The Ministry of Urban Development would involve

financial institutions like the HUDCO and would be responsible in overseeing all aspects of implementation of the programme of replacement of dry latrines and construction of new sanitary latrines, where they do not exist. The Ministry of Welfare would oversee the programme of liberation/rehabilitation of scavengers and their families.

Provision of drinking water and sanitation including solid and liquid waste management facilities in urban areas has been inadequate. A major problem in this regard is the lack of resources with urban local bodies, not only to finance creation of the facilities, but also to operate and maintain them. Almost all urban areas continue to enjoy highly subsidised water, whether it is for domestic use, commercial use or industrial use. The billing and collection mechanism is also weak and faulty and needs considerable improvement. It is necessary to adopt appropriate tariff- structures, as applicable to different strata of population. Cost-recovery should be built in the municipal financial structures and subsidies, where inevitable, kept explicit. Operation and maintenance costs should be fully recovered through adoption of cross-subsidy measures, so that smaller local bodies become self-sustaining, while metropolitan and other big cities are able to meet, in addition, the costs of further developments.

In order to improve efficiency, accountability and public awareness in the management of urban water supply and sanitation, it is desirable to separate the budget for water supply and sanitation from the general municipal budget. The future projects on urban water supply and sanitation should increasingly rely on institutional finance. Cost-recovery through appropriate user-charges under separate budget head, as already tried out in certain municipalities, and strict adherence to time and cost schedule are preconditions for successful implementation of the programme.

In urban areas, apart from strengthening the enforcement machinery to stop theft and pilferage, it is very important to take preventive maintenance measures and ensure that transmission and distribution losses through leakage, are avoided.

It has been felt necessary to evolve and implement a cost-effective special scheme of drinking water supply to small towns with a population up to 20,000 persons with some financial support from Centre on a matching basis under a Centrally sponsored scheme. The details of the scheme and the financing pattern will be worked out by the Ministry of Urban Development in consultation with the Planning Commission, Ministry of Finance and State Govts./U.T.Admns. The MUD will also oversee the management of the scheme.

The Central Plan support to supplement the State efforts in the field of training, research and technology development, management information system, computerised monitoring of rigs as appropriate in rural and urban sub-sectors will need to be continued. Programmes aimed at upgrading the skills of personnel dealing with public health/environmental health engineering activities, transfer of technology from the laboratory to the field, both in regard to material and equipment as well as preventive health, water quality monitoring and surveillance etc., will need to be encouraged. In addition, it will be necessary, particularly in the context of the envisaged large-scale low-cost sanitation programme for elimination of scavenging, to integrate such training with Information, Education and Communication (IEC) support.

Some of the important topics, proposed under the water supply, relate to: community participation, behavioural pattern and technology transfer aspects of water supply; evaluation and assessment of the rural water supply system etc. Studies would be undertaken on the preventive maintenance of water distribution system with reference to leakages and carrying capacities of the mains; leak detection measures; hydraulic analysis and optimum design of the water distribution systems; extension of rapid bacteriological techniques; development of springs for water supplies; development of natural and inorganic coagulants etc. Use of solar energy in the rural water supply; hydraulic rams for the rural water supply in hilly areas; development of package water treatment plants etc. would be given a major thrust. Focus would also be given to R and D on the conversion of brackish water and sea water to drinking water.

In sanitation, the areas for research and development relate to sanitary latrines; integrated bio- gas system for the treatment of excreta and animal wastes and the utilisation of gas; low-cost waste water collection, treatment and recycling for non domestic uses or safe disposal system etc.

Outlays

Keeping in view the constraint of resources and other competing demands, the Eighth Plan provides an outlay of Rs. 16711.03 crore, of which Rs. 10743.03 crore will be under State/UT Plans and Rs. 5968.00 crore under Central Plan for Water Supply and Sanitation Programme. This works out to 3.85 per cent of the total public sector outlays. This includes loan assistance from LIC as well as external assistance from World Bank and bilateral agencies. It is envisaged that sizeable amount of funds will be mobilised outside Plan from the local bodies, the beneficiaries, NGOs, financing institutions like HUDCO etc., particularly for urban sub-sector, in order to achieve the Eighth Plan target.

Ninth Five Year Plan: 1997-2002 (Volume II)

Perspective and Objectives

The level of urbanisation was around 11 to 12 per cent during the first three decades of this century, increasing noticeably in the decade of independence and rising continuously thereafter from 17.3 per cent in 1951 to 25.7 per cent in 1991. The projected scenario indicates a rising trend. The Planning Commission's Technical Group on Urban Perspectives and Policies has projected the urban population at 31.0 per cent of the total population in 1996-97 and 38.0 per cent in 2006-07. During the last four and half decades, some 5-6 million people have been added to urban India every year. The country has one of the largest urban systems with 217.6 million people in 1991, which is projected to increase to 289 million in 2001 and around 605-618 million during 2021-2025. There will be about 40 metro cities in the country in 2001 as against 23 in 1991.

The slow-down in urbanisation during 1981-91 as compared to 1971-81 (36.4 per cent growth as against 46.1 per cent) and the growing concentration of urban population in larger towns are other urban concerns, towards which the Ninth Plan strategies will be directed. The tasks are challenging, for it is mainly in the mega and metro cities that land is a major constraint for undertaking development work. A large part of civic amenities, particularly water supply, sanitation and sewerage, are managed with assets that have outlived their operational efficiency. The required massive upgradation and renovation of these assets, is constrained by high population density and concentrated commercial activities at the locations where these service assets are installed. The lack of comprehensive urban planning in the past to promote regular upgradation and renewal has resulted in a large backlog of development activities.

The key urban concern is the growing gap between demand and supply of basic services. While there has been a steady growth in the housing stock, infrastructure and services, the gaps between demand and supply have been rising, even in terms of conservative norms. It is now well-recognised that these gaps are unlikely to be bridged over the next 5 to 10 years. Many goals of housing, potable water and sanitation that were to be attained by 2001 AD, may require the target point fixed 10-15 years ago to be extended.

In the midst of growing urbanisation, India, nevertheless, continues to live in her villages. As many as 629 million people live in some 580,706 villages, which works out to an average of 1,083 per village. Rural population density is low at an average of 214 persons per sq. km, which brings out the rural development challenges in terms of provision of human settlements-related services of potable water, sanitation, and access to livelihood programmes. Increased per capita cost of the services, Operation and Maintenance (O and M) logistics and recovery of investment are priority concerns.

The rural hinterland has played a critical role in sustaining urbanisation. This is reflected in the indicators of sources of primary inputs, competitively priced labour for urban economic activities, primary funds as reflected in comparative urban and rural credit-deposit ratios and market for urban products. But the unending migration of the rural poor to urban areas may have a destabilising effect on urbanisation and its sustainability. Income and employment opportunities will have to rise in the rural areas, through both the farm and non-farm sectors and habitats and basic services have to be improved so that with rural development and congenial habitats, rural areas emerge as sustainable centres of economic activities and human settlements.

The rural-urban continuum would be strengthened so that gaps between rural and urban lifestyles are reduced. Effective urban strategies and programmes cannot be developed in isolation of those in the rural areas. The Ninth Plan will take cognisance of this ground reality, particularly in respect of three critical components of human settlements development, namely, drinking water, sanitation and housing.

In this perspective, the major sectoral objectives of the Ninth Plan are:

- Development of urban areas as economically efficient, socially equitable and environmentally sustainable entities;
- Accelerated development of housing, particularly for the low income groups and other disadvantaged groups;
- Development and upgradation of urban infrastructure services to meet the needs of a growing population;
- Alleviation of urban poverty and unemployment;
- Promoting accessibility and affordability of the poor to housing and basic services;
- Promoting efficient and affordable mass urban transportation systems in metropolitan cities;
- Improvement of urban environment;
- Promoting private sector participation in the provision of public infrastructure and of the community and NGOs in urban planning and management of specific components of urban services; and
- Democratic decentralisation and strengthening of municipal governance.

Performance Review, Policies and Strategies

The total Plan outlay in the 46 years of planning has been Rs. 8,580 crore on urban development, Rs. 10,430 crore on urban housing, Rs. 15,100 crore on urban water supply and sanitation, and Rs. 19,300 crore on rural water supply and sanitation.

The performance review of the Plan programmes has brought out some of the operational problems. The activities were determined by the availability of funds, which is a common constraint in a resource-scarce economy. This resulted in inadequate coverage of the population and encouraged a top-down approach, with the plans being formulated at the national level on the basis of feedback from the States, with marginal inputs from the functionaries directly working at the grass-roots level. At times, ad-hoc interventions were made, driven often by political and administrative expediencies rather than economic considerations and the ground situation. This has resulted in multiplicity of programmes with varying components directed to the same target group and lack of convergence or proper coordination, sequencing and linkages among them. There has also been poor feedback of experiences from the field to provide the critical ingredients for a peoples-centred and people-oriented planning. The policy framework under the Constitution (73rd and 74th Amendment) Act provides an opportunity to shift the approach in the Ninth Plan.

Some estimates are available on the magnitude of work ahead. In terms of financial indicators, the investment for urban housing has been estimated at Rs. 5,26,170 crore and for rural housing Rs. 1,72,930 crore between 1997 and 2021 for new housing, upgradation and extension, Rs. 70,300 crore to Rs. 3,07,500 crore for different types of urban drinking water systems with the investment being higher for surface than for ground water system. A large part, in some cases, more than one-half, will be the backlog of investment. In a shorter term perspective of 1997-2002, urban housing investment has been estimated at Rs.121,370 crore and for urban water supply at Rs. 26,300 crore and for rural water supply at Rs. 40,000 crore.

In terms of reach-out indicators, new housing stock required is about 9.0 million units in urban areas and 7.7 million units in rural areas during 1997-2002 and about 77.0 million and 63.0 million units in the longer term perspective, extending up to 2021. Housing upgradation has to cover about 7.5 million units and 20.0 million units in urban and rural areas, respectively, during the Ninth Plan period. As regards drinking water, the aim is to cover the total urban and rural population with existing norm and then take up qualitative and quantitative upgradation. Total conversion of dry latrines into low-cost wet latrines is the immediate task in urban areas.

Major sectoral objectives of the Ninth Plan:

- Development of urban areas as economically efficient, socially equitable and environmentally sustainable entities;

- Accelerated development of housing, particularly for the low income groups and other disadvantaged groups;
- Development and upgradation of urban infrastructure services to meet the needs of a growing population;
- Alleviation of urban poverty and unemployment;
- Promoting accessibility and affordability of the poor to housing and basic services;
- Promoting efficient and affordable mass urban transportation systems in metropolitan cities;
- Improvement of urban environment;
- Promoting private sector participation in the provision of public infrastructure and of the community and NGOs in urban planning and management of specific component of urban services; and
- Democratic decentralisation and strengthening of municipal governance.

Water Supply and Sanitation

Drinking water supply and sanitation facilities are very important and crucial for achieving goal of `Health for All'. The Government is committed to provide drinking water to every settlement in the country within 5 years. The Government has also decided to go all out to achieve the goal of expansion and improvement of sanitation facility along with other social infrastructure.

- Government of India (1996), Second United Nations Conference on Human Settlements (Habitat II), National Report, Ministry of Urban Affairs and Employment.
- Planning Commission (1996), Reports of Ninth Plan Working Groups.

Performance Review

Drinking Water (Urban): In the initial period of planning, from the First to the Fifth Plan, the outlay on urban drinking water was considered substantial with respect to the size of the urban population (17.3 to 19.9 per cent) but thereafter, the thrust in the

Plan programme was diverted to rural water supply and sanitation, in spite of the rapidly increasing proportion of urban population which was 23.3 per cent at the time of the Sixth Plan and 25.7 per cent at the time of the Eighth Plan. The proportion of this sector's outlay to total public sector plan outlay marginally increased from 1.28 per cent to 1.38 per cent between the First Plan (1951-56) and the Eighth Plan (1992-97). The likely expenditure in the Eighth Plan was about Rs. 7,000 crore. In terms of the Seventh Plan expenditure, the Eighth Plan expenditure was 274 per cent in nominal terms.

The task in the Eighth Plan was to increase the coverage of access to safe drinking water to about 94 per cent of the urban population from 84 per cent at the end of Seventh Plan and of urban sanitation services to 69 per cent from 48 per cent. While the full feedback on coverage is not available, it has been estimated that in terms of estimated 1997 population, the coverage of urban population is unlikely to increase from the level attained in the Seventh Plan. Adequate investment would be needed to meet the requirements of incremental population for drinking water and sanitation services.

The programme review has brought out the concentration of efforts on State capitals and other major cities and on augmentation and improvement, without any significant additional population coverage, resulting in the efforts being absorbed by population growth. The participation of financial institutions and the private sector was not significant, particularly due to the absence of cost recovery, appropriate tariff rate policies and lack of fiscal and monetary incentives.

In this perspective, a new programme was launched in the Eighth Plan for urban water supply, namely the Accelerated Urban Water Supply Programme (AUWSP), which was targeted to small towns (population less than 20,000, 1991 Census) as these towns had been excluded earlier, had encountered severe problems of water scarcity and the revenue base of the urban local bodies in these was weak. The AUWSP was launched in 1993-94 with a modest outlay of Rs.50 crore, with envisaged funding by

Central and State Governments in the ratio of 50:50. Out of the 2,151 eligible towns (1991 Census), project reports were approved by the Central Ministry for 227 towns for an estimated cost of Rs. 218.50 crore and Rs. 68.62 crore was released to State Governments up to March 31, 1997. The progress was modest, partly because the scheme was launched only in March, 1994 and there were delays in the acquisition of land, change of water sources, procurement of materials and equipments, submission of timely physical and financial reports by States and release of funds by the State Governments to the implementing agencies. These teething problems would be resolved and the activities should go on full stream in the Ninth Plan

Drinking Water (Rural)

The Plan investment during the eight Plans for rural water supply as a proportion of public sector Plan has gone up from 0.15 per cent to 2.47 per cent. The Eighth Plan outlay was Rs. 10,055 crore and the target was to extend the coverage of water supply facilities from an estimated 78 per cent to 100 per cent, covering all the 3,000 spill-over "problem villages" of the 1985 list and 1.5 lakh "partially" covered villages including hamlets. To achieve this objective, schemes were implemented under the State Sector, Centrally Sponsored Accelerated Rural Water supply Programme (ARWSP), Sub-missions for tackling quality problem (QP) habitations suffering from excess fluoride, salinity, iron, arsenic, scarcity of sources, and requiring sustainability of the sources and the systems. The infrastructure and the support programmes like human resource development, education, information and communication, research and development, science and technology, management information system including computerisation of implementing departments and field formations in the States and monitoring and evaluation were taken up.

Subsequently, the State Governments undertook comprehensive surveys during 1991-94 for the Rajiv Gandhi National Drinking Water Mission, which provided the feedback that the tasks ahead were much more than envisaged at the beginning of the Eighth Plan. As on April 1, 1994, there were 1.41 lakh not-covered (NC) villages/habitations and 4.30 lakh partially covered (PC) villages/habitations, apart from 1.51 lakh villages/habitations suffering from acute water quality problems (QP). In addition, the Sundaresan Expert Committee constituted in May 1993 by the Central Department of Rural Development has evaluated the rural water supply programme with special reference to the Mini-Missions and Sub-Missions.

Recent provisional data indicate that the rural water supply programmes have covered 3.40 lakh villages/habitations during the Eighth Plan. The State feedback has further suggested that during the Eighth Plan, after the survey, 1.114 lakh NC, 1.524 lakh PC and 0.11 lakh QP villages/habitations are expected to have been covered leaving a balance of 0.296 lakh NC, 2.776 lakh PC and 1.40 lakh QP villages/habitations as on 1-4-1997. However, keeping in view the field realities, Rajiv Gandhi National Drinking Water Mission in consultation with the State Govts, further revised/updated the number of NC and PC villages/habitations and thus the task for the Ninth Plan would be to cover 0.88 lakh NC, 3.91 lakh PC and 1.40 lakh QP villages/habitations. In terms of population, about 86.74 per cent of the rural population, as per 1991 Census, is expected to have been provided with an access to safe drinking water. The Eighth Plan review has also brought out the short life span of hand pumps, say 5-6 years due to variety of reasons including the general depletion of the ground water table. The Constitution (73rd Amendment) Act, an Eighth Plan initiative, has provided an institutional mechanism for effective decentralisation of activities and the drinking water and sanitation schemes are good candidates for these, especially because community participatory efforts have to play a key role.

There is a need to bring about organisational reforms in the implementation machinery in the Centre and the States to equip them to work effectively in a Mission mode with guidance from the Rajiv Gandhi National Drinking Water Mission Authority and its empowered committees at the Centre and similar Authorities, empowered committees and District Committees in the States to ensure the achievement of goals and inter-sectoral integration and co-ordination.

The Eighth Plan review brings out the need to strengthen the contents of the ongoing Centrally Sponsored Schemes of ARWSP, especially in the light of the lessons learnt, suggestions of the Sundaresan Expert Committee and the feedback from the country-wide evaluation study conducted in 1996 by the Programme Evaluation Organisation (PEO) as also the Comprehensive State Survey on rural water supply. The Ninth Plan strategy would, in this context, give priority to totally uncovered and poorly covered settlements (where the supply is up to 10 lpcd) as well as the severely affected quality problem habitations and then to other habitations. There after progressively raise the present norm of 40 lpcd to 55 lpcd, reduce the distance norm from 1.6 km. to 0.5 km. in plain areas and 100 mtr elevation difference in hilly areas as recommended by the CMs' Conference, held in July 1996 on Basic Minimum Services. Furthermore, installation of piped water supply system should be discouraged, as it has been found to be less dependable by the PEO in their recent country-wide survey. The villagers should be motivated to take over the routine O and M activities and also contribute resources for repair and maintenance.

In rural areas, where piped water scheme is operational or is proposed to be developed, the Maharashtra model may be adopted, which is structured on the basis of strong community participation, through Village Panchayat Committees and Village Water Committees, whose members are directly involved during the construction of different components of the scheme, including in assisting the Maharashtra Water Supply and Sewerage Board in deciding the location of the village works, such as service reservoirs, standposts, etc. and ensuring that the standposts in their jurisdiction are maintained in good running conditions and are properly drained. The Village Water Committees would have at least 50 per cent women members and adequate representation for SC/ST and these local committees are entrusted with the responsibility for house connection. Before these connections are provided, the owner has to ensure that adequate arrangements are made for disposal of sullage water. The village committees are also responsible for ensuring hygienic conditions of all water sources in the villages.

As regards O and M of handpumps, community-based models have been developed in a number of States, particularly in Betul district of Madhya Pradesh, Banda and Barabanki districts of Uttar Pradesh and Midnapore district of West Bengal. The Midnapore model has been recognised as a good practice and is being emulated and adopted by other States. In this model, a Water Committee is established in each village/habitation, two women from the community are trained as caretakers, the beneficiaries raise Rs. 500 per handpump as the initial fund for maintenance and each family contributes 50 paise per month towards maintenance. This has resulted in an optimum level of functional handpumps on a wholly self-sustaining basis with the active participation of the community and the local NGOs.

In this perspective, the Ninth Plan envisages 100 per cent coverage of all habitations with safe water, together with the installation of a quality monitoring and surveillance system all over the country, evolving cost-effective and socially acceptable O and M strategies, re-orienting the structure and functioning of rural water supply planning and implementing agencies and taking all measures to ensure sustainability of drinking water sources. Tackling the problems of drying of sources, providing a role for the beneficiaries and Panchayati Raj Institutions (PRIs) in planning and implementation of the water supply facility are other priority tasks. In view of the resource constraints, it would be necessary to restrict the role of external agencies to priority areas.

Urban Sanitation

The Centrally Sponsored Scheme of Urban Low-Cost Sanitation for Liberation of Scavengers was an important Eighth Plan scheme for urban sanitation. It was first operated through the

Ministry of Home Affairs and subsequently implemented by the Ministry of Welfare. It is being operated through the Ministry of Urban Affairs and Employment (earlier Ministry of Urban Development) since 1989-90. The Eighth Plan provision was Rs. 150 crore in the Central Plan, which was only about 25 percent of the required assistance to meet the objective of conversion of all the existing dry latrines in urban areas of the country numbering 50 lakh units into low-cost pour-flush sanitary latrines and 100 per cent liberation of scavengers on "whole town" coverage basis.

As on March 31, 1997, 760 schemes were sanctioned in 1,155 towns with a total project cost of Rs. 1,062.36 crore, towards which a loan of Rs. 477..09 crore and subsidy of Rs. 363.31 crore was sanctioned. The loan released was only 30.16 per cent (Rs. 143.87 crore) and the subsidy released was 41.23 per cent (Rs. 155.50 crore). The projects were sanctioned to construct 14.52 lakh new units and convert 19.25 lakh dry latrine units into low-cost pour-flush latrines for the individual households and 3,463 community latrines. In terms of actual work done, 6.95 lakh units were completed up to Eighth Plan period out of 33.77 lakh units sanctioned (20.6 per cent). It is expected that at 1991-92 prices, the expenditure during the Eighth Plan was 45.3 per cent of the Plan outlay.

The impact of the programme on the physical and financial front has not been impressive. This is due to a variety of reasons, particularly insufficient schemes provided by the State Governments, delays in preparing documents and papers for sanction of loan and subsidy (separately for each beneficiary), slow release of subsidy due to inadequate physical progress, inappropriate technology, lack of awareness and reluctance of State Governments to give guarantee. An evaluation of the programme in three States, sponsored by the Central Ministry of Urban Affairs and Employment had brought out evidence to show that the objectives of the scheme were not strictly adhered to, the recommended technology was often unsuitable, relatively better-off families took over a substantial number of the pour-flush latrines and funds were inadequate or not available for the superstructure.

Another Centrally Sponsored Scheme, the Ganga Action Plan (GAP), implemented by the Central Ministry of Environment and Forest, has contributed to the improvement of the sanitation facilities in 25 Class I cities along the river Ganga in the States of Uttar Pradesh, Bihar and West Bengal. Interception, diversion and treatment of sewage works and low-cost sanitation units were set up in GAP -I and 792 mld of sewage has been intercepted and diverted and 596 mld of sewage treatment facilities have been installed.

Rural Sanitation

The Eighth Plan outlay for rural sanitation was Rs. 674 crore to cover an additional 2-3 per cent of the rural population, as per the 1991 Census. Recent data show that population coverage by sanitary latrines has increased from 11 per cent to about 16 per cent during the Eighth Plan. This is inclusive of the efforts of IAY, JRY, UNICEF, CAPART and private initiatives, besides the Centrally Sponsored Rural Sanitation Programme (CRSP) and its State counterpart.

As per the existing policy, subsidy under the rural sanitation programme is given to people below the poverty line for construction of individual household latrines and conversion of dry latrines into sanitary latrines. Subsidy is extended to the Panchayats for exclusive sanitation complexes for women, in areas, where adequate space is not available for individual household latrines and other sanitation facilities in the villages/habitations. Interest-free loan is also provided to entrepreneurs/Panchayats to set up sanitary marts and link them to production centres for facilitating easy availability of the materials required for the sanitation programmes. Sensitisation for other sanitation facilities covers drains, soakage/ garbage pits and intensive health awareness through IEC. These activities should be further strengthened and modified, where required.

Ninth Plan Priorities and Strategies

While the provision of drinking water facilities in urban areas in the country has improved over the years, the provision of sewerage and drainage facilities has not received adequate attention. Ideally the water supply and liquid waste management schemes should be integrated. The absence of this integrated approach has resulted in the degradation of the environment, with serious health impact from water-borne and vector-borne infections. In some areas, industrial contamination with heavy metals also leads to severe health hazards. The Ninth Plan Sub-group of the Planning Commission on Environment and Health had concluded that the unsatisfactory progress in supply of safe drinking water and sanitary disposal of solid and liquid waste has contributed to the continued high morbidity from water-borne and vector-borne diseases. The Expert Group on Public Health and the Working Group on Health Care Delivery in Urban and Rural Areas recommended that water quality monitoring and surveillance as well as the projects for urban waste management should be taken up on a priority basis to achieve substantial reduction in morbidity due to water and vector-borne diseases.

Drinking Water (Urban)

The urban drinking water supply strategies in the Ninth Plan would address the priority concerns of universal coverage, adequacy in terms of minimum per capita consumption norms, quality, distance from source as well as regularity of supply, bringing in its wake the policy and operational issues of drying and inaccessible sources of water, recycling of waste water and sewage for non-domestic use, water harvesting, among others. The strategies to promote and strengthen decentralisation of production and distribution systems, privatisation and participation of the community in management and maintenance are expected to not only induct higher efficiency levels and effective reach out but also contain line leakages and wastages. Special attention will be given to strengthen the on going Centrally Sponsored Accelerated Urban Water Supply programme

(AUWSP) to saturate the small towns with population less than 20,000 during the Plan period.

The State and UT Governments should prepare long-term Master Basin River Plans, following the guidelines issued by the Central Ministry of Water Resources, apart from making proper estimates of water needs for drinking, cooking and non-consumption domestic uses like bathing, washing, toilets, gardening, etc. City water management system should have at least a 20-25 year development perspective. Provision should be made to recycle waste water, rain water harvesting, re-use of sewage after appropriate treatment for flushing of sewers and toilets, air conditioning, etc. Over-exploitation of ground water must be avoided to maintain quality and to control water pumping cost. Appropriate legislation and its effective implementation should form an integral part of the strategy. The modified model Bill of the Central Ministry of Water Resources on ground water exploitation may be considered by State Governments for adoption.

Financing of drinking water supply programmes is a crucial issue in urban areas in view of the massive investments required. These are beyond the scope of the Plan, but nevertheless, these would have to come into the sector to meet the goals of the Plan and maintain the sustainability of the human settlements. Further, drinking water and sanitation activities will have to be taken up as an integrated programme, because in the absence of such a linkage, sanitation activities tend to be overlooked. Innovative financial strategies, including alternative leasing instruments and fiscal intervention are called for. Plan funds would be used not only for direct intervention but also as a leverage instrument, a strategy already introduced during the Eighth Plan in case of some urban infrastructure projects. This strategy has to be increasingly adopted to activate and sustain the funds flow from outside the government sector. Equally important is recovery of full cost. New strategies would be gradually developed, in terms of recovery of O and M cost in the first instance and total capital cost later, though subsidy in pricing will continue, more sparingly than in the past.

The delivery and management system has to be strengthened. In the light of the Constitution (74th Amendment) Act, while State agencies may continue to plan and implement capital works, the responsibility of distribution may be progressively decentralised to local bodies, and where feasible, to the private sector, within the policy guidelines of the State Governments. While this process will be initiated with distribution works, in due course capital works may be decentralised. Concerted efforts will be made to enhance the capacity of the municipalities to bridge the gap between their resources and commitments. At the same time, city agencies may continue in mega and metro cities, as long as they operate on sustainable basis.

In view of the massive investment required, it is obviously not possible for either the State Governments or the Central Government to go forward with this magnitude of funds. Institutional sources/ externally aided projects, private sources and community sources would all have to come forward in case we have to provide every body with safe potable water within the stipulated time frame. Alternative strategies, new technologies, cheaper methodologies as also mechanisms like rain water harvesting etc would have to go in a big way to provide alternatives to the present method of handling the work relating to the sector. It is expected that by deferment of some of the less important activities, use of low cost technology, people and private sector participation and better management, the objective of 100 per cent population coverage in Urban area with safe drinking water supply could be achieved with an investment of about Rs. 20,750 crore.

Drinking Water (Rural)

The Ninth Plan strategies for rural water supply would seek to attain universal coverage of drinking water through different programmes and strategies in no source villages/habitations, partially covered villages/habitations and water quality problem villages/habitations. A habitation-driven approach will be adopted in preference to a purely village-centred approach. The highest priority is to be given to all the remaining "no-source" and poorly-served "partially covered" (less than 10 lpcd) villages/habitations as well as those facing acute water quality problems. Thereafter, priority will be given to other partially covered (11-40 lpcd) and water quality problem villages/habitations. In each category, completion of the on-going schemes will be given priority before starting new schemes. The liberalised norms for service level of 55 lpcd and one HP/PSP for every 150 persons as also distance norm of 0.5 km may be adopted only after having covered all the villages/habitations with the existing norms of 40 lpcd, 250 persons per HP/PSP and distance norm of 1.6 km. To cater to the drinking water requirements of cattle in the DDP areas, an additional 30 lpcd of water may be provided.

Water is perceived in the rural areas as a social good, to be provided free by the government rather than as a scarce resource that should be managed as an economic asset. Supply of water to consumers should normally be based on the principle of effective demand which should broadly correspond to the standard of service that the users are willing to maintain, operate and finance. There should be a capital cost recovery of 10 per cent from the users in all the new drinking water supply projects aimed at increasing the service level beyond 40 lpcd.

The present practice is that the water supply projects are designed and executed by the implementing departments and passed on to the end-users. The experience has brought out the unwillingness of the Panchayats to take on the responsibility for operating and maintaining them. The State Governments do not have an effective machinery at the village level to maintain the assets. A radical change in the management system is required. Rather than being supply-driven, the system should be demand-driven, and should take into account user preferences, private connections and related issues. People should be aware of the technologies and given the option to select the technology, as well as meet the expenditure on the project. People's participation at all stages of the project implementation is likely to help get over the problems of sub-standard materials, poor workmanship and inadequate maintenance. These problems should be addressed to in the Ninth Plan.

As an experiment, it may be advisable, in some places, to transfer the funds to the user communities or the panchayats, who may be induced to buy pipes and install handpumps on their own. The Panchayati Raj Institutions and the local administration should be entrusted with the responsibility for the O and M of the installed systems. The PRIs should be given the option to levy and collect user charges for drinking water and sanitation services, so that at least the O and M, if not the further development works too, may become a self-financing activity.

The rapid development in ground water-based irrigation in many States has caused ground water depletion, resulting in a reduction in the life of the drinking water supply sources. The highly subsidised electricity tariff for irrigation has led to an indiscriminate and disproportionate level of ground water extraction. Ground water depletion has aggravated water quality problems due to excess fluoride, arsenic and brackishness in certain areas forcing the engineering departments to abandon the low-cost handpump-based systems and to opt for expensive and complicated piped water supply systems. A number of steps need to be taken up to manage ground water in a more scientific manner, especially in dark and grey zones and the States should bring in a legislation to control over-exploitation of ground water on the lines of the model Bill brought out by the Central Ministry of Water Resources. User groups should be formed, on the pattern of the Joint Forest Management Group, to take up the monitoring of ground water and ensuring that it is managed as a common property resource rather than allowing it to be over-exploited as an open access resource.

As in the urban areas, integrated water supply and sanitation programmes will be increasingly implemented during the Plan in the rural areas also. The implementing machinery in the Centre and the States will require organisational restructuring to work in a Mission mode with guidance from the Rajiv Gandhi National Drinking Water Mission Authority and its empowered committees. Micro water-shed based master plans should be prepared to ensure the sustainability of water sources by taking care of demand and supply. The inputs of professional institutions, NGOs and Community Based Organisations (CBOs) should be inducted into planning, development and management. At the same time, integrated water use and conservation methods should be adopted.

Private sector efforts in construction and maintenance of rural water supply and environmental sanitation should be encouraged and mobilised to the maximum extent. Financing of water supply activities in rural areas might not appear to be as attractive to the private sector as those in urban areas. Nevertheless, Sri Satya Sai Trust of Puttaparthy has set an unparallel example of private initiative in implementing on their own, without any State's budgetary support, a massive water supply project, with an expenditure of Rs. 250 crore, to benefit about 730 scarcity and fluoride/salinity-affected villages and a few towns in Anantpur district of Andhra Pradesh in a time frame of about 18 months. This path-breaking effort should encourage business groups, trusts and foundations. Also full cost recovery might not be a realistic approach during the Plan period. Alternative financial strategies will be evolved as the need to ensure adequate supply, in terms of quantitative and qualitative parameters, is a national commitment.

In view of huge requirement of funds, we have to think of other methodologies for raising other resources and alternative strategies to effect economy, such as adoption of low cost technological solutions using local materials to the extent possible and deferment of programme for quality affected habitation, which are not of severe nature and adoption of liberal norms. Some economy could also be effected by taking into account the privately owned sources which yield sufficient water and are accessible to the common people, involvement of community in O and M and some contribution for capital works, ensuring better sustainability to avoid early failure of HPs etc (presently 15-20 per cent HPs go defunct every year), involvement of NGOs and private sector participation to the extent possible. With these measures and the available outlays, it may be possible to achieve the set objective of providing safe drinking water facility to every settlement in rural areas within 5 years.

Urban Sanitation

In spite of the substantial efforts made to eliminate manual scavenging and bring in total conversion of dry latrines into low-cost pour-flush latrines, with a target of 100 per cent elimination of manual scavenging during the Eighth Plan, the problem remains a challenge to planners on the eve of the Ninth Plan. Consistent with the goal of "Health for All", efforts will be made to provide a reasonable level of sanitation to a larger population in urban areas by rapid expansion and improvement of sanitation facility during the Plan, with the specific objective of elimination of manual handling of night-soil through conversion of all dry latrines into low cost sanitary latrines. The goal of 100 percent conversion of dry latrines, elimination of manual scavenging and total rehabilitation of the liberated scavengers will be a permanent tribute to the Father of the Nation. To ensure this, municipal byelaws would need to be modified to ban construction of dry latrines and States should legislate, on the lines of the Central legislation, to prohibit employment of manual scavengers beyond a specified date in the Ninth Plan.

Low-cost on-site sanitation will be encouraged in unsewered parts of cities, small and medium towns and other locations where this strategy might be feasible. In the larger towns and cities and congested locations, including important tourist places and centres of pilgrimage, it would be desirable to adopt the conventional sewerage and treatment system.

The incidence of plague in some parts of the country stimulated interest in solid waste management. Technological innovations to improve the re-usability of the recycled wastes will contribute to the viability of projects and should be encouraged. This strategy would promote the segregation of different kinds of wastes at the collection point to reduce the cost of disposal. Toxic wastes should be collected and disposed of separately. The "polluter pays" principle should be applied and the proceeds may be used to finance waste disposal programmes. Solid waste disposal can be privatised also. Priority will be also given to the implementation of liquid and solid waste management programmes in the State capital towns.

As far as sanitation is concerned, greater community participation is the most important criterion without which other activities would fail. Drainage, sewerage, treatment of wastes/effluents, sanitary land fills, location and installation of incinerators, low cost sanitation etc are areas of concern, but there can be no uniform solution for the whole country and the State Governments would naturally be expected to play their role in a manner suitable to the needs of towns/cities where the sanitation coverage is far below the required levels. In view of the over all resource-constraint and other competing demands, it may perhaps not be possible to make a very huge investment in the next 5 years and therefore we may have to restrict the target in respect of sanitation to about 60 per cent, which may require an investment of around Rs.5500 crore. Besides sectoral plan outlays under State/UT Plans and Central Plan, a significant amount of Central assistance will also be available under the Central Plan scheme of National river conservation plan. A substantial amount is also expected to be contributed through private participation and institutional finance outside Plan.

Rural Sanitation

While the elimination of manual scavenging is a mandatory requirement in urban areas, in the rural areas, a demand-driven low- cost sanitation approach would be increasingly adopted in preference to a supply-driven approach. A network of production centres and rural sanitary marts would be integral components of the new approach to reach out self-sustainable and people-centred sanitation programmes. It is essential to adopt a "package" approach to rural sanitation, integrating it with rural drinking water programme and providing sufficient motivation inputs for its effective implementation. This is required in view of the late start of the rural sanitation programme.

In this perspective, rural sanitation programmes should be implemented by PRIs and NGOs, who should be directly involved in creation of demand, IEC, training, implementation, including setting of production centres and sanitary marts. Each State should have a nodal State NGO who would coordinate the NGO activities at the district level. Women should be given a special role at all stages and assisted through credit, skill inputs and employment. Equally important is to mobilise the children, especially through schools and anganwadis so that sanitation and hygiene practices are promoted at an early age and the demonstration effect filters within the rural society.

The programme should improve the technology content and also include compost toilet and latrines-based bio-mass activities. The Midnapore programme has been implemented with little or no subsidy or Government intervention, through the efforts of Ramakrishna Mission, an NGO. The demonstrated sustainability of this people-driven approach has stimulated its subsequent replication across West Bengal.

It is therefore proposed to restructure the ongoing exclusively subsidy-driven sanitation programme using valuable field experience on the low cost sanitation with extensive advocacy and people's participation. A number of interesting campaigns have conclusively demonstrated the weaknesses of the subsidy-oriented, top-down sanitation programme and have extensively and successfully co-opted NGOs, Banks, Panchayats to achieve very impressive coverage levels (e.g. Midnapur in West Bengal, periyar in Tamil Nadu , Mysore in Karnataka, Allahabad in U.P). A policy note in this regard, under preparation in the Ministry, envisages the use of the CRSP funds as "Seed Money" to propagate low-cost rural sanitation, based on felt-needs, a greater private sector involvement and using the "vertical upgradation" concept. A campaign approach would be developed on the lines of the literacy/immunisation and the subsidies structure reoriented to specifically target the poorest strata. With the above approach and the available outlays, it may be possible to achieve coverage of about 35 per cent rural population by the end of the Ninth Plan.

Action Points for Consideration

For the attainment of the set objectives/targets within the Ninth Plan, the following action points are called for:

Urban Water Supply and Sanitation

1. Larger external assistance (higher priority to Urban Water Supply and Sanitation) be provided. At present it is estimated to be around Rs.5250 crore for the 9th Plan.
2. The Government of India will play a role of facilitator in policy framework, institutional capacity building and financial reforms so as to enable the State Governments and urban Local Bodies to achieve the desired objective within the prescribed time frame. In addition to this, the Government of India will also provide technical guidance in order to create proper environment for the concerned agencies to plan and formulate water supply and sanitation schemes.
3. As recommended by the Working Group, an 'Urban Development Fund' may be created on the lines of the Tamil Nadu model which could be utilised for creating infrastructure facilities in urban areas and such a fund should act as a catalyst to finance those schemes which are viable and with a little help from this kind of fund local bodies can become eligible to obtain loans from commercial institutions like IDBI, ICICI, IF and LS and from the open market. The assistance from the fund can be provided to small and medium towns in the form of soft loans and grants so as to enable them to take further loans from the open market as most of these small towns otherwise might not be in a position to obtain loans from financial institutions, on their own strength.
4. Since it is difficult to meet the huge resource gap out of State and Central Plan funds, greater emphasis would need to be given for institutional financing through HUDCO, LIC and

other institutions. Widening the equity base of the financing institutions like HUDCO for raising the market borrowings could be encouraged.

5. Some financial support to the ULBs to meet the expenditure towards interest differential on the loan taken from the financing institutions would encourage the ULBs to come forward to take loan even at commercial rate of interest.
6. Rebate on excise and customs duties for purchase of leak detection equipment and other such machinery needed for development and improvement of infrastructure facilities could be of great assistance to the State Governments/ULBs.
7. As a follow up of 74th Constitution Amendment Act, most of the State Governments are likely to entrust the responsibility of operation and maintenance of urban water supply and sanitation systems to local bodies and therefore it would be necessary for the State Finance Commission to explicitly indicate the norms and other financial implications make a realistic assessment of requirement of funds and also to make suitable recommendations for provision of finances by different categories of towns.
8. Private Sector participation in construction and maintenance of water supply and sanitation schemes, to the extent possible be encouraged/mobilised..
9. Involvement of NGOs and community be encouraged by the State Governments.
10. Adoption of improved low cost technology be encouraged to save cost of construction and maintenance.
11. The water tariff be raised substantially to meet at least the full cost of operation and maintenance in smaller towns and to raise some surplus also in bigger towns/cities particularly those having industrial base. This will not only make the running cost self-financing, but also enable the State Governments/ULBs to raise institutional financing.
12. Improved metering systems, particularly in Class-I Cities, would not only help in actual quantification of the water uses

but also the proper billing of the water supply, which would also improve the revenue collection.

13. Each organisation at the State/ULBs level should be encouraged to have its own training plan and adequate infrastructure facilities commensurate with the work plan. Special emphasis should be given to the need for skill upgradation for the personnel responsible for O and M. The Human Resource Development Programme must endeavour to enhance user sensitivity on the part of O and M staff and increase public awareness which will promote NGOs and consumer participation with respect top protection of assets and improved service delivery.
14. The quick and amicable solutions between States through Central intervention for sharing of water resources would avoid delay in implementation of the water supply projects and save the increased capital investment.
15. There is a need for development of National Data Bank and creation of Monitoring Cells at State and Central level for rigorous monitoring of the urban water supply and sanitation system. This would help in detection of bottlenecks and suggest mid-course corrections/reorientation of policies at Central/State level for developmental activities of the sector.
16. Over exploitation of ground water must be avoided to control deterioration of its quality and reduced cost of pumping. Regulatory mechanism for ground-water exploitation be brought in by the State Governments, particularly in all such urban areas which are facing acute shortage of drinking water through out the year, for better sustainability of the sources of water.
17. Conservation of water by better management to reduce leakages and pilferage and re-cycling of treated waste water for non-domestic uses be encouraged by giving incentives. This will not only save precious fresh water but also reduces load on waste water/sewage treatment units.
18. Rain water harvesting structures be encouraged in a big way to increase availability of water and also increase ground-

water recharge for better sustainability of ground water sources.

Rural Water Supply and Sanitation

1. Larger external assistance (higher priority to rural water supply and sanitation) need to be provided to augment State resources.
2. Transfer the responsibility of at least operation and maintenance of Rural Water Supply to the PRIs in line with 73rd CAA.
3. Adoption of improved low cost technology be encouraged to save cost of construction and maintenance.
4. Free supply of water to people in rural areas should be discouraged and some user charges collected through community participation.
5. Private Sector participation in construction and maintenance of water supply and sanitation schemes to the extent possible be encouraged/mobilised.
6. Involvement of NGOs and community be encouraged by the State Governments.
7. The rapid development in ground water based irrigation in many States has caused ground water depletion. Highly subsidised irrigation electricity tariff have led to an indiscriminate and disproportionate level of ground water extraction. To regulate and develop ground water resources in a scientific manner, a Model Bill was framed by the Water Resources Ministry in 1970 and was circulated to the States. The Bill has again been recently revised and circulated to States in 1996. Except for Maharashtra, the implementation of the provision of the legislation was not satisfactory. State Ministers' Conference held in August, 1997 resolved against any strong legal measures of controlling ground water discharge and cropping pattern. Instead, they preferred to rely more on improving recharge and arresting run off through water shed programmes. Rain Water Harvesting Structure, therefore, be encouraged in a big way to increase availability

of water and also increase ground water recharge for better sustainability of water supply schemes.

8. Water supply links with watershed development programmes should be made stronger for better sustainability of drinking water sources.

Housing

Performance Review: The dimensions and problems of housing need to be viewed in the overall environment of human settlements. Housing has been primarily a self-help activity. The housing policies and programmes, while accepting that housing is essentially a private activity, has to recognise that State intervention is necessary to meet the housing requirements of the vulnerable sections and to create an enabling environment in accomplishing the goals of "shelter for all" in a self-sustainable basis.

An important development in the Eighth Plan was the bringing about of a consensus in the approach to human settlements development. The National Housing Policy (NHP) provided the basic approach, the economic reforms stimulated the process and the preparatory process for the Habitat II Conference brought together the key actors through the National Steering Committee, Key Groups of human settlements managers, NGOs and CBOs, private sector and the National Human Settlement Forum, which crystallised and endorsed in the National Report.

The Eighth Plan outlay for urban housing was Rs. 3,581.67 crore in the State Sector and Rs.1,341.35 crore in the Central Sector (Rs.860 crore as IEBR and Rs.481.35 crore budgetary support, inclusive of equity support). The expenditure under the Central Sector was 96 per cent and in the State sector, 112 per cent. However, there were significant inter-State variations in the funds utilisation rate. In terms of the total activities and investment requirement in the housing sector, the Plan outlay was modest.

The Eighth Plan target was 7.80 million new housing stock, including 6.29 million units in Economically Weaker Sections

(EWS) and Low Income Group (LIG) categories. The estimated investment requirement was Rs. 5,779 crore, at 1989-90 prices. Metropolitan cities were estimated to account for as much as 2.75 million units at an investment of Rs. 22,770 crore. The urban upgradation activity was estimated at 1.75 million units at an investment of Rs. 1,130 crore. Housing for the totally houseless population, urban and rural, would require an investment of Rs. 610 crore. Housing has been, therefore, largely a people's activity, but constraints of finance, land, other inputs and the absence of a stimulating environment has pushed the urban housing solutions beyond the reach of the majority of the people.

Recent Habitat II housing and urban indicators for mega cities and secondary towns show that the cost of a median house in terms of the annual household income goes up sharply with the city size: 13 years income in Mumbai, 12 years in Delhi, 11 years in Bangalore and 7 years in Chennai, and it goes down to 3 to 4 years in secondary towns. This is the situation in the formal housing market, but a similar trend is seen in informal housing with 2-3 years income in mega cities and less than one year in the secondary towns. The comparative variations in housing costs in the formal and informal housing sectors and the composition of the population in the latter also bring out a shift from formal to informal housing as costs go up. Rental housing indicator also shows market distortions as reflected in high rental to income ratio, 20-25 per cent in secondary towns and 30-50 per cent in the mega cities. Habitat II National Report that 50 per cent of the units constructed through the cooperatives are in the LIG category.

In this perspective, public housing thrust is, most appropriately, directed towards social housing, to reach out housing solutions to the priority groups. An equally important activity is to provide a policy framework and a legislative, fiscal and financial system that would put into effect the enabling role of the government in stimulating, supporting and promoting other actors to play direct roles in the housing delivery system. These two activities have been the pillars of the Eighth Plan approach and would continue in the Ninth Plan.

It has been estimated that during the Eighth Plan, funds flow from the formal sector was about Rs. 25,000 crore, inclusive of Central and State Governments, Life Insurance Corporation (LIC), General Insurance Corporation (GIC), National Housing Bank (NHB), Housing and Urban Development Corporation (HUDCO), Provident Fund, commercial banks, housing finance institutions and cooperative apex federations. The State level apex cooperative housing federations had disbursed Rs. 884 crore as loan to primary housing cooperatives during the first three years of the Eighth Plan and this enabled the construction of 2.95 lakh units.

The net flow to individuals was about 50 per cent of the total funds flow from the formal sector. The estimation of output of housing stock and serviced sites from the formal sector investment is difficult because the data have to be compiled from different Central and State agencies. There is an element of duplication in the data of financial institutions and housing agencies. While data on individual loans and other resources mobilised, especially for upgraded units and construction on serviced plots are often not collected, the physical achievements have not been monitored closely with reference to the Plan outlays for new housing stock and upgraded units. The only systematic data collection is undertaken for the 20 point programme in respect of EWS and LIG housing units. Their output in the first four years of the Eighth Plan was 4.68 lakh EWS units and 1.87 lakh LIG units.

It is broadly estimated that the housing stock provided by public agencies, cooperatives and private agencies, with the help of institutional finance, budget outlays and internal resources, may be of the order of 7 lakh units of EWS housing and an equal number of slum housing units are estimated to have been upgraded under the Nehru Rozgar Yojana (NRY). The LIG incremental stock may be 6 to 7 lakh units, on the assumption. The output of units for other higher categories may not exceed 5 lakh. Thus, as against the projected physical housing output of 30 lakh units in the urban areas during the Eighth Plan period, the contribution of the formal sector may not exceed 20 lakh units.

In this development perspective during the Eighth Plan, the tasks ahead for the Ninth Plan have to be examined. Several estimates are available of the present housing shortage and the projected shortage at a fairly disaggregated level. The National Buildings Organisation (NBO) has estimated the 1991 shortage at 8.23 million, up from 7.0 million in 1981, but expects the absolute shortage to decline progressively to 7.57 million units in 1997 and 6.64 million 2001. However, other estimates indicate that the shortage will increase to 9.4 million units in 2001 (Habitat II estimates.)

A major initiative was taken in the Sixth Plan, when the public sector was entrusted with a promotional role in housing in general and restricting its direct operations to housing for the urban poor and provision of house sites and construction assistance for rural landless labourers. Development activities were diversified in the Seventh Plan by providing for setting up an institutional financial system for housing and urban infrastructure and thrust was given to slum upgradation in situ, development, in preference to relocation and provision of basic services for the poor. Work on the National Housing Policy (NHP) was initiated in the mid-eighties, together with preparatory work to set up a National Housing Bank and the process gathered momentum during the International Year of Shelter for the Homeless (IYSH), 1987.

Social Housing Schemes are implemented in the State Sector with State Plan provision and loan assistance from HUDCO and other financial institutions. These include Housing Schemes for EWS; LIG; MIG/HIG; and Rental Housing Scheme for State Government Employees. HUDCO provides up to 15 per cent of its resources for EWS housing and NHB refinances the State cooperatives and others involved in this activity. The income, cost and loan ceilings were revised in 1992 and are again under review, keeping in view the cost escalations and changes in the incomes of the target groups.

In the case of the EWS, for example, the income ceiling was raised from Rs. 700 in the Seventh Plan to Rs. 1250 in the Eighth Plan and the loan component to Rs. 19,500 for construction and Rs. 9,500 for repairs. The emphasis in the development strategy for the EWS is on sites and services and self-construction. The LIG housing scheme is primarily a loan scheme and is executed by the State Governments through Housing Boards and Housing Departments, and the budget provision is supplemented by institutional finance. The income eligibility level, which was Rs. 701-1500 in the Seventh Plan, was raised to Rs. 1251-2650 in the Eighth Plan. HUDCO supplements the efforts of State Governments/UT Administrations and its loan component for LIG category housing is Rs. 55,000 for construction and Rs. 37,500 for repairs/additions. There is a need to further revise the ceilings and norms, which would be taken up in the Ninth Plan.

A national network of Nirmithi Kendras (Building Centres) has been established with Central assistance through HUDCO under a Central scheme. These Centres impart training to artisans in low-cost construction skills and produce building materials and components by utilising agro-industrial wastes. A Central grant of Rs. 2 lakh was provided to each Centre till 1994-95 and under a revised funding pattern, effective from 1995-96, the Central grant-in-aid ranges from Rs. 3-5 lakh, depending on the level of the activities and a HUDCO loan is also available. As on 31.12.96, 435 Centres have been identified and 239 Centres have become functional. The total Central grant has been Rs. 5.75 crore and the output of training exceeds 75,000 construction workers. The ultimate impact on the contribution of these trained workers to new housing stock, including upgradation and renewal, has not been made and will form a part of the Ninth Plan agenda. It is necessary to monitor the career path of the outturns of the centres through tracer studies and indicators.

The scheme of Night Shelters/Sanitation Facility to Footpath Dwellers in Urban Areas provides night shelter and sanitation facilities to footpath dwellers. The per capita development cost provided for this is Rs. 5,000, 20 percent of which is financed by Central Government and 80 per cent from implementing agencies or a HUDCO loan. The programmes overall implementing agency is HUDCO and the coverage is all urban areas, having the problem of footpath dwellers. As on 31.12.96, HUDCO had sanctioned loan of Rs. 10.06 crore and subsidy of Rs. 9.13 crore to 56 schemes to provide 19,366 beds, 5,258 pay-and-use toilet seats, 64 baths and 145 urinals. The total number of beneficiaries under this scheme is expected to be about 60,000, but the feedback regarding its impact in terms of actual users, coverage of the footpath dweller population and their satisfaction level is not available and this task will be taken up in the Ninth Plan.

The schemes for other priority groups which include handloom weavers and beedi workers are implemented through Central Government subsidy released by the concerned Ministries and HUDCO loan. HUDCO also provides loan for construction of hostels for working women. The National Housing Bank (NHB) has recently launched housing schemes for slum dwellers and households headed by poor women with the funds mobilised under the Voluntary Deposits Scheme.

Under the one-time scheme of Central Assistance for reconstruction of floods-damaged houses in Tamil Nadu, Karnataka and Kerala, HUDCO has sanctioned construction of 77,969 houses till the end of December, 1996, of which 20,318 houses have been reconstructed. The funding pattern provides for 30 percent Central subsidy, 30 percent State subsidy and 40 percent HUDCO loan.

Rural housing did not receive much attention during the first 25 years of planning. The Central rehabilitation programmes of the Ministry of Refugees Rehabilitation provided, until around 1960, housing to about 5 lakh households, mainly in Northern India. A Village Housing Scheme was also launched in 1957 as part of the community development movement, under which loans were provided to individuals and cooperatives, subject to a ceiling of Rs. 5,000 per house and 67,000 houses were built under this scheme by the end of the Fifth Plan (1980). The Estimates Committee, in its 37th Report (1972-73), expressed distress at the unsatisfactory conditions of kutcha housing in rural areas and the apathy of the Government. In response to this assessment, the Housing Sites-cum-Construction Assistance Scheme was launched as a Central Scheme in the Fourth Plan which was later transferred to the State Sector in April, 1974, on the recommendation of the NDC.

Indira Awas Yojana (IAY) is the most important rural housing scheme. Its genesis can be traced to the rural employment programmes like the National Rural Employment Programme (NREP) and Rural Landless Employment Guarantee Programme (RLEGP), in which construction of houses was a major activity. There was, however, no uniform policy for rural housing. In June, 1985, a specific proportion of RLEGP funds was earmarked for construction of houses for SCs/STs and freed bonded labour. Later in April, 1989, the NREP and RLEGP were merged into the Jawahar Rozgar Yojana (JRY), and up to 1992-93, the IAY was continued as a part of the JRY, with a special provision of 6 percent of the housing units free of cost to members of SC/ST and freed bonded labour living below the poverty line in the rural areas. The proportion of free housing units was raised to 10 percent in 1993-94 and the scope was extended to cover non-SC/ST rural poor, subject to the condition that the non-SC/ST beneficiaries should not receive more than 40 percent of the total allocation.

Further extension of the coverage was made in 1995-96 to include families of servicemen of the armed and para-military forces killed in action. In the identification of the beneficiaries, weightage is given to victims of atrocities, households headed by widows and unmarried women, households affected by natural calamities or displaced by development projects, nomadic, semi-nomadic denotified tribes, internal refugees and disabled families. After the JRY was restructured from January 1, 1996, The IAY has become an independent Centrally Sponsored Scheme for shelter, with the resources being contributed on 80:20 basis by Centre and States.

The output of the IAY is estimated at 37.16 lakh houses during the period 1985-86 to 1996-97 at an investment of Rs. 5,038 crore. The IAY has been recognised as a positive support activity that has provided to the homeless poor in rural areas a feeling of security and has facilitated their integration in the emerging social milieu. An evaluation of the IAY by the Planning Commission in 1993 brought out a high satisfaction rate, with 84 per cent of the beneficiaries being satisfied with their houses. States have accepted it as a major activity and almost every year since its inception, the annual targets have been exceeded. The programme received a major thrust in the Eighth Plan, particularly in 1995-96, when the outlay was substantially enhanced from Rs. 437.69 crore in 1994-95 to Rs. 1368.34 crore in 1995-96. During the Eighth Plan period, the total allocation was Rs. 3821.73 crore, utilisation Rs. 3781.63 crore (99.0 per cent), and houses constructed 26.21 lakh, which was 86.7 per cent of the target of 30.22 lakh.

The cost norms under the IAY have undergone changes during the period 1985-86 to 1996-97. The Chief Ministers Conference in July, 1996 recommended an increase in the construction assistance under the IAY from Rs. 14,000 to 20,000 and this was followed by the Ministry of Rural Areas and Employment enhancing the ceiling for new construction to Rs. 20,000 per unit in plain areas and Rs. 22,000 per unit in hilly and difficult areas, effective from 1.8.1996.

Implementation of Agenda 21

During the Eighth Plan period, significant activities were undertaken towards the implementation of Agenda 21, endorsed at the Rio de Janeiro Environment Meeting of 1992. This document had laid stress on the deteriorating situation in human settlement conditions, assessed to be a result of low levels of investment because of resource constraint and recommended promotion and improvement of activities in eight priority areas. The Government of India has responded positively.

The key objective of the National Housing Policy (NHP) 1994 is to provide access to adequate shelter for all. There is an enormous shortage in the housing sector and major deficiencies in the housing related infrastructure. The Government has been progressively adopting the role of an enabler rather than a direct provider. However, this necessitated a policy shift to encourage private and cooperative sector to play a major role in housing sector, modifying the existing legal and regulatory regime. Keeping in view the above Government has since adopted a new Housing and Habitat Policy (approved by the Cabinet in July 1998). Efforts are also being made by the Central and State Governments to achieve the objective of shelter for all through a number of Centrally sponsored schemes and institutional financing through HUDCO and other institutions. Several enabling programmes have been initiated, such as, the establishment of a housing finance system with a National Housing Bank at the apex level, amendment to the Urban Land (Ceiling and Regulation) Act to expand the supply of land, formulation of a model Rent Control Act, model Apartment Ownership Bill and schemes to link up housing and income generation programmes for the poor.

As a part of the strategy to strengthen the human settlements management activities, the Central Government has introduced several schemes such as : Environment Improvement of Urban Slums, a State sector scheme; Integrated Scheme of Low-cost Sanitation; Nehru Rozgar Yojana (NRY) with three components namely Scheme of Urban Micro Enterprises (SUME), Scheme of Urban Wage Employment (SUWE), and Scheme of Housing and Shelter Upgradation (SHASHU); Urban Basic Services for the Poor (UBSP); Scheme of Integrated Development of Small and Medium towns (IDSMT); Scheme of Infrastructure Development in Mega-cities (IDM); Integrated Rural Development Programme (IRDP); Jawahar Rozgar Yojana (JRY); Development of Women and Children in Rural Areas (DWCRA); Accelerated Rural Water

Supply Programme (ARWSP); Accelerated Urban Water Supply Programme for small towns with population less than 20,000 (AUWSP) and Minimum Needs Programme (MNP)/Basic Minimum Services (BMS).

In order to improve the land-use planning capabilities at the city/town level, the Central Government has launched an urban mapping scheme which utilises advanced technologies such as remote sensing and aerial photography to prepare physical and utility maps on appropriate scales. Two-third of Indian States and Union Territories are vulnerable to natural disasters. In order to develop policies and strategies for planning human settlements in disaster-prone areas, the Government of India has set up the National Centre for Disaster Management. A Vulnerability Atlas is being developed to indicate disaster-prone sites in the country.

The rapidly growing demand for housing and infrastructure is exerting heavy pressures on the natural environment. To promote sustainable development of the construction industry, Government of India has taken several initiatives to promote energy-efficient building materials and shift the reliance from non-renewable resources to renewable resources. The national network of Building Centres is disseminating information on these eco-friendly and energy-efficient building materials and construction technologies and the Building Material and Technology Promotion Council (BMTPC) is promoting large-scale utilisation of agro-industrial wastes. The Council of Scientific and Industrial Research (CSIR) is co-ordinating the R and D activities on the development of new wood substitutes for use in construction activity. The Department of Environment, Government of India has launched a scheme of labelling eco-friendly building materials and the Bureau of Indian Standards has formulated standards, specifications and code of practice on several innovative building materials. Further capacity building programmes are being launched all over the country to improve human resource development. Sustainable energy and transport systems like Mass Rapid Transit System (M.R.T.S.) are being developed in order to tackle pollution and traffic congestion.

Ninth Plan Priorities and Strategies

- While housing needs of all segments of the population will have to be met, the Ninth Plan will focus special attention on households at the lower end of the housing market, the priority groups identified for such support, such as e.g. People below poverty line, SC/ST, disabled, freed bonded labourers, slum dwellers and women headed households.
- Government will, as a facilitator, create an environment in which access to all the requisite inputs will be in time, in adequate quantum and an appropriate quality and standards.
- There will be provision for more direct intervention by the Government in the case of lower segments of the housing market and selected disadvantaged groups.
- A package of incentives and concessions to attract private sectors would be introduced to shoulder the task of housing for the poor.

While the housing needs of all segments of the population will have to be met, the Ninth Plan will focus special attention on households at the lower end of the housing market, the priority groups identified for such support, such as, for example, people below the poverty line, SC/ST, disabled, freed bonded labourers, slum dwellers and women-headed households. Minimum housing adequacy norms will be evolved that would include per capita living space, structural durability, access to drinking water with minimum quantitative and qualitative norms, sanitation facilities and connectivity. The responsibility to fix the norms will be entrusted to the States and it is expected that the State governments will further decentralise the responsibility to Urban Local Bodies (ULBs) and Panchayati Raj Institutions (PRIs), with provision for a participatory process to determine the norms. The norms would be the base for working out State and district housing action plans for both the urban and rural areas.

Housing has been always a people's activity and will continue to be so in the Ninth Plan, both in the urban and the rural areas. Government will, as a facilitator, create the environment in which access to all the requisite inputs will be in time, in adequate quantum and of appropriate quality and standards. All housing delivery systems, such as the cooperatives, private sector, community groups, and people's self efforts, will be stimulated to make their contributions to new housing stock as well as upgradation and renewal of the existing stock. In the case of the cooperatives, the endeavour will be to encourage the formation of cooperatives from the planning stage of the housing programme and maintaining a high continuity rate of the original members.

There will be provision for more direct intervention by the government in the case of the lower segments of the housing market and selected disadvantaged groups, whose needs may not be effectively or adequately met by the market-driven forces, which will, in other cases, be a prime mover of housing development activities, particularly in the urban areas. However, a package of incentives and concessions to attract private sectors would be introduced to shoulder the task of housing for the poor. Up till now private sector has been playing an almost non-existent role in the shelter delivery for the vulnerable group. Cooperative sector and other public housing agencies could also be encouraged to share the responsibility. Subsidy would continue to be provided for some more time and the flow mechanism will be made transparent and increasingly routed outside the financial system. Government has set the goal to provide housing for all and towards this end it proposes to facilitate the construction of 20 lakh additional housing units annually. The focus will be on providing houses to the houseless, inadequately housed and disadvantaged groups below poverty line. Since ratio of housing shortage between rural and urban areas is 65:35 as per the NBO statistics derived from the 1991 census, out of 20 lakh additional houses 13 lakh will be in the rural areas and 7 lakh will be in the urban areas.

Land market reforms will be undertaken through restructuring legal, planning and fiscal provisions, on which considerable work has been done during the Eighth Plan and the results incorporated in several official documents. A work agenda to implement them will be taken up. Land scarcity is one of the key elements to development of housing and infrastructure services. Legislative provisions like the Urban Land Ceiling and Regulation Act (ULCRA) 1976, whose basic objective is to make land available to all income segments in the urban agglomeration, has in practice, led to distortions in the land market operation. The Cabinet has since taken a decision to repeal ULCRA. To promote sustainable human settlements, the Plan will take specific initiatives to promote and adopt in human settlements programmes energy-saving, eco-friendly and environment-friendly technologies and building materials.

Apart from new construction, the Ninth Plan agenda will take up the massive task of upgradation and renewal of old and dilapidated housing stock. In the urban, this is a major challenge in the inner city areas and in the growing slum and squatter settlements, which have become an ingenious solution to get shelter perfected by the people who cannot enter the formal housing market on their own. Within this category, the Plan will look into the needs of the households below the poverty line. Urban renewal in this direction is crucial to the health and sustainability of the urban environment.

To build sustainability into the housing of the urban poor as well as in rural housing, integrated development of settlement should be promoted, on the principle of strengthening the linkages and inter-dependency between shelter and income upgradation. India has made a commitment to this approach in the NHP and the Habitat II National Plan of Action (NPA). To promote this strategy, the Ninth Plan will support the use of composite credit instrument, modify land-use patterns and city master plans and strengthen the linkages between the farm and the non-farm sector in the rural and semi-urban areas. The NGOs and other voluntary organisations would have to play the role of a catalyst.

Some special development needs have to be addressed as regards rural housing. Urbanisation has had an impact on the traditional rural housing development activities, with increased flow of information on housing designs, new technology, and materials. The options and need to upgrade the structure, especially the roof and the wall, has been recognised in the NHP and in rural housing programmes. This would reduce the annual maintenance inputs, including human inputs, and provide better protection against natural calamities. Rural housing is also qualitatively different from urban housing, in that the housing activity is not very much based on the cash economy but depends to a considerable extent on land rights and access to resources. Rural housing has also emerged as a major component of rural development programmes and, as such, is considered to be an integral part of rural development planning. Keeping in view the varied range of geo-climatic conditions and housing typologies in rural areas, the tasks are stupendous in developing and managing rural housing programmes. One set of materials, plans or construction techniques cannot be applicable across the country, and hence rural housing requires grass-root level feedback on housing needs, together with basic amenities like approach roads, internal roads, drainage, water supply, sanitation and work place.

As per 1991 census the total rural household shortage was 13.72 million. Of these 3.41 million households were without shelter and 10.31 million households were living in `Kutcha unserviceable' houses. In addition an estimated increase of 10.75 million households would be required on account of population growth during the period 1991-2002.It has also been estimated that between 1990-91 and 1996-97, about 5.7 million units would have been added to the rural housing stock through the on-going programmes of IAY, State Governments, HUDCO and self-help system. Thus the net housing shortage between 1997 and 2002 is 18.77 millions of which 8.46 millions are new houses and 10.31 million are kutcha/unserviceable houses. Another set of estimates, presented in Habitat II National Report, also brings out a similar scenario with new housing requirement estimated at 7.7 million units and upgradation requirement at 11.2 million units.

An additional estimate was made of extension of existing units, which was 8.7 million units. It is clear that large upgradation activity has to be taken up during the Ninth Plan for which realistic estimates of net housing shortage, State-wise, will be required. The overall housing shortage does not reveal the regional dimension of the problem. While housing shortage exist in almost all States, there is a large concentration in a few States with Bihar accounting for nearly 1/3 of the housing shortage in the country followed by Andhra Pradesh, Assam, Uttar Pradesh and West Bengal, which together account for another 44.65 per cent. In each of remaining States the housing shortage is less than 5 per cent. Therefore in the backdrop of the total housing requirement the housing shortage in selected States is more acute.

Apart from the quantitative dimensions of the rural housing requirements, the qualitative aspects are equally important, particularly those relating to per capita living space, durability and access to amenities. The 1991 Census indicated that 40.8 percent of the 112 million rural households lived in one-room units and the pre-dominant roofing materials used were grass, straw and thatch. These rural housing activities have to be incorporated under the IAY, as a special mechanism for financing is required to facilitate the use of market-sourced materials for increasing the durability of structure and providing access to basic habitat services.

There is virtually no institutional finance in the rural housing sector except what is provided through its scheme by Housing and Urban Development Corporation. The housing finance institutions will have to overcome their reluctance to enter into the rural housing market. The access to rural housing credit, outside the Government schemes like the IAY, would require special attention during the Ninth Plan, as also full access to low-cost materials and appropriate technology. With the growth in the rural housing programme emphasis would also have to be placed on training and development of skills so that skilled masons in adequate numbers are available in the rural areas to carry out construction works, particularly, using new building materials and low cost technology. The financial institutions will have to meet the credit needs of rural housing through innovative credit instruments and delivery systems that take into account the specificities of rural housing, geo-climatic conditions and socio-cultural practices, besides the need to finance the habitat-related services. Multiplicity of institutions to service the shelter and basic needs may not be very much desirable.

The provision of house sites has emerged in recent years as a crucial requirement in some parts of the country, and especially for the rural poor, a large proportion of whom do not have security of tenure nor the right or access to land for building a house. Land should be acquired in places where public land supply may be a constraint and this strategy should take into account the ecology and environmental considerations, as also the appropriateness of the location in terms of the economic activities and access to basic habitat services. Under an on-going programme of House Sites-cum-Construction Assistance, which is implemented by the State Governments, 233.43 lakh house sites have been allotted and construction assistance provided to 77.6 lakh beneficiaries up to 1995-96.The implementation of this scheme has been slow, with most States not being able to keep up the desired pace vis-à-vis the extent of the housing shortage. The IAY may be modified to include a provision for making minimum land available to such rural poor and the land would have to be acquired in the proximity of village habitations. Tenurial arrangements to protect the rights of the rural poor and disadvantaged groups on the houses and lands occupied by them is another priority concern.

The IAY would be the main Government programme for achieving the objective of shelter for all rural poor. It would continue to be a 100 per cent subsidised programme, targeted specifically towards providing shelter for the houseless, inadequately housed and disadvantaged groups. Under the IAY, the funds are allocated to the State/UT on the basis of the proportion of rural poor in the State/UT to the total rural poor in the country. This modality fails to take account of the actual housing shortage and does not take into account the housing needs of the economically weaker section who are just above poverty line. There is need for modification of present IAY.

In view of the massive upgradation activities to be undertaken, the IAY may have to be modified to support these activities, initially utilising up to 20 percent of the total IAY funds for upgradation of unserviceable kutcha houses. The Ninth Plan would also give a thrust on improving the quality of houses under the IAY through cost-effective measures and introduction of appropriate technologies and functional designs to suit the housing needs of different geo-climatic conditions, cultural preferences and lifestyles of the people.

In this effort, the focus of research and development would be on innovative low-cost building and construction technologies, cultural-specific housing designs and appropriate housing materials for building durable and safe houses. Apart from developing new technologies, the rich stock of appropriate technologies will be disseminated to the rural areas. To utilise these technologies effectively a major role will be provided for development of skills by the Nirmithi Kendras (rural building centres) under the aegis of HUDCO for dissemination of rural building techniques and for effective training to rural youth in trades related to low-cost housing. Institutional facilities already available in select rural ITIs, polytechnics and vocational training centres will also be strengthened. NGOs should also participate in conserving and upgrading the traditional housing architecture and should promote development of integrated programmes for the upgradation of artisans' skills and the deployment of unemployed youth in various trades related to low-cost housing.

Integrating the financing of rural and urban housing within a single organisation might not necessarily be in the interest of the rural housing sector. Rural housing finance requires a different type of approach, more development-oriented than a purely financial approach. Rural housing finance might have to take into account the financing of habitat-related services and in the case of housing in poorly connected areas, also economic activities. Kutcha housing units should be eligible for institutional finance and there must be a high level of flexibility in the repayment schedule, linked more to seasonality of income flows than to the conventional monthly repayment programme. There is also the problem of ownership of land as in some parts of the country, particularly in tribal societies, land is owned by the community rather than on an individual basis. The Ninth Plan would examine the feasibility of special integrated rural human settlements finance and development institution, as well as specific programmes like the IAY that would look into the financing and development of upgradation activities.

Several States/UTs are implementing their own housing programmes, in addition the IAY. It is necessary to coordinate all the efforts with a view to addressing the housing shortage in a phased manner. There should be regular and timely data on allocations, cost norms, and the number of houses constructed each year, State-wise. A strong data base and monitoring system is required for this purpose. The Central and State Governments, along with financial institutions would then be able to jointly undertake the tasks of providing a house to all, with basic habitat services, in a time bound manner. Activities will have to be undertaken at the village level through convergence and collective action. This would necessitate the proactive participation of the village community who would formulate an action plan on the basis of identified needs and priorities and in line with the resources available.

The magnitude of the housing task ahead is so great that besides the State Government's efforts at providing land and finance, making available easy access to local construction materials and dissemination of appropriate building technologies, there has to be a more active involvement of several other agencies such as cooperatives, the community, voluntary organisations and the private sector. Public sector undertakings would also be required to participate in the programme as part of their social obligation and commitment. The PRIs have to also play a key role.

A few legislative changes are required particularly relating to tenurial arrangements, including rights to house and land. The "nistar rights" of the poor to access traditional building materials and undertaking cadastral surveys are priority activities to be undertaken during the Ninth Plan. Another concern, in the case of States with large tribal population, is to safeguard the non-alienable property rights of the people and evolving a workable solution to the oft-identified problem of mortgaging of community owned land for individual home loan programme. It is equally important to cover all habitat-related activities presently implemented by various departments into a single programme so that planning, community mobilisation and effective monitoring and impact assessment can be taken up in a more effective manner. The village should be made an effective planning unit, giving full recognition to the Constitution (73rd Amendment) Act.

Special Action Plan- Urban Housing

It has already been mentioned about the target of construction of 20 lakh additional houses every year under the Special Action Plan. The target of additional dwelling units has been broadly bifurcated as 13 lakh units for rural areas and 7 lakh units for urban areas. This division of target is stated to be based upon the ratio of housing shortage in the urban and rural (basis 1991 census). The Government's role is that of an enabler than that a builder. Taking a clue from this approach government may provide necessary fiscal concessions, access to land, appropriate technological support and inexpensive finance to the sector. There would be necessity to bring the legal reforms required for the sector particularly in respect of rent control regulating the activities of builders, Apartment Ownership Act Building Bye-laws and National/Departmental Standards and Codes. Land is most critical input. An integrated programme for land assembly and infrastructure development should be taken up on a priority basis.

Keeping in view the large quantum of low cost funds needed, the finance Ministry would have to consider allowing substantially higher allocation of tax free bonds for resource mobilisation. The banking sector would need to be directed to make available more funds for housing, both by expanding the percentage of incremental deposits as well as earmarking dedicated funds under the priority sector especially for EWS/LIG housing. Fiscal incentives under the Income Tax Act for housing initiatives need to be provided. Further assistance under I.T. Act to the HFIs should be continued. Tax concession under Wealth Tax may be provided for promoting rental housing scheme. Amendments to the NHB Act need to be expedited for early foreclosure procedures.

Based on the average cost of EWS and LIG of Rs. 35000 and I lakh respectively the investment requirement for 7 lakh new units has been worked out to be of the order of around Rs. 4000 crore. The extent of funding from institutional financing is proposed to be 70 per cent and the balance 30 per cent is proposed to be met partly as subsidy from Central/State Governments and partly as beneficiary contribution in cash, kind and labour. This, however, is the assumption that there would not be any change in technology leading to reduction in costs. The investment expected from the institutional financing bodies would be of the order of Rs. 2800 crore. The bulk of institutional finance for housing in the country is provided by HUDCO, NHB, 25 HFIs and Commercial Banks for direct lending and the LIC/GIC for supportive lending for housing sector. There is a need for all financing institutions to lend their helping hand for supporting the additional 20 lakh houses every year.

One of the key demands in the housing programme is active participation of Private Sector. A package of incentives and concessions is needed to attract the private sector. It is proposed that shelter delivery would be through private sector public housing agencies, co-operative sector and NGO/CBOs. The implementation of the programme would require a strong public private partnership in assembly/ development of land provision of infrastructure and shelter delivery.

While the Union government is responsible for policy formulation, the actual implementation lies with the State Governments. At the Central Government level, the Ministry of Urban Affairs and Employment will be directly involved in the policy formulation on urban housing, for the techno-financing dimensions for the whole housing sector and legal and regulatory reforms in the sector. Ministry of finance would be involved in granting various fiscal concessions so as to make the housing sector attractive for investment and in allowing additional resource mobilisation through market borrowings and international assistance. Ministry of Law would need to consider reforms in the regulatory regime particularly speeding up of foreclosure procedures and amendments required on other statutes which have impact on the housing sector.

Requirements of Funds

As has been pointed above, the total investment requirement for the construction of 7 lakh additional units is of the order of Rs. 4,000 crore, annually. This consists of institutional finance of the order of Rs. 2,800 crore including equity support to HUDCO to be provided through central budget and the balance Rs. 1,200 crore consists of subsidy from Central/State Govts. and beneficiary contribution in cash, kind and labour. Assuming that the investment requirement remains constant over a period of time the requirement for implementation of PMSA during IX Plan works out to Rs. 16000 crore because PMSA commences from the second year of the Ninth Plan (1997-2002).

Physical Targets

The physical targets under SAP are 7 lakh additional dwelling units annually starting from second year of the Ninth Plan (1997-2002).

Assuming that physical output of formal sector institutions in the implementation of SAP would be commensurate with the investment requirement of 70 per cent, the target for formal sector financial institutions would be 4.9 lakh dwelling units annually and the balance 2.1 lakh units would be provided by the beneficiary contribution ,subsidy. Out of formal sector institutions HUDCO is expected to build one third of the total target namely 2.33 lakh dwelling units annually. However since there is likely delay in the implementation of the SAP and HUDCO is currently engaged with the task of providing roughly one lakh dwelling units annually through ongoing schemes the additional target for HUDCO has been kept at a reduced level of 1.5 lakh dwelling units for 1998- 99 instead of 2.33 lakh originally proposed. The shortfall in the current year (0.83 lakh dwelling units) may be undertaken by other Formal Sector Institutions. During the remaining years of IX Plan (i.e. 1999-2002), HUDCO could take up one third of the shortfall in 1998-99 (i.e. 0.83 lakh dwelling units) over and above the original target of 2.33 lakh dwelling units.

As an incentive for taking up the additional targets in the formal sector through the various activities/programmes a corpus of approximately Rs. 100 crore could be set up which could be utilised for leveraging additional resources for meeting the requirement of funds for housing of the deprived sections of the society

Housing is a State subject. Given the wide variation in the housing needs in the States and constraint of resources to meet the housing needs, State Govts. and UTs would have to play a critical role in formulating plans and programmes suited to local needs and conditions in consultation with the local bodies. State Governments would need to identify the specific agencies for implementation of the Action Plan. Development of housing infrastructure and services has not kept in tune with the growth of housing. The problem of upgradation and renewal of basic services like potable drinking water and sanitation is serious. An integrated programme for land assembly and infrastructure development particularly water supply, sanitation, drainage and electric supply would require to be taken up on a priority basis. Action of the State Government would need to take into account the resource flow from the private, cooperative and public sectors. The role of the Central Government would be to guide and facilitate the implementation of Action Plan. The synergy created with the efficiency of private sector and experience of the public agencies would ensure that the overall costs is kept at minimum.

Special Action Plan for Rural Housing

Present Status of Construction In Rural Housing: At present it is estimated that approx **12.3 lakh houses** are being constructed annually in rural areas under various housing schemes. Based on this estimation it was projected that approx 61.50 lakh houses (i.e. 12.30 lakh x 5 years) will be added to the overall housing stock between 1997-2002 AD at the 1997-98 level of funding. In addition, from the Additional Central Assistance (ACA) for BMS which includes rural housing as one of the seven components, it is estimated that at least 1.70 lakh additional housing units would be constructed annually from 1998-99 to 2001-02. Therefore, a total of 68.30 lakh units of rural houses were to be constructed as per earlier projections.

Special Action Plan for Social Infrastructure: Targets for Rural Housing: Under the Special Action Plan for Rural Housing, an additional 13 lakh new houses are required to be constructed annually in the rural areas in addition to the existing 12.3 lakh units per year. Therefore, the total houses to be constructed annually would increase commensurately to 25.30 lakh.

Operational Strategy to Achieve the Targets Set Under Special Action Plan for Social Infrastructure: Portfolio of Rural Housing Schemes To Be Implemented: The task for preparing the Action Plan on Rural Housing has been taken up in the second year of the Ninth Five Year Plan i.e. 1998-99. The composite housing strategy for the Ninth Five Year Plan is multi-pronged and includes proposed modifications in the existing housing schemes and certain new initiatives. These are detailed below:

- **Indira Awaas Yojana (IAY)- Main Programme**: The Indira Awaas Yojana is the most important rural housing scheme which aims at providing dwelling units free of cost to the rural poor living below the poverty line. On 1.1.1996 with the restructuring of Jawahar Rozgar Yojana (JRY), IAY became an independent Centrally Sponsored Scheme (CSS) for shelter for the rural poor with resources being shared on a 80:20 ratio between the Centre and States. The main objective of the scheme is to construct dwelling units free of cost for the target group below the poverty line which comprises SC/ST, freed bonded labourers and also non-SC/ST families. The cost norms under IAY have been periodically increased and in the latest upward revision the maximum ceiling of assistance admissible under IAY has been raised from Rs. 14,000 to Rs. 20,000 in plain areas and from Rs. 15,800 to Rs. 22,000 in the hilly/difficult areas.

The existing scheme has a limited format i.e. construction of new houses. As the need for upgradation of unserviceable kutcha houses in the rural areas is acutely felt, the existing pattern of public investment in the rural housing sector is not necessarily the most efficient. In principle, it would be cost effective to provide part financing for upgradation of existing houses as the field level situation supports this. Hence in its modified form it is proposed to implement the IAY in two components namely, (a) construction of new houses (at an average weighted cost of Rs. 20,900) and (b) upgradation of kutcha and unserviceable houses (at a unit cost of Rs. 10,000). States would be allowed to use up to 20 per cent of the funds allocated under IAY for the upgradation of unserviceable kutcha houses.

To correct the regional imbalance, implicit in the overall housing shortage, in the country, it would be imperative to change the existing allocation criterion under IAY from the incidence of poverty to actual housing shortages in States. Also the absorptive capacity of the States both physical and financial in terms of their 20 per cent share would also have to be taken note of as problems of implementation are acute in some States.

- **Credit-cum-Subsidy Scheme (CCS):** There are a large number of households in the rural areas who have not been covered under IAY, since they do not fall within the BPL category. For such households living just above the poverty line, but still constituting the segment of economically weaker sections, a new Credit-cum-Subsidy Scheme (as a sub-scheme of IAY) is proposed to be launched covering people up to twice the income level of the BPL families. The Finance Minister in his budget speech for 1998-99 has also made a reference to the introduction of such a scheme. Under this scheme it is proposed that 50 per cent of the assistance would be in the form of subsidy and 50 per cent as loan but within the IAY cost norms (presently Rs. 20,000 for the plain areas and Rs. 22,000 for the hilly/difficult area). The loan portion would be provided by financial institutions, commercial banks, housing boards, etc. and the refinance facility will be provided from HUDCO, National Housing Bank etc. The funding of the subsidy portion would be shared in the ratio of 80:20 between the Centre and the States. It is proposed to launch this scheme in 1998-99.

- **Innovative Stream for Rural Housing and Habitat Development (ISRHHD):** The Innovative Stream for Rural Housing and Habitat Development (ISRHHD) is proposed to be launched as a sub scheme of IAY on a pilot project basis for the BPL poor. Under this scheme it is proposed to encourage the use of cost effective, environment friendly, scientifically tested and proven indigenous and modern designs, technologies and materials to construct IAY houses suited to the particular location. The Innovative Stream for Rural Housing and Habitat Development would be launched in 1998-99, on a pilot scale.
- **National Housing Bank/Commercial Banks Funding**: The National Housing Bank (NHB) and other banks would have to enhance their performance in rural housing. The Golden Jubilee Rural Housing Finance Scheme (GJRHFS) was launched by the National Housing Bank in 1997-98 with its coverage extending to the rural areas and to small towns having a population up to 50,000. The benefits of this scheme have however been cornered mainly by the small towns. The total estimated contribution of NHB and other commercial banks to rural housing annually is only 0.6 lakh units.

In the Budget speech of the Finance Minister, the NHB has been directed to finance 1.00 lakh rural dwelling units under the

Swarna Jayanti Housing Finance Scheme (SJHFS) as against the existing 50,000 units.

- **Rural Building Centres (RBCs):** To address the primary objectives of technology transfer, information dissemination, skill upgradation through training of rural masons, plumbers etc. and production of cost effective and environment friendly materials, there is a need to establish an institutional network of RBCs in all the districts in the rural areas as has been done in the urban areas.

Rural Building Centres in the rural areas would be taken up initially on a pilot basis. After assessing the viability of this scheme, it would be extended in a phased manner to cover all the districts of the country.

- **Housing and Urban Development Corporation:** The Housing and Urban Development Corporation (HUDCO) is functioning with equity support provided by Government of India, as the apex national techno-financing agency in the housing sector. So far its operations have been largely confined to urban areas. However, at present HUDCO is directing 15 per cent of its total housing resources for financing housing activity in the rural areas and constructing approx. 3.00 lakh rural houses annually. In his budget speech the Finance Minister has enhanced the capital base of HUDCO by Rs. 110 crore so that it may leverage more funds for housing construction in the urban and rural areas.

Equity participation by the Department of Rural Employment and Poverty Alleviation (DREPA), Ministry of Rural Areas and Employment (MRAE) in HUDCO earmarked for rural housing would facilitate HUDCO to raise eight times of the amount from the market for construction of additional houses. By way of illustration Rs. 50 crore equity participation in HUDCO would leverage Rs. 400 crore and which would finance 1.8 lakh houses in rural areas (It may be noted that houses to be constructed by HUDCO with equity participation from Department of Rural Employment and Poverty Alleviation in the remaining 4 years of

Ninth Plan (1998-99 to 2001-2002) would be an additionality over their existing effort at constructing 3 lakh houses annually.

- **Cooperative Housing**: The cooperative housing movement has also contributed to the housing sector by constructing 7.00 lakh units in the rural areas. It is expected to improve its performance in the ensuing years of the Ninth Five Year Plan period.
- **Others including BMS**: The Basic Minimum Services (BMS) programme was launched in pursuance of the recommendations of the Chief Ministers' Conference held in July, 1996. Housing has been identified as one of the seven components of the BMS to provide housing to the shelterless poor in a time bound manner. In addition to the normal State Plan provisions for BMS being made in the States/UTs Annual Plans and the funds routed through the Centrally Sponsored Schemes, the Central Government provided Additional Central Assistance (ACA) for BMS to the States and UTs. It is assumed that from the ACA provided to the States for BMS, at least 1.70 lakh additional housing units would be constructed annually under BMS in the rural areas. Further, it is projected that outside IAY 5.80 lakh housing units will be constructed by various financial institutions like NHB/Commercial Banks and State Governments rural housing programmes. It is therefore estimated that 7.50 lakh additional units would be constructed annually outside IAY by various housing agencies.

Ninth Plan: Physical targets

In the first year of the Ninth Plan i.e. 1997-98 the Central outlay for rural housing (i.e. IAY) was Rs. 1190.00 crore. With this financial provision approximately 7.00 lakh IAY houses were constructed during that year. Approx. 5.30 lakh units have been constructed outside the IAY by various housing agencies and by the State Governments. Therefore the total houses constructed in 1997-98 were approx 12.30 lakh.

In the financial year 1998-99, a Central outlay of Rs. 1600.00 crore has been provided in the Budget for Rural Housing. Based on this Central provision it is estimated that 13.28 lakh houses can be constructed under the IAY and other housing schemes. In addition 7.50 lakh houses would be constructed under other rural housing schemes implemented by the State Governments, including rural houses constructed under BMS, thereby cumulating a total of 20.78 lakh units in the current year.

At the end of the Ninth Plan i.e. 2001-02, 109.53 lakh units would be constructed under various housing schemes in the rural areas.

Tenth Plan

By the end of the Ninth Plan, 109.53 lakh units would be constructed leaving a residual gap of 78.17 lakh units (i.e. 187.70 – 109.53= 78.17 lakh units). It may be noted that at the end of the Ninth Plan the housing shortage would be only in terms of unserviceable and kutcha houses needing upgradation in the Tenth Plan. However, housing shortages during the Tenth Plan are likely to be surfaced on account of population growth. These shortages would be taken care of during the Tenth Plan.

Implementation

The IAY is implemented through District Rural Development Agencies (DRDAs) specially set up in each district of the country for the implementation of rural development programmes or through Zilla Parishads. At the field level the block machinery is entrusted with the responsibility of ensuring that targets for construction of houses under IAY are achieved. At the village level the onus is on the gram sabha to identify and select the beneficiaries. However, given that most State Governments also have their own rural housing programmes, in order to facilitate the implementation of a composite housing plan in the States, it is proposed that the Centrally Sponsored Scheme of Indira Awas Yojana be transferred to the State sector, to be implemented by the State Governments with Central assistance specifically earmarked for this purpose.

The Credit-cum-Subsidy Scheme and the Innovative Stream for Rural Housing and Habitat Development would also be implemented by the DRDAs/Zilla Parishads. The former scheme would be implemented in collaboration with financial institutions/commercial banks, housing boards with the refinance facility being provided by HUDCO and the NHB. The Innovative Stream for Rural Housing and Habitat Development would be implemented on a project basis through HUDCO/NGOs.

The scheme of Rural Building Centres would be implemented by HUDCO/well known State rural housing organisations and NGOs through the DRDAs.

Among the other housing schemes being implemented in the rural areas, the Golden Jubilee Housing Finance Scheme, which has a rural component, is being implemented by the NHB. The NGOs engaged in construction of rural houses are financed through CAPART.

Monitoring

The Department of Rural Employment and Poverty Alleviation in the Ministry of Rural Areas and Employment is responsible for release of Central share of funds, overall guidance, policy-making, monitoring and evaluation of the rural housing programme at the National level.

The programme is continuously monitored by Department of Rural Employment and Poverty Alleviation, on the basis of the monthly reports received from the States/UTs. Senior Officers of the rank of Deputy Secretary and above in the Ministry are appointed as Area Officers for different States/UTs. These Area Officers visit the allotted States/UTs from time to time and inspect among other programmes the actual implementation of the rural housing programme in the field. They also participate in the State Level Coordination Committee (SLCC) meetings providing thereby, an effective link between the policy makers (Government of India) and the implementing agencies (State/UT Governments).

The programmes are also reviewed at the meetings with the State Secretaries of Rural Development and with the Project Directors of DRDAs in the Workshops which are held annually.

The State Level Coordination Committee (SLCC) monitors the programme at the State Government level.

In addition to the regular monitoring of the programmes by the Ministry, the Programme Evaluation Organisation (PEO) of the Planning Commission also periodically evaluates programmes in the rural development sector. The PEO has carried out a quick study of IAY in 1992-93. A system of Concurrent Evaluation has been evolved by the Ministry of Rural Areas and Employment under which reputed independent institutions/research organisations are involved in undertaking the evaluation work. A Concurrent Evaluation of the IAY is being undertaken on the initiative of Department of Rural Employment and Poverty Alleviation.

Urban Development

Performance Review: The National Commission on Urbanisation (1988) had provided an assessment of the urban scenario and a long-term perspective. With this document as the base, and on the feedback of major sectoral developments and urban sector projects, the range of economic reforms initiatives, the New Delhi Declaration of ESCAP countries, 1994, Habitat II national report and UN Habitat Agenda, 1996, the formulation of a National Urban Policy was taken up as a priority activity. The preparation of State urbanisation strategy documents was another important activity, providing an insight into the future development needs in terms of new assets required to meet the anticipated demand for urban services. These State level documents have not, however, brought out the urban renewal and upgradation requirements. The Ninth Plan will seek to incorporate this aspect in the State urbanisation strategy documents so that, if required, these activities may be given special attention in on-going and future programmes, particularly relating to water supply, sanitation, sewerage and waste disposal. At the same time, the Plan would seek to strengthen the preparation and updating of State urbanisation strategy documents, with technical assistance, where necessary. The adoption of a commercial and market approach to infrastructure planning, development and management will be encouraged. For this purpose, suitable capacity building inputs would be provided to State and city officials. Within this macro urban agenda, various on-going schemes like the IDSMT, Mega City, UBSP, Slum Development, NRY, PMI-UPEP, Urban Mapping and any new schemes that might be introduced, will be dovetailed to attain the goals of the State macro urban development model.

The two aspects of urban development activities, namely the creation of new assets and upgradation of existing assets, would need to be taken up simultaneously to maintain the healthy urban environment, prevent the further process of deterioration and reduce the inequity in access to basic civic amenities. This deteriorating urban situation is reflected most glaringly in the extension of the "city within a city" syndrome of vastly varying urban environment conditions in different parts of the urban agglomerations. Action will be directed to positively contribute to the reduction of the existing level of these disparities and the State urban strategy will provide a valuable policy and operational framework.

Among the major legislative contributions of the Eighth Plan was the Constitution (74th Amendment) Act, 1992, also known as the Nagarpalika Act, which was passed by Parliament in 1992 and received the assent of the President on April 20, 1993. This landmark legislation provides a common framework for the structure and mandate of ULBs for effective democratic decentralisation. The Act provided a period of one year to amend or modify the existing municipal laws to bring them in conformity with the provisions of the Nagarpalika Act. The State and UT Governments have taken measures to establish State Finance Commissions (SFCs) and State Election Commissions (SECs). All States have established the SFCs and by March 1997, 10 SFCs have submitted their reports to their respective State Government.

There is, however, a long time lag between the submission of the SFC Report and its placement in the State legislature. The SECs have been established and have conducted elections in all ULBs except in Bihar and Orissa. In the case of Punjab, elections have been held in only two municipalities and 29 nagar panchayats. By January, 1997, about 60,000 elected representatives are in municipal corporations, municipal councils and nagar panchayats in 15 major States. The responsibilities and functions of the elected representatives have, however, yet to be articulated and defined by the State Governments. The District Planning Committees have been set up in only West Bengal, Kerala and Madhya Pradesh, where separate legislations have been enacted for this purpose. In none of the States has the government notified an area as a metropolitan area for the purposes of the Amendment.

Major efforts were made during the Eighth Plan to identify the lacunae and operational constraints in the Urban Land Ceiling and Regulation) Act, 1976 and these have been documented in the Habitat II National Report. The feedback on the implementation indicates failure to curb or prevent concentration of urban land holdings, profiteering, and ensure equitable distribution of land. Out of 4,06,282 applications filed in relation to excess vacant land, less than two-third were dealt with by the State/UT Governments and only 7.5 per cent of the 220,774 hec. of land declared surplus had been taken over. In terms of other indicators also, the performance has not been satisfactory. Exemption under Section 20 of the Act was provided in 53,963 cases, which was 42.1 per cent of the total application number submitted under this provision and only 2,984 schemes out of 9,638 (31.0 per cent) received approval under Section 21 of the Act for construction of dwelling units for the weaker section of society. The approved activities are expected to result in the construction of 4.83 lakh tenements on 5,327 hec. of land. There has been a slow-down in housing development due to delays in acquisition and transfer of surplus land. The Central Government should take up the rationalisation of the Act during the Ninth Plan and the thrust of the new approach would be guided development rather than regulation per se.

The NCR Planning Board was established with the object of containing Delhi's population within a manageable level and developing the National Capital Region in a harmonious and planned manner. As a part of its Regional Plan - 2001, the Board is finalising extensive land acquisition and development of physical infrastructure. It has prepared functional plans for Delhi Metropolitan Area as well as basic strategies and financial mechanism for use of funds. Sub-regional plans for Uttar Pradesh and Rajasthan sub-regions were approved by the Board in June, 1992 and April, 1994 respectively, while those for Haryana sub-region and for Delhi are under preparation and finalisation. An important functional plan for transport sector seeks to bring out a coordinated development of transport networks and shift the modal share from road-based to rail-based transport, which is likely to be more efficient, economic and environment-friendly.

The NCR is an innovative effort at regional planning and development is the only urban initiative to encompass several States. The approach is inter-sectoral, covering various components of regional infrastructure like road and rail transportation, power, communication, among others, apart from local level town-specific infrastructure and civic amenities. The regional development initiative is dependent on timely release of funds and convergence of the various activities of different organisations and partner governments so that the requisite infrastructure can be speedily developed and made operational. This is critical because any delay would lead to an increase in the population who may have to be deflected from Delhi and may create a situation which may be beyond the capacity of the 6 DMA and 8 priority towns in the NCR to properly absorb in terms of providing them adequate and affordable shelter, civic amenities and opportunity to take up a sustainable income-generating activity. Delay in implementation of the programmes carries the risk of making the regional planning initiative a non-viable activity within a short period.

Recognising the potential of the NCR strategy to promote and sustain effective regional development, the NCR programme will be further strengthened to promote regional development in the identified locations. Similar programmes of developing new townships will be promoted in other parts of the country where regional disparities and economic backwardness are critical concerns and also where there is a need to develop viable townships around metropolitan cities.

The IDSMT scheme, an extremely valuable development instrument for small and medium towns, was initiated in the Sixth Plan in 1979-80 to develop the infrastructure, primarily the physical components, in selected towns with population up to 5 lakh, that were assessed to have the potential to emerge as regional centres of economic growth and employment and serve as catchment centres to arrest migration to large towns and cities. The guidelines were revised in August 1995 to make its implementation more effective. A major change was in the financing strategy. Prior to the revision, the entire funding was in the form of loan and a large proportion, 40-70 per cent, was to be mobilised from financial institutions, which was found to be a major operational constraint for most of the municipalities. The revised guidelines provide for varying levels and mix of grant (Central and State) in the ratio of 60:40 and institutional finance /internal revenues to the extent of 20-40 per cent of the project cost. Grant-in-aid for the preparation of town development plans and project reports has also been provided for.

The IDSMT scheme has covered 904 towns up to the end of the Eighth Plan and the cost of the approved schemes, as on March 31, 1997, was Rs. 1427.38 crore and the Central assistance released was Rs. 283.96 crore. During the Eighth Plan, 387 towns were covered, with approved cost of Rs. 890.65 crore and as much as Rs. 403.68 crore was on commercial shops and stalls. The Ninth Plan would develop mechanisms to ensure a better mix of projects.

The revised scheme is expected to be a major instrument of urban sector reforms in the selected growth centres, as envisaged under the Constitution (74th Amendment) Act, as it promotes the use of Central and State grant components to leverage resources internally through the project and externally from financial institutions. The internal resources will develop a Revolving Fund, which would strengthen the municipal financial base for the future. Also, special attention is now paid to economic analysis of the projects, based on cost-benefits techniques.

The performance review brings out a concentration of project activities in a few areas like market complex/shopping centre, tourist facilities, roads and bus terminals. There is no feedback on the impact of these developments on city/town development as well as regional development. The efforts of the implementing agencies have been to see that the number of towns earmarked for coverage in the Plan has been largely covered, but even in respect of the numerical targets of coverage, the annual Plan sanctions have not been as per the provisions made in the Plan. The release of funds has not been satisfactory.

It is too early to get a feedback on the introduction of the cost-benefit analysis in the IDSMT activities, as this component was introduced in the revised guidelines in August, 1995 and is being actually included in the project reports from 1996-97. The Ninth Plan would monitor the progress on this important component since the social and economic benefits should be higher than the cost of the special initiatives taken through the IDSMT at the town and regional level.

One reason for the shortfall has been identified to be the failure of the State Governments to make their contribution and in some cases, the Central funds have not been properly utilised. This has happened because of inadequate monitoring, as the monitoring exercise was limited to administrative reports from the State Government and occasional visits by Central officials to the State capital and some project sites, where there was not much opportunity for Central officials to directly interact with the beneficiaries independently.

The Mega City Scheme, introduced in 1993-94, covers five mega cities of Mumbai, Calcutta, Chennai, Bangalore and

Hyderabad. As on April 30, 1997, 163 projects were sanctioned for an approved project cost of Rs. 1,439.22 crore. Work has been completed in 14 projects, is in progress in 136 projects, and is to be initiated in 13 projects. An expenditure of Rs. 493.99 crore had been incurred, even though the Central and State governments had released Rs. 703.80 crore as their share. The balance is to be raised by the projects from the capital market and financial institutions, using the Central and State government's contribution for leverage. HUDCO had approved a loan of Rs. 383.56 crore to 20 projects (26.6 percent of approved project cost), and only 31.1 percent of this had been released (Rs. 119.16 crore). The Ninth Plan will strengthen the follow-up and monitoring functions so as to accelerate the development of projects at all the stages and ensure that the leverage effect is a minimum of 50 per cent. To facilitate the attainment of this target, the scope of more financial institutions providing institutional finance, including from the private sector, will be explored.

The Scheme takes up three categories of projects, namely, remunerative, user charge-based and non-remunerative or service-oriented. The recommended mix is 40:30:30 among the three categories so that the total city project is financially viable. A study of the project mix shows under-realisation of the ratio of remunerative projects in the case of Calcutta, Bangalore and Mumbai, where the ratio is in the range of 16-18 per cent and it is 35 per cent in Chennai. However, it is 51 per cent in Hyderabad. In contrast, the ratio was attained in all cities except Calcutta for the non-remunerative projects, suggesting that the concern of total city-level project viability does not appear to have been given due attention. This aspect in project selection will be taken up in the Ninth Plan projects.

Project selection criteria should also take into account the inclusion of only those projects which are not likely to receive funding from other accessible sources, especially under the remunerative projects category. Housing, truck terminal, market, shopping and office complexes may have to be given a lower priority. Some non-remunerative category projects have a good potential to be covered under user-charge category, such as flyovers, bridges, public conveniences. The Ninth Plan would focus on development of urban fringes, urban renewal, sanitation, sewerage and drainage, ring roads, while other activities in the illustrative guidelines will have to be taken up through other financial strategies. Thus, for example, city beautification may be given for adoption by major corporates in the public and private sectors, with advertisement rights; wastes collection and disposal through commercialisation of the recycling of solid wastes; slum improvement through alternate programmes; and truck and bus terminals, housing, land development and commercial complexes through privatisation.

While the period of implementation of the Mega City Scheme may not be adequate to assess the impact, the Ninth Plan would take up impact assessment as an activity before extension of the programme within the selected cities and to other mega cities that are likely to emerge in the country. The impact assessment inputs would also facilitate the project components to become more focussed. The initial flow of projects brings out the need for a comprehensive City Urban Agenda on infrastructure requirements, new as well as in the renewal category, together with proper estimates and the cost-benefit analysis. The mega city nodal agencies should also take into account the metropolitan and regional aspects and not restrict their activities to land development and housing. In this context, the state and city town planning laws, urban development authority acts, etc, should be amended to facilitate planning reforms and permit schemes like land adjustment, for example, to promote the use of land as a resource.

This macro approach to mega city planning is essential to decide upon the projects that may be undertaken under the Mega City Scheme and those that may have to be marketed for implementation by other agencies and sources of financing, including the private sector. It is also necessary to break up the massive activities during the Ninth Plan and thereafter into a well-defined time schedule, to ensure the completion of the total infrastructure development on which the sustainability of the mega city depends.

The project feedback brings out that the leverage activity has not yet become fully operational. The Plan will review the reasons for inadequate leverage effect in the project funding and, in that context, consider modifications in the scheme and any other inputs, including fiscal instruments, and professionalising the financial functions that may be required to make the instrument of leverage funds an effective mechanism. Special attention should be paid to strengthen the monitoring of the scheme, which presently is being done through informal reviews and reporting mechanism. The regular monitoring and impact assessment functions may be institutionalised in an independent agency, outside the project for the effective implementation of the scheme.

Cost recovery is another crucial factor for the success of the scheme and for this purpose direct as well as indirect methods will be introduced. The latter may include, for example, conversion charges for change of land use, development and betterment charges related to impact of on-site and off-site activities, Tradable Development Right (TDR) as per the Mumbai model, extra FAR/FSI surcharge, Shelter Tax on large and luxury housing to finance low-income housing, etc. These innovative strategies will be preceded by specific assessment of the real estate market situation and potential revenue generation analysis to determine the type of instruments to be used and the most suitable timing for mobilising resources to meet the cost of the project, and possibly for generating a surplus.

Slum Development is another major activity taken up to upgrade the urban environment and see that the proliferation of slum and squatter settlements does not further deteriorate it. In the past, several schemes have been introduced to improve the living conditions in the slums, where an increasing proportion of the urban poor and migrants live and often work. Recognising the poor access to basic urban services in these settlements, the UBSP and EIUS have been provided some specific Plan support to improve the access to basic services. During the Eighth Plan, a new Centrally assisted Scheme was introduced in 1996, with an initial outlay of Rs. 250 crore for the year and this amount was raised to Rs. 330 crore for 1996-97. The funds have been provided as additional Central assistance to the States/UTs. The Planning Commission has constituted a Working Group to examine the mechanism for determining the State allocations under this Scheme and to examine, among other issues, the possibility of going beyond the conventional criterion of the share of urban population in the State for funds allocation. The NHB introduced a Slum Redevelopment Scheme during the Plan period to provide financial assistance to the implementing agencies for housing development and upgradation and provision of habitat infrastructure like drinking water and sanitation.

The Environment Improvement in Urban Slums (EIUS) scheme is a high priority programme to provide seven basic amenities to slum households, namely, water supply, storm water drains, community baths and latrines, widening and paving of existing pathways and street lighting and other community facilities. The scheme was introduced in 1972 as a Centrally sponsored scheme but was transferred to the State sector in 1974. The ceiling on per capita expenditure has now been raised to Rs. 800/per slum dweller in consultation with the Planning Commission effective from 1.4.1995. The programme is integrated with the existing urban poverty alleviation scheme and seeks the involvement of resident associations.

A scheme for provision of infrastructural facilities in the Displaced Persons (East Bengal refugees) Colonies in West Bengal is in operation. After considering a note submitted by the Ministry of Rehabilitation in 1976, the Cabinet approved the proposal to fund infrastructural development for 1,03,157 plots in 612 colonies at a cost of Rs.23.85 crore. The development components included provision of water supply, drainage, roads and pathways, sanitation and other items. A revised ceiling cost of Rs. 17,777/per plot for development, reimbursement of Rs. 2.33 crore to the State Government and provision of Rs.78 crore in the Central budget as grant for completing the work on the remaining

44,025 plots (originally approved in 1976) was approved by the Cabinet in January, 1995.

Several programmes are on stream with international assistance and cooperation. The KFW loan and grant assistance to HUDCO is for undertaking housing schemes for EWS, Building Centre Programme, low-cost housing in rural and urban areas, low-cost sanitation, slum improvement, reconstruction in Latur and to HDFC for low cost housing and urban infrastructure. The OECF (Japan) has provided assistance for city water supply project in Sholapur and New Mumbai and some other infrastructure activities. The World Bank has extended a grant of US$ 1.0 million to HUDCO for strengthening its infrastructure-related operations, in particular, technical assistance for the preparation of the proposed Urban Infrastructure Financing Project. The World Bank has also provided a line of credit to the Government of Maharashtra for reconstruction of the housing stock and other infrastructure damaged in the Latur earthquake. According to the latest report, 15,713 houses have been completed and 9,292 houses are under construction. Under the repairs and retrofitting component 57,196 houses have been retrofitted, and 86,999 houses are under development.

The Overseas Development Administration (ODA, UK) supports slum improvement projects in seven Indian cities, in collaboration with the Ministry of Urban Affairs and Employment, Government of India. The Programme started in 1983 in Hyderabad, and since 1988, additional projects have been approved in Vishakapatnam, Vijayawada, Indore, Calcutta, Cuttack and Cochin. The project components include development of physical infrastructure, provision of civic amenities, community development and provision of social, economic and educational inputs to contribute towards raising the standard of living of inhabitants in slum settlements. The Government of Netherlands supports a pilot project, Bangalore Urban Poverty Alleviation Project (BUPP), at an estimated cost of Rs.1.5 crore in phase -I, which commenced in November 1993 and is likely to be completed by the end of March 1997. The second phase is likely to commence soon. The project is being executed jointly by the Central Ministry of Urban Affairs and Employment, HUDCO and the Government of Karnataka.

The Urban Mapping Scheme, a Eighth Plan programme, with an outlay of Rs. 6 crore, was undertaken for preparing, on a pilot basis, base maps for 25 identified towns, using the aerial photographing and remote sensing techniques so that urban maps could be updated with the Geographic Information System (GIS). The Town and Country Planning Organisation (TCPO) is the national nodal agency for this task, which is to be undertaken by the National Remote Sensing Agency (NRSA), Hyderabad. The task ahead is enormous, including preparation of new maps, apart from updating some existing maps in some urban centres. This would constitute an important Ninth Plan activity to provide a strong base for effective implementation of the Constitution (74th Amendment) Act provisions relating to a three-tier planning structure at the local, state and regional level.

Other Programmes include research on urban policy, land use planning and development, municipal governance, housing, etc, with an outlay of Rs. 1 crore per annum during the Eight Plan. Impact assessment of the research output has not been made. The Ninth Plan will review these activities and make the funding of research through this outlay as per an urban research agenda, which will be prepared by sectoral experts, keeping in view the priority concerns in the Ninth Plan. A transparent system of funding policy and research impact assessment will be developed.

The World Bank and the Asian Development Bank have provided external assistance for urban sector projects, the former in Tamil Nadu and Uttar Pradesh and the latter in Karnataka. While Uttar Pradesh Urban Development Project was closed on 31.3.96, Tamil Nadu Urban Development Project is under implementation, with a revised project outlay of Rs. 988.50 crore. Negotiations were held with the World Bank for restructuring the existing Tamil Nadu Municipal Urban Development Funds (MUDF) into Tamil Nadu Urban Development Funds (TNUDF) to be set up under the Companies Act.

The ADB is funding the Karnataka Urban Infrastructure Development Project, whose estimated cost is $ 132 million. The project aims to decongest Bangalore through decentralisation of economic activities to four project towns of Mysore, Tumkur, Channapatnam and Ramanagaram to be developed as counter-magnets and maintain the status of Bangalore as a centre for high-tech industry, reduce the pressures on the infrastructure of Bangalore and improve living conditions in the city. Another ADB project in the pipeline is the Development of West Coast Districts of Karnataka. The Department of Economic Affairs, Central Ministry of Finance has recommended to the ADB, the proposal with having an estimated cost of Rs. 758 crore and an external assistance component of Rs. 430 crore. The Bank has since approved in principle to provide a Project Preparatory Technical Assistance of US$ 800,000 during 1997. Another ADB activity is the India Urban Sector Profile (TA Study), for which an agreement was signed in October, 1994 with ADB for financial assistance of US$ 435,000.The project will review India's Urban Sector policies and programmes and suggest areas/projects for future ADB involvement in urban infrastructure in India. Another Technical Assistance (TA) agreement has been signed between Government of India and ADB to determine the scope of investment in six selected towns in Rajasthan.

Ninth Plan Priorities and Strategies

Urban India presents a classic example of a developing scenario with high concentration of urbanisation and economic growth in certain parts of the country, as well as in certain parts of a State. While the IDSMT scheme, special industrial development programmes in backward regions and fiscal incentives have sought to reduce disparities in regional development, the regional disparities have continued.

The priority concern is not only to stop the growing deterioration in the urban environment, reflected in key urban indicators on housing conditions, pollution levels, traffic congestion, informal sector, among others, but to positively change the trend and ensure an improved, healthy and congenial environment. The wide gap between the demand and supply of basic civic amenities like potable water, sanitation, transport and housing, which has shown an increasing trend over the last five decades, will be reduced, through creation of new assets, upgradation and renewal of existing assets, attaining better operational and management efficiency and stimulating flow of resources into all urban development activities.

Regional development, strengthening of the rural-urban continuum and development of new centres of human settlements and economic activities as an alternative to the highly congested metro and mega cities will be among the priority tasks in the Ninth Plan. An increasing proportion of these activities will be financed from outside the Plan resources. The Eighth Plan had initiated a few innovative practices, most notably the use of Plan funds to leverage non-Plan resources from the financial system, through leveraging funds from financial institutions and the capital market. Conceptually, the strategy is well-founded; how effective it has been in the Indian urban situation has to be ascertained. The instrument has been effectively used in the industrial sector for a considerable period, though the leverage base has been the equity capital that has to be serviced and not a grant. If the impact assessment of the urban infrastructure leverage instrument brings out a performance that is lower than anticipated, the reasons should be identified so that the Government, as a facilitator, would be in a position to take appropriate steps to ensure the effectiveness of the leverage strategy. Fiscal instruments, legal provisions and strengthening of professionalism in the municipalities and urban local bodies will be some illustrative areas for suitable intervention with the aim of formulating financially viable projects, undertaking rigorous techno-economic appraisal and facilitating efficient implementation of projects.

The matching of the Central Plan outlays with State finances was another positive participatory endeavour. These activities will be strengthened and the observed operational constraints would be removed. The new approaches to urban finance, initiated during the Eighth Plan, together with an integrated approach to planning and management, should be supported by an equally strong system of monitoring the project and periodic assessment of its impact, to ensure the reach out, especially of the subsidised non-remunerative projects to the specific target groups. The much-required sustainability in financing urban development is expected to be attained through this route. A composite approach to urban development that encompasses inter-dependent urban basic services will further strengthen the development process. These, indeed, are the challenges for the Ninth Plan.

In the context of a regional approach to urban development, the activities of NCR Planning Board are critical to contain deterioration of the environment of Delhi and the participatory efforts of the States should be effectively mobilised. At the same time, development of small and medium towns should gather further momentum and there is clear need to improve the package of remunerative and non-remunerative projects in IDSMT scheme to go beyond the conventional activities like shopping plaza and bus terminal to take up also activities that would bring in sustainability to the urban environment. Critical among them are drinking water, sanitation and waste management as the sustainability of small and medium towns has to be ensured not only in terms of the economic viability parameter but also the environmental sustainability parameter. The standard of cost-benefit analysis to assess the viability of projects, introduced during the Eighth Plan, will be improved through capacity building for inducting a high level of professionalism in the project contents.

It is equally important to improve the composition of the projects under the Mega City scheme and shift the focus to development of urban fringe, urban renewal, sanitation, sewerage and drainage, ring-roads in preference to the Eighth Plan activities like housing, truck terminal, market, shopping and office complexes, which should be given lower priority in the product mix, as they can be supported through commercial and privatisation routes. The slow pick-up of the Mega City scheme was to an extent due to the teething problems but in view of its significant potential to become a catalyst of infrastructure development, the Plan will seek to accelerate project development and implementation processes. It would be desirable in the Ninth Plan to evolve the criteria for funds allocation under the scheme and going beyond the present population criterion to give weightage to indicators like decadal population growth rate, performance in project implementation, resource mobilisation, credibility of the nodal agency and development needs. More emphasis will also be given to promote integrated land use development planning with regard to mapping, use of remote sensing and Geographic Information System (GIS) for preparation of city maps and city/town, metropolitan and district 3-tier Development Plans, covering the annual, five year and long-term perspectives (20-25 years).

Planning and development of urban infrastructure in mega cities as well as elsewhere should be properly structured and the basic requirement is a comprehensive city agenda which would estimate the current infrastructure requirements as also the projections for the next two decades, covering new assets as well as renewal of existing assets. The operational plan, particularly the activities to be undertaken by the key actors should be formulated at the city level and participatory approach should be adopted to earmark the tasks of implementation of tasks among the various agencies, including the private sector. The massive investment activity should be broken up into a well-defined time schedule so that the physical and financial targets are attained and the anticipated impact realised. Cost recovery has to be a major concern though in certain cases, the concept may have to be gradually introduced and subsidy in the provision of certain services may have to be continued during the Plan.

A process of rapid urbanisation invariably places pressures on land, resulting in an increase in land cost, and consequent impact on cost of all land-based activities and services required for sustainable urban development and environment. A choice has to be often made between high-rise and low-rise urban planning strategies. Within each of the alternatives, there is the planning option to promote high or low densities, though the tendency, a priori, is to relate high density with high-rise planning and low density with low-rise planning.

It will not be desirable in this perspective, to recommend a single strategy in the planning of cities. There has to be a different approach in urban planning in small and medium towns, where land may not be a scarce resource as compared to that in metro and mega cities. Several parameters should be given appropriate weightage in conceptualising and developing the city plans and these may include, for example, the affordability of the people to absorb the high-rise and low-rise housing solutions, the impact on the urban environment and quality of life, the implications on energy consumption, travel time from home to workplace, recreation facilities, open spaces, linkage with habitat-related services, etc. Equally important is the financial implication and the cost of funds that might be required for different types of city development programmes.

It was in this context, that the National Commission on Urbanisation had recommended Low-Rise High Density (LRHD) development to be the pre-dominant built up form in urban India. The adoption of this strategy would require a good understanding of the socio-economic conditions of the city dwellers and often modification in existing building bye-laws, zoning regulations, developments codes and land use and management systems. The advantage of low-rise settlements is the low cost of construction, efficiency in energy consumption, socially and psychologically more acceptable and environment-friendly neighbourhoods. From the operational point of view, a high density component in low rise structures might give rise to management challenges. Operational and financial implications of spread of essential utilities and services, including transport, have to be taken into consideration.

The Ninth Plan will follow up on the progress made during the Eighth Plan in creating an urban development-friendly planning and fiscal environment. The Constitution (74th Amendment) Act and the liberated economic policies have ensured an era of democratic decentralisation of the planning and a greater degree of involvement of the private sector. In this changed operational scenario, the urban planning system in vogue should be made more dynamic and participatory and the process of decentralisation has to be extended from the State to the urban local government. The institutional framework for financial and other intermediation, including planning and project development and management, has to recognise the key role assigned to the elected urban local bodies. The Plan will seek to promote and strengthen this approach.

It will, for example, encourage the constitution of the District Planning Committees (DPC), with an elected official as chairperson. The roles and functions of the DPC would include the consolidation of the plans of the panchayats and the municipalities to prepare the development plan for the district, coordination of all inter-related activities and funds, and monitoring the implementation of the district plans, schemes and projects and related activities. The Plan funds would be increasingly decided on the feedback from the DPC.

The Town Planning, Municipal and urban Development Authority and other State Parastatals Acts and regulations should be speedily amended and legal framework strengthened to assign the planning and development functions to the urban local bodies, facilitate planning reforms, permit schemes like land adjustment, for example, to promote the use of land as a resource and include all the emerging needs of planning and development in the light of the Constitution (74th Amendment) Act. The municipal/ city/town development plan will form a key component of plan financing at the local level and seek to maximise the linkages between infrastructure, land use, urban growth and economic growth.

The massive tasks of development and renewal of housing, urban infrastructure and civic amenities requires their integration into the urban and metropolitan planning system as well as in the broader State and city economic and financial plans. There should be complete integration of spatial, economic and financial planning at the city and regional levels. This has been a weak part in the urban development agenda. The Ninth Plan will take positive steps in this direction.

Within this macro framework, an integrated urban planning approach would require integration of planning and development of inter-dependent infrastructure components such as, for example, water supply, sewerage and sanitation, and wastes collection and disposal, which in their totality, determine the quality of the urban environment. A total package should be prepared, which would also facilitate the financing of the programme as it would have a judicious mix of projects that have the potential to provide commercial returns, recover full-cost user charges and provide zero return on certain critical social services. While the commercial projects would not be eligible for any subsidy, the user-charge projects should recover O and M and debt servicing cost, though subsidy through the financial package and other facilities may be provided on case-to-case basis, related to the extension of the services to the disadvantaged groups in the urban society.

The massive urban growth and the resource constraints would, together, result in a situation where the availability of funds would not keep pace with the growing demand. The State Government's efforts would have to be supplemented with larger participation by the private sector. Financing of urban infrastructure is bound to pose new challenges to the different constituents of the financing system. Innovative mechanisms and practices will have to be encouraged and supported to stimulate the flow of finances such as the municipal bond system, municipal financial reforms, fiscal and monetary incentives for the creation of investment-friendly environment, specialised infrastructure development and financial institutions, participation of cooperatives, community groups and NGOs, and public-private partnership in the development and management of urban services and social infrastructure facilities.

The fiscal provisions at the Central, State and local level should be made investment-friendly and conducive towards the flow of funds for urban infrastructure assets creation and renewal. Privatisation of activities in the social service sector as well as projects with long gestation period should be stimulated through the fiscal route rather than through direct subsidy in term loans and other development inputs. This will make the subsidisation of programmes not only transparent but will also speed up the development work and ensure the creation/renewal of the assets, as the fiscal instrument is ex-post and not ex-ante. Monitoring the effective reach out and periodic impact assessment would be also facilitated.

The Ninth Plan will strengthen the activities relating to data base, monitoring and evaluation as the existing system has been found to be inadequate. There is no single agency that is responsible for compiling and maintaining data and information and undertaking regular monitoring and evaluation work at the national, regional, state or city/town levels Even the Plan provisions have not been fully utilised. By way of illustration, the outlay of Rs. 1 crore to Central Public Health Engineering and Environmental Organisation (CPHEEO) and State/UTs during the Seventh Plan for creating a monitoring and MIS Cells was not utilised due to technical problems and procedural delays, and a similar provision in the Eighth Plan did not lead to the establishment of these Cells. .For development of the data base for housing and undertaking housing census, the Eighth Plan outlay was under-utilised . In the case of the Urban and Regional Information System (URIS), the TCPO as a nodal agency for many Centrally Sponsored Programmes like the IDSMT, has taken up the task of developing the urban data bank. These activities will be further strengthened and the scope for privatisation of certain components of the activity within the overall supervision of the TCPO would be explored.

Apart from these activities, where the Plan provisions for data base, monitoring and MIS were provided but were not effectively utilised, in all other major urban sector programmes, the Plan will seek to develop a strong data base and monitoring and impact assessment systems. This is a key requirement for efficient urban management. Regular feedback on the reach out of activities of all the actors, some of whom may not be subject to normal administrative monitoring, becomes crucial for the Government to decide when, where and how to intervene and the extent of the intervention. An effective partnership of the government and non-government agencies in this activity would be promoted and the UNCHS housing and urban indicators would be adopted to build up this activity.

Urban Transport

Performance Review: Urban transport has been a sector whose development and investment requirements have been largely overlooked in the past. The Central Plan allocation till the Eighth Plan was a modest Rs.4.6 crore, as urban transportation system was essentially perceived in the Plans to be an appendage to inter-city rail/road transport systems. It was not recognised that the development programmes in urban transportation were critical to the sustainability of the urban systems. This basic need has been acknowledged now as the rapidly deteriorating transport systems have been seen to affect the urban lifeline. Recent urban transport indicators have shown that the average travel time between home and work place is as much as 44.34 minutes in Delhi, 33.37 minutes in Mumbai, 21.62 minutes in Chennai and 17.60 minutes in Bangalore. The transport indicators also show that transport services utilise 13.6 per cent of the total land area in urban agglomerations, with 11.0 per cent in mega cities and 20.0 per cent in metro cities and 17.1 per cent in secondary towns.

A review of the mass transport modes in metropolitan cities has brought out that except in Mumbai, Chennai and Calcutta, which have suburban rail systems, the bus has been the main mode. Some metropolitan cities do not even have an intra-city bus system. Except for mega cities, modal split in favour of mass transport is poor and generally less than 20 per cent. Share of walk trips and mechanised non-motorised modes in total transport demand is quite high in metropolitan cities. Measures to promote non-motorised modes through provision of footpaths and other pedestrian facilities, cycle tracks and priority treatment at intersections should be an integral part of city transport plans. Land use and transport are strongly inter-related. Integrated Land Use-Transport Plans should be prepared for all metropolitan cities during the Ninth Plan period.

During the Eighth Plan, Central assistance was mainly confined to support the preparation of feasibility and other studies relating to urban transport systems in metro cities, DPR for Delhi MRTS project and contribution towards equity capital of Hyderabad LRT project. The total expenditure, as on March 31, 1996, was Rs. 18.32 crore and Rs.16.80 crore was spent during the Eighth Plan period.

The major urban transport projects that were approved or proposals were initiated during the Eighth Plan are in Delhi, Mumbai, Calcutta, Chennai and Bangalore. The Modified Phase I of the Delhi MRTS project was approved by the Union Cabinet in September, 1996. It consists of 11 kms of underground and 44.3 kms of surface/elevated railway tracks. The total cost of the modified Phase-1 project is estimated at Rs. 4,860 crore at April, 1996 prices. The project is to be implemented by Delhi Metro Rail Corporation Limited, a joint venture of Government of India and Government of National Capital Territory of Delhi. The OECF (Japan) has agreed to provide loan assistance up to about 60 per cent of the project cost. Initially, a loan of Rs. 478.78 crore (14.76 billion Yen) will be provided at 2.3 per cent rate of interest per annum.

The Mumbai Urban Transport Project-II consists of construction of fly-overs, roads, bridges, optimisation of suburban railways, and is being planned by the Government of Maharashtra and the Mumbai Metropolitan Regional Development Authority (MMRDA) in consultation with the Ministry of Railways. Studies on relocation and resettlement, community environmental management plans, among others, are being conducted by the Government of Maharashtra and further activities will be taken up by the State Government on completion of these studies. The Calcutta Metro Rail System, covering a length of 16.5 kms. from Dum Dum to Tollygunge, is operational. The system has been constructed by the Ministry of Railways out of their own budgetary sources. Government of West Bengal have proposed extension of this facility by 8.4 kms., from Tollygunge to Garia. As the Central Government's budgetary resources would not be adequate, the Government of West Bengal has been requested to meet 50 per cent of the project cost.

The Government of Karnataka has mooted a proposal for introduction of a Light Rail Transit System in Bangalore, covering a length of about 90 kms. at an approximate cost of Rs. 4,200 crore. A rail-based surface-cum-elevated MRT system already exists in Chennai from the Beach to Chepauk (5.05 kms.) This system is being extended up to Luz (3.5 kms.)by the Ministry of Railways. A proposal for construction of rail-based MRT system from Luz to Velacherry has also been approved and will be funded jointly by the Government of Tamil Nadu and Government of India (Ministry of Railways).

Ninth Plan Priorities and Strategies

It is now widely recognised that as cities grow in population and size, the demand for transport increases more than proportionately. A good network of roads, coupled with an efficient mass urban transport system makes a substantial contribution to the ``working efficiency" of the cities and enables them to become catalysts of economic, social and political development. An efficient transportation system is, thus, critical for productivity and economic growth in cities. It has been estimated that inefficient traffic and transportation system in the urban areas currently results in an annual loss of Rs. 20,000 crore in vehicle-operating costs and travel time costs.

Recognising the inter-dependence between the sustainability of urban systems and the transport network, the Ninth Plan would have a major focus on planning and development of a viable mix of transportation systems including road transport, MRTS and

LRT, making full use of all travel modes that would utilise underground, surface and elevation systems.

The development activities in the Ninth Plan would give a thrust to multi-modal transport programmes in order to meet the requirements of all categories of passengers, rather than giving priority to single modal transportation systems such as exclusive expressways which would primarily benefit only a small segment of the population, even though, these activities may be commercially viable through the levy of high user charges. The Ninth Plan strategy would, in this context, seek to reduce the role of private modes, owned by individuals and promote public transportation system, keeping in view the road density, pollution, travel time, parking facilities and other operational concerns.

There is also a need to regulate the entry of private vehicles in the central business districts as part of a demand management strategy. Disincentive measures may be introduced to restrict the entry of low passenger occupancy vehicles. The operational policy instruments may include high entry and parking charges and special levies for low occupancy. This has been already demonstrated as an efficient transport management strategy in several countries. The annual registration of new vehicles should keep in mind the holding capacity of the cities and the availability of the parking spaces. Proliferation of personalised modes like cars and scooters needs to be contained by measures such as penal registration rates.

Equally important is to strengthen the organisational and institutional systems to provide for planned and efficient intra-urban transportation system in the cities. A series of initiatives are required, such as, the setting up of an urban transport unit in the nodal ministry and in the Planning Commission, along with similar units at the State level.

The financing of transportation programmes is a critical issue. The initiatives of the Eighth Plan in regard to financing of urban infrastructure programmes should be made an integral part of the financing strategy for urban transportation. Effective public-private partnership will be promoted through appropriate fiscal and other stimulating initiatives so that the massive investment requirements, which are definitely beyond the capacity of the Plan can be mobilised from other sources as well as the domestic and international capital markets. These financing systems may include different types of leasing finance.

It must be recognised that the high costs, low profits and long-gestation periods of rail-based mass urban transportation projects do not make them financially viable nor do they yield commercial returns that would be as attractive as in the surface-based/elevated urban MRT projects. The Central/State Governments would have to necessarily participate in the equity of such projects and also consider making certain provisions for interest-free/low interest subordinate debt, incentives for property development, tax exemptions/ concessions, freedom to fix fares, etc. Budgetary and Plan support from the Central and State Governments will be required for these purposes. The resource mobilisation strategy that the Central and State Governments may adopt for financing these activities may include a mix of dedicated levies and taxes on user and non-user beneficiaries of mass transport systems, which may be in the form of additional excise duty/sales tax on petrol/diesel, surcharge on motor vehicle tax, entry fee on motor vehicles entering metropolitan areas, passenger terminal tax (rail, road, sea and air), surcharge on property tax and a mass transportation tax. The proceeds from these levies may be used to finance the capital costs of MRT projects, and also to discharge part of the long-term loan liabilities.

The exploitation of air space above and around the metro stations, depots, sheds etc, for commercial and residential purposes could generate a substantial amount towards the project cost, which can form a part of the State Government's capital contribution to MRT projects. Keeping in view these possible developments, there is a need to set up a National Urban Transport Development Fund during the Ninth Plan. This Fund would provide financial assistance for mass urban transport projects in the country, preparation of feasibility studies and project reports and training and R and D activities. Similar Funds at the city level may also be encouraged to meet the share of contribution of the State and the Urban Local Governments in urban transport projects.

Financial Resource Mobilisation

The wide range of activities that have to be undertaken in the sectoral programmes relating to urban development, housing, water supply, sanitation and transport would require not only a large quantum of financial resources but also their mobilisation on varying terms with respect to their cost and servicing conditions. The funds should be available in such a quantum and on terms that would meet the capacity/potential of the user sectors in absorbing and servicing them. In some cases, such as housing development and urban transport, there is a strong case for mobilising funds at market cost and then adopting a strategy of cross-subsidisation through different market segments. New housing construction has a good potential to absorb market-sourced/cost funds, especially for the upper market segments, as also public transport services. The lower end of the housing market would need subsidised funds, which should be provided through cross-subsidisation within the housing market. A large part of the rental housing market is also in a position to absorb market-sourced funds. Fiscal incentives such as income tax and property tax would, of course, be a good stimulant.

In the case of other sectoral activities like those relating to water supply, some portion of the funds may have to be mobilised at less than market cost, especially for augmentation of capacity of water supply, but for distribution, which generates immediate income flows, market-sourced funds are likely to be a feasible proposition. This is an activity suitable for privatisation and for accessing funds from thee private sector. The Ninth Plan would promote this route of resource mobilisation.

Plan resources by themselves cannot be expected to meet all the requirements. The well-structured financial sector reforms during the Eighth Plan have opened up the urban sector to a wide range of financial instruments including leasing finance and bond issues, even to urban local governments. International financial institutions are now keen to provide long-term credit, including on soft terms, to urban sector programmes. The Asian Development Bank has provided this type of assistance for the first time in India for some urban projects in Karnataka during the Eighth Plan. Specialised financial institutions have developed a range of term assistance programmes in the areas of housing, urban development, water supply, sanitation and urban transport. A strong financial system has been put into place which can play a significant role in providing the large quantum of financial resources on different terms and conditions to meet the requirements of the sector during the Ninth Plan.

Apart from mobilisation of funds from the domestic and global capital market, it would be necessary during the Ninth Plan for the implementing agencies to reduce the cost of their projects through careful planning of the details of the project, proper monitoring of the implementation so as to minimise, if not totally eliminate, time and cost overruns and ensuring efficiency in operational management. It is important to optimise the utilisation of the assets created, eliminate operational losses and play special attention to recovery of user charges and other tariffs, which also require a significant degree of rationalisation in terms of base and rate. The guiding principle should be full-cost recovery. There is a point of view that full-cost recovery in the initial period may have to be restricted in some sectors to O and M and it may be gradually extended over the Ninth and Tenth Plan periods. The important policy issues are to reduce project cost, optimise utilisation of assets and introduce a realistic pricing policy. These major steps would generate significant amount of internal resources, which could finance the developments in the sector, as well as reduce the total investment requirement.

The implementation of the Constitution Amendment Acts that empower urban local governments and panchayati raj institutions, has to be followed up by reviewing the resource-base of the local governments, both urban and rural, improving tax/revenue administration and rationalising some of the major income sources that have not kept in tune with developments in their areas as well as other economic realities. Active participation of the people in the planning and management of the sectoral programmes is also likely to improve the financial management system and thereby contribute to generation of internal funds for investment.

In this emerging economic and financial scenario, the Plan funds and other subsidised funds should be effectively used as a leverage to mobilise funds from other sources and for very specific programmes included in the Basic Minimum Services (BMS) and those that are targeted to identify priority groups. The leverage strategy was specifically introduced during the Eighth Plan in the Mega city project and the IDSMT scheme. It would be necessary to assess its impact, and if necessary, remove the operational constraints and then extend the strategy to all other sectors.

Tenth Five Year Plan: 2002-07 (Volume II)

Status of Urban Local Bodies

The Constitution (74th) Amendment Act, 1992 was intended to give a more focussed thrust to decentralisation and the creation of a democratic governance structure with local responsibilities being assumed and managed at the local level. It was to address the inadequacies of the existing system of municipalities, redefine the relationship between the states and municipal bodies and lay the foundations of a new approach to urban management and governance that could fulfil the needs and aspirations of urban residents for development. Article 243W of the Act mandated the setting up of elected municipalities - urban local bodies (ULBs) - as the 'institutions of self-government'. The important features of the Act are well-known but bear repetition since all of them have not been acted upon. These are:

- Regular elections under the supervision of the state Election Commission;
- a clear tenure of five years for the elected body;
- protection for the elected body against arbitrary dissolution;
- constitution of Wards Committees for greater proximity to the citizens;
- mandate to state legislature to endow the ULBs with such powers and authority as may be necessary to enable them to function as 'institutions of self-government';
- the Twelfth Schedule which illustrates the range of responsibilities to be given to the ULBs;
- the constitution of State Finance Commissions (SFCs) to review municipal finances and make recommendations regarding distribution of the proceeds of state-level taxes between the state governments and the ULBs, criteria for grants-in-aid, measures needed to improve the financial position of the municipal bodies, etc.;

- setting up District Planning Committees and Metropolitan Planning Committees for integrated as well as coordinated planning for urban and rural areas by the various agencies involved in providing civic, transport, economic and social services.

It is significant that apart from the traditional municipal functions, Article 243W allocates to ULBs the function of 'preparation of plans for economic development and social justice', and the Twelfth Schedule contains 'urban poverty alleviation' as a municipal responsibility. These take municipal bodies from being mere providers of civic amenities to a much wider arena of action encompassing economic and social planning. The Constitutional amendment has designed the ULBs as comprehensive institutions of urban self-government, and has left the details to be worked out by the state legislatures.

The state governments have carried out the required amendments to the municipal laws in accordance with their own requirements and some states have even enacted fresh legislation. Elections under the new dispensation have been held in most states, more than once in many. The enthusiasm among urban residents for the ULBs has been amply demonstrated by the fact that voter turnout in elections has been in the range of 65 to 70 per cent, much higher than the participation in elections to Parliament and state legislature. There are around 73,000 elected representatives in the ULBs all over the country. It has, therefore, rightly been observed that 'the democratic structure of the country is no longer limited only to the Parliament and the state legislatures'. Now there is no denying the fact that the elected ULBs are full-fledged institutions of local self-government, a key part of democratic decentralisation in the country.

The challenge to be met in the Tenth Plan period is to assist these elected bodies to grow organically to fulfil the demands of urban residents for a quality of life in line with world standards. There is no doubt that the urban governance will progressively be managed at the local level ensuring better opportunities for people to express their needs and expectations, and with professional competence and capacity supplementing the democratic nature of the ULBs. The credit for this goes to the 74th Constitutional amendment, though it has been the subject of much debate from the outset.

Urbanisation Scenario in India

The Provisional Census Data of the 2001 Census reveals several significant facets of urbanisation over the last decade. Of the 1.02 billion population, 285 million or 27.8 per cent live in the urban areas which comprise 5,161 towns, an increase of 2.1 per cent over the proportion of urban population in the 1991 Census.

There is wide variation among states in urbanisation. At one end of the spectrum is the National Capital Territory of Delhi, with 93 per cent of its population living in urban areas. At the other end, Himachal Pradesh is the least urbanised state with only 9.8 per cent of its population in urban areas. Tamil Nadu is the most urbanised among the larger states with 43.9 per cent urban population, followed by Maharashtra with 42.4 per cent and Gujarat with 37.4 per cent. Among the larger states, Bihar has the lowest proportion of urban population (10.5 per cent), below Assam (12.7 per cent) and Orissa (14.9 per cent).

In terms of absolute number of persons living in urban areas, Maharashtra leads with 41 million persons. Uttar Pradesh comes next with 35 million followed by Tamil Nadu with 27 million.

There are 27 cities with more than one million population, while the Urban Agglomerations (UAs)/Cities with population of more than one million number 35. About 37 per cent of the total urban population live in these Million Plus UAs/Cities. In Maharashtra, West Bengal and Gujarat, more than half of the urban populations live in the Million Plus UAs/Cities.

The decadal growth of population in rural and urban areas during 1991-2001 is 17.9 per cent and 31.2 per cent respectively, indicating a relatively higher growth in urban populations. However, it has been observed that the degree of urbanisation in India is among the lowest in the world. United Nations estimates for 2000 show that 47 per cent of total population of the world live in urban areas. While the proportion of urban population in developed countries range between 75 and 80 per cent, it is 36.7 per cent in Asia. Within Asia, countries like China and Indonesia, starting from lower levels of urbanisation in 1950, have now overtaken India with urbanisation of 32.1 per cent and 40.9 per cent respectively.

This is partly explained by one demographic fact: In India the decadal growth of urban population has been declining, from 46.1 per cent in 1971-81 to 36.4 per cent in 1981-91 to 31.2 per cent in 1991-2001. Correspondingly, the average annual exponential growth in UAs/Towns has also dropped from 3.8 per cent to 3.1 per cent and 2.7 per cent respectively. While this, to some extent, reflects a declining trend in total population growth, the fact still remains that urbanisation in India is proceeding at a fairly modest pace, though some states and cities are reporting exponential growth.

The moderate growth rate gives some breathing space to set the house of urban governance in order. However, there are cities where there is no time to lose.

Major Issues in Urbanisation for the Tenth Plan

Attitudes to urban growth within the country tend to swing between two extremes. Cities are seen either as an unavoidable evil or in a more positive way as 'engines of growth'. The former view is held by those who focus on the growth of slums and squatter colonies, the congestion on the roads and environmental degradation. The others, in contrast, focus on the bustling formal and informal sectors in urban areas and their contribution to the economy, the diversification of occupations away from traditional land-based ones to newer forms of production and services, and the lower levels of poverty as compared to rural areas.

There is, in fact, evidence to show that urbanisation is likely to have been a key determinant of economic growth in the 1980s and 1990s, boosted by economic liberalisation. From this point of view, the moderate pace of urbanisation in the country has been a cause of disappointment. There is, however, no rural vs. urban conflict either in terms of national growth, or in development priorities. In fact, perhaps because of the success of rural development programmes along with the limited availability of land for squatting in central urban areas, there seems to be no runaway migration from rural to urban areas.

Impact of Growth

The impact of the growth of population on urban infrastructure and services has mostly been adverse. Cities with high rates of growth would be expected to have more resources for investment in the cities, but the fact is that much of this potential has remained untapped. On the other hand, smaller cities with less economic growth face inadequacies of financial and other resources to cope with increasing demands on services, and this may call for supplemental support from the budget. Are the existing institutional arrangements adequate to ensure that the cities can cater to present demand as well as future needs? How far have the provisions of the 74th Constitutional amendment been implemented and how have the new institutional arrangements helped? The institutional arrangements for urban management and the quality of services are closely linked. Strengthening the decentralised ULB structure to cope with the demand for civic services, is identified as the priority task of the Tenth Plan.

Urban Governance

Urban governance today is characterised by fragmentation of responsibility, incomplete devolution of functions and funds to the elected bodies and ULBs, unwillingness to progress towards municipal autonomy, adherence to outmoded methods of property tax and reluctance to levy user charges. State governments continue to take decisions on such matters as rates of user charges, property tax, octroi, role of parastatals in water supply and sanitation services, etc., with little reference to the ULBs that are affected by these decisions. Far from strengthening the constitutional role of the elected ULBs, such developments only reinforce the perception that ULBs are subordinate entities under the day-to-day control of the state governments, beholden to them not only for the development of the cities but often for their very survival. There appears to be a lack of confidence that many of the ULBs are capable of meeting their obligations as institutions of local self-governance. In the present set up, initiatives for local developmental activities rarely come from the ULBs. Experience shows that functional autonomy becomes a reality only when it is accompanied by financial independence. State governments, therefore, need to strengthen the autonomous functioning of the ULBs through positive measures, and in particular, ensure their financial self-reliance.

The role of the ULBs in the immediate future will be:

- To be responsive and accountable to the community;
- to develop cities with standards of service comparable to the best in that particular category;
- to constantly improve their capabilities so as to equip themselves to undertake their tasks in resource-raising, service provision, and poverty alleviation,

Good urban governance calls for adequate policy and legal frameworks, the existence of regulatory and planning authorities, human skills, a sound revenue base, accounting and accountability. Substantial work has already been done to upgrade the urban infrastructure and several parastatals and urban development authorities have acquired considerable skills in planning and executing projects. Programmes such as the Mega City project for five selected cities, the Integrated Development of Small and Medium Towns (IDSMT), and the Accelerated Urban Water Supply Programme (AUWSP) have shown varying degrees of success in meeting some of the urban needs. In particular, parastatal agencies and bodies such as development authorities, need to play a supportive role to the elected bodies rather than taking over functions which properly belong to the ULBs. The objective of devolution and decentralisation should be carried forward by making parastatals and authorities partners and agencies of the democratically elected ULBs, thus making a gradual transition to local management while continuing to use the expertise of the organisations set up and supervised by the State Governments. Initiating the necessary processes for partnerships between the State and its agencies on the one hand, and the ULBs on the other, is a part of the exercise of 'capacity building' in the ULBs.

Importance of Transparency and Right to Information

Since ULBs are closer to the tax-payers who depend on and are affected by the standards of services and infrastructure, there is need for a greater accountability in matters relating to municipal management and transparency in their functioning. The urban development sector is required to develop processes whereby information on all important decisions impinging on the life of urban residents are made available to them. Citizens must be kept informed about the application of funds and other assets and resources of local bodies, decisions relating to land use, construction and other development activities in the cities, taxation/ user charge policy and performance and facts of financial health of the city. The people can be kept in the picture through the media, the Internet, and by the participation of municipal councillors and other personnel in meetings of residents' associations, as well as through more formal means of public information to be laid down in municipal rules.

Sources of Urban Finances

The system of a smooth sharing of resources between the State Governments and the ULBs on the one hand, and between different municipal bodies on the other, which is one of the objectives of the institution of the SFCs must ensure that the transfer of funds to the municipalities is both adequate and stable. The second round of SFCs are in place in most states and, hopefully, as the system evolves, there will be greater simplicity and transparency in the process of devolution of resources to local bodies, without undue transaction costs.

The objective of the system of SFCs would be fulfilled if an adequate level of resource transfers to ULBs takes place. It would, however, be unrealistic to expect ULBs' finances to be healthy when State Governments themselves face acute fiscal and resource constraints. Further, the allocations by SFCs may well tilt towards areas like rural development, irrigation, etc., and may not adequately meet the needs of the cities. The Finance Commissions at the Centre are now increasingly alive to the growing needs of urban areas. The effectiveness of the system of SFCs will depend on adoption of certain healthy conventions by the State Governments. The conventions relate firstly to the choice of persons with adequate knowledge and expertise for appointment to the Commissions, and secondly to the practice of willingly adopting and fully implementing the recommendations. The different approaches adopted by the SFCs in various States to the tasks of assessing the critical needs of urban areas and making recommendations, and the policy of states in regard to acceptance and implementation of these recommendations, would be an area for study. Such a study would also show how far the objective of autonomy of the ULBs is being fulfilled.

Striking a balance between own resources of the ULBs and transfers from the state, is of critical importance. The system of transfer from the State Government should not lead to dilution of the seriousness and adequacy of the ULBs' own effort to raise resources. Misguided 'populism' is a game that the ULBs can also play, and inefficiency in collection, leakage of funds, and violations of fundamental financial principles, are dangers which have been experienced in our municipal entities. There is, therefore, every need to link the transfers under SFC formulations to the degree of efficiency ULBs exhibit in raising resources which the law allows them to generate, and in conforming to proper accounting and financial principles.

In order to help ULBs raise their own resources, the reform of the property tax system should be completed during the Tenth Plan period. The coverage of the property tax net is far from adequate, and this calls for serious attention. Alternatives to the 'annual rateable value', frozen in fiscal terms and discredited in implementation, are available in the form of area-based assessment, and capital value-based assessment. These initiatives should be further refined to develop transparent and buoyant systems of assessment with total coverage of all properties in a city, for which self-assessment by the property owner can be a useful instrument. The levying of user charges, increasing non-tax revenues, control of costs and in particular of establishment costs, and better utilisation of municipal assets are essential measures to make ULBs financially stronger. Municipal accounting systems should be overhauled and made acceptable to lending agencies and financial markets by making it accrual-based. This is especially important for those ULBs wanting to access debt funds.

Plan Assistance for Infrastructure

Assistance from the Centre is an important addition to ULBs resources, though thus far it has been visibly less effective in bringing about reforms in the urban sector. A larger degree of central assistance, including external assistance routed through the Centre, as well as institutional finance from agencies like the Housing and Urban Development Corporation (HUDCO) would be necessary during the Tenth Plan in order to take up a vigorous programme of upgrading infrastructure and services. It is also necessary that these forms of assistance strengthen the elected ULBs as the legitimate institutions of governance at the local level. The assistance must be made conditional on sector reforms, in particular, better standards of service and the collection of user charges.

The coverage of central assistance in the past has been uneven and inadequate, both because of procedural issues as well as limited budgetary allocations. The number of cities/towns which received central assistance under IDSMT, AUWSP, and Mega City scheme up to the end of the Ninth Plan are:

- AUWSP: Between 1993-94, when it was initiated, and 2001-02, 654 schemes have been sanctioned with central assistance worth Rs. 337.37 crore;

- IDSMT: Since it was launched in 1979-80, 1,172 towns have been assisted and central assistance worth Rs. 531.62 crore released;
- Mega City Scheme: Initiated in 1993-94, the scheme covers only Mumbai, Kolkata, Chennai, Hyderabad and Bangalore. Central assistance to the tune of Rs. 714.75 crore has been released.

Other programmes through which the Centre channels funds for urban improvement are:

- NCR PLAN: Rs 360.92 crore have been released as Central contribution towards provision of infrastructure in the National Capital Region.
- HUDCO, which received substantial injection of fresh equity during the Ninth Plan and has been used to leverage funds from market sources, is the other source of loan assistance to urban infrastructure projects.
- The Tax-Free Bonds scheme was introduced in February 2001, rather late in the Ninth Plan period. Since then, two ULBs (the Ahmedabad Municipal Corporation and the Hyderabad Municipal Corporation) have got approval to raise Rs 100 crore and Rs. 82.5 crore respectively.
- External assistance for the urban sector has continued to flow in from multilateral lending agencies like the Asian Development Bank (ADB), World Bank and bilateral agencies.

Infrastructure assistance through the IDSMT and Mega City schemes should aim at overcoming the worst features of neglect of urban requirements, take care of unmet needs in water supply, sanitation, solid waste management, urban transport, and the development of new extensions like residential colonies and satellite towns to relieve congestion. There is a wide variation in the availability of infrastructure and services, between cities and within the cities. The bigger cities tend to have better institutional arrangements and quality of service. In the hierarchy of cities, capital cities tend to get more attention, followed by other cities with greater economic activity, while the very small towns with extremely limited resources rarely see any improvement. The larger cities often have the capacity to raise resources from the market and from domestic as well as international funding agencies. Planning and financial support will need to be targeted at reducing the notable disparities of urban centres with significant limitations resources and glaring lack of civic amenities.

During the Tenth Plan, it is necessary to achieve a substantially higher, if not, total coverage of cities in need of infrastructural upgradation. A substantial step up in Central allocation to the urban sector is, therefore, required. This assistance should be contingent on the achievement of certain reforms, and an overall improvement in the ULBs' own efficiency in resource mobilisation, both through taxes and user charges, as well as service delivery. Municipal bodies need to be motivated to reduce expenditure, and improve the productivity of employees. A review of the working of on-going schemes, in particular IDSMT, Mega City, AUWSP, and Tax-Free Bonds schemes, will be undertaken in order to improve their working. The existing schemes for assistance for infrastructure such as the IDSMT and the Mega City Project, leave a significant number of cities between them without any Central support. During the Tenth Plan, these schemes will be extended to cover the cities which have been outside their purview.

Urban infrastructure cannot be funded by budgetary support alone. While market borrowings are not yet a viable source of financing for urban infrastructure in most instances, a beginning has to be made for building up creditworthiness in ULBs. If this cannot be done for ULBs as a whole, then it should be attempted at least for individual sectors such as water supply, and wherever else user charges and the general resource position makes for it feasible to use debt funds to supplement grants or own resources. Assistance should be provided from budgetary sources as well as from external funding agencies, to defray the costs of implementing reform measures. This will enable the utilities to improve their performance and their finances. A City Challenge

Fund was announced in the Union Budget 2002-03 and is in the process of being designed.

Broad-Based Reforms in the Urban Sector

The objective of reforms in land and housing policy, and of pricing of utilities, should be to augment the resources of the ULBs, provide for adequate maintenance of civic services, and undertake expansion of infrastructure to meet growing needs.

Cities everywhere are recognised as contributing substantially to economic, social, educational and infrastructural needs of the country. While they offer a higher standard of amenities to city-dwellers, they also have an important role in providing a range of services to the rural hinterland creating demand for rural output and providing inputs. Towns and cities act as nodal centres for providing services in marketing, health-care, education, and providing a window to the wider world, serving people other than their permanent residents.

In the past, the approach to urban growth, and in particular urban land issues, has been restrictive, based on the rigid comprehensive development plans, zoning and regulation of land use, with a predominant role in land assembly and development for urban development authorities. The role of the private sector was extremely limited. The inability of the urban development authorities to meet the total housing needs of the urban residents has driven large numbers of people in need of housing in every city, to seek housing in unauthorised colonies. These colonies are now posing a serious problem in urban management. Slums are only the most extreme form of this problem.

It is necessary to set in motion a virtuous circle of urban growth leading to better resources which are then used for improving infrastructure, which, in turn, will lead to further growth of the cities, resulting in enhanced economic activity and growth. Meeting the needs of the urban poor also necessitates ULBs having more resources at their command. The impediments to urban growth, as well as the necessary policy reforms, have been broadly identified.

Land Policy and Housing

The repeal of the Urban Land (Ceiling and Regulation) Act, 1976 has been a significant step towards reform in the urban land market. Following the repeal of the central legislation, a number of state governments have also repealed the state-level law. However, the Act still exists in some states, while several other state laws like the Land Revenue Act, Land Reforms Act, Stamp Duty Act, and Urban Development Authorities Acts/Town Planning Acts continue to hamper the availability of land for housing and other construction, pushing up land prices.

There is a need to take measures to ease the availability of land so that growth can take place through increased construction and housing activity, and land prices can be brought down to moderate levels making affordable shelter available to the lower income groups. This will also help prevent the proliferation of unauthorised colonies. This is by no means a measure to dilute urban planning, where enforcement has often been the weakest link. On the contrary, it will make urban planning more in tune with the changing nature of cities.

More flexible zoning regulations to permit change of land use where justified, easier subdivision regulations, and extension of trunk services to new areas/new townships will help to reduce congestion and develop the cities in an orderly fashion. Innovative measures for land assembly, land pooling, and use of land as a resource to build up infrastructure will need to be continued and their administration made more efficient and transparent.

Since 2001, 100 per cent foreign direct investment (FDI) has been permitted in the development of integrated townships. However, investments may not materialise unless the conditions relating to land procurement are made simple. In urban areas, especially those with Master Plans, the needs of urbanisation should have precedence over land revenue and land reforms legislations in which restrictions on land ownership, transfers, and land use are incorporated in order to prevent the conversion of agricultural land. Other problems relate to the lack of clear titles, old, protected tenancies and rent control. All these problems, working together, have made it impossible for land to be procured for development in city centres, barring in small quantities. In prime areas, much of the land is used well below its potential.

The system of maintenance of land records and registration of property transactions are outmoded and need to be modernised through computerisation so as to speed up the process. There is need to develop and implement a system of authentication of property titles on the lines of the Torrens system now in vogue in many countries. This will make it easier for interested parties to enter into land transactions confidently. Together with the rationalisation of stamp duty, these measures will help in the development of a genuine property market, which ultimately will prove beneficial for the assessment of taxes where property values are the basis.

Rent control and tenancy laws also prevent the development of rental housing, thus contracting housing stock. Reform of these laws is a politically sensitive issue, as evidenced by the history of recent efforts to amend the Delhi Rent Act. However, there is some awareness that rent control at absurdly low levels with virtually no relation to market rates and extraordinary protection to tenants over generations not only hinder the development of rental housing but also act as barriers to the growth of cities. Dilapidated structures cannot be renovated because of the difficulty in evicting tenants, with the result that rejuvenation of inner city areas is not taking place. Transitory arrangements can be made to help those who will face hardships, but zoning regulations should take into account the changing nature of inner city areas and permit their redevelopment.

Fiscal Balance

Poor management of assessment and collection has ensured that the yield from properties in the form of property tax is a fraction of the potential. In many cities, either property tax is not levied at all, or the rates are extremely negligible, as a result of which the resource position of the municipal bodies is extremely poor. On the other hand, stamp duty levied on transactions in land at 8 to -10 per cent is too high, in comparison with other countries. This has resulted in the use of 'black money' in property transactions and the practice of 'power of attorney 'prevent the emergence of a genuine property market, with resultant losses to the exchequer. A further fall-out is the unreliability of information on property values.

Another cause of the fiscal imbalance of ULBs is the highly subsidised supply of services, in particular, water and sewerage. Insufficient revenue income prevents civic authorities from investing in services, leaving existing and future needs unfulfilled and this, in turn, hinders growth. During the Tenth Plan, emphasis will have to be placed on initiating and furthering broad-based reforms to overcome the impediments to urban growth. The reform agenda, initially mooted through the new programme of Urban Reforms Incentive Fund, will, in order to make a serious impact, need to leverage all schemes in the urban sector. Therefore the conformity to an agreed reform programme will be made obligatory for Central assistance to the sector during the Tenth Plan.

Capacity Building

Capacity building in urban institutions is one area which is much talked about but has been relatively neglected in terms of action. The restructuring of the roles of the elected ULBs has to initially come about in the form of partnerships with the parastatals which have been handling a variety of services. The public service element needs to be made more professional and accountable to the people. As resources are the biggest problem of ULBs, measures for comprehensive and rational levy of property taxes and user charges are needed urgently. Adoption of modern accounting systems, improved practices of budgeting and planning, effective use of wards committees and other means of peoples' participation, and programme assistance under the schemes such as the SJSRY, should be put to use for improving urban governance.

Studies have emphasised that in a programme such as Low-Cost Sanitation, provision of subsidies and loan assistance have to be backed by substantial work on designs and materials relevant to each regional context, and by education, training, and propagation in the basic concepts of sanitation and hygiene. Water supply schemes have been transferred to ULBs from parastatals but without creating an ownership structure or building up the capacity to undertake operations and maintenance functions. Participatory management is still a relatively novel concept as bureaucratic approaches insulate public functionaries from public scrutiny or accountability. These are all areas that any programme of capacity building has to tackle.

Water supply and sanitation are the biggest challenges before ULBs and there is an urgent need to step up investment in this sector during the Tenth Plan. The tasks include efficiency improvement, better customer satisfaction, levy and collection of reasonable user charges, accessing institutional and market borrowings to provide sufficient investment funds, and institutional improvement at all levels. A number of states have shown interest in arranging public-private partnerships in this sector and these must be pursued prudently to enhance service quality and efficiency. The Low Cost Sanitation programme needs a new thrust as the sanitation problem has defied a solution so far.

While encouraging the entry of the private sector, the key role of public functionaries should not be overlooked as the progress towards private sector participation is bound to be slow and may not happen at all in many urban centres. The growth of urban capabilities has to be ensured with the support of bodies such as the Central Public Health and Environmental Engineering Organisation (CPHEEO), HUDCO, National Environmental Engineering and Research Institute (NEERI), NIUA, Regional Centres at Hyderabad, Mumbai and Lucknow, the IIPA, and the various training institutions relating to the urban sector. Where needed, the institutions need to re-orient their approach with a view to strengthening the ULBs in the performance of their tasks.

The leading role of parastatals has to be scaled down to give the initiative to the local bodies themselves.

Mapping, Urban Indicators and Data from the Urban Sector

Two of the most important tools of urban managers are maps and data. There is a need to step up the availability of both these basic requirements. While there have been individual efforts, both within and outside the Government to devise and set up a system of collection of urban data or indicators the Town and Country Planning Organisation (TCPO) has been implementing a scheme of urban mapping based on aerial photography. In the Tenth Plan, there is need to widen the availability of maps and urban data so as to cover all urban centres. City personnel as well as policy makers at the Central and State levels need basic urban data relating to settlements, slums, population, housing, transport, environmental issues such as disposal of solid and liquid wastes, and network of services such as water, sanitation, roads, public transport, drainage, streetlights, parks and playgrounds, parking areas etc. on a day-to-day basis.

In addition, the status of municipal personnel, resources, assets, etc. are also required. Currently few maps of any significant scale are available. This could be remedied by using maps generated from satellite data, which are readily available. These maps can be used to supplement ground-level work on property listing for taxation purposes, as well as to monitor trends of urban growth especially in the peri-urban areas. Data on existing service levels are a sine qua non for inter-city comparisons, for bench-marking service standards, for urban planning, and for authorities such as the SFCs who have to make recommendations regarding allocation of resources for the augmentation and maintenance of these services.

Efforts to secure data at the national or state level are unlikely to succeed unless data are systematically collected, validated and updated at the local level. In order to be comprehensive, data should emerge from a process of diagnosis at the municipal level, out of a felt need of municipal functionaries to get to know the requirements and status of various urban services. A scheme to generate city-level data and city maps derived from satellite imagery will be implemented during the Tenth Plan.

Summing Up

The approach to urban management issues in the Tenth Plan has to revolve around the strengthening of the democratic structure, with the assistance of the very agencies-state governments, parastatals and the urban development authorities - who have continued to take over the functions that rightly belong to the ULBs. The task is not easy, not the least because the ULBs do not have the wherewithal to imbibe the concepts and capabilities needed for their responsibilities. These will need to be built up, and legislative and institutional arrangements to achieve this task will have to be made. That the ULBs are not yet in a condition to take on all their responsibilities is no argument against making the necessary transition. On the other hand, the challenge lies in building up the ULBs, because without that there will be neither accountability nor sustained development in the urban sector.

The major thrust areas for the Tenth Plan can be readily identified:

- Investments over the years and institutional effort have resulted in the setting up of a variety of urban infrastructure and services. However, there is a grave danger of these investments being rendered ineffective because of poor operations and maintenance and poor institutional TENTH FIVE YEAR PLAN 2002-07 620 capacity. An extra effort has to be made to ensure that the capacities created in such areas as water and sanitation, transport systems, and planned city development are not permitted to degenerate.
- Public-private partnerships should be brought on to the urban agenda for improving efficiency and better service delivery. However, capacity building in the public services has to be given highest priority, through training both elected and appointed officials, and by restructuring of municipal entities

for more efficient management. Performance of the ULBs in their allotted tasks, apart from being watched by the citizens, should also be closely monitored by the State Governments.

- Finances of the ULBs need strengthening through smooth working of the SFC awards, rationalisation and improvement of the property taxation system, and a sufficient level of levy of user charges. Transfers from State budget should be linked to defined levels of performance of the ULBs in resource-raising, expenditure control, proper financial management, and transparency in functioning.
- Broad-based urban sector reform measures should commence during the Tenth Plan. The fundamental need is to strengthen the autonomy - functional as well as financial - of the ULBs. There is need for improving the debt-servicing capabilities of ULBs so that investment funds from financial institutions and market borrowings can be made available for urban infrastructure works. Plan support in the form of centrally sponsored schemes should be linked to the willingness in the state and local bodies to implement reform programmes.
- The 2001 Census data provide basic information on the trends in urban growth and this will help establish the needs of the ULBs, which has to be balanced by capabilities. Future programmes of assistance should be based on these two factors. But first, studies to develop the disaggregated picture of urban growth in different size categories, different states and types of cities should be taken up immediately based on the Census data. Planning of urban growth projects should be based on these studies.

Housing

Housing is a basic necessity as well as an important economic activity, in that it is a part of the construction industry,. Construction activity accounts for more than 50 per cent of the development outlays. A study by the Indian Institute of Management, Ahmedabad, commissioned by HUDCO, to evaluate the impact of investment in the housing sector on GDP and employment, has found that the sector ranks third among the 14 major sectors in terms of the direct, indirect, and induced effect on all sectors of the economy.

The Housing and Habitat Policy, 1998 has specifically advocated that Government create a facilitating environment for growth of housing activity instead of taking on the task of housing itself. Housing is largely a private sector activity in both the rural and urban sectors. This is not to rule out the need for a high degree of involvement of the Government and its agencies in meeting the housing needs of the urban poor. The nature of this involvement - it may in some instances extend to house construction itself - is to be determined by the needs of a given situation.

The National Agenda of Governance also emphasised that housing activity would be an engine for substantial generation of employment, and all legal and administrative impediments that stand in the way of vigorous housing activity should be removed forthwith. What is undisputed is that governmental initiatives - and its 'facilitating role' - have a significant impact on the provision of housing and growth of the sector. These initiatives and interventions relate to legislations concerning ownership, transfers and development of land; stamp duty and registration laws; rent control legislation; tax policy particularly relating to housing loans; property and land tax laws; town planning law and its actual implementation, i.e., Comprehensive Development Plans, zoning regulations, land use change; and building bye-laws. It also covers urban development activities through parastatals and urban development authorities; sites and services schemes; slum policy; provision of urban infrastructure; urban transport policy and facilities; the institutions in the public sector relating to housing development and housing finance; and house construction in the public sector.

With the anticipated entry of FDI into the real estate sector, care has to be taken that the needs of the urban poor and marginalised sections are not ignored. Given the large number of activities impinging on housing directly and indirectly and the multiplicity of agencies involved, designing a framework for orderly and dynamic growth in the housing sector in the Tenth Plan is a challenge to the planners.

The Working Group on Housing for the Tenth Plan has observed that around 90 per cent of housing shortage pertains to the weaker sections. There is a need to increase the supply of affordable housing to the economically weaker sections and the low income category through a proper programme of allocation of land, extension of funding assistance and provision of support services. The problem of the urban shelter-less and pavement dwellers has not been given the consideration that is necessary in a welfare or pro-poor State, as seen from the lack of progress in the Night Shelter Scheme. Regulation of building quality and its assurance, especially in areas prone to disasters is an issue whose urgency was reiterated after the earthquake in Gujarat in January 2000. Building designs also need to be gender sensitive and should accommodate the requirements of physically challenged population.

In order to increase the proportion of household savings in the housing sector, as well as to provide houses to those who cannot as yet afford to have their own houses, there is need to encourage the promotion of rental housing by the private sector, public sector, cooperatives and individuals. This requires legislative changes in the existing rent control laws, something on which very little progress has been achieved.

Availability of land has been constrained by certain provisions contained in a variety of laws such as the Land Revenue Act, the Land Reforms Act, the Urban Land (Ceiling and Regulation) Act (ULCRA), the Town Planning Act and the Urban Development Acts. Each of them has, often through its provisions and equally through the manner in which they were implemented - created hurdles for legitimate transactions in land urgently required for expansion of the housing stock. The repeal of ULCRA was expected to ease the situation to some extent. This needs to be followed up by other changes whereby legally valid availability of land for urbanization is speeded up, and people are not driven to adoption of short-cuts to obtaining housing plots and other uses.

Balancing the liberal availability of land, with the demands of orderly growth with adequate provision of infrastructure is no easy task, and the 'land sharks' are invariably one step ahead of the authorities that enforce regulations and provide of amenities. This has led to the proliferation of 'unauthorised layouts' and 'informal settlements'. The efficacy of town planning and urban development programmes lies in meeting the growing demand for housing in urban areas within the framework of the tenets of orderly growth. Public and private initiatives in various parts of the country have already demonstrated that, given the will and efficiency of implementation, it is possible to plan ahead and promote orderly growth. These efforts need to be made more widely known and replicated.

Institutional Financing of Housing

The substantial thrust on housing laid by Government through the facilitating measures including Reserve Bank of India (RBI) regulations relating to priority sector lending, fiscal concessions and budgetary incentives has started to bear fruit. Institutional credit disbursals have grown from Rs. 5,767 crore in 1997-98 to Rs. 12,626 crore in 2000-01. These disbursals are through the 28 Housing Finance Institutions (HFIs) under the ambit of the National Housing Bank (NHB).

HUDCO

HUDCO earmarks 55 per cent of its housing portfolio funds for the economically weaker sections (EWS) and low income groups (LIG), with differential interest rates, high loan component for lower cost units, and longer repayment period. Though its releases are somewhat less than sanctions, it is noteworthy that HUDCO has sanctioned 12.46 million urban housing units (till September, 2001) in both urban and rural areas. During 1998-2001, under the Additional 2 Million Housing programme, against a total target of 30 lakh housing units, HUDCO has supported 33.82 lakh units.

The other factor in HUDCO operations for the mass housing programmes is the dependence on State Government guarantees, which as noted elsewhere, disqualifies some states who have defaulted. Such states will need to take steps to fulfil their obligations under the guarantee. HUDCO is also a large player in retail lending for housing, and in two and a half years has sanctioned a total loan amount of Rs. 2,331 crore to 2,62,550 beneficiaries. HUDCO has been in the forefront of the Government's efforts to come to the aid of disaster-affected households, and has provided financial assistance for disaster rehabilitation housing to the tune of Rs. 2,360 crore for construction of over 4 million houses for earthquake, cyclone, and flood victims.

In order to undertake housing programmes for the poorer sections, states must create an environment favouring loan-based house construction for the EWS categories, and strengthen the state-level machinery for lending and loan recovery. EWS housing in urban areas has long remained a neglected area in relation to the demand, and without arrangements in place for credit support to this section, states will find it difficult to continue giving State guarantees to loans from HUDCO. To ensure recovery of loans, conferment of ownership rights in the name of the beneficiary family (jointly in the names of wife and husband) could be done only after the entire loan is recovered, till which time the house may be held on a rental basis. To augment housing supply for the poor, there is also need to enlarge private initiatives and public-private sector partnerships.

Cooperative Sector

The National Cooperative Housing Federation operates through 26 apex cooperative housing federations in the states. There are nearly 90,000 primary cooperative housing societies with 6.5 million individual members. Up to 31 March 2001, the apex federations have mobilised Rs. 6,407 crore from LIC, NHB,

HUDCO commercial and cooperative banks etc., and disbursed loans of Rs 6,800 crore to housing cooperatives and individual members. This has led to the construction of approximately 2.13 million dwelling units (completed and under construction). Housing cooperatives have been given a target of construction of one lakh houses each year under the 2 million housing programme for the EWS/LIG, and they have been able to construct a total of 2.92 lakh units in the 1998-2001 period.

Urban Housing Shortage in the Tenth Plan

The Working Group on Housing has estimated the urban housing shortage at the beginning of Tenth Plan at 8.89 million units. While this is indeed an alarming number, it includes the 'congestion' needs of joint families, obsolescence and replacement of old houses, and upgrading of all the kutcha houses. The total number of houses required cumulatively during the Tenth Plan period is assessed at 22.44 million. There is, therefore, a good case for continuing the Two Million Housing scheme during the Tenth Plan period, as it will take care of about 3.5 million houses for the urban poor.

Strengthening of Housing Stock in Vulnerable Regions

About 54 per cent of India's land area is vulnerable to earthquakes, 8.4 per cent to cyclonic wind and storm surges, and 4.9 per cent of the area is vulnerable to flood damage. The Working Group on Housing has suggested a scheme for strengthening of the vulnerable house in the EWS and LIG category in 107 districts which face highest risk of damage because they are multi-hazard prone. According to an estimate, these houses can be strengthened and retrofitted at 10 per cent of the cost of construction of a new house on an average. What is equally important is to demonstrate retrofitting technologies relevant to the specific disaster-prone area.

The problem of housing slum-dwellers in decent surroundings is dealt with separately. In view of the growing problems of the housing sector, and particularly the urban poor, the following measures are necessary and should be implemented during the Tenth Plan period:

- The first priority in urban housing, particularly for the urban LIG and EWS, is the provision of land at affordable prices. Increased availability of developed land in urban areas through adoption of various innovative approaches like land bank for the poor and land assembly methods, vacant land tax and transferable development rights and simplification of sub-division regulations is called for.
- Unauthorised settlements have become a part of the urban scenario. They house a large number of people and there is ambivalence regarding regularisation of these settlements and extension of services to them. In many cities, they are not brought under the property tax net. Pragmatic solutions leading to security and extension of civic services are required. To prevent proliferation of such colonies, the land use and sub-division policies need to be streamlined, and their implementation rendered speedy and smooth without undue hassles to those in need of land for housing.
- The city planning provisions need to be tuned to the requirements of the weaker sections in urban areas through adoption of appropriate and affordable standards and norms, use of cluster housing and 'growing house' concepts.
- The feeling that urban planning ignores the needs of the urban poor, must be dispelled through effective action to meet these needs. The urban development authorities who acquire and develop large tracts of land for the growth of the cities, should reserve a major part of such land to meet the requirements of the EWS/LIG population. At present, there is little evidence that these authorities - who are often the sole organisation for development of serviced land - are providing the due share of land to the urban poor.
- Housing and economic activities have to go hand in hand with the provision of housing for the workers close to work places. There is need for coordinating the development of industrial areas and housing areas. Layouts should be mixed in nature

with the urban poor-providers of services-being enabled to live and integrate with the rest of the community.

- Schemes such as the Two Million Housing scheme and the new scheme of housing with Central assistance for the slum population (Valmiki Ambedkar Awas Yojana or VAMBAY) should be used to provide immediate benefit to the most disadvantaged urban segments.
- HUDCO assistance is not available to several states which are unable or unwilling to stand guarantee for these loans. A solution has to be found so that the urban poor in these states do not find themselves at a disadvantage in comparison with other states where there is greater willingness to use HUDCO loans.
- Urban housing should mostly be based on savings and credit from HFIs. The workers of the informal sector and other urban poor including slum-dwellers are generally not served by these Institutions. At the same time, public institutions such as Housing Boards and Housing Co-operatives, have not been able to meet the needs of these sections. This will only increase the growth of unserviced housing and of slums. There is a need to make housing loans available to the EWS in the cities. Credit activity by state agencies and housing co-operatives need to be revived. HUDCO and the HFIs should be encouraged to finance self-help groups or groups who have the support of an NGO and who can be of assistance in loan recovery.

Costs of urban housing are likely to be higher in comparison with rural housing programmes because of the higher land costs standards of construction in urban areas. It is for this reason that a scheme such as VAMBAY, launched in the final year of the Ninth Plan, has a combination of subsidy and loan. Expectations of fully subsidised housing should be discouraged.

Urban Poverty Alleviation and Slum Improvement

Reduction and alleviation of poverty, if not its complete eradication, including poverty in urban areas, has long been one of the objectives of planning. There have been encouraging trends in urban poverty in both percentage and numerical terms, though the urban poor still face age-old problems at the ground level. Besides, there are wide regional variations as well as differences among different size-class towns with regard to the extent and nature of urban poverty.

According to the 2001 Census, the total urban population is 285.35 million, which accounts for 27.78 per cent of the total population. While the total population in the country increased by 21.34 per cent in 1991-2001, urban population grew by 31.36 per cent during the same period. The somewhat moderate growth of the urban population is explained by the declining rate of urban growth in the last two decades.

The encouraging feature is that apart from continuation of the fall in the proportion of the urban poor, for the first time in the 1991 Census, there is also a reduction in the absolute numbers of the urban poor. According to the large sample survey data on consumer expenditure (55th Round) of the NSSO using a 30-day recall period, 67.1 million or 23.62 percent of India's urban population were below the poverty line in 1999-2000. While the percentage of persons below poverty line in urban areas had been steadily declining since it was first estimated at 49 per cent in 1973-74, the absolute number of persons below the poverty line had been rising, touching 76.3 million in 1993-94. This trend has been reversed in the latest Census.

Though, at the national level, the percentage of the poor in rural areas is significantly higher than in urban areas, only a few of the larger States conform to this pattern. States such as Andhra Pradesh, Goa, Gujarat, Haryana, Karnataka, Kerala, Madhya Pradesh, Maharashtra, Rajasthan, Tamil Nadu, Delhi and the Union Territory of Pondicherry have reported levels of urban poverty that are higher than rural poverty. States where rural poverty is higher than in urban areas are Arunachal Pradesh, Assam, Bihar, Himachal Pradesh, Orissa, Uttar Pradesh and West Bengal. Analysis shows that poverty reduction among States has been uneven. The most important point about the interstate variations in poverty is that it shows no correlation with per capita income or other development indicators like per capita consumption, levels of industrial and infrastructural development, etc., in urban areas during the nineties. While the lack of development is the cause of urban poverty in many States, the nature and sectoral composition of development is responsible for poverty in others.

Unemployment data show that the overall unemployment rates are not high, though they are higher in urban areas than in rural areas. The unemployed person-day rates are higher than the rates obtained for persons, thereby indicating a high degree of intermittent unemployment. This is mainly due to the absence of regular employment for many workers. Studies have shown that casualisation of labour is the main, and increasing, source of urban poverty. The dynamics of development in urban areas of many States during the past two decades has been such that rapid economic growth has not led to a corresponding decline in poverty. While income levels are rising to meet the basic nutritional needs, other equally basic needs of shelter, civic amenities, health care, educational and social needs, etc. are not being met in an adequate fashion. Urban poverty, thus, emerges as a more complex phenomenon than rural poverty. Some aspects of the complexity of urban poverty are:

Level of Basic Amenities: There are serious deficiencies in urban infrastructure as a result of the rapid growth of urban population and low investment in urban development. In general, the smaller the town, the less likely it is to have a wide coverage of amenities, and the poor in such towns face correspondingly higher deprivation. It has been noted that the percentage of households having flush toilets exhibits a strong positive correlation with economic development, much more than any other indicator of amenities. The coverage of civic amenities, specifically electricity, drinking water and toilets, is uneven and variation across size class of urban centres shows regularity and a distinct pattern. The percentage of households covered by each of the three amenities increases systematically with the size class of the urban centres except for Class VI towns. Class V towns (population between 5,000 and 10,000) register a high percentage of households not covered by toilets, electricity and drinking water (61 per cent, 41 per cent, and 28 per cent respectively) in 1991. The shortages are very serious for urban centres with population of less than 50,000. This emphasizes the need for greater involvement of the State and Central Governments in upgrading the infrastructure of the small towns. Most of the small and medium towns are not in a position to generate funds to provide civic amenities to all sections of population. These towns, particularly those located in less developed states, should, therefore, be the major focus of government policy in terms of providing basic amenities.

Town or City Size: There is evidence to show that the incidence of poverty in a town, as measured by Head Count Ratio (HCR), declines steadily with increasing size. In 1987-88, the HCR in towns with less than 50,000 population was 47.40 per cent while that in towns with population of more than one million was 26.73 per cent. In 1993-94, the corresponding figures are 43.16 per cent and 20.57 per cent. The National Capital Territory of Delhi (where the urban population accounts for 93 per cent of the total population according to the 2001 Census), experienced a population growth of 51.3 per cent during the decade of 1991-2001. The percentage of people below the poverty line in Delhi stood at 49.61 per cent in 1973-74 and declined steadily over the years to 16.4 per cent in 1991 and now stands at 9.42 per cent.

A larger incidence of secondary and high-value tertiary activities in large cities gives people residing there a higher level of income. In contrast, the income levels of people in small and medium towns tend to be low because of the poor economic base and lack of employment opportunities in the organised sector. In the changing economic scenario, care has to be taken to ensure that the process of structural adjustment does not lead to an increase in urban inequality. For poverty alleviation in the broader sense, encompassing both income and environment, within a framework of balanced regional development, it would be important to restructure priorities in favour of small and medium towns and slums in larger cities, where a large majority of the urban poor live.

Household Size: The fact that household size affects the poverty status of a household is well known. Larger households tend to have a higher probability of being poor.

Features of Urban Poverty

Poverty can take specific forms of deprivation and misery among individual households. The degree of poverty can also differ, and attempts have been made to categorise the urban poor on a declining scale such as core poor, intermediate poor and transitional poor. Another study classifies them as declining poor, coping poor and improving poor, with different degrees of priority for the three basic needs of survival, security, and quality of life.

Approach to Urban Poverty Alleviation

In an environment where the poor are exploited and ignored, there is a major role for the State and its agencies, including the ULBs and the parastatals, in the field of urban development and provision of services such as water supply, health, education, sanitation, legal protection and employment generation. This is an immense challenge because of the known weaknesses of the system like the lack of accountability, corruption, and the dominant role of elite groups who wield substantial power in urban governance.

The first formal attempt to experiment with the community development approach in cities was the Urban Community Development project started in 1958. The Environmental Improvement of Urban Slums scheme was started in 1972 at the Central level to provide basic physical facilities like safe drinking water, sanitation, storm water drains, street lighting and roads. This scheme was transferred to State Governments in 1974. Following experiments with a variety of combinations of schemes for employment generation, formation of beneficiary groups, training, community organisations and thrift/ self-help groups, finally the integrated programme of Swarn Jayanti Shahri Rozgar Yojana (SJSRY) was launched in 1997.

The implementation of programmes for the urban poor is beset with enormous problems. The problem of inadequate funding has been compounded by under-utilisation of Central funds, diversion of funds released for specific programmes, and infructuous expenditure. Monitoring at the Central level has been weak and ineffective. Success stories have not been publicised or adopted on a wider scale. The understanding of the programmes, their objective and modalities relating to implementation has been weak and superficial, leading to inaction in many areas that are of vital concern to the urban poor. There are few master plans and very little effort at monitoring the benefits that are expected to flow to the target communities. In addition, there has been too much emphasis on engineering or the 'works' aspects of programmes without adequate understanding of the social, psychological and other dynamics of poverty. The beneficiaries have not been consulted nor given a voice in the implementation of programmes. When there is a deceleration of economic growth, especially when governments experience fiscal constraints and need to reduce deficits, allocation of funds for the social sectors suffers. This should not to happen.

Slums

Provisional data relating to slums in the 2001 Census throw some interesting light on the slum population. Nearly 28 million persons lived in the slums in 1981, accounting for 17.5 per cent of the urban population. The estimates for 1991 were 45.7 million slum dwellers accounting for 21.5 per cent of population. According to the 2001 Census, there are 40.6 million persons living in slums in 607 towns/cities, and they account for 22.8 per cent of the population of these cities. However, the latest Census data also reflect the problems inherent in not having an accepted definition of slums and absence of proper listing of slum settlements in the urban offices concerned with slum improvement and civic amenities. The practice of notifying slums under relevant laws is not being followed, especially where the land involved belongs to Government or any of its agencies. As a result of these lacunae, these data are not definitive because towns with less than 50,000 population, and slum clusters which are not formally or informally recognised if the population was less than 300 are excluded.

While demographic data on slum populations and on civic amenities to slum dwellers from the Census are still awaited, there appears to be no change in the basic level or improvement in the features of slum settlements despite several decades of programmes for the environmental improvement and upgradation of slums. There is cause to wonder whether 'Cities without Slums' is a slogan about an objective, which, however desirable, is believed to be unreachable, or whether it is a serious planning and urban development concern. Certainly the degree of effort to upgrade slums to a more habitable level, does not indicate a serious effort in this direction.

The Draft National Slum Policy drawn up by the Department of Urban Employment and Poverty Alleviation in the Ministry of Urban Development in April 1999, had been widely debated and many comments received. It needs to finalised. A National Policy on Slums is of great significance given the degree of wrong perception regarding the nature and extent of the slum problem. Such a policy can help bring an attitudinal change among the authorities and the people at large, including the urban poor and the slum-dwellers, regarding measures to improve their quality of life and make our cities free from the worst features of slums. Slums are generally treated as the inevitable outcome of continuing migration of unskilled labour, but, in fact, most slum-dwellers are permanent residents of the city. In many instances, families in slums span several generations. The main objectives of a slum policy would be.

- To create awareness of the underlying principles that guide the process of slum development and improvement and the options that are available for bringing about the integration of these settlements and the communities residing there with the urban area as a whole.

- To strengthen the legal and policy framework to facilitate the process of slum development and improvement on a sustainable basis; to ensure that the slum population are provided civic services, amenities, and economic opportunities to enable them to rise above the degrading conditions in which they live.
- To arrive at a policy of affirming the legal and tenurial rights of the slum-dwellers.
- To establish a framework for involving all stakeholders in the efficient and smooth implementation of policy objectives.

Focusing on slums enables planners to look beyond income levels to neighbourhood and environmental considerations and this results in a more multi-dimensional view of urban poverty. In view of the progress made in decentralised urban governance through the 74th Constitutional Amendment, it is necessary ask how this has benefited the slum-dwellers and provided them an increased opportunity to articulate their needs, and obtain assistance from civic authorities and urban planners. It does appear that the effort has been more towards providing some amount of civic services in an un-coordinated fashion than towards devising all-embracing programmes with participation of the slum-dwellers themselves, and finding solutions which provide not only a decent quality of life with prospects of further improvement, but also make slums redundant in our urban habitations. Slum dwellers need not perennially be at the receiving end of selected doles but must be made part of the urban economic and social processes with adequate opportunities for improving their lives, while contributing what is acknowledged to be a major share in the economic activities of the cities. Upgradation of living conditions of the urban poor has to be recognised as part of the national development process. Some of the obvious lapses in slum programmes are:

- Non-listing of all habitations, big or small, which should be classified as slums.

- Lack of basic information on the number of households in such habitations, and the status of basic amenities.
- Absence of a master plan for a period of five years to gradually increase the level of civic amenities.
- Adherence to outdated and totally inadequate standards of services to the slum-dwellers, under the EIUS component.
- Failure to provide specific provisions in municipal laws for dealing with issues relating to the urban poor, slums, and economic planning for poverty alleviation, etc., which flow from the 74th Constitutional Amendment; failure to build up capacity in municipal bodies to provide the required services to slum communities and the urban poor.
- Uncertainty regarding agency arrangement for various slum improvement tasks between the municipal authority, development authority, slum board, housing board, parastatals, etc., and failure to provide a coordinating institutional arrangement;
- Failure to implement provisions made in Comprehensive Development Plans for the housing, and economic needs (production and marketing activities) of the urban poor, especially provision of land, and facilities for street vendors and hawkers. In the absence of such planning, unplanned growth takes place leading to 'informal' or unauthorised low quality settlements, and unauthorised hawking which subjects the poor to harassment from petty officials. It is often said that 'there is no place for the poor in town planning process' and even existing provisions are not implemented for the benefit of the urban poor.
- Failure on the part of land-owning agencies on which slums are located to take decisions on permission to make environmental improvement and in situ upgradation of slum clusters.
- Failure to converge available civic services in sanitation, paved access and drainage, streetlights, health-care, water supply, education, etc., by organising responsibility cells and involving the beneficiaries in planning of services.

- Lack of a commitment to achieve a breakthrough in bringing slum-dwellers out of the stigma and misery of living in slums. and instead, use funds such as National Slum Development Programme for tinkering with the symptoms.

Importance of Slum Upgrading

Action taken so far for slum improvement or in situ upgrading is inadequate. Re-designing and re-constructing settlements with the participation of residents and assistance from public bodies is a viable option with the least amount of disturbance to the settlers or their livelihood. This method of slum improvement needs to be practised on a much wider scale. The VAMBAY project permits in situ upgradation, and it is necessary that an early decision is taken regarding land on which slums are situated in order to facilitate upgradation.

Various Central Government schemes -National Slum Development Programme (NSDP), Swarna Jayanti Shahri Rozgar Yojana (SJSRY), VAMBAY, Night Shelters, Two Million Housing Scheme, Accelerated Urban Water Supply Programme (AUWSP), Low-Cost Sanitation -provide for a wide range of services to the urban poor including slum-dwellers. They include identification of the urban poor, formation of community groups, involvement of non-government organisations (NGOs), self-help/thrift and credit activities, training for livelihood, credit and subsidy for economic activities, housing and sanitation, environmental improvement, community assets, wage employment, convergence of services, etc. What is needed is to ensure that the task of meeting the needs of the slum-dwellers is better organised and effectively administered, and duly monitored at both State and Central levels.

Approach and Programmes of Urban Poverty Alleviation in the Tenth Plan

The 74th Amendment is intended to increase the participation of the people and accountability in administration. State Governments should legislate the requisite amendments to the municipal laws, to clearly devolve the tasks of urban poverty alleviation and slum improvement to the ULBs.

A multi-dimensional strategy is called for, which will focus on empowerment of the urban poor. The community structure under the SJSRY should be made the common pattern and the foundation of all programmes for the urban poor and slum dwellers. This would be an effective way to give the poor a forum to talk about their needs and, given the empowerment of the poor when organised, ensure that their demands are then met.

Services required by the urban poor -physical infrastructure as well as human development services - are simple to enumerate and, over the years, most of them have been attempted at least in a rudimentary fashion. During the Tenth Plan, the focus has to be on upgrading these services, and on convergence for achieving synergy. Convergence of services such as water supply, drainage, solid waste management, as well as for health care, family welfare, education, anganwadis and crèches should be the main plank of urban poverty alleviation. Outlays on water supply and sanitation should, in particular, focus on the needs of the urban poor. Setting up basic health and education units such as crèches, anganwadis, primary schools, public health units and primary health centres (PHCs) in areas where the urban poor live, is equally important.

At the state level there is need to:

- Set up urban poverty and slum improvement task forces. The first task should be to upscale the old standards of services under EIUS and make them more relevant to the average level of services available to the residents of the town/city.
- City administrations should create urban poverty alleviation (UPA) cells at the municipal level. The cell should have representation of all the services required by slum-dwellers, as well as of the Community Development Societies set up under SJSRY, and NGOs active in the field. The UPA cell should be in overall charge of urban poverty and slum related programmes.

- The UPA cells should draw up City Poverty Alleviation Plans in which the community organizations of the poor created under the Swarn Jayanti Shahri Rozgar Yojana (SJSRY) should be involved. The tasks of various agencies should be well-defined and coordination should be effective. The thrust should be on the provision of all basic services such as potable water and sanitation services, including household taps, toilets with septic tanks, covered drains, waste collection services etc. to the slum settlements. Other activities for the socio-economic upliftment of the slum populations should also be taken up, making maximum use of the SJSRY and similar schemes.
- City-wide master plans for slum improvement should be drawn up with the objective of removing the slum characteristics of the selected settlements. The annual programmes and projects, including those to be financed out of NSDP funds, should be based on such master plans.

Programmes for urban infrastructure supported by the Central Government, such as the IDSMT and the Mega City Scheme should have adequate provisions for meeting the infrastructural deficiencies of settlements of the urban poor.

The personnel who deal with UPA programmes must appreciate the many forms urban poverty can take. These programmes must also deal with the policy-related causes of urban poverty such as inappropriate framework of urban services, inadequate coverage of education, health, infrastructure and transport, lack of labour rights and unemployment benefits, land and housing regulations which make it unaffordable for the poor to find housing and push them to disaster-prone and unhygienic areas, lack of safety nets and social support systems, etc.. The designated UPA cell in the ULBs should be sensitised to ensure that the needs of the poor are provided for in investment plans and maintenance provisions.

The community structures created under SJSRY need to be strengthened and further diversified. One method would be to form associations of specific groups such as street vendors, who could have their own self-help groups, and network to create a financial interface with the formal sector financial institutions in order to gain access to credit. Social security benefits would be another area to cover. During the Tenth Plan, the scope of SJSRY should be expanded to include a scheme of contributory social security assistance such as insurance against death of the bread-winner, sickness, disability, and old age benefits to members of the community structures, in which there will be a matching contribution from the Government.

Capacity building is required for developing communication and inter-personal skills among the people responsible for providing for the needs of the urban poor, for improving the level of services and satisfaction of the beneficiaries, and for providing coordinated services from a number of line agencies. The creation of UPA cells has to be followed up by exposing personnel to techniques of convergence and team formation, communication and planning.

The positive aspect of SJSRY is that it contains the two basic requirements of any programme of poverty alleviation namely, community involvement and empowerment, and employment generation. Evaluation studies show that the progress of the scheme has not been remarkable, but that is no reason to give up the scheme itself. What is needed, instead, is to take corrective measures and improve implementation. Some areas of improvement are:

- The wage employment component should be used only for building assets and infrastructure relating to the urban poor, and not for general municipal works. The requirements should be selected by beneficiaries themselves and implementation should be from such lists of works identified by the beneficiaries.
- The guidelines need to be simplified and made more concise, removing all ambiguities and contradictions.
- The component of vocational training should be revamped and the quality of training improved;

- Community organisers and project coordinators should be appointed wherever they are not present, and the persons must be qualified in social work. The role of NGOs in projects should be strengthened. The community structures created under the scheme should be fully involved in the activities under the scheme, including selection and implementation of works, thrift and credit groups, group economic activities, etc. These community structures should be encouraged to fulfil their role as pressure groups for highlighting issues relating to their upliftment.
- Monitoring of the project at both the Central and State levels should be strengthened.

There is, in general, despondency among agencies responsible for programmes such as SJSRY with regard to availability of credit. There is a feeling that the increased emphasis on the viability of banks and reduction of non-performing assets (NPAs) is beginning to affect the availability of credit for the urban self-employed. This would be an unfortunate development. There is an urgent need to restore the banking sector's role in providing credit support to the urban informal sector, especially the self-employed urban poor. As the Task Force on Employment Opportunities noted, banks can meet the credit needs of the informal sector by financing self-help groups which provide micro credit for informal sector activities.

The concept of micro-finance essentially rests on the premise that (a) self-employment/ enterprise formation is a viable alternative means of alleviating poverty, (b) lack of access to capital assets/credit acts as a constraint on existing and potential micro-enterprises and (c) the poor are capable of saving despite their low level of income. Micro-finance could be referred to as providing credit support, usually in small amounts, along with other components such as training and other related services to people with poor resources and skills but who are in a position to undertake economic activities. Significant progress has been made in this area in recent years and the effort needs to be extended.

Such self-help activity can be strengthened with the assistance of NGOs with a good track record.

The other area requiring a thorough review and overhaul is vocational training under SJSRY, much of which is in the government sector and fails to equip the candidates with any sustainable level of skills or for self-employment. Innovative areas of employment, as has been developed in Kerala under the Kudumbasree programme, needs to be emulated in other states.

Land-owning agencies should be set a strict time limit to decide whether or not they wish to retrieve the land under slums and participate in a resettlement programme. If they fail to decide, the slums should be brought under in situ development without further reference to the agency.

The National Slum Policy which has already been subjected to wide debate and discussion, should be given a final form, followed up by implementation.

Performance of NSDP

The National Slum Development Programme (NSDP) initiated in the year 1997 as a scheme of Special Central Assistance, has been providing additional central assistance to State Governments for slum improvement. However, its performance has not been satisfactory mainly because of the delays at the State level in releasing the funds to implementing agencies. The monitoring of the programme at the Central level requires strengthening. To ensure proper utilisation, during the Tenth Plan the NSDP funds should be released for specific projects. States should submit annual plans for projects which will upgrade selected slums to get over the slum characteristics. The existing practice of releasing the funds to the states should be modified to this extent.

Night-Shelters for the Homeless

The programme of construction of Night Shelters for those without homes in urban areas requires rejuvenation. The provision of subsidy under the scheme has to be adequate to make it feasible for NGOs working in the field of housing for the poor, to take up construction and operation of the shelters. The NGOs will also need assistance in procuring land, though the maintenance of the shelters can be left to the NGOs themselves. Hence there is need to revise the scheme, raising the grants per bed to realistic levels, so as to achieve the objective of providing a sufficient number of night-shelters. Establishment of special night shelters for shelterless women and children will be a focal area for the Tenth Plan.

Mid-Term Appraisal of the Tenth Five Year Plan: 2002-2007

Urban Infrastructure

The poor quality of urban infrastructure in our major cities is an aspect of infrastructure deficiency that has come to be increasingly recognised in recent years. Urban infrastructure problems are likely to intensify as our cities expand and our urban population grows. Besides, in an environment in which states are increasingly interested in attracting foreign direct investment, it is inevitable that the quality of infrastructure in urban areas will be one of the critical competitive aspects that investors will consider in making location decisions.

National Urban Renewal Mission: The Budget for 2005-06 includes a provision of Rs. 5,500 crore for National Urban Renewal Mission. The basic approach of the Mission is that States willing to undertake urban sector reforms will be provided with assistance that would help finance critical urban infrastructure. A key assumption in designing the urban reforms is that the urban infrastructure should be financially self sustaining subject to the provision of a reasonable amount of viability gap funding. It must be recognised however that the provision of Rs. 5,500 crore is far from adequate if indeed a number of states seek funds under this program. This is one of the areas where funding requirements could increase substantially in the years ahead.

Urban Development

The Tenth Plan had, in the context of urban development, laid stress on improving the functional and financial autonomy of urban local bodies (ULBs), strengthening of their finances through smooth implementation of State Finance Commissions (SFC) awards, rationalisation of the property taxation system and levy of user charges. The Plan advocated broad-based urban sector reform measures and emphasised that public-private partnerships (PPP) should be brought on the urban agenda in order to improve the efficiency and delivery of services.

Although some states have made earnest efforts in this regard, the progress in these thrust areas is below expectations. Not much headway has been made in the area of urban reforms, which need to be brought on the agenda of urban governance. State governments have not given full effect to the recommendations of SFCs. State governments and ULBs have been generally reluctant to levy reasonable user charges. The property tax system is not only outdated but its coverage is far from adequate. As far as functional autonomy is concerned, most state governments have shied away from implementing several provisions of the Constitution (Seventy Fourth) Amendment Act, 1992, which envisaged a decentralised governance structure at the local level. Though PPP projects have been taken up in some cities, their impact has been limited because of a lack of properly designed PPP models and the absence of a regulatory framework to govern such arrangements.

Status of Urban Infrastructure

The process of urbanisation has gathered considerable momentum over the last 50 years. The growth of population has put urban infrastructure and services under severe strain. Smaller cities have found it particularly difficult to cope with the increasing demands on services because of inadequate financial resources. Urban areas in India, present a grim picture with regard to availability of basic infrastructure.

- About 21 per cent of the urban population is living in squatter settlements, where access to basic services is extremely poor.
- Although 89 per cent of the urban population is reported to have access to safe drinking water but there are severe deficiencies with regard to equitable distribution of water.
- Nearly 46 per cent of urban households have water toilets, but only 36 per cent of the urban households are connected to the public sewerage system.

- Average per capita generation of waste is estimated at 0.4 kg per capita per day in cities ranging from 1 lakh to 50 lakh population and the garbage collection efficiency ranges between 50 to 90 per cent of the solid waste generated.
- City roads are inadequate for traffic requirements, leading to congestion and fast deterioration in quality of roads due to excess loads.

The Rakesh Mohan Committee on the investment requirements of infrastructure had estimated the annual requirement of funds (1996-2001) for providing infrastructure (water supply, sanitation and roads) to the urban population at Rs. 28,298 crore. The annual requirement for the period 2001-2006 was estimated to be Rs.27,773 crore. During the Ninth Plan period, Rs. 5,200.01 crore under the Central Plan and Rs.20,838.00 crore under states Plan were spent on housing and urban development. In the Tenth Plan, an outlay of Rs. 11,510 crore as gross budgetary support (GBS) for the ministries of Urban Development and of Urban Employment and Poverty Alleviation) under Central Plan and Rs. 43,138.67 crore under states Plan has been provided. This represents an increase of 121 per cent in Central Plan and 107 per cent in the state Plan over the Ninth Plan realisation but the present level of funding is not even tackling the fringes of the problem.

Democratic Decentralisation of Urban Local Bodies

The Constitution (Seventy-Fourth) Amendment Act, 1992, aimed at decentralisation and creation of a democratic governance structure at the local level. Its objective was to redefine the relationship between the states and the municipal bodies, in order to firmly establish elected ULBs as the institutions of self-government (Article 243W).

The states have carried out the required amendments to the municipal laws and elections have been held in several states more than once under the supervision of State Election Commissions. The objective of political decentralisation has been accomplished to a substantial degree but the existing institutional framework for urban planning has not been realigned in accordance with the provisions of the Seventy-Fourth Amendment. Most state governments have shied away from implementing several provisions of the Act. The Twelfth Schedule (Article 243W) lists 18 functions to be transferred to the ULBs. However, only six states (Bihar, Chhattisgarh, Himachal Pradesh, Madhya Pradesh, Punjab and Tripura) have devolved all these functions. Only 21 states have set up District Planning Committees and only West Bengal and Maharashtra have established Metropolitan Planning Committees. Functional and financial autonomy of ULBs remains a distant dream.

Experience of State Finance Commissions

The effectiveness of the SFCs depends on the implementation of their recommendations by the respective states. The ultimate objective of the exercise should be the transfer of adequate level of state resources on a multi-year basis to ULBs in a manner that is free from procedural hassles and uncertainties. Importantly, there is a need for the transfers, based on the recommendations of SFC, to be linked to the degree of efficiency in raising resources, proper accounting and conformity to urban reforms.

However, experience shows that state governments have not fully complied with the recommendations of SFCs. Most SFCs have recommended a proportionate share of state tax and non- tax revenue to be devolved to the ULBs but the actual transfers are much less and uncertain. This has led to a precarious situation for the ULBs, which have also suffered because of the abolition by most state governments of octroi which was their main source of revenue.

Urban Governance

The devolution of functions to ULBs is incomplete and the financial resources with ULBs are inadequate. State governments are unwilling to provide autonomy to ULBs, the methods of property taxation are outdated and, in general, the attitude towards levy of user charges is indifferent.

A number of cities have involved the private sector in the provision of urban services. PPP projects, particularly in Tamil Nadu, Karnataka, Maharashtra, Andhra Pradesh and Gujarat have covered conservancy, sanitation, garbage collection/disposal, compost plant, street lighting, water supply, collection of local taxes, development and maintenance of gardens and parks, bus terminus, land development and market development etc. A majority of PPP initiatives are in water supply, sanitation and solid waste management. Lack of properly designed PPP models and the absence of a regulatory framework to govern such arrangements have inhibited the full utilisation of the PPP arrangements for urban development.

The Tenth Plan laid emphasis on transparency and right to information for both of which information technology (IT) can prove useful. Information technology can also bring about improvement in the service delivery mechanism and the revenue base of ULBs. Various municipalities have adopted e-Governance initiatives for property tax, grievances redressal, procurement, tap connection status, double accounting system, water charges, service tendering, birth/death certificates, building plan status, etc. The National Informatics Centre (NIC) has been instrumental in carrying out various e-Governance initiatives in most of the cases. Ministry of Urban Development is in process of preparing a National Mission Mode Project on e-Governance in Municipalities. The main objectives of the Mission are to improve efficiency and effectiveness in interaction between local government and its citizens and other stakeholders, improve quality of internal local government operations to support and stimulate good governance and bring about transparency and accountability in the governance of ULBs.

A scheme to generate city-level data and city maps - two of the most important tools of urban managers which are generally not available - derived from satellite imagery was to be implemented during the Tenth Plan. Digitised maps have not been generated from satellite data and little work has been done on ground-truth surveys. Similarly, basic urban data relating to settlements, slums, population, housing, transport, disposal of solid and liquid waste, water supply, sewage and sanitation, roads, drainage, street lights, parks and playgrounds, parking areas, etc. are lacking. A new scheme - National Urban Information System (NUIS) - proposed by the Ministry of Urban Development remains to be finalised.

The Tenth Plan acknowledged that there is a pressing need for capacity building of municipalities through training of elected and appointed officials and by restructuring of ULBs for efficient management of civic services. The public service element needs to be made more professional and accountable to the people. Community involvement not only results in effective implementation of the projects but also leads to better designing and substantial reduction in operational costs. 'Ward Committees and Area Sabhas' are ideal for participatory management. By making ward plans mandatory, the ward councillors become accountable, thus improving urban governance.

Urban Reforms

Given the emphasis on urban reforms in the Tenth Plan, an Urban Reforms Incentive Fund (URIF) was launched for providing incentive to state governments to carry out reforms in the following areas:

- Repeal of the Urban Land Ceiling and Regulation Act.
- Rationalisation of stamp duty in phases to bring it down to no more than 5 per cent by the end of the Tenth Plan period.
- Reform of rent control laws to stimulate private investment in rental Housing Schemes.
- Introduction of computerised process of registration.
- Reform of property tax so that it becomes a major source of revenue for ULBs, and arrangements for its effective implementation with collection efficiency of 85 per cent by the end of the Tenth Plan period.
- Levy of reasonable user charges, with full cost of operations and maintenance (O and M) being collected by the end of the Tenth Plan period.

- Introduction of double entry system of accounting.

Under URIF, 28 states/Union Territories have signed the Memoranda of Agreement (MoA) with the Ministry of Urban Employment and Poverty Alleviation. Of these, 20 have agreed to repeal the Urban Land Ceiling Act and rationalise the stamp duty, 22 States/UTs have agreed to reform the Rent Control Act, 27 States/UTs have agreed to computerise the registration process and levy of reasonable user charges. All 28 States/UTs have agreed to adopt the double entry system of accounting and reform the property tax. According to the URIF guidelines, the first instalment of assistance is released on the MoA being signed and subsequent releases are based on the achievement of the prescribed milestones. While Rs. 188.15 crore was released as first instalment on signing MOA, an amount of Rs. 68.18 crore only was released as second instalment which indicates that all the milestones have not been carried out in line with in the MoA.

Review of Plan Schemes

Urban Water Supply and Sanitation: Safe drinking water supply and sanitation are basic human needs and are crucial for achieving the goal of "Health for All". The Tenth Plan envisaged the augmentation of water supply in urban areas in order to reach the prescribed norms, higher degree of reliability, assurance of water quality, a high standard of operation and management, accountability to customers and, in particular, special arrangements to meet the needs of the urban poor as well as levying and recovery of user charges to finance the maintenance functions and to facilitate further investment in the sector. These achievements are to a large extent, dependent on the willingness of the state governments and ULBs to restructure water supply organisations, levy reasonable water rates, take up reforms in billing, accounting and collection and become creditworthy in order to have access to market funding.

Financial Performance: Urban water supply and sanitation is being handled mostly under the state Plan, except for the Accelerated Urban Water Supply Programme (AUWSP), which is a centrally sponsored scheme (CSS) for small towns with population less than 20,000. There is no Central scheme or CSS in operation relating to sewerage/sewage treatment except under National River Conservation Plan (NRCP) which is meant for towns/cities located at the banks of important rivers. The Tenth Plan outlay for urban water supply and sanitation was Rs. 18,749.20 crore (excluding the states of Arunachal Pradesh, Tamil Nadu, Uttaranchal and the Union Territory of Lakshadweep) under state/Union Territory Plans.

Key Issues and Recommended Strategy: Paying adequate attention to operation and maintenance (O and M) of the created assets could result in a 40-50 per cent improvement in their useful life. There are a variety of reasons for the neglect of O and M: inappropriate system design, multiplicity of agencies and overlapping of responsibilities, inadequate training of personnel, lack of performance evaluation and monitoring, lack of operation manuals etc. The Ministry of Urban Development has brought out a manual on "Operations and Maintenance of Urban Water Supply System".

Several pilot studies have shown that water losses in distribution account for between 20 and 50 per cent of the total flow in the system, with the maximum leakage being caused in the house service connections. In India, the water supply is by and large intermittent (supply hours ranging from three hours to ten hours), and external pollution may get sucked into the system at the points of leak during non-supply hours (when the system is not under pressure), causing health hazards. A systematic approach to the reduction of wastage of water from leaks and preventive maintenance would obviate the need for augmentation and also help in increasing revenue.

The principal reason for the persistence of these problems is that the urban water supply and sanitation service providers are not financially viable. They cannot maintain the quality of services without large subsidies. Their inability to impose a reasonable user-charge, itself a reflection of political constraints, is the major obstacle to their becoming financially viable. In view of the pressure on budgetary resources, there is no alternative to making suppliers of these services charge more reasonable tariffs thus creating an environment in which they can access institutional finance with government budgetary support limited to meeting viability gap requirements

Two other problems with urban water supply and sanitation service providers are lack of autonomy and accountability. In many cases, their personnel also lack the necessary managerial skills. A shift to professionally managed financially viable bodies will help address these problems. Environmental degradation is also a problem. The exploitation of water resources is not sustainable at present.

Solid Waste Management

The management of urban solid waste is one of the most neglected areas of urban development in India. India produces about 42 million tons of urban solid waste annually. The current municipal solid waste generation is estimated to be approximately 0.4 kg per capita per day. There has been a decline in the standard of services in collection and disposal of household, industrial and hospital waste. In most cities, nearly half the solid waste remains unattended. Lack of financial resources, inadequate manpower, fragmentation of administrative responsibility, non-involvement of community and lack of awareness are major constraints in solid waste management. Considering the complexity of the problem, it is necessary to evolve a suitable national strategy even though its implementation can best be handled at the level of ULBs.

Bird hits are among the major causes of air crashes in the country. An Inter-Ministerial Joint Sub-Committee constituted by the Ministry of Defence recommended proper sanitation facilities, including solid waste management and drainage, to overcome the bird menace in the towns where Indian Air Force (IAF) airfields are located. A Central scheme has been formulated to cover ten selected IAF airfield towns at a cost of Rs.99.34 crore. The O and M of the scheme would be borne by the respective ULBs/state governments. An expenditure of Rs.99 lakh during 2003-04 and Rs.40 crore during 2004-05 was incurred.

In October 2000, the Ministry of Environment and Forests notified the Municipal Solid Wastes (Management and Handling) Rules, 2000, which lay down the procedures/ guidelines for collection, segregation, storage, transportation, processing, and disposal of municipal solid waste. The rules require that all cities should set up suitable waste treatment and disposal facilities by 31 December 2001.The rules also specify standards for compost quality, leachate control, and management and closure of landfill sites. The Ministry of Urban Development has also brought out a comprehensive manual on municipal solid waste management for the guidance of ULBs.

In view of the urgency and importance of solid waste management in urban areas, the Tenth Plan had suggested a new mission-mode state sector programme named 'Urban Sanitation Mission', with focus on setting up sanitary land- fills and composting plants for urban solid waste, and improvement of drainage in urban areas with special Central assistance, subject to availability of additional resources. However, no funds could be tied up so far. Therefore, under the proposed National Urban Renewal Mission and Urban Infrastructure Development Scheme, solid waste management has been accorded priority with focus on projectised approach.

Urban Transport

A good network of roads and an efficient mass urban transport system make a substantial contribution to the working efficiency of a large city for its economic and social development. However, there are no coherent urban transport plans in most cities and the urban transport infrastructure is grossly inadequate. According to the 2001 Census, there are 35 metropolitan cities with million plus population. Except for Mumbai, Kolkata and Delhi, none of the Indian cities has a Mass Rapid Transit System (MRTS).

The Delhi Metro Project is progressing according to schedule and is expected to be fully operational by March 2006. Other metropolitan cities are also in the process of preparing detailed project reports (DPRs) for a metro-rail system. In Kolkata, the State Govt. is considering an Elevated Mass Rapid Transit System (EMRTS), in Hyderabad, the State Govt. has got a DPR prepared for Metro system, and in Mumbai, a Master Plan for Metro system has been prepared and a 15 km long Varsova-Andheri-Ghatkopar corridor through BOOT is under consideration. However, it needs to be borne in mind that the metro-rail projects are highly capital intensive and require long gestation periods. There is one point of view that metro-rail projects can be commercially viable only in cities with skyscrapers.

The concept of Bus Rapid Transit (BRT) system has now been adopted worldwide. The BRT achieves reduced travel times through the use of transit-only lanes, signal priority, prepaid fares and buses designed for easy boarding.

Central Sector Scheme in Urban Transport

The only Central scheme under way since 1996 is the Delhi MRTS project executed by the Delhi Metro Rail Corporation (DMRC) Ltd. The revised cost of the Delhi Metro is Rs. 10,571 crore. The requirement of funds during the Tenth Plan, estimated by the Ministry, was to the tune of Rs. 8,927.65 crore. During the first two years of the Tenth Plan, an amount of Rs. 1,050 crore was provided and Rs 3,339.30 crore was utilised, the additional funds being provided by means of supplementary budget by the Ministry of Finance. Further, in the Annual Plan of 2004-05, Rs. 480 crore has been provided against the requirement of Rs. 2,030 crore. There is a provision of Rs. 200 crore for other schemes of Urban Transport in the Tenth Plan but there has been progress only in case of the Bangalore MRTS. While, the Bangalore MRTS has got the Planning Commission's 'in-principle' approval, the funding aspects and the role of the Government of India as an equity partner are yet to be finalised by the Ministry of Urban Development.

Key Issues and Recommended Strategy

In view of the poor urban transport facilities in Indian cities, there is an urgent need for a National Urban Transport Policy and road-rail network planning for improving urban connectivity. In developed countries, cities start planning and building an MRTS when they reach a population level of one million and start operating MRTS by the time they are two million strong. By that reckoning, all million plus cities should be either operating an MRTS or at least have one on their drawing board. It is estimated that on an average, the elevated metro-rail costs Rs. 100 crore/ km while the underground/underwater metro-rail costs Rs. 275 crore/km. Therefore, viability and suitability factors should be kept in mind while selecting the modes of transportation for a city. The Ministry of Urban Development provides grant assistance of 40 per cent of the cost of studies for addressing traffic and transportation problems of a city. The Ministry of Urban Development is also in the process of formulating a National Urban Transport Policy to address various issues involved in urban transport.

States need to draw up urban transport plans for all million plus cities and state capitals, by studying various modes of public transport. City-specific projects including the BRT system and a rail-based urban transport system need to be critically evaluated along with other sustainable modes of transportation whereby the urban transport problems need to be considered by the planning agencies as an integral component for land use planning.

Integrated Development of Small and Medium Towns

The CSS of Integrated Development of Small and Medium Towns (IDSMT) was initiated in 1979-80 with the objective of improving the economic and physical infrastructure in small and medium towns so that they become capable of generating economic growth and employment and slow down migration to larger cities. The scheme is applicable to cities with population up to 500,000. The ratio of Central assistance to state assistance is

60:40 and there is a loan component of 20 to 40 per cent (depending on the size of the city) from financial institutions.

An outlay of Rs. 1,304.65 crore was approved for the Tenth Plan to assist 925 new and on-going towns under IDSMT scheme. During the first three years of the Plan period, only 30 per cent (assuming full utilisation of 2004-05 allocations) of Tenth Plan allocation is expected to be utilised. In terms of physical achievements, 67 per cent towns (621 towns) are expected to be assisted during the same period. This thinning of resources has led to a lack of appreciable results on the ground.

Mega City Scheme

The Mega City Scheme, applicable to Mumbai, Kolkata, Chennai, Bangalore and Hyderabad, was initiated in 1993-94 with the objective of undertaking infrastructure development projects of city-wide/regional significance. The projects cover a wide range of components like water supply and sewerage, roads and bridges, city transport, solid waste management etc. The Central Government and respective state government share 25 per cent each of the project cost with the balance 50 per cent being met through institutional finance.

An outlay of Rs.1,050 crore was approved for the Tenth Plan. During the first three years of the Plan period, 44 per cent (assuming full utilisation of 2004-05 allocations) of the Tenth Plan allocation is expected to be utilised. It is evident that the amount provided is grossly inadequate to take care of the problems of these cities. It has also been observed that the institutional finance is invariably short of the required 50 per cent share. There is need to re-evaluate the resource requirements, if any serious attempt is to be made to deal with the problems of mega cities.

National Capital Region Planning Board

The National Capital Region Planning Board (NCRPB) was established in 1985 with a view to containing the pressure of population on Delhi and to attain balanced and harmonious development of the National Capital Territory (NCT) of Delhi and adjoining areas. An outlay of Rs.350 crore has been earmarked for this scheme in the Tenth Plan. During the first three years of the Plan, 46 per cent (assuming full utilisation of 2004-05 allocations) of Tenth Plan allocation is expected to be utilised. However, the objectives of arresting the migration to NCT Delhi and achieving the dispersal of economic activities are yet to be met.

Recommended Strategy for Urban Development

It is evident from the mid-term appraisal that the Tenth Plan strategy for urban development is reflected unevenly in the schemes under way and their level of funding does not meet the requirements of this sector and the enormous challenges it pose. The urban development sector has the following general deficiencies:

- The systems at the city level are not financially viable.
- Existing schemes are patchy and the allocated resources are grossly inadequate to the magnitude of the problems.
- Issues are not addressed in a holistic manner.
- There are many schemes with similar/overlapping objectives.

The following two-track strategy is recommended with the focus on urban reforms and e-governance:

- Convergence of urban development schemes
- National Urban Renewal Mission

Convergence of Urban Development Schemes

A single comprehensive scheme - Urban Infrastructure Development Scheme (UIDS) -needs to be evolved for providing assistance for improving urban infrastructure. The proposed scheme should have the following features:

1. Central sponsorship
2. Financial assistance under the proposed scheme should be in the ratio 80:10:10 (Centre:State:financial institutions/own resources).
3. Grants from the Government of India and state governments need to flow to a special revolving fund at the state level, with

a stipulation that at least 25 per cent of such grants (Centre and state) released to ULBs should be ploughed back to this revolving fund for sustainable development.

4. The allocations available under IDSMT, Mega City, City Challenge Fund, Pooled Finance Development Facility and AUWSP should be subsumed under the new scheme.
5. Areas like, water supply, sanitation, drainage, sewerage and solid waste management, roads, street lighting, urban transport and other civic amenities will be covered under the new scheme.
6. The state governments would execute Memoranda of Agreement (MoAs) with the Government of India and ensure that the reforms prescribed in the scheme are undertaken by the ULBs

The urban reforms that should be made conditional for eligibility for assistance under UIDs are:

- Implementation of decentralisation measures as envisaged in the Constitution (Seventy-Fourth Amendment) Act to establish elected ULBs as institutions of self-government.
- Adoption of modern, accrual-based double entry system of accounting in ULBs.
- Passage of a public disclosure law to ensure preparation of medium-term fiscal plans of ULBs and release of quarterly performance information to all stakeholders Passage of community participation law to institutionalise citizen participation and introducing the concept of the Area Sabha in urban areas
- Transferring all special agencies that deliver civic services in urban areas to ULBs over a period of five years and creating accountability platforms for all urban civic service providers in transition
- Introduction of e-governance using IT applications like, Geographical Information System and Management Information System for various services provided by ULBs
- Reform of property tax with GIS, so that it becomes a major source of revenue for ULBs and arrangements for its effective

implementation to ensure that collection efficiency reaches at least 85 per cent within the next five years. Complete revamping of the property tax system through detailed data gathering process, tracking and monitoring system

- Levy of reasonable user charges by ULBs with the objective of recovering the full cost of O and M within the next five years

National Urban Renewal Mission

The impact of the growth of population on urban infrastructure and civic services has been adverse. For the cities to realise their full potential and become true engines of growth, it is necessary that focused attention is given to the improvement of urban infrastructure and, more importantly, to improving the institutional service delivery mechanism at the city level.

Sub-optimal structures continue to exist in cities partly because the landlords do not have any incentive of maintaining them, because of low rental income and partly on account of difficulty in evicting tenants. This hampers the rejuvenation of inner city areas. Transitional arrangements can be made to avoid hardship cases but zoning regulations should take into account the changing nature of inner city areas and permit their redevelopment, paving the way for urban renewal. In the developed countries, when an area is declared under law as an Urban Renewal or Urban Redevelopment Area, all land transactions and building activities within that area are stopped, land is requisitioned by the government and a general plan for reconstruction is prepared by the designated authority. The authority is empowered to move occupants from a renewal region on the condition that other suitable premises should be provided outside of other prospective renewal or redevelopment regions. However, in the Indian context, much more is needed than mere redevelopment of inner city.

The National Urban Renewal Mission (NURM) would be a reforms-driven, fast track, planned development of identified cities with focus on efficiency in urban infrastructure/services delivery mechanism, community participation and accountability of ULBs towards citizens. The following broad framework is proposed for the Mission:

1. Central sponsorship
2. The sector-wise DPRs would be prepared by the identified cities enumerating projects for various components along with their priorities.
3. The funding pattern would be 35:15:50 (between Centre, States/ULBs and financial institutions) for mega cities (>40 lakh population), 50:20:30 for cities with million plus but less than four million population and 80:10:10 for other cities.
4. The grant assistance (both Central and state) would act as seed money to leverage additional resources from financial institutions/capital market. In addition, various PPP models with viability gap funding would also be explored to further supplement the resources. The scheme would be implemented through a designated state level nodal agency.
5. Every identified city would prepare planned urban perspective frameworks for a period of 20-25 years (with five yearly updates) indicating policies, programmes and strategies of meeting fund requirements. This perspective plan would be followed by the preparation of Development Plans integrating land use with services, urban transport and environment management.
6. The menu of urban reforms would include both mandatory and optional items of reforms. The cities seeking assistance under NURM would have to undertake all the mandatory reforms within the prescribed time frame, even as they have the freedom to opt for any five items of reforms from the optional category. The state governments and the identified city would execute MOA with the Government of India and ensure that such reforms are actually undertaken. This tripartite MOA would be submitted along with the DPRs.
7. Apart from the reforms listed under the UIDS, the mandatory reforms would include the following:

- Drawing up PPP models for development, management and financing of urban infrastructure for different sizes of ULBs.
- Introduction of independent regulators for urban services.
- Rationalisation of stamp duty to bring it down to no more than 5 per cent within next five years.
- Repeal of the Urban Land Ceiling and Regulation Act.
- Reform of rent control laws to stimulate private investment in rental housing schemes.
- Implementation of a system to improve the efficiency of drinking water supply on the basis of water audit.

8. The five optional reforms would be chosen from among the following:

- Revision of by-laws to streamline the approval process for construction of buildings, development of sites etc.
- Simplification of the legal and procedural frameworks for conversion of agricultural land for non-agricultural purposes.
- Introduction of Property Title Certification System in ULBs.
- Earmarking at least 25 per cent of developed land in all housing projects (both public and private agencies) for the economically weaker sections (EWS)/low-income group (LIG) category with a system of cross subsidisation.
- Introduction of a computerised process of registration of land and property.
- Revision of by-laws to make rainwater harvesting mandatory in all buildings to come up in future.
- Reuse of reclaimed water.
- Adoption of water conservation measures.
- Administrative reforms i.e. reduction in the establishment cost by voluntary retirement schemes, not filling up of posts falling vacant due to retirement etc. and achieving specified milestones in this regard.

Urban Housing

Housing is a basic necessity as well as an important economic activity. The Housing and Habitat Policy of 1998 has specifically advocated that the government create a facilitating environment for growth of housing activity, rather than taking up the task of housing itself. In both rural and urban sectors, housing is largely a private sector activity. This is not to rule out the need for a high degree of involvement of the government and its agencies in meeting the housing needs of the urban poor. It has to be recognised that there is a need for massive expansion of social housing in towns and cities, paying particular attention to the needs of the slum dwellers.

The Working Group on Housing constituted for formulation of the Tenth Five Year Plan had observed that around 90 per cent of housing shortage pertained to the weaker sections. Therefore, there was a need to increase the supply of affordable housing to the economically weaker sections and the low-income category. The substantial thrust on housing manifested in facilitating measures including Reserve Bank of India regulations relating to priority sector lending, fiscal concessions and budgetary incentives, has started bearing fruit. The Housing and Urban Development Corporation (HUDCO) earmarks 55 per cent of its housing portfolio to weaker sections and low-income groups, with differential interest rates, higher loan component and longer repayment period. The Government of India provides equity support to HUDCO with a view to leveraging more funds from the market. Under the Two Million Housing programme of the Government of India, which was started in 1998-99, HUDCO has been entrusted with the responsibility of providing annual loan assistance for the construction of 6 lakh houses in rural areas and 4 lakh houses in urban areas. Till now, Government of India has been extending equity support to HUDCO which has been stopped since August, 2004 on declaration of HUDCO as Mini Ratna.

Financial Performance

For the Tenth Plan, an outlay of Rs. 1,000 crore was approved for providing equity support to HUDCO. During the first three years of the Plan, Rs. 620.60 crore i.e. 62 per cent (assuming full utilisation of 2004-05 allocations) of Tenth Plan allocation is expected to be utilised. In terms of HUDCO's mandate of providing loan assistance to the extent of 55 per cent of its housing portfolio to EWS/LIG categories, the financial achievement during the first two years of the Tenth Plan has been only 24.29 per cent (in 2002-03) and 33.25 per cent (in 2003-04), which is far below the target. However, in physical terms/ numbers, over 90 per cent of the loans under housing are going to EWS/LIG categories. Under the Two Million Housing Programme, 8.87 lakh dwelling units in the urban areas and 9.53 lakh dwelling units in the rural areas were sanctioned by HUDCO in the first two years of the Tenth Plan.

The CSS, Night Shelter Scheme, which is funded on the basis of 50:50 between Centre and the states, aims to provide construction of composite night shelters with community toilets and baths for urban shelter-less with 50 per cent subsidy from the Government of India and 50 per cent as contribution from implementing agencies or through HUDCO as loan. During the first three years of the Tenth Plan, Rs.8 crore i.e. 26 per cent (assuming full utilisation of 2004-05 allocations) of Tenth Plan allocation of Rs. 30.97 crore is expected to be utilised under the scheme. This shows that the problem of urban shelterless and pavement dwellers has not been given the consideration it deserves. Since the land is a State subject, on the recommendation of the Ministry of UEPA, the scheme of Night Shelter has been transferred to State sector w.e.f. 2005-06.

Issues and Recommended Strategy

In order to increase the proportion of household savings to be invested in the housing sector, as well as to provide houses to those who cannot afford to have their own, the promotion of rental housing by the private sector, public sector, as well as cooperatives and individuals needs encouragement. This requires changes in the existing laws relating to land ceiling, stamp duty, registration of land and properties as well as rent control laws. This would unleash investment in the housing sector on a large scale, resulting in a positive effect on employment generation as well.

For providing affordable housing to the 'urban poor', states need to earnestly address certain key issues. They need to adopt a three-pronged strategy involving easy availability of land and transfer of tenurial rights, cheap and easy access to-credit and promoting low-cost building material and technology for construction of houses.

The various urban development authorities, which acquire and develop large tracts of land for the growth of the cities, should provide a major part of such land to meet the requirements of the EWS/LIG categories. At present, there is little evidence that these authorities - which are often the sole organisation for development of serviced land - are doing so. States need to formalise a system of earmarking at least 25 per cent of developed land in all housing projects (both public and private agencies) for EWS/LIG category with a system of cross subsidisation.

The mandate of providing credit for housing to EWS/LIG categories has, more or less, been confined to HUDCO whose performance has not been satisfactory. Much more needs to be done and other housing finance institutions must also supplement efforts that are being made in this sector. Similarly, not much serious efforts have been made to popularise low cost building material and technology for the construction of houses. State governments need to adopt a definite strategy regarding this in consultation with technical institutions.

Sometime back, 100 per cent foreign direct investment (FDI) was permitted for development of integrated townships but not INDIA'S FIVE YEAR PLANS 12 Urban Infrastructure much headway has been made in this regard. This has been mainly on account of the problems relating to land procurement. There is a need to ease the availability of land to check land prices, which have been high on account of restrictions on availability. More flexible zoning regulations to permit change of land use, easier subdivision regulations, and extension of trunk services to new areas/new townships, would reduce congestion and develop the cities in an orderly fashion. Innovative measures for land assembly/ land pooling, use of land as a resource to build up infrastructure and adoption of methods such as vacant land tax and transferable development rights (TDR) need to be studied and replicated wherever feasible. Further liberalisation in FDI for integrated township, housing and construction sector/real estate need to be examined in consultation with various stakeholders. The State Governments need to play proactive role in providing necessary clearances in a time bound manner to attract FDI.

Slum Development

The existence of slums in urban areas essentially reflects urban poverty and, despite the efforts to discourage slum dwellers, their number has been increasing. This puts tremendous pressure on urban basic services and infrastructure. Nearly 28 million persons lived in slums in 1981 accounting for 17.5 per cent of the urban population. In 1991 the number of persons living in slums increased to 45.7 million accounting for 21.5 per cent of the urban population. According to the Town and Country Planning Organisation (TCPO) Estimates 2001, the slum population number 61.82 million.

The National Slum Policy has not yet been finalised. There has, over the years, been a paradigm shift in the government's slum policy prescriptions. Originally, a 'slum free cities' policy was prescribed. However, looking at the social dimensions of the whole problem and the various economic activities carried out by the slum dwellers, this concept has given way to rehabilitation of slum dwellers. The rehabilitation involves either relocation or in-situ development of the slum areas. Most state governments and municipalities prefer in-situ development of slum areas. In the initial years of the slum development, the focus was on provision of infrastructure in slums through the National Slum Development Programme (NSDP) and now there is renewed stress on provision of shelter to urban slum dwellers through the Valmiki Ambedkar Awas Yojana (VAMBAY).

The Maharashtra Government has widely used the TDR concept to rehabilitate slum dwellers, which does not envisage any contribution either from slum dwellers or from the state government. On the other hand, in Karnataka, the beneficiary is required to make an upfront contribution. Further, some state governments provide credit either directly or through the ULBs and incentive in the form of interest subsidy to the beneficiary. Therefore, there is an urgent need to formulate a National Slum Policy with emphasis on similar action by states for state-specific situations.

Financial Performance

VAMBAY was introduced in 2001-02 to meet the long-standing gap in programmes for slum-dwellers, viz. provision of a shelter or upgrading the existing shelter of people living below the poverty line in urban slums. Under VAMBAY, the Government of India provides 50 per cent subsidy while the States have the option of mobilising their matching portion of 50 per cent from other sources, such as their own budget provision, resources of local bodies, loans from other agencies, contributions from beneficiaries or non-government organisations (NGOs) etc. Under this scheme, 20 per cent of the total allocation is provided for sanitation and community toilets to be built for the urban poor and slum dwellers. During the first three years of the Tenth Plan, Rs. 727.58 crore i.e. 36 per cent (assuming full utilisation of 04-05 allocations) of the Plan allocation of Rs. 2,040 crore is expected to be utilised.

Recommended Strategy

- For integrated slum development, the existing schemes of NSDP, low cost sanitation and VAMBAY need to be INDIA'S FIVE YEAR PLANS 13 integrated under one platform and financial institutions and/or private sector should be involved in this effort to the extent possible.
- The projectisation approach needs to be adopted so that emphasis is given to project-related schemes that are

identified by the municipalities or the state governments in consultation with the slum dwellers. This would ensure that only viable projects are taken up and community participation is forthcoming. This would also ensure that the resources are put to optimum use. Considering the constraints on resources, prioritisation of various projects to be included in the slum development programme is necessary.

- To ensure that viable projects are identified, an authentic database and a clear-cut government policy on land where the slum dwellers are squatting (whether to provide tenurial rights/ownership rights) need to be evolved.
- To provide sustainability to slum development/upgrading programmes, the contribution of beneficiaries has to be ensured and the involvement of public sector/private sector/financial institutions under the overall patronage of the state governments/Central government is necessary to enlarge the resource base. PPP models for such integrated housing and slum development programme need to be evolved.
- The issues of livelihood, infrastructure, education, health, environment and more importantly sanitation have to be addressed in a holistic manner. Such an approach is essential, as the relocation of slum dwellers to the far-off areas would prove to be counter-productive.

The Way Forward

- Step up investments in urban infrastructure in a major way to bring our cities on par with those in the emerging economies of Asia. Intensify urban reform efforts on a substantial scale. Enhance Central assistance for urban development and link all such assistance with urban reforms to be undertaken by the states and ULBs.
- Encourage each city to prepare a perspective plan encompassing all aspects including water supply, sanitation, drainage, sewerage and urban transport. This is necessary to enable enhanced investment. Build a reliable database on

urban infrastructure and services must be an integral part of the plan.

- Implement reforms in urban governance. These are needed for augmenting the resources of ULBs to undertake investment and for maintaining the assets that are created. The goal must be to set in motion a virtuous cycle of urban growth leading to better resources, which are then used for improved infrastructure and further growth of the cities. Include, as part of the reforms measures for decentralisation, making the elected ULBs institutions of self-governance. In addition, the reforms must encompass, among other things, accounting reforms, enactment of laws for public disclosure and community participation, transfer of all civic services to ULBs, introduction of e-governance, reform of property tax and levy of reasonable user charges
- Design a two-track approach for Plan assistance with focus on urban reforms and e-governance.
- On the first track, merge all schemes of the Government of India for urban infrastructure and civic amenities. In future, make normal levels of assistance available on a platform of reforms. Such allocations would be conditional on urban reforms being carried out by the state governments and the ULBs.
- On the second track, take up the million plus cities, the capital city in every state and a small number of other cities that are of historical importance for a considerably enhanced level of Plan assistance through the National Urban Renewal Mission.
- Undertake reforms of urban land ceiling, rent control and stamp duty in order to unleash housing activity in the urban areas. For the urban poor, a three-pronged approach is needed, involving availability of land, cheap and easy credit and promotion of low cost building material and technology.
- Formulate a National Slum Policy. A single comprehensive Integrated Housing and Slum Development Programme should be evolved, merging the existing schemes of VAMBAY and NSDP.

- Formulate a National Urban Transport Policy and undertake road-rail network planning for improving connectivity.

Eleventh Five Year Plan:
(Approach Paper Released in November 2006)

Construction, housing and real estate industry provides a large scope for direct and indirect employment of persons with a wide range of skills and also of unskilled persons; it employs over 30 million people and has been growing at over 10 per cent per year over the last five years. It covers rural and urban infrastructure, roads, airports, sea-ports and commercial and residential buildings. The 11th Plan therefore, put special focus on this sector so that its potential to create employment and growth is fully realised.

In housing we have a large unmet need and a growing demand due to growing working population and nuclear families. Availability of housing loans at low interest rates has stimulated this demand. Construction has great possibilities for creating employment which need to be fully exploited. Growing at 9 per cent per annum since the mid-1990s, the services sector accounts for 54 per cent of GDP and is currently the fastest-growing sector of the economy. This sector is estimated to have the potential for creating 40 million jobs and generating additional US$ 200 billion annual income by 2020. The sector has the unique opportunity to grow due to its labour cost advantage reflecting one of the lowest salary and wage levels in the world, coupled with a rising share of working age population Infrastructure development has been identified as a major thrust area emphasised through such projects as Bharat Nirman, Pradhan Mantri Grameen Sadak Yojana, National Highways Development Programme, Modernisation of Airports etc.

The Urban Land Ceiling Act which is still in operation in some states is one among several constraints on land development in many states which need to be reconsidered. Non-transparent land use policies, which are almost ubiquitous, also add to the problem. Urban Rent Control, high stamp duty and other transfer costs also restrict construction. State governments and Municipal

Bodies should undertake a comprehensive review of such policies and amend necessary laws/regulations in line with the requirement of modern city development to formulate their Master Plans and Zonal Plans in a given timeframe. State governments should also make their rural/urban land-use conversion processes simpler and quicker.

The situation is aggravated by low investment in urban roads and rapid transport systems, which if developed can help disperse population and mitigate the high cost of urban properties. The issue of enlarging the scope of FDI in this sector has to be viewed in light of the fact that even in China nearly half the FDI inflows are in the housing sector alone. Investment in the sector can be stimulated if government and SEBI bring about refinements in the financial markets by developing sophisticated financial instruments, customised for real-estate sector.

Increasing Investment in Infrastructure Sector

Public Private Partnerships (PPPs) are increasingly becoming the preferred mode for construction and operation of infrastructure services such as highways, airports, ports etc., both in developed and developing countries. PPPs offer significant advantages in terms of attracting private capital in creation of public infrastructure as well as in improving efficiencies in the provision of services to users. PPPs can be undertaken through a range of alternatives such as BOT, BOOT etc. They enable governments to transfer construction and commercial risks to the private sector which is best suited to manage them. However, considerable work is needed to create an enabling environment which should not only attract private investment but must also be seen to be in the public interest and this is best assured if the process is seen to provide services at reasonable cost and in a transparent manner. If we adopt best practices, it will be possible to create credible PPP projects that evoke a positive public response and do not require re-negotiation or payment of unforeseen liabilities by the government or the users.

PPPs are best implemented through standardised arrangements that constitute a stable policy and regulatory regime where private capital derives greater comfort and seeks the least possible risk premium. Model Concession Agreements (MCAs) would be used for providing a stable regulatory and policy framework. The MCA for PPP in highways has already been approved and published. Similar work is nearing completion in other sectors.

Because PPPs involve dealing with the private sector, they sometimes give rise to suspicion that corporate investors are getting a favoured treatment. Transparent processes and consultations with stakeholders combined with effective competitive bidding for PPP projects help in improving perceptions and enhance the acceptability of PPP projects. This approach also provides the requisite comfort to public servants who are responsible for awarding projects to private entities.

The key to making PPPs acceptable is to create an environment where PPPs are seen to be a way of attracting private money into public projects, not putting public resources into private projects.

Roads

The 10th Plan stressed the need for improving mobility and easy accessibility. Accordingly, the National Highway Development Programme (NHDP) consisting of 4-laning of the Golden Quadrilateral [NHDP I] with a length of 5,846 km. and the North-South and East-West Corridor [NHDP II] with a length of 7472 km. coupled with Pradhan Mantri Gram Sadak Yojana (PMGSY) for rural roads were taken up. The PMGSY programme has been recently expanded to achieve the Bharat Nirman target of connecting 1000+ habitation (500+ for hilly and tribal areas) by 2008-09 with all weather roads. This programme will help bring India's villages into the market economy. Similarly the "Special Accelerated Development Road Programme for the North Eastern Region (SARDP-NE)", will help in developing and integrating these regions with the rest of the country.

Keeping in view the need for nationwide connectivity and mobility, it is proposed to undertake an expanded programme for highway development going beyond NHDP I and II to include NHDP III to VII. This programme will involve substantial resources from public private partnerships based on build, operate and transfer (BOT) model which has many advantages over the traditional construction contracts. All contracts for provision of road services for NHDP Phase-III onwards would be awarded **only on BOT basis**, and the traditional construction contracts will be awarded only in specified exceptional cases. A model concession agreement has been developed to facilitate speedy award of contracts. This is a very significant innovation in the area of public-private partnership.

The National Highway Development Programme (NHDP) approved by the Committee on Infrastructure is estimated to require a total investment of Rs. 220,000 crore. Some of the projects in the programme will, however, spill over beyond 2011-12. Compared to an investment of Rs. 59,490 crore projected for the Tenth Plan (likely actual of Rs. 51,000 crore), investment during the Eleventh Plan is likely to be Rs. 180,000 crore. The programme has been divided in seven phases/ segments as indicated below:

The present traffic mix consisting of non-motorised and low-powered vehicles compels low speed. Furthermore most of the National Highways pass through habitations and ribbon development is a perennial problem. It is, therefore, necessary to establish a network of access controlled Expressways across the country for which advance planning would be undertaken during the 11th Plan. The actual construction (except for 1000 kms already taken up) would be undertaken during the 12th Plan period and would be prioritised according to the density of traffic. The increased emphasis on rural roads would also continue and a major proportion of the 1.72 lakh unconnected habitations would be connected with all weather roads under the PMGSY.

The maintenance of roads has not been given adequate importance by the states mainly due to paucity of resources. This has resulted in poor riding quality of the road network which is highly uneconomic. A rupee spent on maintenance saves two to three rupees in vehicle operating costs, besides improving traffic flow. Keeping this in view, the 12th Finance Commission has recommended additional grants to the tune of Rs. 15,000 crore for maintenance of roads and bridges for the four-year period 2006-07 to 2009-10.

The National Highway Authority of India (NHAI) has an enormous task before it to implement a road programme involving a total cost of over Rs. 220,000 crore. The Authority is being restructured to give it greater professional skills combined with a measure of autonomy and accountability.

Indian roads are considered very accident prone and claim a large number of casualties representing an enormous human and economic loss. It is proposed to establish a dedicated organisation for promoting road safety. One per cent of the cess is to be earmarked for safety-related measures.

Urban Infrastructure

Congested roads, poor public transport, inadequate availability of water, improper treatment of sewage, uncollected solid waste and above all grossly inadequate housing that forces more than 50 per cent of our population in some metropolis to live in slums, all these severely decrease the quality of life and lower the well being of urban population. They also affect the investment climate since India cannot expect to make a favourable impression on foreign investors and the international business community generally, if India's cities appear to be falling behind those in other developing countries. The state of urban infrastructure in the country has deteriorated to an extent that we are not able to fully benefit from these economies. Rapid economic growth will inevitably lead to an increase in urbanisation as cities provide large economies of agglomeration for individual activity. Poor urban infrastructure inflicts a severe hardship on people.

In order to cope with massive problems that have emerged as a result of rapid urban growth, the Jawaharlal Nehru National Urban Renewal Mission (JNNURM) was launched by Govt. on 3rd December, 2005 for a seven year period beginning 2005-06. It envisages urban renewal projects in a mission mode approach. The mission envisages providing focussed attention to integrated development of infrastructural services in 63 selected cities to secure effective linkages between asset creation and asset management, to ensure adequate investment of funds to fulfill deficiencies, to scale up delivery of civic amenities on universal access to urban poor and to encourage planned development of cities. The 11th Plan will have to make substantial provision of funds under the JNURM if the momentum of urban reform linked to infrastructure creation really takes off as we hope.

Jawaharlal Nehru Urban Renewal Mission involves a total allocation of Rs. 50,000 crore by the Central government in the form of ACA Grant to states/UTs. The state would be provided Additional Central Assistance (ACA) in the form of 100 per cent grant as a %age of project cost ranging from 35 per cent (for Mega Cities) to 90 per cent (for NE states). In order to ensure outcomes, the state has to prepare city development plans, detailed project reports and sign MOA indicating milestones for implementation of reforms, with the Ministries of Urban Development and Urban Employment and Poverty Alleviation to access the funds from the Central government.

At the end of the 11th Plan, all mission cities would achieve the following:

1. Modern and transparent budgeting, accounting, financial management systems, designed and adopted for all urban services and governance functions.
2. City-wide framework for planning and governance will be established and become operational.
3. Access for urban residents to a basic level of urban services.
4. Financially self-sustaining agencies for urban governance and service delivery.

5. A women friendly environment by ensuring proper lighting, better transportation and adequate safety measures.
6. Transparency and accountability of local services and governance to citizens.
7. E-Governance applications in core functions of ULBs/Parastatals resulting in reduced cost and time of service delivery processes.
8. Telecom and Connectivity.

One sector has brought the improvement in the quality of life of the people in India, i.e. the telecom sector. It has improved then quality of life for poor as well as rich people. India has witnessed an impressive telecom revolution during the last decade. From one of the highest telecom charges in the world, India has moved to one of the lowest telecom charges. During the last two years, we have been adding on an average 3 million mobile connections per month, with private operators playing a major role. The tele-density presently stands at 14.4 with major contribution coming from tele-density in urban areas. The 11th Plan must ensure continued expansion in this important area, especially in rural areas, so that the gap with other countries is reduced.

In addition to telephone connectivity, which is predominantly used for voice, we also need to establish internet connectivity for data. Access to the internet in urban areas increased significantly due to its affordability but it is still low and in rural areas it is negligible. We need to make special intervention to connect rural areas and develop a strategic plan to carry text, data and video to make rural telephony a viable proposition.

Expansion in investment and economic restructuring of existing enterprises accelerates growth. Indian financial system comprising commercial banks, non-bank financing organisations, capital market institutions and insurance and pension funds is very strong. We have to continuously strengthen our financial system and support its development through a combined effort at improving the regulatory system in line with international best practices and liberalising the system to encourage competition. This liberalisation should include an increased role for foreign financial institutions in the domestic market and a carefully calibrated opening of the economy to international capital markets.

Then load on environment increases with the growth in population. The fast economic and industrial growth intensifies degradation of environment. We can have the resources to prevent and deal with environmental problems, but we must also ensure that rapid growth is environmentally benign. This can be achieved through greater awareness, starting with school children, and appropriate policies. The 11th Plan must integrate development planning and environmental concerns, providing the use of economic instruments based on the polluter pays principle, supplemented by command and control policies where these are more appropriate.

This includes improving Air and Water Quality. Real time monitoring environment sustainability of air and water quality is crucial for devising programmes and policies related to pollution management. The existing 300 monitoring stations for air and 850 for water quality need augmentation in number and technology. Establishing a reasonably adequate monitoring network with contemporary technology will be a priority.

The objective of river cleaning is to restore the water quality of all the major rivers to the designated best use which is the 'bathing class' (category B). We are very far from achieving this objective. The National River Conservation Plan needs a critical review of the present strategy of central assistance to states for creation of facilities. Sustainability and operational issues remain unresolved in most cases. Ways of linking treatment of sewage and industrial effluents to the urban and industrial development planning need to be worked out. The goal should be to ensure that by the end of the 11th Plan no untreated sewage or effluent flows into rivers from cities and towns. Studies on minimum essential flow in the rivers and plans to maintain it must be drawn up. This should include workable mechanisms to expedite solution of water sharing problems between states.

The demands of river cleaning increase with population and expansion of townships and success depends on the efforts of all stakeholders. Civic bodies should have a pivotal role to play in this context. This must be ensured through policy/legislative means. The impact on water quality of the "Water Quality Assessment Authority (WQAA)" constituted in June 2001, in different states is yet to be ascertained. A workable mechanism will be developed for monitoring and early warning systems for improving water quality.

Another aspect of environment sustainability is Solid Waste Management. The increasing generation of solid waste is a growing problem in all cities. Uncollected garbage is not only visually ugly, it also causes diseases. Dumping garbage into landfills is not an attractive option in our land scarce cities and should be minimised. Most industrial countries now require their citizens to segregate wastes at home into recyclable products. While recycling is done by rag pickers in India, their lives can be made less unpleasant if citizens sort out organic and inorganic waste and dispose of organic waste in local compost or vermiculture pits. Cities and towns must be encouraged to evolve systems with citizen participation, for segregation of waste at point of origin, maximising recycling and safe disposal of the rest. Preservation of wildlife and bio-diversity with the participation of people is needed. An interface with communities will be developed, communication and surveillance of forests and wildlife will be augmented through Integrated Forest Protection scheme of MoEF. People living in deep forests will be encouraged to shift to fringes voluntarily for providing inviolate space for wildlife. To facilitate this process, an appropriate programme including provision for livelihood opportunities will be formulated as suggested by the Tiger Task Force.

Mitigating Land Degradation through Green Cover is also an important area, which will be taken care of in the 11th Plan. Overuse of resources has been identified as a major cause of land degradation. Creation of forest/biomass resources in all the culturable vacant lands will be taken up for strengthening life support system of communities and maintaining soil/water regimes. A programme for social forestry will support development and sustainable management of the common property resources through Panchayati Raj Institutions. Encouraging agro/farm forestry and building interface between industry and farmers is an important strategy suggested in the National Forest Policy 1988. An enabling environment will be created for encouraging tree growing by farmers. Subsidised supply of raw material to industries from government forests will be discouraged. Domestic and international trade of the farm forestry produce by support price mechanisms and exim/tariff regulation will be considered. Forest management will be encouraged to withdraw from raising farm forestry plantations in government forests to provide better market opportunities to the farmers.

Following initiatives are to be pursued in the 11th Plan:

1. Encourage PRIs to revive common property resources through social afforestation.
2. Rationalise forest regulations to allow industry to partner farmers in undertaking agro-forestry for augmenting the raw material base for forest based industries like paper & pulp.
3. Encourage the corporate sector to participate in development of degraded land for forestry, without compromising communities priorities.
4. Rationalise rules and procedures under environmental laws to expedite investment, production and employment growth.

11th Plan proposes for a comprehensive review of environmental clearance procedures to ensure that the system is transparent and avoids unnecessary delay. It is required for the large increases in investment required for accelerated growth.

The Jawaharlal Nehru National Urban Renewal Mission (JNNURM) launched in 2005-06 is directed to provide improved urban services. The above programmes will require substantial allocation of funds, mainly by the government. The question arises whether these outlays compromise public investment in other needed areas and reduce growth? In fact, if targeted effectively and implemented efficiently, these programmes and the outlays envisaged will stimulate the economy and raise its growth rate. The Rural Employment Guarantee Scheme, for example, can create productive assets and provide additional income to the poor and increase demand for food and other consumer goods, which in turn would also stimulate growth. Increasing demand for agricultural goods is important to raise agricultural growth, which is otherwise likely to face a demand constraint. Growth of agriculture in turn is vital to bridging rural urban divide. Similarly, the backward districts development programme can be mobilised to increase growth and reduce disparity.

Part III
Select Urban Development and Housing Schemes in Operation

1

Jawaharlal Nehru National Urban Renewal Mission

I. Need for Development of the Urban Sector

1. Background:

(1) Need for Urban Sector Development: According to the 2001 census, India has a population of 1027 million with approximately 28per cent or 285 million people living in urban areas. As a result of the liberalization policies adopted by the Government of India is expected to increase the share of the urban population may increase to about 40 per cent of total population by the year 2021. It is estimated that by the year 2011, urban areas would contribute about 65 per cent of gross domestic product (GDP). However, this higher productivity is contingent upon the availability and quality of infrastructure services. Urban economic activities are dependent on infrastructure, such as power, telecom, roads, water supply and mass transportation, coupled with civic infrastructure, such as sanitation and solid waste management.

(2) Investment Requirements in the Urban Sector: It is estimated that over a seven-year period, the Urban Local Bodies (ULBs) would require a total investments of Rs. 1,20,536 crore.

This includes investment in basic infrastructure and services, that is, annual funding requirement of Rs. 17,219 crore. It is well recognised that in order to fructify these investments, a national level initiative is required that would bring together the State Governments and enable ULBs catalyse investment flows in the urban infrastructure sector.

2. Need for Reform Initiatives

(1) Harnessing the Potential of Reforms in Urban frastructure: While several reform initiatives have being taken e.g. the 74th Constitutional Amendment Act and model municipal law, there is potential for further reform-oriented steps in order to meet the development objectives. Reform initiatives also need to be taken further and articulated by the State Governments in order to create an investor-friendly environment.

Urban Sector Investment Requirement

(Rs. crore)

Category	Number of cities	Investment requirement (over 7 years starting 2005-06)	Annual Funds Require-ment
Cities with over 4 million population	7	57,143	8163.3
Cities with 1-4 million population	28	57,143	8613.3
Selected Cities with less than 1 million population	28	6,250	892.9
Total	63	1,20,536	17219.5

(2) Need for National-Level Reform-Linked Investments: There is a need to integrate the reform initiatives and scale up the effort to catalyse investment in urban infrastructure across States in the country. There is a felt need to set up an initiative that will provide reformlinked assistance to State Governments and ULBs in the country.

(3) Need for Sustainable Infrastructure Development: Another crucial aspect requiring immediate attention is that physical infrastructure assets created in urban areas have generally been languishing due to inadequate attention and/or improper O&M. The fiscal flows to the sector have laid emphasis only on the creation of physical assets. Not much effort has been made either to manage these assets efficiently or to achieve self-sustainability. It is therefore necessary that a link be established between asset creation and management, as both are important components for ensuring sustained service delivery. This is proposed to be secured through an agenda of reforms.

(4) Need for Efficiency Enhancement: Concurrent with statutory reforms, such as the enactment of a model municipal law, reduction in stamp duty, repeal of the Urban Land (Ceiling and Regulation) Act, 1976 (ULCRA) etc, there is an urgent need to take measures to enhance efficiencies in urban service deliveries.

3. Rationale for the JNNURM

(1) National Common Minimum Programme of the Government of India: The National Common Minimum Programme attaches the highest priority to the development and expansion of physical infrastructure. Accordingly, it is proposed to take up a comprehensive programme of urban renewal and expansion of social housing in towns and cities, paying attention to the needs of slum dwellers.

(2) Commitment to Achieving the Millennium Development Goals: The Millennium Development Goals commit the international community, including India, to an expanded vision of development as a key to sustaining social and economic progress. As a part of its commitment to meet the Millennium Development Goals, the Government of India proposes to: (i) facilitate investments in the urban sector; and (ii) strengthen the existing policies in order to achieve these goals.

(3) Need for a Mission-led Initiative: Since cities and towns in India constitute the second largest urban system in the world, and contribute over 50 per cent of the country's GDP, they are central to economic growth. For the cities to realise their full potential and become effective engines of growth, it is necessary that focused attention be given to the improvement of infrastructure.

II. Jawaharlal Nehru National Urban Renewal Mission

1. The Mission

Mission Statement: The aim is to encourage reforms and fast track planned development of identified
cities. Focus is to be on efficiency in urban infrastructure and service delivery mechanisms, community

participation, and accountability of ULBs/Parastatal agencies towards citizens.

2. Objectives of the Mission

(1) The objectives of the JNNURM are to ensure that the following are achieved in the urban
sector;.

a) Focussed attention to integrated development of infrastructure services in cities covered under the Mission;
b) Establishment of linkages between asset-creation and asset-management through a slew of reforms for long-term project sustainability;
c) Ensuring adequate funds to meet the deficiencies in urban infrastructural services;
d) Planned development of identified cities including peri-urban areas, outgrowths and urban corridors leading to dispersed urbanisation;
e) Scale-up delivery of civic amenities and provision of utilities with emphasis on universal access to the urban poor;
f) Special focus on urban renewal programme for the old city areas to reduce congestion; and
g) Provision of basic services to the urban poor including security of tenure at affordable prices, improved housing, water supply and sanitation, and ensuring delivery of other existing universal services of the government for education, health and social security.

3. Scope of the Mission

The Mission shall comprise two Sub- Missions, namely:

(1) Sub-Mission for Urban Infrastructure and Governance: This will be administered by the Ministry of Urban Development through the Sub- Mission Directorate for Urban Infrastructure and Governance. The main thrust of the Sub-Mission will be on infrastructure projects relating to water supply and sanitation, sewerage, solid waste management, road network, urban transport and redevelopment of old city areas with a view to upgrading infrastructure therein, shifting industrial and commercial establishments to conforming areas, etc.

(2) Sub-Mission for Basic Services to the Urban Poor: This will be administered by the Ministry of Urban Employment and Poverty Alleviation through the Sub-Mission Directorate for Basic Services to the Urban Poor. The main thrust of the Sub-Mission will be on integrated development of slums through projects for providing shelter, basic services and other related civic amenities with a view to providing utilities to the urban poor.

4. Strategy of the Mission

The objectives of the Mission shall be met through the adoption of the following strategy:

(1) Preparing City Development Plan: Every city will be expected to formulate a City Development Plan (CDP) indicating policies, programmes and strategies, and financing plans.

(2) Preparing Projects: The CDP would facilitate identification of projects. The Urban Local Bodies (ULBs)/ parastatal agencies will be required to prepare Detailed Project Reports (DPRs) for undertaking projects in the identified spheres. It is essential that projects are planned in a manner that optimises the life-cycle cost of projects. The life-cycle cost of a project would cover the capital outlays and the attendant O&M costs to ensure that assets are in good working condition. A revolving fund would be created to meet the O&M requirements of assets created, over the planning horizon. In order to seek JNNURM assistance, projects would need to be developed in a manner that would ensure and demonstrate optimisation of the life-cycle costs over the planning horizon of the project.

(3) Release and Leveraging of Funds: It is expected that the JNNURM assistance would serve to catalyse the flow of investment into the urban infrastructure sector across the country. Funds from the Central and State Government will flow directly to the nodal agency designated by the State, as grants-in-aid. The funds for identified projects across cities would be disbursed to the ULB/Parastatal agency through the designated State Level Nodal Agency (SLNA) as soft loan or grant-cum-loan or grant.

The SLNA/ULBs in turn would leverage additional resources from other sources.

(4) Incorporating Private Sector Efficiencies: In order to optimise the life-cycle costs over the planning horizon, private sector efficiencies can be inducted in development, management, implementation and financing of projects, through Public Private Partnership (PPP) arrangements.

5. Duration of the Mission

The duration of the Mission would be seven years beginning from the year 2005-06. Evaluation of the experience of implementation of the Mission would be undertaken before the commencement of Eleventh Five Year Plan and if necessary, the program calibrated suitably.

6. Expected Outcomes of the JNNURM

On completion of the Mission period, it is expected that ULBs and parastatal agencies will have achieved the following:

(1) Modern and transparent budgeting, accounting, financial management systems, designed and adopted for all urban service and governance functions.

(2) City-wide framework for planning and governance will be established and become operational.

(3) All urban residents will be able to obtain access to a basic level of urban services.

(4) Financially self-sustaining agencies for urban governance and service delivery will be established, through reforms to major revenue instruments.

(5) Local services and governance will be conducted in a manner that is transparent and accountable to citizens.

(6) E-governance applications will be introduced in core functions of ULBs/Parastatal resulting in reduced cost and time of service delivery processes.

III. Assistance under JNNURM

1. Financial Assistance under JNNURM

The Government of India has proposed substantial assistance through the JNNURM over the seven-year period. During this period, funds shall be provided for proposals that would meet the Mission's requirements.

Under JNNURM financial assistance will be available to the ULBs and parastatal agencies which could deploy these funds for implementing the projects themselves or through the special purpose vehicles (SPVs) that may be expected to be set up.

Assistance under JNNURM is additional central assistance, which would be provided as grant (100 per cent central grant) to the implementing agencies.

Further, assistance from JNNURM is expected to facilitate further investment in the urban sector. To this end, the implementing agencies are expected to leverage the sanctioned funds under JNNURM to attract greater private sector investments through PPP that enables sharing of risks between the private and public sector.

2. Areas of Assistance under JNNURM

(1) Assistance for Capacity Building, City Development Plan (CDP), Detailed Project Reports (DPRs), Community Participation, Information, Education and Communication (IEC)

The JNNURM will provide assistance for the above-stated components with a provision of 5 per cent of the total central assistance or the actual requirement, which ever is less. In addition, not more than 5 percent of the Central grant or the actual requirement, whichever is less may be used for Administrative and Other Expenses (A&OE) by the States

For capacity building, ULBs and parastatal agencies could engage consultants, in consultation with the SLNA, and seek reimbursement from the Ministry of Urban Development (MoUD) of the Ministry of Urban Employment and Poverty Alleviation (MoUEPA).

(2) Investment Support Component

Investment support will be provided to implementing agencies on a project-specific basis for eligible sectors and projects proposed to be undertaken in eligible cities subject to approval of the Central Sanctioning and Monitoring Committee (CSMC) of MoUD/MoUEPA.

As part of the process for seeking investment support, each ULB seeking assistance from the JNNURM would be required to prepare a CDP that shall *inter alia* include strategy to implement reforms, city-level improvements and an investment plan to address the infrastructure needs in a sustainable manner.

Assistance under investment support can be deployed in the following forms:

a) **Enhancing Resource Availability:** The JNNURM assistance can be used to leverage additional resources available with the ULBs in addition to their existing resources and transfers from the State. These resources could be utilised for capital investment and O&M investments in a project.

b) **Enhancing Commercial Viability of Projects:** In respect of projects, which are not commercially viable on a stand-alone basis, assistance under the JNNURM may be sought for enhancing project viability. This assistance could be in the nature of viability gap support to projects.

c) **Ensuring Bankability of Projects:** Cash flows of infrastructure projects having long gestation periods are susceptible to variations in cash flows, rendering a project non-bankable. To enhance predictability of underlying cash-flows, credit enhancement mechanisms such as establishing liquidity support mechanisms, up-front debt-service reserve facility, deep discount bonds, contingent liability support and equity support are required in order to make the projects bankable. The JNNURM assistance could therefore be used for funding such support mechanisms.

IV. Eligible Cities, Sectors and Projects

1. Cities Eligible for Assistance under the JNNURM

(1) Eligible Cities: The JNNURM shall give assistance for infrastructure development in the eligible cities/Urban Agglomerations (UAs) (refer Annex) across States in the country.

These cities/UAs have been selected based as per the following criteria:

A. Cities/UAs with 4 million plus population as per 2001 census

B. Cities/UAs with 1 million plus but less than 4 million population as per 2001 census

C. Selected Cities/UAs (State Capitals and other cities/UA of religious/historic and tourist importance)

The cities should have elected bodies in position.

2. Sectors and Projects Eligible for Assistance under the Sub-Mission Directorate for Urban Infrastructure and Governance

The sectors and projects eligible for JNNURM assistance would be as follows:

(1) Urban renewal, that is, redevelopment of inner (old) city areas [including widening of narrow streets, shifting of industrial and commercial establishments from non-conforming (inner city) areas to conforming (outer city) areas to reduce congestion, replacement of old and worn out pipes by new and higher capacity ones, renewal of the sewerage, drainage, and solid waste disposal system etc.] ;

(2) Water supply (including desalination plants) and sanitation.

(3) Sewerage and solid waste management.

(4) Construction and improvement of drains and storm water drains.

(5) Urban transportation including roads, highways, expressways, MRTS, and metro projects.

(6) Parking lots and spaces on PPP basis.

(7) Development of heritage areas

(8) Prevention and rehabilitation of soil erosion and landslides only in cases of special category States where such problems are common; and

(9) Preservation of water bodies.

3. Sectors and Projects Eligible for Assistance under the Sub-Mission Directorate for Basic Services to the Urban Poor.

The sectors and projects eligible for JNNURM assistance in eligible cities would be as follows:

(1) Integrated development of slums, housing and development of infrastructure projects in slums in the identified cities.

(2) Projects involving development, improvement, and maintenance of basic services to the urban poor.

(3) Slum improvement and rehabilitation of projects.

(4) Projects on water supply, sewerage, drainage, community toilets, and baths etc.

(5) Projects for providing houses at affordable cost for slum dwellers, urban poor, economically weaker sections (EWS) and lower income group (LIG) categories.

(6) Construction and improvement of drains and storm water drains.

(7) Environmental improvement of slums and solid waste management.

(8) Street lighting.

(9) Civic amenities like community halls, child care centres etc.

(10) Operation and Maintenance of assets created under this component.

(11) Convergence of health, education and social security schemes for the urban poor

4. Inadmissible Components for JNNURM Assistance

Projects pertaining to the following are not eligible for JNNURM assistance:

(1) Power

(2) Telecom

(3) Health

(4) Education

(5) Wage employment programme and staff components.

(6) Creation of fresh employment opportunities

V. Agenda of Reforms

The thrust of the JNNURM is to ensure improvement in urban governance and service delivery so that ULBs become financially sound and sustainable for undertaking new programmes. It is also envisaged that, with the charter of reforms that are followed by the State governments and ULBs, a stage will be set for PPPs.

The agenda of reforms is given in the section below. The National Steering Group (NSG) may add additional reforms to identified reforms. A Memorandum of Agreement (MoA) between States/ULBs/Parastatal agencies and the Government of India, a prerequisite for accessing the Central assistance, would spell out specific milestones to be achieved for each item of reform.

All mandatory and optional reforms shall be completed within the Mission period.

1. Mandatory Reforms

(1) Mandatory Reforms at the Level of ULBs, and Parastatal Agencies

a) Adoption of modern accrual-based double entry system of accounting in ULBs and parastatal agencies.
b) Introduction of a system of e-governance using IT applications, such GIS and MIS for various services provided by ULBs and parastatal agencies.
c) Reform of property tax with GIS. It becomes a major source of revenue for ULBs and arrangements for its effective implementation so that collection efficiency reaches at least 85 per cent within next seven years.
d) Levy of reasonable user charges by ULBs and Parastatals with the objective that the full cost of O&M or recurring cost is collected within the next seven years. However, cities and towns in the North East and other special category States may recover only 50 per cent of O&M charges initially. These cities and towns should graduate to full O&M cost recovery in a phased manner.
e) Internal earmarking, within local bodies, budgets for basic services to the urban poor.
f) Provision of basic services to the urban poor including security of tenure at affordable prices, improved housing, water supply and sanitation. Delivery of other existing

universal services of the government for education, health and social security is ensured.

(2) Mandatory Reforms at the Level of States

a) Implementation of decentralisation measures as envisaged in 74th Constitutional Amendment Act. The State should ensure meaningful association and engagement of ULBs in planning the function of parastatal agencies as well as the delivery of services to the citizens.
b) Repeal of ULCRA.
c) Reform of Rent Control Laws balancing the interests of landlords and tenants.
d) Rationalisation of Stamp Duty to bring it down to no more than 5 per cent within next seven years.
e) Enactment of the Public Disclosure Law to ensure preparation of medium-term fiscal plan of ULBs and parastatal agencies and release of quarterly performance information to all stakeholders.
f) Enactment of the Community Participation Law to institutionalise citizen's participation and introduce the concept of the Area Sabha in urban areas.
g) Assigning or associating elected ULBs with "city planning function". Over a period of seven years, transferring all special agencies that deliver civic services in urban areas to ULBs and creating accountability platforms for all urban civic service providers in transition.

2. Optional Reforms (common to States, ULBs and Parastatal Agencies)

The following optional reforms are expected to be undertaken by ULBs, parastatal agencies and State governments:

a) Revision of bye-laws to streamline the approval process for construction of buildings, development of site etc.
b) Simplification of legal and procedural frameworks for conversion of land from agricultural to non-agricultural purposes.
c) Introduction of Property Title Certification System in ULBs.

d) Earmarking at least 20-25 per cent of developed land in all housing projects (both public and private agencies) for EWS and LIG category with a system of cross subsidisation.
e) Introduction of computerised process of registration of land and property.
f) Revision of byelaws to make rain-water harvesting mandatory in all buildings and adoption of water conservation measures.
g) Byelaws for reuse of recycled water.
h) Administrative reforms i.e. reduction in establishment costs by adopting the Voluntary Retirement Scheme (VRS), not filling posts falling vacant due to retirement etc., and achieving specified milestones in this regard.
i) Structural reforms.
j) Encouraging PPP.

Annex
List of Identified Cities Eligible for JNNURM

Category A: Mega Cities/UAs
(1) Delhi
(2) Greater Mumbai
(3) Ahmedabad
(4) Bangalore
(5) Chennai
(6) Kolkata
(7) Hyderabad

Category B: Million plus Cities/UAas
(1) Patna
(2) Faridabad
(3) Bhopal
(4) Ludhiana
(5) Jaipur
(6) Lucknow
(7) Madurai
(8) Nashik

(9) Pune
(10) Cochin
(11) Varanasi
(12) Agra
(13) Amritsar
(14) Vishakhapatnam
(15) Vadodara
(16) Surat
(17) Kanpur
(18) Nagpur
(19) Coimbatore
(20) Meerut
(21) Jabalpur
(22) Jamshedpur
(23) Asansol
(24) Allahabad
(25) Vijayawada
(26) Rajkot
(27) Dhanbad
(28) Indore

Category C: Cities/UAs with less than one million population
(1) Guwahati
(2) Itanagar
(3) Jammu
(4) Raipur
(5) Panaji
(6) Shimla
(7) Ranchi
(8) Thiruvananthapuram
(9) Imphal
(10) Shillong
(11) Aizawl
(12) Kohima
(13) Bhubaneshwar
(14) Gangtok

(15) Agartala
(16) Dehradun
(17) Bodhgaya
(18) Ujjain
(19) Puri
(20) Ajmer-Pushkar
(21) Nainital
(22) Mysore
(23) Pondicherry
(24) Chandigarh
(25) Srinagar
(26) Mathura
(27) Haridwar
(28) Nanded

2

Night Shelter Scheme for Urban Shelterless

The ultimate goal of the National Housing & Habitat Policy, 1998 is to ensure that the basic need to Shelter for All is fulfilled in a time-bound manner and a better quality of life is provided to all the citizens of the country by harnessing the unused potential in the public, private and the household sectors. Till such time this goal is achieved, it is necessary to provide some kind of shelter to the absolutely shelterless urban population, including street children, destitute women, and migrant labourers etc., who are in urgent need of shelter to protect themselves against the vagaries of nature all through the year.

The Scheme of Night Shelters for the Urban Shelterless is in operation since 1988-89.

The scheme was further modified in August 1992 to cover all urban centres having concentration of footpath dwellers/homeless and renamed as **Scheme for Shelter & Sanitation Facilities for Footpath Dwellers**. A component for Pay & Use toilet was added to the scheme.

The Scheme is in nature of a demand driven scheme and implementation of the scheme as the land owning agency is undertaken by the State Government or local municipal bodies or State sponsored agencies.

Since **October, 2002** the scheme has been renamed as **Night Shelter for Urban Shelterless** and the component of Pay & Use Toilets has been withdrawn.

Present Financing Pattern/components included in the scheme and financial progress of the scheme: In the present shape, a Central Government subsidy @ 50 per cent of the cost of construction subject to cost ceiling of Rs. 20,000 per bed is provided through HUDCO. The balance is required to be arranged by the State Government/implementing agency. The project is appraised by a Departmental Sanctioning Committee headed by Joint Secretary (Housing).

Physical Progress of the Scheme: As already mentioned, the scheme is a demand driven scheme and progress of the Scheme depends on the proposals mooted by the State. Cumulatively, as on 13.10.2004, HUDCO has sanctioned 99 Night Shelters/Pay and Use Toilets schemes. On completion, these projects would provide 17,599 beds, 17,165 WCs, 2637 baths and 2372 urinals. A subsidy of Rs. 1580.21 lakh has been released by HUDCO for these schemes apart from loan release of Rs. 1159.05 lakh.

3

Two Million Housing Programme

In accordance with the National Housing & Habitat Policy 1998 which focuses on Housing for All as a priority area, with particular stress on the needs of the Economically Weaker sections and Low Income Group categories, the Two Million Housing Programme was launched during 1998-99. This is a loan based scheme, which envisages facilitating construction of 20 lakh additional units every year (7lakh DUs-in Urban areas; 13 lakh DUs in Rural areas). HUDCO is to meet the target of 4 lakh dwelling units in Urban areas and 6 lakh dwelling units in Rural areas annually. The target of 2 lakh dwelling units in Urban areas is to be met by Housing Finance Institutions [HFIs] recognised by the National Housing Bank & Public Sector Banks and the balance 1 lakh dwelling units in Urban areas by the Co-operative Sector.

The primary responsibility for fulfilment of the targets in physical terms rests with the State Governments, while HUDCO and other agencies make the funds available in the form of loans. Hence the successful implementation of the scheme largely depends upon the cooperation of the agencies of the State Governments responsible for launching and implementation of various housing schemes. Housing Cooperative societies and private sector will also be encouraged to participate in the housing activity in a big way provided a facilitating environment is created by the State Governments in the form of legal, administrative and fiscal reforms.

4

Urban Reforms Incentive Fund (URIF)

In his Budget Speech 2002-2003, the then Union Finance Minister announced the creation of an Urban Reforms Incentive Fund (URIF) with an initial allocation of Rs. 500 crore to provide Urban Reform linked assistance to States. The scheme was approved by the Govt. on 28-6-2003 with an annual allocation of Rs. 500 crore. The fund seeks to provide incentives to the States to have urban reforms in the first phase (2003-2004) in the following areas with weightage indicated against each:

Sl. No	Reform Area	Weightage
1.	Repeal of ULCRA	10 per cent of State's Share out of URIF
2.	Rationalization of stamp Duty	20 per cent of State's Share out of URIF
3.	Reform of Rent Control	20 per cent of State's Share out of URIF
4.	Introduction of computerised process of registration	10 per cent of State's Share out of URIF
5.	Reform of Property Tax	10 per cent of State's Share out of URIF
6.	Levy of reasonable user charges	20 per cent of State's Share out of URIF
7.	Introduction of double entry system of accounting in Urban Local Bodies	10 per cent of State's Share out of URIF

Amount under URIF is released as Additional Central Assistance to Annual Plan of States. The State-wise allocation of funds is released on the basis of share of each State in the urban population. A Memorandum of Agreement is required to be signed between State and this Ministry. The funds are released by the Finance Ministry on the recommendations of the Ministry of Urban Employment & Poverty Alleviation. 50 per cent of the fund is released on signing of the Memorandum of Agreement (MOA) and the remaining after assessing the progress of each State by the Empowered Committee set up under the Chairmanship of Secretary (UEPA). The composition of the Empowered Committee is as under:

1. Secretary (Ministry of UEPA) - Chairman
2. Secretary (Department of Expenditure) - Member or his representative not below the rank of Joint Secretary.
3. Secretary (Planning Commission) - Member or his representative not below the rank of Joint Secretary.
4. Joint Secretary (UD), Department of UD - Member
5. Joint Secretary (Housing) - Member Secretary

Progress achieved under URIF Scheme during 2003-2004 and 2004-05

During the year 2003-2004, Memorandum of Agreements were signed between Government of India and 24 States/UTs viz Tamil Nadu, Madhya Pradesh, Chattisgarh, Tripura, Karnataka, Maharashtra, Manipur, Kerala, Haryana, Andhra Pradesh, West Bengal, Orissa, Nagaland, Arunachal Pradesh, Gujarat, Uttar Pradesh, Goa, Meghalaya, Bihar, Rajasthan, Himachal Pradesh and UTs of A&N Islands, Chandigarh, Govt. of NCT of Delhi.

During 2004-05 Govts of J&K, Jharkhand and Punjab have signed MOA. Further, Govts of Tamil Nadu & Rajasthan have signed Supplementary MOA for the remaining reforms. Ministry of Home Affairs in consultation with Ministry of Law informed that there is no need to sign MOA with UTs and an Executive Order from the Centre would suffice. Thereafter UT of Pondicherry was also recommended for release of funds during 2004-2005 on the basis of the reforms they were willing to carry out.

Till date, 25 States and 3 UTs have signed MOA/truncated MOA under URIF scheme. Out of these 20 States have agreed to repeal Urban Land Ceiling Act and Rationalisation of Stamp Duty; 22 States have agreed to implement Rent Control Reforms; 27 States have agreed to implement computerised Registration and Levy of Reasonable User Charges and 28 States have agreed to adopt Property Tax reforms and Double Entry System.

Ministry of Finance (Department of Expenditure) was requested for release of Rs. 188.145 crore towards 1st Instalment to the 24 States/UTs during 2003-04. Ministry of Finance and Ministry of Home Affairs (for UTs) have been further recommended for release of Rs 188.742 crore to 21 States/UTs during 2004-05 under URIF after assessing the progress.

World Bank Assistance and Second Generation Reforms under URIF

The World Bank is interested in supporting urban reforms primarily in the context of development of urban infrastructure. As the major part of the urban infrastructure is in the domain of the M/o UD, it has been decided not to pursue the matter with the World Bank for the time being.

5

Fiscal Concessions for Housing

This Ministry has been pursuing with the Ministry of Finance the matter of provision of various fiscal incentives for the Housing Sector. Many of the suggestions had been accepted and the following concessions under Income Tax and Wealth Tax have been given during the financial year 1998-99.

- Urban vacant land held as stock in trade has been exempted from Wealth Tax for a period of 7 years.
- Rental properties have been exempted from Wealth Tax provided the houses had been rented out for at least 300 days.
- 25 per cent of rental income to be deducted for repairs and collection charges (under Section 24 of Income Tax Act).
- Deductions for interest on borrowed capital in case of self occupied properties increased from Rs. 15,000 to Rs. 30,000.
- Carry forward of losses from `House Property' against future income under the same head to be allowed for 8 years.
- Reintroduction of Section 80 GG in respect of deduction for rents paid.
- Tax holiday for approved housing projects 100 per cent deduction from profits for first 5 year and 30 per cent deduction for subsequent 5 years.
- Infrastructure status to housing industry subject to certain conditions.

The Government has also been successfully granted various concessions under Excise Duty and Custom Duty which will go a long way in stimulating increased productions of low cost building materials and components based on utilisation of industrial wastes and other cost effective technology.

During the presentation of Budget for the year 1999-2000 Finance Minister has announced the following fiscal concessions:

- The Reserve Bank of India will advise the scheduled commercial banks to lend up to 3 per cent of their incremental deposit for housing sector as compared to the existing 1.5 per cent. This Ministry will regulate monitor actual lending by scheduled commercial banks in the housing sector.

- In the Budget speech of the Finance Minister it has also been announced that the foreclosure laws in the housing sector will be suitably simplified under the National Housing Bank Act for more investment in this sector. This will also help to develop the primary as well as secondary mortgage market in the housing.
- For encouraging the middle class investor the budget process the interest on a loan for self occupied property be exempted from tax up to a ceiling of Rs. 75,000 instead of present provision of Rs. 30,000.
- Under 88-I of the Income Tax Act the present condition of dwelling units up to the existing 1000 square feet has been increased to 1,500 square feet in all the locations except Delhi and Mumbai.
- To encourage the viability of housing Finance Companies it has been proposed that to tax their income on actual basis rather on accrual basis.
- To encourage the corporate sector to invest in housing for their employees the budget has proposed the increase or depreciation rate from 20 per cent to 40 per cent on new dwelling units purchased by corporate sector.
- Tax-free municipal bonds to a limited amount will be permitted to boost the urban infrastructure facilities.
- The following concessions under Income Tax and Wealth Tax have been given during the financial year 2000-2001.
- Under section 24(i)(iv), interest on borrowed capital is available as a deduction from house property income where property is acquired or constructed with borrowed capital. The available deduction was raised to Rs. 1,00,000 from Rs. 75,000.
- Under section 80-IB 100 per cent of profits is available as deduction in case of an undertaking an building housing projects approved before 31.03.2001 by local authority

subject to the condition that such undertaking has commenced or commences development and construction on or after 1st day of October, 1998 and completes the same before 31st day of March, 2003. The project should have a minimum plot area one acre and each unit should have a maximum built up area of 1500 sq.ft. (for Delhi and Mumbai 1000 sq.ft.).

- Under section 88, a rebate of 20 per cent is provided to individuals and Hindu undivided families in respect of payment of instalments or repayment of amount borrowed for construction or purchase of residential houses. Also, a similar rebate is available to subscriptions made to notified deposit schemes of the National Housing Banks which in turn provides credit to the housing sector. The exemption given under Section 88 of IT Act has been increased from Rs. 10,000 to Rs. 20,000.
- All the concessions given in the previous two budgets have been retained which are Concessions given under Section 80-IA, 10 (23)(G), concessions given for rental housing by way of exemption on interest paid on housing loans etc, concessions given for cost effective and environment friendly building materials have been retained. Further concessions have been extended for pre-fabricated building material.
- Capital Gains Tax on sale of immovable property is now exempted for purchase of more than one house.
- Interest Tax imposed on loans given by housing finance institutions has been dispensed with.
- Equity to HUDCO to build more houses in rural areas (95 lakh houses) increased (Rs. 350 crore).
- Benefit to NHB and HUDCO under Section 54 EA and 54 EE withdrawn.

The budget 2001-2002 provides a new thrust for major investments in the housing and infrastructure sector by offering following:

- The 10 year tax holiday to be availed in the first 20 years, announced in respect of water treatment, sanitation, roads, highways, railway and solid waste management systems among others, would help in promoting the much needed infrastructure for improving the quality of life and development of healthy and sustainable cities. This would encourage an increased participation of private sector.

- The increasing of the limit of exemption of tax on payment of interests in respect of housing loans for self-occupied houses from the existing Rs. 1 lakh to Rs. 1.5 lakh would enable and promote larger investment by the people at large in ownership housing.
- Further the withdrawal of the present requirement of obtaining NOC for transfer of assets including immovable properties, would also remove the obstruction environment bringing in increased buoyancy in the housing market. This removes the requirement for tax clearance certificate under section 230A from the assessing officer before transfer of immovable property.
- As far as the Corporates like HUDCO are concerned, the reduction of the present surcharge level of 16 per cent to only 2 per cent would substantially improve the profitability of the organisations and will be a stimulant to industrial growth. The reduction of surcharge on personal income tax from 17 per cent to 2 per cent would also give additional disposable income to the people for increased investments in other areas including housing.
- The additional equity infusion of Rs. 230 crore during 2001-2002 for HUDCO would enable HUDCO to continue its efforts for providing massive housing in rural and urban areas.
- The approval given for raising low cost resources through the HUDCO Gujarat Punarnirman Tax Free Bonds to the extent of Rs. 1500 crore would substantially help in extending financial assistance by HUDCO for the reconstruction, retrofitting and rehabilitation requirements of both housing and the damaged infrastructure in Gujarat.
- The opening up of long term funds for infrastructure through insurance sector would substantially ease the difficult situation the Housing and development Financing Institutions

were facing in raising resources of longer repayment tenure. Further, the reduction in the interest rates on small savings including Provident Fund will give a strong signal to the market to reduce interest rates.

- The proposal for bringing in comprehensive legislation for providing an enabling framework for the much needed securitisation initiatives is very timely and would result in a larger buoyancy in the financing of housing and infrastructure sectors.
- The customs duty reduction on cement from 35 per cent to 25 per cent would definitely help in softening of domestic prices of cement.

Following recommendations of this Ministry were accepted in the Budget 2002-03:

Continuing the thrust given to the housing sector over the last four years, the deduction for interest payable on housing loans for self-occupied houses even where such houses are acquired or constructed after 31.3.2002, will be allowed as long as the acquisition or construction is completed within three years from the end of financial year in which the loan was taken. For giving a further impetus to investment in the housing sector, the capital gains exemption provided in section 54EC of the IT Act has been extended to bonds issued by the NHB. However, the facility available to local authorities under section 10(23)(G)) has been withdrawn.

Exemption is available from custom duty for import of critical machinery for production of building materials based on Fly ash, Phospogysum, Timber substitutes and Pre-fabricated building components. Partial exemption from excise duty is available on building materials using 25 per cent of fly ash or more. Exemption from excise duty on Pre-fabricated building components produced at site, lightweight concrete building blocks, mosaic tiles and articles of mica, sandlime bricks roofing tiles and glazed tile, building products manufactured by Building Centres.

Following recommendations of this Ministry were accepted in the Budget 2003-04.

- For concessions available to undertakings developing housing projects under Section 80IB(10) of the Income Tax Act, the cut off date for approval by local authorities has been extended to 31st March,2005.
- Under Section 24 of the IT Act, it has been agreed in the Budget that the interest continues to be deductible up to Rs. 1.5 lakh.

6

Shelter and Sanitation Facilities for Footpath Dwellers in Urban Areas

As per the 1991 census, the total number of houseless households in the urban areas is 3 lakh and most of them are in the metropolitan cities. A majority of the houseless in the urban areas comprises footpath dwellers who are unable to secure any kind of shelter against the vagaries of weather e.g. rain and winter. They comprise also single women and children.

To meet their minimum housing needs, a centrally sponsored Night Shelter Scheme for Foot Path Dwellers was initiated during the VII Plan with the under mentioned components:

- Construction of Community night shelters with water supply and sanitary facilities.
- Pay and use toilets/baths
- Renovation of existing structures, like market places etc. as Night Shelter.
- Temporary or mobile night shelter of adequate standards on the basis of justification provided by State Governments considering the prevailing local factors.

The scheme was modified in August 1992. The modified scheme has the following components

- Construction of community night shelters with community toilets and baths.
- Construction only of community pay and use toilets/baths for the homeless.

These two components can be part of an overall complex of commercial or remunerative facilities or civic infrastructure.

Modality of Operation

The projects under the scheme will be formulated, constructed and operated by the municipal bodies or agencies designated by

State Governments. Voluntary organisations recommended or concurred in with the State Government or its agencies can also be involved with the implementation and management of the schemes. To make the composite night shelter scheme self supporting for maintenance purpose, commercial places like shops and godowns can be provided in the ground floor of such complexes and existing structures can be renovated to create such integrated units. HUDCO will be responsible for approval, financing and monitoring of the scheme under the supervision of the Ministry.

Construction of Community Night Shelters with Community Toilet/Bath Facilities

These buildings besides providing space for sleeping, would also include facilities for common bathing, W.C., drinking water and lockers etc. Wherever required, open parking of rickshaws, hand carts or rehries etc. can be provided near the shelter. The facility can be designed as part of an integrated complex having remunerative components. Model designs as well as technical help in design as per local conditions will be provided by HUDCO. The upgradation and renovation of existing market places or buildings in disuse can also be proposed. Land will be provided by State/Local Government or through agreement with private owners. The cost of construction should be limited to Rs. 5,000 per beneficiary. Central Government through HUDCO will provide up to Rs. 1,000 per capita as subsidy and the balance Rs. 4,000 per capita may be either the contribution by the local body from its own resources or State budget or to be secured from HUDCO as loan at terms applicable for social infrastructure or found from the overall cost of execution of the integrated complex by the executing agency. The subsidy element alone would not be released, unless HUDCO has ensured through appraisal that adequate funds to cover balance cost has been or is being mobilised by the agency. Where the agency seeks the balance cost from HUDCO beyond Rs. 5,000 only 50 per cent of the excess cost beyond Rs. 5,000 will be financed by HUDCO and the balance will be provided by Municipal body/State Government or the executing agency.

7

National Policy for Urban Street Vendors

1. Introduction

Street vending as a profession has been in existence in India since time immemorial. However, their number has increased manifold in the recent years. According to one study Mumbai has the largest number of street vendors numbering around 250,000, while Delhi has around 200,000. Calcutta has more than 150,000 street vendors and Ahmedabad has around 100,000. **Women constitute a large number of street vendors in almost every city.** Some studies estimate that street vendors constitute approximately 2 per cent of the population of a metropolis. The total number of street vendors in the country is estimated at around 1 crore. Urban vending is not only a source of employment but provide 'affordable' services to the majority of urban population. The role played by the hawkers in the economy as also in the society needs to be given due credit but they are considered as unlawful entities and are subjected to continuous harassment by Police and civic authorities. This is reported to be continuing even after the ruling of the Supreme Court that "if properly regulated according to the exigency of the circumstances, the small traders on the side walks can considerably add to the comfort and convenience of the general public, by making available ordinary articles of everyday use for a comparatively lesser price. An ordinary person, not very affluent, while hurrying towards his home after a day's work can pick up these articles without going out of his way to find a regular market. The right to carry on trade or business mentioned in Article 19(1)g of the Constitution, on street pavements, if properly regulated cannot be denied on the ground that the streets are meant exclusively for passing or re-passing and no other use."

Further **Articles 39 (a) and (b)** of the Constitution clearly mention that the State shall in particular direct its policy so that -

(a) the citizens, men and women equally, have the right to an adequate means of livelihood.
(b) the ownership and control of the material resources of the community are so distributed as best to sub serve the common good.

Street vendors provide valuable services to the urban population while trying to earn a livelihood and it is the duty of the State to protect the right of this segment of population to earn their livelihood. This policy aims to ensure that this important section of the urban population finds recognition for its contribution to society, and **is conceived of as a major initiative for urban poverty alleviation.**

2. Definition

A street vendor is broadly defined as a person who offers goods or services for sale to the public without having a permanent built up structure but with a temporary static structure or mobile stall (or headload). Street vendors may be stationary by occupying space on the pavements or other public/private areas, or may be mobile in the sense that they move from place to place carrying their wares on push carts or in cycles or baskets on their heads, or may sell their wares in moving bus etc. In this policy document, the term urban vendor is inclusive of both traders and service providers, stationary as well as mobile vendors and incorporates all other local/region specific terms used to describe them, such as, hawker, pheriwalla, rehri-patri walla, footpath dukandars, sidewalk traders, etc.

3. Overarching Objectives

The overarching objective to be achieved through this policy is to Provide and promote a supportive environment for earning livelihoods to the Street vendors, as well as ensure absence of congestion and maintenance of hygiene in public spaces and streets.

3.1 Specific Objectives

The basic objectives of the policy are:

- **Legal:** To give vendors legal status by amending, enacting, repealing and implementing appropriate laws and providing legitimate hawking zones in urban development/zoning plans.
- **Facilities:** To provide facilities for appropriate use of identified space including the creation of hawking zones in the urban development/zoning plans
- **Regulation:** To eschew imposing numerical limits on access to public spaces by discretionary licenses and instead moving to nominal fee-based regulation of access, where market forces like price, quality and demand will determine the number of vendors that can be sustained. Such a demand cannot be unlimited.
- **Role in distribution:** To make Street vendors a special component of the urban development/zoning plans by treating them as an integral and legitimate part of the urban distribution system.
- **Self Compliance:** To promote self-compliance amongst Street vendors.
- **Organization:** To promote, if necessary, organizations of Street vendors e.g. Unions/Co-operatives/Associations and other forms of organization to facilitate their empowerment.
- **Participation:** To set up participatory mechanisms with representation by urban vendors' organizations, (Unions/Co-operatives/Associations), Voluntary organizations, local authorities, the police, Residents Welfare Association (RWAs) and others for orderly conduct of urban vending activities.
- **Rehabilitation of Child Vendors:** To take measures for promoting a better future for child vendors by making appropriate interventions for their rehabilitation and schooling.
- **Social Security & Financial Services:** To facilitate/ promote social security (pension, insurance, etc.,) and access to credit for Street vendors through promotion of SHGs/co-operatives/Federations/Micro Finance Institutions (MFIs) etc.

4. Elements of the Policy

4.1 Planning Norms

Following the Supreme Court orders, some cities drafted guidelines for regulating urban vending activities. However, the provisions made so far do not generally recognize the fact that demand for their wares/services is highly specific and varies as to location and time, manifesting as a **natural propensity of Street vendors to locate in various places at particular times.** On the contrary, the present urban planning norms completely disregard the formation of such natural markets. They also do not have implementation systems in place. Planning norms should be supportive of such natural markets.

4.1.1 Spatial Planning norms - demarcation of vending zones

The demarcation of hawking zones should be city/town specific. To make the plans conducive and adequate for the hawkers of the respective city/town, the following should be adhered to:

- It should take into account the natural propensity of the Street vendors to locate in certain places at certain times in response to patterns of demand for their goods/services.
- City authorities should provide sufficient spaces, designated as 'vendors markets' in layout plans at locations of such natural markets, for the number of vendors (static and mobile) which can cater to demand for their wares/services. If aspirants to such location exceed the number of spaces available, excess may be regulated by fees or lottery and not discretionary licenses. In any case market forces relating to price, quality and demand will automatically curtail the number of vendors to sustainable levels.
- Mobile urban vending should be permitted in all areas even outside the designated vendors' markets, unless designated as 'no-vending zone' through a participatory process. The 'no-vending zones' may be notified both in terms of location and time. Locations should not be designated as 'no-vending' zones for frivolous reasons; the public benefits of declaration

of a no-vending zone should clearly outweigh the potential loss of livelihood and non-availability of goods and services that it would involve.

- With the growth of city/town every new area should have adequate provisions for Street vendors.
- Designation of vendors markets/no-vending zones should not be left to the sole discretion of any civic or police authority but must be accomplished by a participatory process by a **Town Vending Committee** (which for large towns/cities may be constituted on the basis of wards) whose membership may be as follows:

➢ Municipal Authority
➢ Traffic and Local Police
➢ Public Land Owning Authority
➢ Associations (Market, Traders, Resident Welfare, slum & chawl etc.)
➢ Representative from associations of Street vendors (static & mobile)
➢ Representative from lead Nationalized Bank/Commercial Bank.

The hawker's representatives should preferably constitute at least 25 per cent to 40 per cent of the total number of members of the Committee. At least 1/3rd of the representatives of street vendors should be women. Process for selection of street vendors' representatives should be based on the following criteria:

- **Membership based organisations**
- **Financial Accountability**

The Committee should ensure that provisions for space for vendors' markets are pragmatic, consistent with formation of natural markets, sufficient for existing demand for vendor's goods and services, as well as likely increase in line with anticipated population growth. Provisions of space may include temporary designation as vendors' markets (e.g. as weekly markets) whose use at other times may be different (e.g. Public Park, parking lot). Timing restriction on urban vending should correspond to the needs of ensuring non-congestion of public spaces/public hygiene.

The Committee should ensure continuation and up-gradation of weekly markets

Other functions of the committee are described below:

4.1.2 Quantitative Norms refer to the norms on amount of space to be provided for vendors' markets. At the town/city level enough space should be designated for vendors' markets at least to the extent of 2 per cent to 2.5 per cent of the total city population. Each town/city may evolve its own quantitative norms, but after proper surveys.

4.1.3 Qualitative guidelines refer to facilities to be provided at vendors' markets by the civic authorities. They would invariably include:

- Provide provisions for solid waste disposal
- Public toilets to maintain cleanliness.
- Aesthetic design of mobile stalls/push carts
- Provision for electricity
- Provision for drinking water
- Provision for protective covers to protect their wares as well as themselves from heat, rain, dust etc.
- Storage facilities including cold storage

4.2 Regulatory Process

Traditionally issuing licenses to vendors was seen as an instrument to give some of them 'legal' status, **in an environment where urban vending is *ipso facto* illegal**, which would in turn remove the very basis of their harassment, extortion and eviction by the concerned authorities. However, numerical limits to such licenses, which are sought to be justified on the argument that congestion in public places would thus be avoided, has given rise to an elaborate regime of rent seeking. In the first instance, rent is derived from the issue of licenses, since the demand exceeds the (often arbitrary) numerical limits of such licenses. Second, given the demand for services of Street vendors exceeds the supply from licensed vendors, a number of unlicensed vendors seek to operate, and rents are extracted during enforcement by allowing them to operate without licenses. Given these inadequacies of the licensing system and the associated rent seeking, doing away with licensing system is the appropriate course. However, the alternative should not only prevent rent seeking but also enable the livelihood – congestion trade-off to be resolved. The demand for vending in a particular area can be matched with the supply without over-congestion if zoning plans provide adequate vending spaces both with respect to location and time. **A system of registration of hawkers and non-discretionary regulation of access to public spaces in accordance with the planning standards and nature of trade/ service should be adopted. This is described in greater detail below.**

4.2.1 Registration System

- The power to register would be vested with **Town vending committee/Ward vending Committee.**
- All vendors in each city should be registered at a nominal fee to be decided by the ULBs based on any reliable means of identification. There should preferably be no numerical restriction or quotas, or prior residential status requirements of any kind.
- Registration should be renewed after every three years.
- The registration process must be simple.
- The vendors will be issued **Identity Cards** which would contain:
- Photographs of the husband and wife
- Name of any one nominee from the family
- Names of other members in the family (may be used for health or other social security programme)
- Nature of business
- Children below 14 years would not be allowed in the card for conduct of business.

4.2.2 The Town vending Committee/Ward vending Committee

It would be composed of representatives of hawkers, planners, police, local councillors, resident welfare associations, traders associations and municipal functionaries and would be empowered to:

- Set the terms and conditions (planning) for hawking.
- Take corrective action against defiant hawkers.

4.2.3 Collection of Revenue: The vendors would be charged a monthly fee for access to various services. There should be direct linkage between the urban local bodies (ULBs) and hawkers for collection of:

- Registration fee
- Monthly maintenance charges – differentiated according to location/type of business
- Fines, if any, etc
- The Town Vending Committee/Ward Vending Committee should be made available a proportion of revenue generated from registration fees and monthly fees from their ward to run their operations subject to a minimum grant from the local authority.

4.3 Monitoring Mechanism: The Town vending Committee/Ward Committee would be entrusted with adequate powers and resources to:

- Monitor the hawking activity of a particular ward and the quality of the services provided
- Take corrective action, if required
- Report to City level Committee, if required
- Recommend revaluation/changes in specified norms for hawking
- State level nodal officer to monitor and report to the Central Ministry on the functioning of the Street vendors of the State.

5. Relocation and Rehabilitation

Street vendors are most vulnerable to forced eviction and denial of basic right to livelihood. It causes severe long-term hardship, impoverishment and other damage including loss of dignity. Therefore, no street vendor should be forcefully evicted. They would be relocated with adequate rehabilitation only where the land is needed for a public purpose of urgent need. Therefore:

a) Eviction should be avoided wherever feasible unless there is clear and urgent public need in the land in question.

b) Where relocation is absolutely necessary, notice of minimum 30 days should be served to the concerned vendors.
c) Affected vendors/representative's involvement in planning and implementation of the rehabilitation project.
d) Affected vendors should be assisted in their efforts to improve their livelihoods and standards of living or at least to restore them, in real terms to pre-evicted levels.
e) Loss of assets should be avoided and if possible compensated.
f) State machinery must take comprehensive measures to check and control the practice of forced evictions.

No hawker/street vendor should be arbitrarily evicted in the name of 'beautification' of the cityscape. The beautification and clean up programmes undertaken by the states or towns should actively involve street vendors in a positive way as a part of the beautification programme.

6. Municipal and Police Laws – Required Interventions

6.1 There are certain sections of the Police Act and Indian Penal Code, which are the main deterrents to the profession of vending. They are as follows:

- **Section 283 of the IPC** (Danger or obstruction in public way or the line of navigation) Whoever, by doing any act or by omitting to take order with any property in his possession or under his charge, causes danger, obstruction or injury to any person in any public way or public line of navigation, shall be punished with fine which may extend to two hundred rupees. **The offence punishable under this section is the nuisance of causing obstruction.**
- **Section 34 of the Police Act** No person shall cause obstruction in any street or public place by
- Allowing animals or vehicle
- Leaving any vehicle standing or fastening any cattle in the street or in the public place
- Using any part of a street or public place as a halting place for vehicles or cattle

- Leaving any box, bale package or other things whatsoever or upon a street for an unreasonable length of time or contrary to any regulation
- By exposing anything for sale or setting out anything for sale in or upon any stall, booth, board, cask, and basket or in any other way whatsoever.

These two provisions create the contradiction between a legal 'licensed' vendor and 'illegal' obstruction or causing nuisance resulting in physical eviction of even licensed vendors.

6.2 The policy recommends that Central Government and all States should amend the Police Act and Rules/Regulations there under and add a rider as follows:

"Except in case of street vendors/hawkers and service providers with certain reasonable regulations"

6.3 The Central Government should also amend the **Section 283 and Section 431** of IPC **and include the rider as mentioned above.**

6.4 The state government should also remove the restrictive provisions in the Municipal Acts to make street vendors inclusive in the city plan/cityscape.

7. Self Regulation

Besides, monitoring by external authorities, it is extremely important for the street vendors to practice Self-Regulation especially with respect to the following:

7.1 Hygiene and quality control: It is most important with respect to food vending especially in sensitive areas like near schools, parks etc where there is considerable exposure to children. Though quality control is essential, the practice of 'health inspector' may not necessarily be suitable or productive.

7.2 Cleanliness: The street vendors should assume responsibility to keep the environs clean – by properly disposing the waste etc.

7.3 Scale of operation (Number of vendors to operate in specified area). Every land use has a ceiling and it is true for hawking also. Overuse can cause complications drawing stringent actions, which can be avoided if the specifications are adhered to. Therefore, the quantitative norms should be respected by hawkers as a measure of self-regulation in terms of number of a typical trade to be allowed in a place. Registration system in participation with hawkers' union/association may be used to regulate the scale of operation so that the ceiling limit is not crossed.

8. Others

8.1 Access to Credit

Street Vendors being a part of the unorganized sector have little or no access to credit from the formal sector financial institutions particularly for their economic activities without which they will have to depend on private moneylenders borrowing at higher interest rates. NABARD has already started refinancing banks in rural areas for on-lending to Self-Help Groups (SHGs) for income generation activities. Likewise, banks should be encouraged to extend credit to SHGs of vendors.

The Vendors' Associations should be assisted by NGOs and under SJSRY Scheme for organizing SHGs, networking and federating the SHGs to create a financial interface between the vendors and formal sector financial institutions to gain access to larger credit not only for income generation but also for housing whenever the need arises.

8.2 Insurance/Social Security

While the Insurance Sector has opened up in a big way, according to IRDA, only 12 per cent of the insurable population in India is covered by insurance, which means an average Indian is abysmally underinsured. Insurance is not just a privilege but also a social responsibility. The Street Vendors being a part of the unorganized sector, the vulnerability is very high. Hence, they should be brought under insurance cover through the federation.

Various products that are offered by the Insurance Companies include death, illness, disability, group insurance, pension fund etc.

In our country, though the need for social security is very high, provision of extending social security to the unorganized sector through governmental sources with meager sources would be a difficult proposition. So far, Government efforts have been restricted to Old Age Pension. Hence, it is imperative that the unorganized sector should evolve a mechanism to mobilize funds to invest in extending social security to the clients in the unorganized sector.

Social security generally covers medical care, sickness, maternity benefits, employment injury, inability and survivors' benefits, old age pension etc. Social security laws in our country are broadly divided into two categories viz. contributory and non-contributory. The contributory laws are those which provide for financing the social security programmes by contribution paid by workers and employers and in some cases supplemented by contributions/grants from the government. Important contributory schemes include ESI, Provident Fund, Pension and Deposit Linked Insurance schemes etc. Non-contributory laws are workmen's Compensation Act, Maternity Benefit Act and Payment of Gratuity Act. Most of these acts are applicable to organised sector labour.

The Street Vendors are not only a part of the unorganized sector but also are self-employed and the contribution has to come only from the Street Vendors themselves. Though insurance schemes are available to the unorganized sector of which Street Vendors are a part, as the workers are dispersed, it is difficult for the promoters of these schemes to create/gain access for their assets/products.

Basically, two options are available for enlisting Street Vendors for the social security benefits:

A. Collection of the contribution of Street Vendors by the registration office on monthly basis.

- Creation of Welfare Board for Street Vendors. Either bank should be instructed to collect the money from vendors, or the vendors can deposit their contribution in banks on monthly basis. At the end of the month, the banks will transfer the money to the Welfare Boards. Ministry of Labour should take initiative for creating Welfare Boards on the lines of Welfare Board for Construction Workers/Beedi Workers

- A fixed amount will be deposited for a variety of social security benefits including health, medicare, family pension. This kind of arrangement would require enactment of an Act.

B. Other option is that the Street Vendors' unions should be assisted by NGOs or other agencies to promote Self-Help Groups and networking and federating them to emerge as a financial institution, which will look into extending credit and also delivering other products such as insurance, old age pension etc.

The products under social security programme could interalia also cover the following:

- insurance for health facilities;
- maternity benefits
- old age pension
- child care facilities

Street vendors are vulnerable to loss of goods due to natural as well as manmade disturbances that adversely hampers their economic situation. There should be special insurance schemes to cover their products.

8.3 Training and Skill Upgradation: Street vendors being micro enterprises should be provided with training to upgrade their technical and business skills so as to increase their income as well as to look for alternatives.

9. Organizing the Street Vendors

9.1 The Street Vendors are part of the unorganized sector. The main objective to get the street vendors to get organised is for providing the following services:

- Access to group insurance for a variety of insurance products
- Access to financial services
- Development of small and medium enterprise
- Housing
- Vocational Training and Capacity Building for awareness as well as skill up-gradation

9.2 In addition, it is also important to organise them for creation of a united front for negotiation/protection of their rights. In this regard, it is required to promote organisations of street vendors' e.g. SHGs, Co-operatives and other forms to facilitate their empowerment. The organisation should build adequate systems for managing finances/investment to be handled by professionals.

10. Role of State Governments

All State governments should ensure that institutional arrangements, legislative frameworks and other necessary actions achieve conformity with the National Policy for Street Vendors

11. Action Plan

A comprehensive survey of street vendors to build an adequate database on street vendors particularly in large and medium cities should be undertaken by the State Governments.

8

Social Aspects of Housing Development

Housing is the third basic priority of life after the food and cloths. Provision of the houses should therefore be a priority for any economy whether under-developed or developing. Every body should have an affordable shelter of his own. There are many natural calamities like earthquakes, flood, heavy rain, hailstorm and recent addition sunami, which destroy the houses. It also becomes the responsibility of the State to assist such people. Besides the house the encircling environment is also necessary. More and more people migrate to cities in search of employment. Being uneducated they have to work as labour and live in unhealthy conditions in slums. A statistics of the world as well as India will open our eyes.

Lot of work is being done in India and abroad to improve the housing and the encircling environment to improve the quality of life. Some of the areas of such improvement experiments are given below:

Assistance for People Affected with Sunami Tidal Waves

The Tsunami tidal waves struck the coastal areas in the states of Andhra Pradesh, Tamil Nadu and Kerala and Union Territories of Pondicherry and Andaman and Nicobar Islands on December 26, 2004. Central bank of the country Reserve Bank of India has suggested the banks on being proactive in providing relief to the Tsunami affected. It has advised that the bank managers should, on the basis of their experience and in consultation with other agencies operating in the areas, identify the victims who are in need of assistance and provide them necessary relief and that they need not wait for any list of victims to be formally made available by any authority before providing relief to the affected persons. This would include taking help of good NGOs working in the areas to identify borrowers as also increase the limit of consumption loan to be provided to the affected persons up to Rs. 5,000 without any collateral. The limit may be enhanced to Rs. 10,000 at the discretion of the branch manager, depending on the repaying capacity of the borrower.

Further, banks may allow opening of savings bank accounts with a nominal balance of say, Rs.10, so that victims can receive relief cheques in their accounts. In the case of loss of passbooks/ cheque books, fresh ones should be immediately issued. In addition, the Reserve Bank has permitted its staff in the affected states to undertake relief work in the affected areas.

The National Housing Bank has formulated a concessional scheme for financial assistance to banks and housing finance companies for providing finance for construction, repair and renovation of houses.

The National Bank for Agricultural and Rural Development (NABARD) has proposed to provide refinance at concessional rate to banks for financing the affected persons. NABARD has also been requested to advise the banks that the unit costs (presently being circulated among banks by NABARD) for providing term loans for purchase of boats, fishing nets, *etc.*, were only indicative rates and as such, should be flexible and should be decided by the banks depending on the local conditions.

Community Policing in Mumbai

The Community Policing programme in slums was launched on 11th of June 2004.in Kokari Agar, Wadala, where the federation has resettled a number of communities that used to live along the railway tracks. About 10,000 people attended this function and they came from all over Bombay and even as far as Pune and Pimpri. In September 2004, 65 slums in Mumbai had 'slum police panchayats', each made up of ten representatives from the slum - seven women, three men and a local police officer. There is need for comparable changes in the relationships between slum dwellers and government agencies/municipalities who are responsible for providing water, sanitation and health care. Coverage of slum police panchayats is expanding rapidly in Mumbai, with training sessions for both police and community volunteers as well as frequent reviews of the experience to date, to see what improvements can be made.

In Pune and Mumbai committees are set up in slums with 7 women and 3 men to work in close coordination with a designated police official. These committees are selected by slum communities themselves and the idea is that as far as possible disputes should be resolved at the community level itself through the intervention of these committees. It can be implemented on a very large scale without requiring additional resources from the government.

These committees deal with issues like petty quarrels amongst people standing in a queue for water, alcoholism and the resulting domestic violence and other disputes among slum residents. The community intervention prevents small incidents from being blown out of proportion. It saves the time and energy of the police by such dispute resolution since the formal legal system of criminal law and courts of justice could be avoided. The slum policing scheme transforms the relationship between the poor and the police and perceptions are changing. Work in underway to see how the police rooms within each slum might also provide a location of doctor's consultation and for more constructive relationships with local utility providers.

Mahila Milan has been exploring a pro-active and positive relationship with the police for many years. These women have had to regularly deal with police stations which routinely pick up their men on 'loitering' charges. Getting their men out of these situations always left them feeling helpless. However, this situation changed with gradual and increased engagement through Mahila Milan initiated dialogues with Police stations and working as a collective to ensure peace in neighborhoods.

In some slums, police committees have brought pressure on locals who illegally brew and sell alcohol to shit their shops down. This is to contribute to reducing drunkenness and related violence. The local Mahila Milan has supported those who previously made illegal alcohol to develop new livelihoods. Without community volunteers, the police would find it impossible to control this.

Delhi Development Authority Shows the Way

In Delhi a fire destroyed the entire settlement of Lakshmibai Nagar, in February 2004, where 140 residents of this slum lived. An alliance had been working for 3 years in this settlement and was quick to send a team to Delhi to provide some immediate relief. When attempts were made to rebuild temporary shelters, the police came and arrested several community members. Subsequently, a proposal was made to the Delhi Development Authority (DDA), the main government agency owning land in Delhi; to resettle these families in ground +3 structures. By pooling physically the areas offered to individuals and going upwards, it would be possible to quadruple those areas. The DDA is very interested in this proposal and has asked for a concept note with drawings and costing. The DDA is committed to the project and this is a very positive sign.

Working with the Municipality in Cuttack, Orissa

The Cuttack Development Authority had started approaching Mahila Milan to lead slum surveys and low-cost housing development. After successfully negotiating with the municipality to prevent the eviction of hundreds of families from four different settlements, MM actually managed to secure some land and begin building low-cost housing for one of these communities. This experience is expected to form the basis of many more such city-poor joint ventures.

Resettlement and Relocation -From Transit To Permanent

Thousands of families that have been living in transit camps for the last four years are about to move into permanent buildings across the city in Mumbai. All these families used to live along the railway tracks and were moved when the Railways initiated the Mumbai Urban Transport Project - to expand the rail networks in the city. It was an enormous undertaking to survey, resettle and thereafter support the thousands families that moved into transit camps, but it's also been an important and useful time to prepare and organize for the changes this permanent shift would bring.

Oshiwara Tenements Project

At Oshiwara, 800 tenements are being constructed as part of MUIP. Each tenement has a separate kitchen, common room, bedroom, toilet and bathroom. The corridors are five feet wide and have been built to allow maximum light and breeze.

Federation leaders regularly accompany project affected people to visit project sites and examine the tenements. Preference of floors is given to people who are not well or elderly and the rest of the floors and flats are assigned based on a lottery system.

Bharat Janata in Dharavi Gets a 5 Crore Loan

The National Housing Bank is mandated to widen access to finance for housing The BHARAT JANATA Housing Cooperative, located in Dharavi is a very special and tough project that serves as a precedent in many ways. It is a community which has been a member of the Dharavi Vikas Samittee (Dharavi Development committee) for over 10 years. National Housing Bank sanctioned a 5 year loan of Rs. 5.89 crore for Bharat Janata @ 6.5% interest in May 2004. SPARC, Mahila Milan and NSDF have begun to work with many communities to take on housing and infrastructure projects. In Mumbai,

Bharat Janata Coop completed the various procedures and documentation needed. This cooperative is special because it represents the real and tough ground realities why developers with commercial interest will never touch such a project. The settlement itself is very dense, and the issue of where people will stay when the construction gets started has been a difficult one. It is right in the middle of the dense Dharavi Township, and although the development plan foresees a road, this may well materialize only in the distant future.

NHB is mandated to work on housing for the poor, and it has very little experience in lending to the urban poor, both because banks which could get refinance from NHB don't have such projects and the agency itself has very little experience in such lending. However NHB itself took the initiative to approach the SPARC to understand its work, and examine the kinds of projects emerging from its activity with federations. This was in July 03, after which a series of meetings and discussions followed on the basis of which the Chairman of NHB and his staff presented this proposal to the Board. Hope that this project once comes up with all the hurdles will be replicated at other places also. will

Panvel Building Project

Panvel is a large town which is just outside Mumbai city that falls within the larger Mumbai Metropolitan Region. The plan is to redevelop land which will be provided by MHADA and build ground plus two storeyed buildings - similar to the housing we have constructed at Hadapsar in Pune. It's expected that each tenement will cost about Rs. 60,000. Already, 2 informal settlements have been identified to be relocated. The federation is already working there, and will soon begin the survey. Contractors interested in working in Panvel have been asked to see the land available, and visit Pune to see the VAMBAY project there.

In Pune, the RCC contract was given at Rs 141 per sq foot to regular contractors while Mahila Milan contractors managed the rest of the construction, supervised the overall project, worked to identify and survey households, shift these households and negotiate with the city. Our success in Pune has shown us that VAMBAY projects like these are an attractive housing option and we need to develop a system by which we can manage these projects at scale. The estimated cost of the project is Rs. 3.48 crore. Based on the VAMBAY experience we believe we will need about 35 per cent to start construction. Our plan is to seek this fund first from CLIFF, and then negotiate with a bank for the loan, thereby being able to develop a trend for future projects.

Housing Project in Kanjur Marg

The Alliance has been asked to build about 112 tenements for families affected by the MUTP project and living in Kanjur Marg are to be build. . It's a small project but very significant because the families that are affected belong to the very same group of families that demonstrated that the MUTP would be possible. At that time, in 1998, nobody believed that the poor communities living along the railways would ever willingly move. 800 families from the Railway Federation decided to pioneer this process and demolished their homes along the tracks and built their own transit houses at Kanjur Marg. It was based on their strategy that the shifting of another 12,000 households took place. Now, six years later, they are finally going to move into their permanent buildings, on a plot that is adjacent to where they are currently living. The financing of this project is typical to most PAP housing. The land owner, Jolly Board, will get the land TDR and Nirman will get the construction TDR. We will even build a few extra tenements - using our NGO incentive - which we will sell on the open market.

Pushing for a Slum-free Delhi

When over a hundred houses in a slum in Delhi were unilaterally demolished, the members of a federation were quick to help them. They made a presentation before a high level committee appointed by the Government of India to look into how to make Delhi 'slum-free'. The exercise was to introduce the officials to the idea of SRA and the importance of slum rehabilitation in situ, and to recommend that Lakshmibai Nagar be treated as a pilot project by the Committee. However, there was reluctance to consider in situ rehabilitation as an option and there was talk of shifting the residents to some other location.

Community Toilets in Tirupur

Tirupur, a city in Tamil Nadu, is a successful industrial town, accounting for 75 per cent of the exports of knitwear from India, employing hundreds of thousands of people in its factories. There is hardly any public sanitation in the slums of the town. NTADCL had raised funds from the market to develop infrastructure for Tirupur and given a contract to build 2000 seats to L&T, a major professionally managed engineering firm. Project faced a number of problems. Although 88 slums had been identified for this work, land had only been secured at 9 locations. And second, that L&T had no experience in constructing community toilets before. Then the alliance took the work and cities are now recognizing that that building toilets is not simply a mechanical or technical construction exercise, but rather, the success of community sanitation programmes rests on strong communities who are organized and trained in maintenance and supervision. Finally, the project made an inroad into Tamil Nadu - a state that we have not worked on sanitation before and Tirupur may become a model and inspiration for other cities in the region to explore sanitation.

CIVIC Bangalore

CIVIC Bangalore is a trust, with people from a range of backgrounds: business, development and social sciences, academic and professional, was and remains largely voluntary in nature. It was first established as an association. The institution promotes partnerships for a collective effort towards a better planned, administered and managed Bangalore City. It is an outcome of regular discussions held by a group of diverse individuals who asked themselves the question: How can we participate to make Bangalore a better place, by improving the quality of life It was set up in 1992, This is supported and funded by The Urban Management Programme- UMP, South Asia and the Ford Foundation, New Delhi.

It was recognised as an Urban Forum for Bangalore by UN-ESCAP in 1994, is battling on a variety of issues of democratic, peoples' participation processes, by bringing in citizens groups, NGOs', local and state officials, business and industry, academics and others to the discussion. This lead to the formation of a Stakeholder Forum for Bangalore. In this network its activities support NGO's in other parts of Karnataka state as well.

The main objective of CIVIC Bangalore is to generate and disseminate empowering information to the citizens of Bangalore in general, so that they have better control over the processes of decision making that affect their lives, resulting in a demonstrable improvement in the quality of their lives. We also activate and mobilise participation of the local people in the planning, administration and management of the affairs of the Local Authorities.

The methods adopted by CIVIC Bangalore create better living conditions are:

1. Sharing empowering information.
2. A joint initiative by CIVIC and Janasahayog to study the current status of provision of services in 77 BMP slums. The study has been completed and the report is ready which will be discussed.
3. Lobbying for politico-administrative reform through greater democratisation in matters related to city administration.
4. Improvement and decentralisation of civic services in an ecologically sustainable manner supporting local groups and their initiatives.
5. Pressing for public meetings/ hearings to reveal the implications of major new plans, actions and development efforts by Local Government and private enterprises, to improve transparency and to mobilise public opinion for or against depending on how the proposed development serves the public interest.
6. Focussing on the special socio-economic problems of vulnerable groups within the context of urban planning and administrative reform.
7. Demanding environmental improvement and betterment in quality of life of the citizens.
8. CIVIC invite public to share in the vision by joining them.

CIVIC Bangalore publishes newsletters and research papers. The subscription for the newsletters and research papers and for getting added to their mailing list and for invitation to our meetings Individuals have to share Annual subscription of Rs.

100, For Life subscription: Rs. 2,000; for NGOs/Resident Groups: Annual subscription: Rs. 200, and for Corporate the annual subscription is Rs. 2,000. The life subscription is Rs. 15,000.

Prabhat Pheris (Morning Processions) in Ahmednagar

Municipal president Lata Lodha is all set to revive the practice of morning marches by the city elders and civic officials giving on the spot reprieve to the citizens. The morning marches would give an impetus to resolve the civic problems.

The assurance came from the civic chief during her thanksgiving speech after she was felicitated by the residents of Premdan. Nagar Urban Bank director Brijlal Sarda presented the civic chief with flowers. Meanwhile, the residents of Siddharthnagar have embarked on a self-help drive to clean the gutters in their vicinity as the Ahmednagar Municipal Council turning a Nelson's eye towards their repeated pleas for cleansing the area. The civic chief called for citizens' co-operation for solving civic problems, while she disclosed that water supply, roads and cleanliness top her agenda. The council has expedited planning on a few major schemes which she said would accelerate the development of the city. She would ensure a balanced development for all the civic wards without any favoritism or bias, she vowed.

Besides revival of morning marches, endeavours would be to guarantee a concerted association between the civic officials and municipal council members, she said.

Social Initiatives by TCS

Be it girl child education in South Asia in collaboration with UNICEF or adult literacy programs in South India, TCS believes in using Information Technology as an instrument for social development and change. Other TCS' community initiatives have been in areas addressing environmental and civic problems; setting up and maintaining infrastructure for urban beautification, pollution reduction and healthcare; waste management in the office environment, tree plantation and water treatment. TCS has always recognized the responsibility corporates should have towards the wider communities they operate in. TCS' Environment Policy aims at improving environment management by setting higher standards, and optimising the use of power, water, consumables, and other natural resources. It also aims at reducing pollution by minimising the waste generation from business operations. The policy focuses on environment conservation as an essential element of TCS' business philosophy and infrastructure.

9

Facts about Housing

- If we go by the definition of today, the urbanisation process will continue and by 2030, over 60 per cent (4.9 billion) of all WORLD people (8.1 billion) will live in cities.
- By the end of 21st century most of the people in the world will be living in urban areas.
- Between 1950 and 1990, the cities grew more than twice as fast as villages.
- The last decade, 1990-2000, saw an increase of about 83 per cent in the world urban population.
- The cities have added, on an average, about 81 million people annually.
- In 1950, had about 39 per cent of the world's urban population.
- By 1990, this percentage had gone up to 63 %.
- Now it is estimated to be 70.
- The number of big cities is rising, without proper infrastructure and basic services.
- Improper policies are resulting in unhealthy and unsustainable urbanization.

At the beginning of the new century and millennium the world has:

1. 19 cities with 10 million or more people;
2. 22 cities with five to 10 million people
3. 370 cities with one to five million people;
4. 433 cities with 0.5 to one million.
5. Another 1.5 billion people live in urban areas of less than half a million people.

- World would witness mega-cities of about eight million or hyper-cities of 20 million or more population.

- Villages are turning into semi-urban settlements and second-tier cities becoming larger ones with virtually no civic amenity.
- Due to urbanization, the urban poor will increase to constitute as much as 50 per cent of the total population living in cities by 2020.
- In informal sector workers whose living conditions are marked by low status, low wages, long hours, and insecure habitats giving rise to a new social class.
- The cities of developing countries have become a dumping ground for a surplus population working in unskilled, unprotected and low-wage informal service industries and trade.
- The cities of the developing world faces today one of the most awesome tests in our history.
- India is no exception to the general trend of fast increase in the population of cities and the mind-boggling complexity of the problems that it is causing.
- In India the percentage of urban population to the total population has moved from about 14 per cent in 1951 to about 28 per cent in 2000 (30 crore).
- At present, the urban population of India is more than the total population of 1947.
- During the last 50 years, on an average, India been adding about five or six million people to its towns and cities.
- There are already four mega-cities (five million plus), 19 metro-cities (one million plus) and 300 large towns, besides 3,396 small and medium-size urban settlements.
- The number of metro-cities is at present 40, and four of the Indian cities — Mumbai, Delhi, Kolkata and Chennai — are among the 30 largest cities in the world.
- Mumbai is the sixth largest city of the world (1990).
- Between 1990 and 2020, India would add 418 million people to its urban population.
- A special feature of the Indian scene has been that the dramatic increase in the size of our metropolitan cities has not

reduced the pressure of population or poverty in the rural areas.

- The per capita availability of arable land in villages has been declining.
- The city-dwellers continue to groan under spatial tyranny, particularly in the metropolitan towns.
- The average space occupied by an inhabitant in those towns is about 1/40th of the average national space available to an individual.
- In India no place is too filthy, slushy or dangerous for a large no of huts to be put up and for living purpose.
- In fact, mini-tragedies of this nature are happening all the time.
- Most of the urban centers do not enjoy modern sanitation facilities, portable and safer water supply.

Result of Poor Quality of Life in Indian Cities

1. About 30,000 pre-mature deaths.
2. 17 million respiratory hospital admissions.
3. 2 billion restricted activity days are occurring.
4. New and more virulent forms of diseases are appearing. Till the cure is found, many lives are lost.
5. Delhi, Mumbai and Kolkata account for 44 per cent of these deaths.
6. These unhealthy conditions are estimated to cause an annual loss of 30.5 million 'Disability Adjusted Life Years' which is equivalent to Rs. 36,000 crore.
7. There are more fatalities each year from road accidents in India than in the United States, though we have only about a twentieth of road vehicles as compared to the latter.
8. Urban environment, too, has suffered deep degradation. The suspended particulate matter in the air now exceeds the safe level even in smaller cities.
9. The dust-load in the air of our cities is the highest in the world.

Few years ago, cities were treated as the heaven for living by the villagers. Electricity, roads, shops, hospitals, cinema, good buildings, courts, schools; everything was available nearby. People need not walk and spent half a day to purchase the goods or to go to court. Children need not walk to long distances for school. There ware all luxuries of life in the cities.

Now hundreds of people, multi-storeyed buildings, traffic jams, a few trees, maybe a park, and hordes of civic problems from water shortage and power cuts to irregular public transport services - that in essence describes most Indian cities.

Towns are the focal points of trade and administration. Administrative compulsions, economic and commercial necessities influence the location and development of towns. Strategic requirements also determine the setting up of new and small towns.

- The urban population in India is now about 28.5 crore (2001). The cities with more than 1 million populations have also increased from 23 in 1991 to 35 in 2001. The problems of the cities have also increased.
- An Urban Reforms Incentive Fund has been set up to provide reform-linked assistance to the States with an initial allocation of Rs. 500 crore.
- The Ministry of Urban Development and Poverty Alleviation has issued Property Tax Guidelines in 1988 to all State Governments with the objective of rationalising and simplifying the property tax, considered as one of the best sources of revenue for the urban local bodies.
- In 1992, the 74th Constitutional (Amendment) Act was promulgated seeking to empower the urban local bodies namely the municipal council and corporations in the different size class cities.

World's Most Beautiful Cities

Cape Town (South Africa), Venice, Paris, San Francisco, Granada, Perth, Western Rio de Janeiro, Vancouver, are regarded as most beautiful Harbour Cities in the world.

World's Most Dense Cities

- Hong Kong is the world's most dense major urbanized area. About 3,500,000 people live in 70 square kilometers (27 sq miles). It comes to a population density of 48,571 per square kilometer (128,000 per sq mile).
- Manhattan borough of New York City has about 1,800,000 people in 22 square miles.

List of Metropolitan Areas by Population

Most of the data for this list was compiled from the 2005 urban agglomeration population figures from the United Nations 2005 World Urbanization Prospects Report. These figures include suburban areas immediately surrounding a major city and sometimes multiple major cities which may be close enough together to function essentially as one area. Figures with notations are from the indicated sources.

Rank	Metropolitan City and Country	Area (Km2)	Population estimate	density per km²
1.	Tokyo - Japan	13,500	35,197,000	2,610
2.	Seoul - Korea	11,790	22,770,000	1,996
3.	Mexico City - Mexico	4,980	19,411,000	3,898
4.	New York City – USA	17,405	18,747,320	1,077
5.	Sao Paulo - Brazil	8,050	18,333,000	2,277
6.	Mumbai - India	4,360	18,196,000	4,206
7.	Delhi - India	1,480	15,048,000	10,360
8.	Shanghai – China	3,920	14,503,000	3,700
9.	Kolkata - India	1,780	14,277,000	8,033
10.	Moscow - Russia	2,150	13,400,000	6,232

Number of Top 100 Metropolitan Areas in Various Countries

India has 9 metropolitan areas among the 100 metropolitan areas in various countries of the world. People's Republic of China has 15, United States14, Brazil 8, and Mexico has 3 metropolitan areas in various countries of the world. Rest of the countries have either no city among 10 biggest metropolitan cities in the world or one or two.

Index

Index